THE GOLDEN

HOME AND

THE GOLDEN HOME AND HIGH SCHOOL ENCYCLOPEDIA, while sufficiently comprehensive and detailed for family use, has been created principally for students at the high school level.

The aim of this reference work is twofold: first, to serve the student's immediate need for authoritative information on a wide range of subjects, and, second, to set forth and explain the many areas of knowledge, so that a student may explore them and thus more competently plan his educational future.

Arranged alphabetically in twenty volumes, here are thousands of full, accurate entries, written and reviewed by experts. The text is abundantly illustrated with full-color photographs and paintings.

Designed to complement the high school curriculum, this encyclopedia offers help with assignments and valuable guidance in the use of other reference tools —dictionaries, atlases, and various library materials. Extensive cross-references and a complete index direct the reader quickly to the information he seeks. A special feature of this work is the sound career information it offers in scores of job and professional fields.

Among the many subjects encompassed in these volumes are the newest developments in science, from microbiology to radioastronomy; fine arts and literature; history and government; religion and philosophy; the physical world, its plants and animals; the social sciences; invention and industry. Four-color maps and latest census figures contribute to an up-to-date view of the world, its continents, nations, and peoples.

Every care has been taken to make *The Golden Home and High School Encyclopedia* lively and stimulating, without sacrifice of accuracy. It is the hope of the editors that these volumes will be used with both advantage and pleasure.

VOLUME VI

HIGH SCHOOL
ENCYCLOPEDIA

in 20 Volumes

Degas, Edgar • Euripides

GOLDEN PRESS • NEW YORK

FIRST PRINTING, 1961

Library of Congress Catalog Card Number: 61-13292

© Copyright 1961 by Golden Press, Inc. Designed and produced by Artists and
Writers Press, Inc. Printed in the U.S.A. by Western Printing and Lithographing
Company. Published by Golden Press, Inc., New York.

DEGAS, EDGAR (1834-1917), a French artist, was born in Paris. He was a pupil of Ingres and Lamothe at the Ecole des Beaux-Arts. His first publicly exhibited work was a pastel, "War in the Middle Ages." Although he continued to work with pastel throughout his career, he soon drew upon contemporary life for his subjects and used oils and the tools of etching, aquatint, and lithography. He completed "Steeplechase" in 1866 and "Family Portrait" in 1867. In 1868 he began the long series of studies and portraits of ballet dancers for which he is most famous. With Monet and Manet, Degas was a leader of the new impressionist school from its first important exhibition in 1874 through the sequence of exhibitions which followed. In 1880 he produced a series of "Portraits of Criminals." Continuing with his studies of contemporary life, he produced paintings of nudes, workingwomen, jockeys, singers, and behind-the-scenes night life. Many of Degas' works are exhibited in American art galleries, especially in the Metropolitan Museum in New York, but most of them are in the Jeu de Paume in Paris. Among Degas' best known paintings are: "The Ballet of Robert the Devil," "Dancers Practicing at the Bar," "Woman with Chrysanthemums," "Interior of a Cotton-Broker's Office at New Orleans," and his portraits of Manet.

Museum of Fine Arts, Boston—Librairie Hachette

This is one of the numerous paintings Edgar Degas made of jockeys and race horses.

A difficult problem Charles de Gaulle had to cope with as president was the Algerian war.

DE GAULLE, CHARLES (1890-   ), president of France. As prime minister and minister of defense of France from June, 1958, to January, 1959, he brought an end to the Fourth Republic, a series of ineffective coalition governments in existence since 1946, and gave France a new constitution. In January, 1959, de Gaulle became president of the Fifth Republic.

Born in Lille, he was the son of a professor of philosophy and literature at a Jesuit school in Paris, where he spent most of his boyhood. In 1911 he was graduated as an honor student from Saint-Cyr, the West Point of France. He was thrice wounded in World War I and spent some time as a prisoner in Germany. After the war he taught military history, wrote his first book, and received special training designed for officers who would later be appointed to command armies. He served on the general staff and in the early 1930's was sent on several military missions.

In 1934 de Gaulle published his book *The Army of the Future*, advocating the creation of a mechanized army based upon the armored column. France turned a deaf ear, but the Germans adopted some of his ideas and converted them into the panzer divisions that overran France in 1940. De Gaulle, then a brigadier general, escaped to London and there founded the French Committee of National Liberation. The British government recognized him as a commander of the Free French army.

After the defeat of Germany de Gaulle returned to France and held the presidency of the provisional government until January, 1946. When the National Assembly refused to adopt his policies, he resigned and founded his political party, the Rally of the French People (RPF). After repeated failures to gain control of the government this party was dissolved, and de Gaulle retired to his country estate until he was called upon to form a new government in 1958. See FRANCE.

A man of strong character and definite ideas, de Gaulle had a large share in the liberation of France. He believed that only a strong executive could unite France and restore the past greatness of that nation.

DEHYDRATED FOOD is food in which the water content is so reduced by drying that micro-organisms and enzymes are unable to initiate spoilage. In reducing the water content of food to less than 5 percent, other factors that cause deterioration are also reduced, as are both weight and volume to make the food more easily stored and shipped. The largest percentage of dried food products in the United States is made up of beans and peas; fruits and vegetables are next in order of production, followed by milk and eggs. The two general methods of dehydration are sun drying and artificial drying. Sun drying on a large scale is used mainly for fruits. Artificial-drying equip-

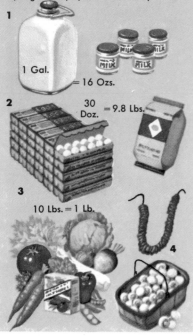

Dehydration of foods drastically reduces their weights and volumes. The amount of this reduction is illustrated below for milk, 1; eggs, 2; vegetables, 3; and mushrooms, 4.

1
1 Gal.
= 16 Ozs.

2
30 Doz. = 9.8 Lbs.

3
10 Lbs. = 1 Lb.

4

ment includes cabinet, kiln, tunnel, and vacuum types of dryers. This equipment must be designed with respect to the effects of drying on flavor, nutritional value, and color of the processed food.

A third method of food preservation, called dehydrofreezing, or freeze drying, is a combination of the dehydrating and freezing processes and has certain advantages over both. Storage space for the dehydrofrozen product is less than that required for the directly frozen product, and rehydration and thawing can be accomplished simultaneously by placing the dehydrofrozen food in boiling water.

DE LA MARE, WALTER (1873-1956), English poet and novelist, was born at Charlton, Kent. He studied at St. Paul's School and there founded the school magazine. In 1890 he became a bookkeeper for the Standard Oil Company. His first short story was published in 1895 and his first book, *Songs of Childhood*, in 1902. His *Collected Poems* was published in 1941 and his *Collected Tales* in 1950. His most noted novel is his *Memoirs of a Midget*. In 1948 de la Mare was made a Companion of Honour by King George VI. He has compiled two noted anthologies, *Come Hither* and *Behold This Dreamer*.

DELAWARE, the Diamond State, was one of the original 13 colonies and the first state to ratify the Constitution in 1787. Dover is the capital and a major food-processing center in the state. Wilmington is by far the largest and most important city.

Delaware is the second smallest state with an area of 2,057 square miles. It is about one-fourth the size of New Jersey. From north to south it measures 99 miles, and from east to west it varies from 9 to 36 miles. In 1960 the population of the state was 446,292. Well over half the population is located in the Wilmington metropolitan area.

Delaware, for the most part, is flat. The only elevation is the low, hilly section in the extreme north, which rises to 440 feet. The coast varies from marshes and sandy beaches to lagoons. The principal streams, Brandywine Creek and the Christina River, are small. The Great Pocomoke Swamp extends across the southern border into southeastern Maryland. The northern part of Delaware has a humid, continental type of climate, while the south is of a humid, subtropical type.

Farming is a major enterprise in Delaware. In the northern sections of the state such field crops as wheat, corn, rye, oats, barley, and hay are grown. Dairying is also important. In the south the moderate temperatures and sandy soil are suitable to the growing of fruits, such as peaches, apples, strawber-

ries, and melons and also such vegetables as peas, asparagus, cucumbers, and beans. The raising of poultry, particularly broiler chickens, is important throughout the state. Chickens account for about 60 percent of the agricultural income. The coastal waters provide excellent fishing. Products of com-

mercial importance include oysters and other shellfish, shad, menhaden, herring, and rockfish. Clay, sand, and gravel are the chief minerals of economic significance in Delaware. The chief products of the state are chemicals, textiles, rubber, iron and steel products, machinery, and paper. Wilmington is the industrial center of Delaware. Picturesque towns of historic interest and coastal resorts, such as Rehoboth and Bethany beaches, are among the major attractions of the state.

Delaware Bay was discovered by Henry Hudson in 1609. The first Dutch settlement, founded near modern Lewes in 1631, was destroyed by Indians. In 1638 a permanent settlement, Port Christina, was made on the site of present-day Wilmington by the Swedes. These colonists are presumed to have introduced the log cabin to America. The Dutch, under the leadership of Peter Stuyvesant, built Fort Casimir (now New Castle) in 1651 and by 1655 had taken control of all the Swedish colonies.

Delaware's official flag bears the state's seal. The sheaf of wheat, ear of corn, and ox represent the early agriculture. The farmer on the left symbolizes agriculture, a basic industry. The hunter on the right represents another early activity and occupation. The state motto is below the symbols.

The Dutch, in turn, were expelled by the English in 1664, and Delaware became part of the territory of the Duke of York. It was transferred to Pennsylvania under William Penn's jurisdiction in 1682, and in 1703 the region was granted a degree of autonomy. In 1776 it became the state of Delaware.

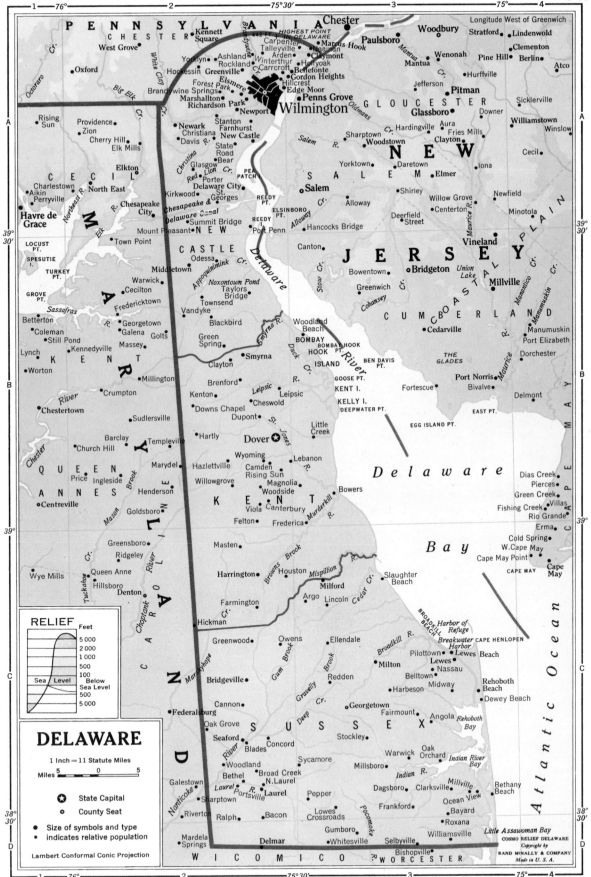

DELAWARE

1 Inch = 11 Statute Miles

Miles 5   0   5

✪ State Capital

○ County Seat

● Size of symbols and type

● indicates relative population

Lambert Conformal Conic Projection

RELIEF

Feet
5 000
2 000
1 000
500
100
Sea Level
Below
Sea Level
500
5 000

COSMO RELIEF DELAWARE
Copyright by
RAND McNALLY & COMPANY
Made in U.S.A.

Courtesy of Delaware State Development Department

In addition to the chambers of the state legislature, Legislative Hall in Dover contains the governor's suite and the secretary of state's offices. Dover has been the capital of Delaware since 1777.

Strawberries, shown below boxed and ready for market, are a major truck crop in Delaware. With the exception of the industrialized Wilmington area in the northern part of the state, Delaware is agricultural.

Courtesy of Delaware State Development Department

Courtesy of Delaware State Development Department

At the left, costumes of an earlier day are being modeled before a historic house in Odessa, Del. The state has a wealth of well-preserved 18th-century and 19th-century buildings.

Early industries were lumber and grain mills, found most often on Brandywine Creek. E.I. Du Pont established a powder mill on the Brandywine in 1802—the start of the U.S. chemical industry. After 1800 Wilmington developed as an industrial center and carried on a thriving trade with the West Indies. Delaware, a border state, fought with the Union during the Civil War, although there were many pro-slavery elements throughout the state. The development of transportation facilities after 1860 expanded industries, especially in the northern sections of the state.

DELAWARE

Nickname: Diamond State
Seal: Farmer and rifleman on either side of shield containing ox, Indian corn, wheat, symbols of early agriculture—motto below—sailing ship above
Flag: State seal on yellow diamond in center of flag's blue field—at bottom, date of Delaware's admission as state
Motto: Liberty and Independence
Flower: Peach blossom
Bird: Blue hen chicken
Capital: Dover
Largest city: Wilmington
Area: 2,057 sq. mi. (including 79 sq. mi. inland waters)
Rank in area: 49th
Population: 446,292
Chief university: University of Delaware
Average temperature: Wilmington, 33° F. (Jan.), 76° F. (July)
Average annual rainfall: 40 to 45 inches
Chief economic activities: Agriculture (including dairying, poultry raising), manufacturing
Chief crops: Apples, peaches, truck crops, corn, wheat
Chief manufactures: Chemicals, textiles, leather, machinery, iron and steel products
Notable attractions: Fort Christina and Delaware Dunes state parks
Important historical dates:
    1631 Earliest settlement by Dutch
    1638 First permanent settlement at Fort Christina, now Wilmington, established by Swedes
    1664 Dutch territory under rule of Peter Stuyvesant seized by English
    1682 Under control of William Penn
    1787 First state to ratify Constitution

DELAWARE RIVER, of the eastern United States, is formed in the Catskill Mountains in southeastern New York. It flows southeast, separating New York and Pennsylvania, then south to form the New Jersey–Pennsylvania border. The river empties into Delaware Bay. It is about 315 miles long and is navigable to Trenton, N.J. It has long been important in commerce. Such cities as Philadelphia, Pa., Camden, N.J., and Wilmington, Del., are situated on its banks.

DELIAN LEAGUE, an alliance of Greek city-states led by Athens. It was organized in 478-477 B.C. to oppose the Persian invasions. Within 17 years Athens and Sparta, which had both been fighting the Persians, fell out, and the Delian League came to rival the Peloponnesian League, led by Sparta, for dominance in Greece. By this time also the Delian League had changed from an alliance of equal city-states to a group of city-states subject to Athens.

The rivalry between the two leagues resulted in several wars starting about 460 B.C. and concluding with the Great Peloponnesian War, which continued intermittently from 431 to 404. This war brought victory in Sparta and defeat to the Delian League. See PELOPONNESIAN WARS.

DELPHI, a small town of ancient Phocis in central Greece, on the southern slope of Mt. Parnassus, was the seat of a famous oracle of the god Apollo. The answers to questions were delivered by a priestess called Pythia, who sat on a tripod and repeated the words inspired by the god. The message was then passed on, in verse or prose, by the priests of the shrine. The oracle

held a position of great influence throughout ancient Greece and was also visited by people of other nations. The gifts brought by pilgrims over the years made Delphi the richest treasury in Greece. The oracle continued to give its answers and prophecies even after the Greek states bowed to the rule of Rome. Its activities were ended A.D. 390 by a decree of the Christian Emperor Theodosius I. Excavations since 1840 have unearthed the temple, sculptures, inscriptions, and other valuable remains, many of which are now in the Delphi museum.

DELPHINUS, or the Dolphin, is a small constellation near the celestial equator lying between Pegasus and Aquila near Sagitta. It is visible in the evening sky from midnorthern latitudes between June and November. It is sometimes called Job's Coffin, but the origin of this name is not known.

Photo by Jerome Wyckoff

This shale (above) was once clay in a delta.

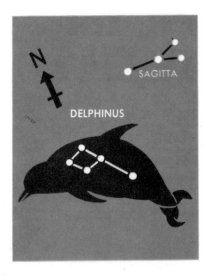

According to legend, Delphinus, or the Dolphin, enabled the poet and musician Arion to escape from a ship manned by a crew that was plotting to kill him. Delphinus, attracted to the ship by Arion's lute playing, bore the musician safely ashore. As a reward the dolphin was placed in the sky.

DELTA, the triangle-shaped area of land at the mouth of a river. It is formed by deposits of clay, silt, sand, and gravel brought down to the sea or lake by the current of the river. The name was first applied to the triangular island formed by the Nile River where it flows into the Mediterranean Sea and afterward to other similarly shaped areas at the mouths of other rivers.

The word *delta* is also the name of the fourth letter of the Greek alphabet. It corresponds to the English D and is shaped like a triangle.

The formation of a delta is shown below. As the silt-laden water approaches the river mouth, its velocity decreases. Heavy sediment is deposited to form seaward-sloping foreset beds; light sediment is deposited farther out to sea. New channels are cut through the delta when the river floods.

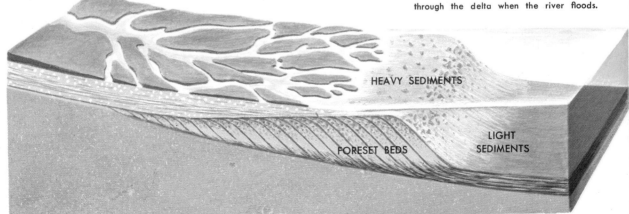

HEAVY SEDIMENTS

FORESET BEDS

LIGHT SEDIMENTS

DEMOCRACY, government by a majority of the people that respects the rights of the minority. A democratic government, to survive, demands a democratic outlook and way of life from its citizens. Democracy may be present in many types of governmental structures—in a monarchy or an aristocracy as well as in a republic. Democratic decisions may be reached by a direct vote of the people, as in a town meeting, or by a vote of the representatives of the people, as in the government of the United States and Great Britain. The word *democracy* has been perverted in its applications by ideologists to the "people's democracies" under communism. However, its meaning can be recaptured by a reading of such authors as Thomas Jefferson or Walt Whitman.

Democracy implies that the majority of people can choose well and can respect the rights of a minority. A democrat believes that a minority can have the patience to seek power by legal means. Democracy considers the individual the most important human unit, and the democrat feels that the individual's self-respect will grow into a respect for others. In short, democracy is optimistic and is based on a high evaluation of people. In contrast, tyranny, such as it is expressed in Hitler's *Mein Kampf*, is based on pessimism and a contempt for men.

During the French Revolution three fundamentals of democracy were expressed in such documents as the *Declaration of the Rights of Man and of the Citizen*. These fundamentals are still valid: fraternity, liberty, and equality. Fraternity has to do with brotherhood and means that men will pursue their goals in toleration and friendliness. But there can be fraternity, as among slaves, without democracy. Therefore, liberty is important. Liberty means that people may develop their talents, personalities, and points of view with only as much restraint as is necessary to allow others to share in liberty. Liberty demands constant vigilance and interest in government on the part of citizens. Equality is part of the principle of fraternity. It means that each man will have one vote in elections and that all men will be treated in the same way before the law. Equality does not imply that all men are exactly the same. Not all men, for example, can be good musicians. But with equality all men will have an equal opportunity to nurture their individual talents.

Democracy demands intelligence and sophistication. Sportsmanship is a major ingredient of a democracy. Sportsmanship implies that all people will play the game of living according to the rules. It means that a political election or victory in a debate will not be followed by the extermination of those with different views, as under communism or fascism. The end, in other words, contrary to Machiavelli, does not justify the means. A person pursues his goals according to the rules.

Greek democracy recognized order and the security of the individual and his property. The philosopher Aristotle did not accept democracy fully, but he recognized some of its merits. Rome's great genius for government was not expressed through democracy. The Roman Stoics and the early Christians, however, developed the ideal of equality. During the Middle Ages the idea of contract was developed. Thus, the feudal lord ruled his serfs, but he was bound to certain responsibilities toward them. The idea that kings were bound by a divine law was the beginning of constitutionalism, and it was first expressed in England in the Magna Charta. In the 17th century defenders of the constitutional government arose in Holland (Johannes Althusius) and England (John Locke). French democratic thinkers rose in the 18th century to defend constitutionalism (Montesquieu), human rights (Voltaire, Diderot), and the general will of the citizens (Rousseau). In the 19th century men were concerned with the practical problems of democracy. Outstanding contributions to democratic thought were made by Thomas Jefferson in the United States, Jeremy Bentham and John Stuart Mill in England, and Alexis de Tocqueville in France. Great strides toward the more democratic society of the 19th century included the birth of public education and the labor movement. In the 20th century democracy was faced with profound challenges from totalitarianism, which arose out of modern industrial conditions. Great problems still remain to be solved by democratic thinkers in a changing world. See ACADEMIC FREEDOM; CIVIL RIGHTS.

DEMOCRATIC PARTY. The Democratic party in the United States originated with the faction of the Democratic-Republican party that successfully backed Andrew Jackson for the presidency in 1828. During Jackson's two terms as president the name Democrat became popular. The party of Jackson, supported by southern small planters and hill farmers and western frontiersmen, was often called the Democratic party. It stood at that time for Jacksonian democracy. The new party name, however, was not officially used until 1844, the year James K. Polk was elected president.

The Democratic party won all but two presidential elections until 1860. In that year the party split over the issue of slavery, which had been a source of conflict within the party since 1840. In 1860 the party divided into a northern wing and a southern wing and lost the election to Abraham Lincoln, a Republican.

However, the Democratic party remained strong in the Congress, although it did not win a presidential election again until 1884 and 1892, when Grover Cleveland was elected president. During the post-Civil War years the Solid South was created. This was a bloc of ten southern states that consistently delivered their electoral votes to the Democratic candidate for president.

After the Civil War several other Democratic traditions grew up. It became usual for the party to hold an annual Jackson Day dinner on January 8, the day that General Jackson's men defeated the British at New Orleans in 1815. In 1870 a political cartoon by Thomas Nast that appeared in *Harper's Weekly* showed the Democratic party as a donkey. The symbol caught on as the popular emblem of the party.

After Cleveland the Democratic party was led by William Jennings

Below is the Democratic nominee, John F. Kennedy, during the 1960 presidential campaign.

Courtesy of the White House

The donkey symbolizes the Democratic party.

Bryan, who tried to make it a farmer-labor party. Bryan, who was thrice defeated for the presidency, advocated first a cheap-money policy for the benefit of debtors and finally took an anti-imperialism stand. In spite of Bryan's eloquence the party's strength dwindled under his leadership. In 1912 the Republicans divided their votes between the Progressive party, led by Theodore Roosevelt, and the Republican party, led by President William Howard Taft. The Democrats, profiting by the split in their political opposition, elected Woodrow Wilson to the presidency. In 1916 President Wilson repeated his victory.

But the political drift following World War I was again to the Republican party. The depression of 1929-1933, however, reduced the popularity of President Herbert Hoover. In 1932 the Democrats elected Franklin D. Roosevelt to the presidency. Gradually the Democratic party built the political platform that still characterizes it. Most of its programs have retained the flavor of President Roosevelt's New Deal.

In 1948 Democratic President Harry Truman won the presidency in a victory that surprised most political seers. Truman appealed strongly to farmers and wage earners, and his vigorous whistle-stop campaign won him votes. In 1952 and 1956, however, Adlai Stevenson was unable to repeat Truman's victory. The Republican party began to make inroads into the Solid South; the New Deal impetus had begun to lose its vigor; and the support from farmers dwindled. See BRYAN, WILLIAM JENNINGS; CLEVELAND, STEPHEN GROVER; DEMOCRATIC-REPUBLICAN PARTY; JACKSON, ANDREW; NEW DEAL; POLITICAL PARTY; REPUBLICAN PARTY; ROOSEVELT, FRANKLIN DELANO; TRUMAN, HARRY S.; WILSON, WOODROW.

DEMOCRATIC-REPUBLICAN PARTY.

George Washington had not wanted the new United States to break into political factions. However, by 1790 certain groups that opposed Alexander Hamilton's Federalists united behind Thomas Jefferson, then secretary of state. The party called itself the Republican party, although the Federalists in ridicule dubbed its members democrats. Some of the Jeffersonian Republicans were proud of this title, however, and sometimes called the party the Democratic-Republican party. Jefferson himself seldom used this name.

The party's strength was drawn partly from among small tradesmen and skilled workers in the coastal cities but mainly from among the frontiersmen in the agricultural South and West. It proposed that the Constitution should be strictly interpreted and that powers should not be extended to the federal government at the expense of the states. Democratic-Republicans also accused the Federalists of aristocratic leanings.

In 1800 Jefferson was elected president. Thereafter the Republicans, or Democratic-Republicans, overwhelmed the Federalists in presidential elections. Jefferson was followed in the presidency by James Madison, James Monroe, and John Quincy Adams, all of whom were Democratic-Republicans.

During Adams' presidency, which began in 1824, the Democratic-Republican party split into two groups. The first, forming around Adams, Henry Clay, and the remnants of the Federalist party, called itself the National Republican party (later the Whigs). The other group was headed by Andrew Jackson (who had had more popular and electoral votes than Adams in 1824, although Adams had been chosen president by the House of Representatives). This group retained the Democratic-Republican title. Jackson won the 1828 election. While he was president, the name Democrat became popular, and the party changed its name to the Democratic party. See DEMOCRATIC PARTY; FEDERALIST PARTY; STATES RIGHTS.

DEMON STAR. See ALGOL.

DEMOSTHENES

(383?-322 B.C.), the great Athenian statesman and orator, was born at Athens, the son of a wealthy arms manufacturer. Traditionally, he was a poor speaker in his first appearance in the Assembly, but through strenuous efforts he became a masterful orator.

In 351 Demosthenes became prominent by opposing Philip II of Macedon. In his later career Demosthenes was discredited when Alexander the Great's treasurer, Harpalus, landed at Athens with 5,000 stolen talents and, at Demosthenes' urging, was arrested. Commissioners, of whom Demosthenes was one, were put in charge of the money, and half of it disappeared. If guilty of nothing more, Demosthenes was at least negligent. He was imprisoned but escaped and went into exile. After Alexander's death he returned to Athens, but Antipater later asked for his and other anti-Macedonians' lives. He attempted to escape but was pursued and took poison.

Courtesy Wrestling World

"Jack" Dempsey was one of the greatest fighters in the history of boxing.

DEMPSEY, JACK

(1895-   ), real name William Harrison Dempsey, U.S. boxer, was born in Manassa, Colo. He spent a good part of his young life learning to become a boxer. In 1919, at the age of 24, Dempsey reached the goal of every aspiring fighter: He won the world heavyweight championship. The fighter's opponent was Jess Willard, who was knocked out in the fourth round.

Known as the "Manassa Mauler," Dempsey defended his title against Georges Carpentier, who was defeated in the fourth round; Tom Gibbons, who fought hard and long for 15 rounds; and Luis Firpo, who went down in the second round. In 1926 Dempsey lost his hard-earned title to boxer Gene Tunney. Dempsey's fighting skill had disappeared after three years of idleness. Dempsey was outboxed, and by decision Tunney, in the tenth round, was named the new heavyweight champion. During the late 1920's Dempsey refereed fights, announced matches, and advised young boxers. In 1931 he decided to reenter the ring, but he discovered he could not keep up his rigorous schedule. In 1932 he retired from boxing.

DENEB is an enormously bright star estimated to be 10,000 times brighter than our sun. Only two stars—Rigel and Betelgeuse—are known to be brighter than Deneb. It appears in our sky as a bright first-magnitude star, but not so bright as about 18 other stars. This is because Deneb is many times farther away from us than the others—almost 600 light-years. You can find Deneb in the constellation Cygnus. It has a second name, Alpha Cygni. See CYGNUS.

DENMARK is a small Scandinavian kingdom situated in the northwestern part of Europe. Copenhagen, the capital, has more than one-fourth of the country's population. Chief cities are Aarhus, Odense, and Aalborg. The kingdom of Denmark is composed of Denmark proper, Greenland, and the Faeroe Islands. Denmark consists of the peninsula of Jutland (about 70 percent of the area) and a group of about 500 islands, of which about 100 are inhabited. The total area of the country is approximately 17,000 square miles. It is about one-tenth the size of its neighbor Sweden. Denmark has a population of about 4,500,000.

Except for its short southern boundary with Germany, Denmark is surrounded by water. The western coast of Jutland is lined with white sand dunes, broken by many fiords. The eastern coast of Jutland and the islands are the most productive areas, with the best soil. Denmark has no mountains but presents a gently rolling countryside.

Denmark has a humid, marine climate. Mean temperatures range from an average of 59° F. in the summer to 32° F. in the winter.

Most people in Denmark are farmers or fishermen or are employed in industry. Agriculture and stock-raising have been a tradition in the country. Denmark's climate and soil conditions are very favor-

Denmark's national flag and royal coat-of-arms are among the oldest in Europe.

able for dairying, grain growing, and the production of root crops. The majority of the farms are small or of medium size. There are many agricultural cooperatives, which serve the farmers.

Danish industry is a very important element of the economy. If processed foods are included among manufactures, industry now contributes more to the national income than agriculture. Meatpacking has developed rapidly. Chemicals, cement, textiles, ships, ceramics, furniture, and silverware are among the chief products.

Foreign trade is vital to Denmark. Imports such as fuel, fertilizers and feeds, and raw materials for industry are of great importance to Denmark's economy and its exports. The county is shifting its emphasis on the export of agricultural products to the export of industrial goods. Food products are of high quality and are limited in variety. Important exports include machinery and meat and dairy products.

Western Europe receives the bulk of Denmark's foreign trade. The United Kingdom is, by far, the chief customer. The United States has increased its volume of Danish imports. The outstanding item has been canned hams, in addition to metal alloys, furniture, mink furs, and ceramics.

The Danish population is very homogeneous. Visitors find the Danes to be friendly, hospitable, and generous people, who have a keen sense of humor. They live well. The people are intensely interested in education, as well as in sports.

Folk costumes are not worn except occasionally on the islands of Amager and Fano or at folk festivals. The bicycle is the universal means of transportation. Even new streets and highways are laid out with special bicycle lanes. The language everywhere is Danish, although differences in dialect are present. The Lutheran church is the established church in Denmark. A large majority of the population are members.

Denmark is a constitutional monarchy and is the oldest kingdom in Europe. Legislative power rests in the king and the Folketing, the one-chamber parliament. Executive power, theoretically in the hands of the king, actually is exercised by the cabinet.

The historical period of Denmark began about 800. The Danes in these years were roving seafarers. They were the vikings who raided Britain, The Netherlands, France, and the Mediterranean countries. King Gorm the Old was the first historically known king of Denmark. He

Fish vendors selling eels on a sunny street in Copenhagen sit patiently while customers select whatever they desire.

Philip D. Gendreau

lived at the beginning of the 10th century. Since Gorm, Denmark has had an unbroken line of kings.

In the early 11th century Denmark reached its peak of power. England, Norway, and part of Scotland were conquered. The Scandinavian union was dissolved in 1523, but Norway remained united with Denmark until 1815. During the reign of King Christian X (1912-1947), Denmark, on Apr. 9, 1940, was occupied by the Germans. It was liberated by the Allies in May, 1945. For detailed map, see SWEDEN.

DENMARK

Area: 16,576 sq. mi.
Population: 4,500,000
Capital: Copenhagen
Largest cities: Copenhagen, Aarhus, Odense, Aalborg
Chief river: Guden
Climate: Mild winters, the coldest month averaging about 32° F.—cool summers, the warmest month averaging about 60° F.—frequent light rains
National flag: Red, with white cross
National anthem: *Kong Kristian*

The Danes sell their dairy products all over the world. These cheeses are being cured.

stod ved højen Mast (King Christian Stood by the Lofty Mast)
Form of government: Constitutional monarchy
Unit of currency: Krone
Language: Danish
Chief religion: Lutheran
Chief economic activities: Livestock raising, dairying, farming, manufacturing, fishing, international shipping
Chief crops: Wheat, barley, other grains, potatoes, sugar beets, peas and beans, hay and forage
Chief manufactures: Processed foods, machinery and metal products, ships, chemicals, textiles, clothing
Chief minerals: Peat, limestone, chalk
Chief exports: Bacon and other meats, butter, cheese, eggs, machinery
Chief imports: Fuels, metals and machinery, grains and other foods, animal feed, textile fibers and yarns

Turck—Shostal

Town Hall Square is the hub of Copenhagen. The tower with the clock is the Town Hall. From its top one can view the spires of the city.

Philip D. Gendreau

DENSITY is a term used by scientists to refer to the quantity of matter in a given unit of volume.

A block of stone weighs more than a block of wood of the same size because the matter in it is more closely packed, and a block of lead weighs even more because the matter in it is yet more closely packed. The densest natural metal known is uranium, and the least dense is lithium. In other words, a cubic inch of uranium would weigh more and a cubic inch of lithium would weigh less than a cubic inch of any other solid substance we could find.

For scientific purposes it is customary to compare the density of a specific material with the density of some standard substance, usually water. The ratio thus obtained is called specific gravity. For example, the weight of a cubic foot of iron is 490 pounds, and that of a cubic foot of water is 62.4 pounds. If the density of water, with which we will compare the iron, is set at 1, the specific gravity of iron is said to be 7.8. See ARCHIMEDES.

DENTISTRY is the health profession concerned with the care and treatment of the teeth and mouth. Just as a medical doctor has the letters M.D. after his name, dentists use D.D.S. (Doctor of Dental Surgery) or D.M.D. (Doctor of Dental Medicine).

The work of the dentist is varied. Besides the familiar tasks there are seven recognized specialties within the profession: pedodontics, caring for the teeth of children; orthodontics, straightening crooked teeth; periodontics, diseases of the gum;

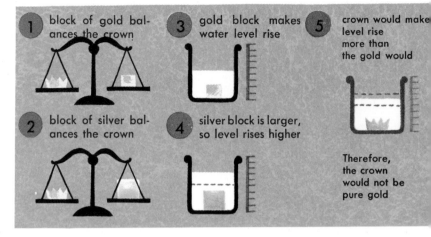

prosthodontics, providing and fitting dentures; public health dentistry; oral surgery; and oral pathology.

The treatment of dental diseases had its origin in ancient times. The early Egyptians and others had fanciful toothache remedies. It was not until the 19th century, however, that dentistry began to make rapid scientific and technical advances. For example, two dentists, Horace Wells and W. T. G. Morton, played important roles in the development and use of anesthesia.

Advancements in the 20th century have been notable. Among them are: the discovery that fluoridation of water can reduce dental decay by as much as 65 percent; more and more general research into the causes of decay; and high-speed drilling equipment, which has enabled the dentist to treat more patients with less discomfort to them and less fatigue to himself.

By these steps Archimedes proved that the crown of the king of Syracuse had been alloyed with silver.

OCCUPATION: Dental Hygienist

NATURE OF WORK: Promoting oral health by preventive treatment and instruction under direct supervision and control of a licensed dentist

PERSONAL FACTORS—ABILITIES, SKILLS, APTITUDES: Hygienist should possess tact and a pleasant manner, as well as manual dexterity, a sense of responsibility and orderliness, a liking for detail, and the ability to master basic scientific subjects.

EDUCATION AND SPECIAL TRAINING: A high-school graduate must have a minimum of 2 years' training in an approved dental-hygiene school, with preference given to women students with college preparatory courses. All states require licensing of dental hygienists after an examination and payment of a fee ($10 to $75).

WORKING CONDITIONS:
1. **INCOME:**
   COMPARED WITH OTHER CAREERS WITH EQUAL TRAINING: Average to high
   COMPARED WITH MOST OTHER CAREERS: Average
2. **ENVIRONMENT:** Most work in private dental offices, but some in schools, public-health agencies, hospitals, and industry
3. **OTHER:** Regular hours with vacation, sick leave, and retirement benefits in most cases; not too strenuous; open exclusively to women; increasing opportunities

WHERE TO FIND MORE INFORMATION: American Dental Hygienists' Association, 100 East Ohio Street, Chicago.

Courtesy of Marquette University

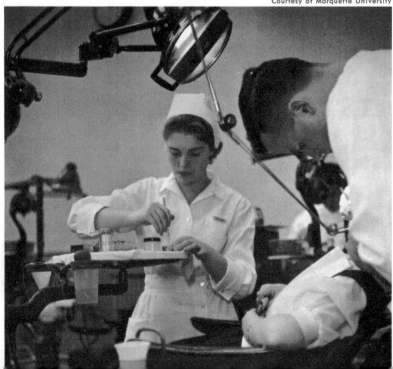

This dental hygienist is assisting the dentist by preparing filling compound for his use.

OCCUPATION: Dentist

NATURE OF WORK: Maintenance, repair, and reconstruction of the teeth and mouth

PERSONAL FACTORS—ABILITIES, SKILLS, APTITUDES: A good visual memory, excellent judgment of space. and shape, delicacy of touch, and a high degree of manual dexterity are required. The ability to master scientific subjects is essential. A liking for people and a good business sense are helpful.

EDUCATION AND SPECIAL TRAINING: A high-school graduate must have from two to three years of predental college work, followed by four years of professional training in a dental school. All dentists must be graduates of· an approved school and must pass state-board examinations.

WORKING CONDITIONS:

1. INCOME:
   COMPARED WITH OTHER CAREERS WITH EQUAL TRAINING: High to average
   COMPARED WITH MOST OTHER CAREERS: High

2. ENVIRONMENT: Private office, hospital, armed forces, or public-health agencies

3. OTHER: Hours, about 43 per week; excellent job opportunities because of increasing demand for dental services

WHERE TO FIND MORE INFORMATION: American Dental Association, Council on Dental Education, 222 East Superior Street, Chicago 11, Ill.

A dentist helps his young patient into the dentist's chair in a clean, modern office. A principle of modern dentistry is that frequent checkups should begin at an early age. Two visits a year are recommended.

Amer. Dental Assoc.

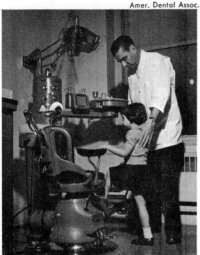

DENVER, the capital of Colorado, is a commercial, financial, and transportation center. It is also the administrative headquarters for many federal agencies, with more federal offices and employees than any city except Washington, D.C. Its population in 1960 was 493,887.

Denver is a large resort city, situated east of the Front Range of the Rocky Mountains. The dry, healthful climate is one attraction, and many mountain resorts are nearby.

The city is engaged in the distribution of livestock, the shipping of coal, and the refining of silver and gold from nearby mines. Farm machinery and rubber and food products are among the leading manufactured goods.

Denver was founded about 100 years ago and became the state capital in 1867. Its development came in the 1870's and 1880's when silver and gold strikes were made in the vicinity. Denver was a base for mining operations, especially during the rush to Pikes Peak. By the end of the 19th century the city had become a distribution point and commercial center for an extensive agricultural area. In recent years it has witnessed a rapid expansion.

DEPARTMENT STORE, a retail store selling many lines of merchandise, organized so that each type of goods is sold in a specialized shop or department. Each department has its own buyer and budget but follows a store-wide operating policy. The store has central accounting, advertising, and personnel departments. In addition to providing charge-account service, free delivery, and a phone and mail-order shopping service, the store may have restaurants, a beauty parlor, and other services.

Department stores evolved from more specialized shops. Some famous ones are: Macy's, New York; Marshall Field and Company, Chicago; T. Eaton and Company, Ltd., Toronto; Bon Marché, Paris; and Selfridge and Co., Ltd., London.

Before 1850 there were buildings containing several shops, but they were owned by different people. The first department store was Bon Marché of Paris, founded in 1852.

One of the first department stores in the United States was that of Rowland H. Macy. He began the system of "shaded prices," for example, charging $1.98 instead of $2.00.

Alexander T. Stewart, another New York department store pioneer, introduced the one-price system. After this there could be no more haggling over prices.

DEPRESSION OF 1929-1933, one of the worst periods of unemployment and financial loss in modern history. Although this depression was worldwide and affected different countries differently, it was most severe in the United States. World War I, like all great wars, had left an aftermath of cynicism and disillusionment for Americans. As a consequence there developed, during the 1920's, widespread skepticism about time-honored precepts of morality, ethics, and even personal and business finance. Along with other kinds of bizarre behavior, people overspent their incomes; they went into debt far beyond reason, confidently hoping that their incomes would rise to meet their "needs." Business firms, too, over-expanded their plants—and their debts—in a fever of optimism about the prospects for business activity. These forces worked together to produce an almost unprecedented inflation of prices, particularly corporation-stock prices.

Prosperity during the 1920's was not entirely unalloyed. In 1923-1924 both business and agriculture underwent a mild recession, from which agriculture did not recover. During 1928 and early 1929 doubts began to spring up even in some areas of business. The failure of certain important European financial firms in the summer of 1929 suddenly jolted many people into a realization that what they had thought was a new era might be just a pipe dream. Early in the fall some stock prices began to decline. Soon the downward movement became general and so rapid that it was like a landslide, carrying everything before it. On October 24 more than 16 million shares were traded, and the decline of prices was so catastrophic that the day is remembered as "Black Thursday." Prices continued dropping, and many people had their entire fortunes wiped out, particularly those who had purchased stocks on the margin, that is, on credit.

Overoptimism was soon replaced by overpessimism. Business firms began to cut down their production, leaving thousands of workers unemployed. People and business firms tried to "protect" their money by drawing it out of the banks (whose whole method of managing their loans and deposits was based on the presumption that people would never behave in this irrational way). These withdrawals caused banks to fail by the hundreds. Distress literally fed upon itself. Thousands upon thousands of people lost their homes, and farmers lost their farms, because they could not pay their taxes and mortgage debts. Industrial production continued to decline, and by 1933 there were between 12 and 15 million workers unemployed. Thousands of homeless people lived in cardboard shacks they had built themselves; others sneaked onto railway freight cars and traveled from place to place in search of work. Breadlines were a common sight, as were people selling apples on street corners to earn a living. In 1934 more farmers lost their farms because duststorms in the Southwest ruined their land. John Steinbeck's famous book *Grapes of Wrath* is about these people. (See DUST BOWL.) One of the bitterest incidents of the depression was the Bonus March in 1932. In June several thousand jobless and homeless veterans marched from all over the country on Washington, D.C., to demand immediate payment of a veterans' bonus. Many left after Congress refused to vote the bonus, but others stayed because they had no place to go. A riot caused President Herbert Hoover to order out troops. These troops under General Douglas MacArthur cleared the marchers and their families from their shacks and burned the shacks down.

The Federal Reserve System, which had been unsuccessful in its efforts to hold down the inflation, proved equally powerless to stem the deflation. President Hoover attempted to combat the disastrous overpessimism by pleading with industry and labor to keep business going and with banks and other mortgageholders not to foreclose their mortgages. Most of these efforts were dismally unsuccessful; but the Reconstruction Finance Corporation, which he organized in 1931, later proved to be one of the most effective instruments for pouring out government money in aid of distressed business firms. As a result of the depression Franklin D. Roosevelt defeated President Hoover in the 1932 presidential election. His program, the New Deal, was devoted to curing the depression and preventing another. (See NEW DEAL.) Although the severest part of the depression ended by about 1934, the country did not fully recover until about 1939, when preparations for the entry of the United States into the war that had already broken out in Europe brought industry back to full production.

DEPTH CHARGE, an underwater-explosive device for use against hostile submarines. It is a thin-skinned, cylindrical case containing high explosive. It is detonated by a hydrostatic fuse, which can be set to activate at any predetermined depth. Depth charges can be dropped from any surface ship or aircraft equipped with launchers. Fast surface ships have ramps in the stern over which the charges are rolled into the sea. Depth charges are launched abeam from mortar-type guns called Y-guns or K-guns by placing them on T-shaped expendable racks that fit in the gun muzzles.

In making an attack an antisubmarine vessel will maneuver to pass ahead of the enemy submarine and lay a pattern of depth charges. The distance ahead depends upon the speed and depth of the submarine and the sinking rate of the depth charges. Enough speed is used to prevent damage to the attacking ship if part of the pattern is launched off the stern.

The location and depth of the enemy submarine is determined by special detection equipment. Ships normally use acoustic echo-ranging or listening equipment called sonar; aircraft employ sonobuoys and magnetic anomaly detectors. Conventional depth charges, which detonate at preset depths, disturb the water and interfere with echo ranging. For this reason as well as the increased speed of nuclear submarines, smaller, faster sinking, ahead-thrown depth charges have been developed. These are fired by rocket or mortar devices ahead of the attacking ship in scatter patterns and do not explode unless they hit the submarine. These smaller charges have been given odd names such as Mousetrap, Squid, Hedgehog, and Limbo. The latest development in depth charges is the use of an atomic bomb to replace the high explosive.

DERRICK, a frame used in drilling oil wells. The derrick holds boring equipment in place and serves as a storage area for the tools and pipes that must be lowered into the well. A derrick may be located on a barge or a pier as well as on land. Derricks are of various heights; some may be as high as 200 feet.

A derrick is also a type of crane used on cargo ships and in the construction of large buildings. The arm, or jib, and an upright pole, or mast, are attached to each other at their bases. The movement of the jib is controlled by guy wires attached to the top of the mast.

Library of Congress

René Descartes

DESCARTES, RENE (1596-1650), French philosopher and mathematician, born at La Haye. He is regarded as a founder of modern epistemology, or the branch of philosophy dealing with the origin, limitations, and methods of human knowing. As a boy, Descartes had a critical and inquisitive mind. He attended the Jesuit school of La Flêche, where his delicate health excused him from the school's morning duties and allowed him to lie abed thinking. After La Flêche, Descartes went to Paris to become acquainted with the mathematician Claude Mydorge. The departure from Paris of a friend, Father Marin Mersenne, caused him to seek seclusion for several years, during which time he studied mathematics. In 1617 he became a soldier in The Netherlands, and in 1619 he joined the Bavarian service. That year, in

These derricks in an oilfield hold drilling equipment and store tools and pipes.

Fred Bond—FPG

his comfortable room at Neuburg on the Danube, he gave free play to his mind and developed ideas that were later put into his *Discourse on Method*.

Following many travels and a futile attempt to seclude himself again in Paris, Descartes settled in Holland to devote himself to philosophy. He left his financial affairs in the hands of Abbé Picot and his publishing in charge of Father Mersenne so that he could be free to meditate, discuss, and argue. Descartes' residences, always located near universities, were usually divided into a reception room for visitors and a scientific workshop. He was never an avid reader—he preferred to think, to experiment, and to discuss. His first work in Holland was a book on the physical universe, *The World*. He published the *Meditations on the First Philosophy* in 1641 after he had subjected it to the criticisms of other thinkers. His *Principles of Philosophy* was published in 1644. Descartes was called to Sweden in 1649 to tutor young Queen Christina, who demanded her philosophical instruction at 5 o'clock each morning. He died there in 1650.

The life of this quiet philosopher was rich in contributions. He founded analytical geometry, made a number of innovations in algebra, and added to the knowledge of music and optics. His philosophy was founded on systematic doubt. He discovered that he could doubt all things save the reality of God and the statement, *"Cogito ergo sum"* (I think, therefore I am). From this point he set about to construct his concept of man and the universe in accordance with geometry and mechanical laws.

DESERT, a region where few forms of life can exist because of cold or dryness. Thus the ice-covered island of Greenland and the arctic wastes of Siberia are really deserts. However we are accustomed to thinking of a desert as a waste of sand where there is so little rainfall that only a few especially adapted animals and plants can live.

There are two principal bands of desert land around the earth, one in the Northern Hemisphere and one in the Southern Hemisphere. The northern one includes the Sahara, with its offshoots the Libyan and the Nubian, and the great desert of the Arabian Peninsula, which stretches up into Iran and across Central Asia, where it becomes the Gobi, reaching almost as far east as Manchuria. Then, on the other side

Union Pacific Railroad

Visitors tramp over the sand dunes of Death Valley, California, toward the blue wall of the Panamint Range. Especially adapted plants and animals inhabit this desert area.

of the Atlantic we have the desert areas of the southwestern United States and northern Mexico. Below the Equator are the Kalahari Desert in southern Africa, a desert region in coastal Peru and northern Chile, and the great desert of the interior of Australia.

Not all deserts are sandy; even where there is a large amount of sand, the surface is broken by areas of rock and occasional bare hills or mountains. Dotting the stretches of sand are small spots called oases, where grass and trees are watered by springs. Most rivers in deserts flow only when there is a sudden rainstorm. But where the river is fed by water from a mountain region, it is often able to maintain a steady flow entirely across the desert to the sea. The Nile, Indus, Tigris, and Euphrates rivers are mountain-fed streams. The dry climate of the Gobi Desert of Central Asia has preserved large deposits of extinct animal and plant forms.

DESK, a flat-topped table used for writing and reading and equipped with drawers for storing equipment and supplies. The desk is an important piece of furniture in both homes and offices. Professional people, officeworkers, and students do much of their work at desks.

Desks are made of either wood or steel. Desk tops may be linoleum, glass, plastic, or wood. Many desks are adapted to the special needs of their users; for example, desks often include deep drawers for filing letters and other documents. Others contain special storage areas for typewriters or other business machines.

The desk developed from the writing box of the Middle Ages. The writing box was a wooden box with a slanted top; the top was hinged so that it could be lifted and writing materials could be stored inside. The first desk was produced by mounting a writing box on legs and reversing the hinging of the top so that the top opened toward the writer.

The practice of filling the space beneath the desk with drawers began in the 17th century. In the 18th century the addition of bookcases to the top of the desk resulted in a massive piece of furniture called a secretary. At the same time a small writing table, called a lady's desk, became fashionable. Both the secretary and the lady's desk often contained many small drawers, pigeonholes, and secret compartments.

Today's table desks developed from simple writing tables to which one or more banks of drawers were added. A major difference between these desks and older models is that the newer ones provide enough leg room for the user of the desk. Today's desks also have much more writing space.

DES MOINES, the capital of and largest city in Iowa, is an industrial, transportation, and printing and publishing center. The city is also a national financial and insurance center. It is located on both banks of the Des Moines River in central Iowa. The city is situated in a region containing extensive bituminous coal mines and is in the heart of the Iowa corn belt. It had a population in 1960 of 208,982.

Points of interest in the city include the state Capitol; the State Historical, Memorial, and Art Building, which houses pioneer relics as well as art treasures; and the Iowa State Fair Ground, where each August one of the world's largest agricultural exhibits is displayed. Des Moines is the seat of Drake Univer-

Courtesy Iowa Development Comm.

The state Capitol of Iowa, located in Des Moines, is crowned by a large gilded dome.

sity. Fort Des Moines, a WAC training center during World War II, and the U.S. Army's Camp Dodge are near by.

The city's manufactures include farm equipment, rubber products, leather goods, clothing, and processed food. Des Moines is an important wholesale and retail center for the state.

The city developed from a military outpost that was established in 1843. The community prospered not only as a resting point for California-bound pioneers but as a river port. Des Moines became the state capital in 1858.

DE SOTO, HERNANDO (1500?-1542), Spanish explorer, was born in Barcarrota and was educated at the University of Salamanca. When he was about 19 years old, he sailed for Central America. He served with Pizarro and Almagro in the conquest of Peru and retired from there with a share of the fortune stolen from the Incas.

In 1537 he obtained from Charles V permission to conquer Florida

Brown Brothers

After discovering the Mississippi River, De Soto went west to what is now Oklahoma.

and at the same time was made governor of Cuba. Using Cuba as his base, de Soto sailed for Florida in 1539. From Florida he and his small contingent traveled through what are now various southern and southwestern states in a search for another Peru. In 1541 de Soto reached the Mississippi River, the first white man knowingly to do so. On the return trip home de Soto died, and his body was ceremoniously committed to the river.

DETECTIVE, a person engaged in the investigation of violations of the criminal statutes and the activities of criminals. A detective unit is an important part of a police department. It is charged with the prevention and detection of crime. Detectives perform their duties in civilian clothes. They are usually assigned to investigate the more serious criminal offenses and assume responsibility of investigation after the uniformed policeman, who is often the first to arrive at the scene of a crime, has made preliminary investigation. The detective conducts his investigation for the purpose of identifying and apprehending the offender and securing and preserving evidence; and he assists the prosecuting authority in preparation of the case for the grand jury and the subsequent court trial. Business firms and individuals frequently hire, from private agencies, investigators commonly known as private detectives. Private detectives employ methods and procedures similar to police detectives, but ordinarily they are not vested with police authority. One of the best known private agencies is Pinkerton's National Detective Agency, founded in 1850, the first private agency in the United States. See CRIMINOLOGY.

DETERGENT, a "soapless soap." The word *detergent* has two meanings. The first, used until about 1941, was "anything that cleans," that is, any soap or scouring powder. Then about 1941 the word acquired a more specialized meaning: a new type of cleaning agent that does not produce a scum in hard water. This meaning was taken up by the automobile-oil industry to describe certain new types of engine oils that would hold the gummy products of combustion in suspension.

As late as 1947, just after World War II, almost no tallow and grease were used in the production of synthetic detergents; but approximately five years later 120 million pounds were used in the manufacture of detergents.

Just how a detergent cleans is still a subject of intense scientific investigation. It seems that a detergent has a superior so-called wetting power that lowers the surface tension of water and because of this property loosens the dirt. See SOAP AND SOAP MANUFACTURE; WATER.

DETROIT is the world's automobile-manufacturing center. This Michigan city is also a busy port on the Detroit River, which connects Lake Erie and Lake St. Clair. Bridges and tunnels join the city with Windsor, Ontario. Detroit's population in 1960 was 1,670,144. Detroit is the fifth largest city in the United States.

Detroit's growth is mainly the result of the automobile industry developed by Henry Ford and others in the early 1900's. The industry has expanded to other cities in Michigan, such as Flint and Lansing, and to the suburbs of the Detroit metropolitan area.

Detroit's cultural and educational institutions include Wayne State University, University of Detroit, and the Detroit Art Institute.

The city was settled in 1701 by French colonists. The French controlled it until 1760 when the English took possession. The Americans occupied Detroit in 1796, although it had been granted them by the Treaty of Paris in 1783. The British held it for one year during the War of 1812. The United States assumed final command in 1813 after Commodore Perry's victory on Lake Erie. From 1805 to 1847 Detroit was first the territorial and then the state capital. With the development of both water and rail transportation after 1830 the city underwent rapid expansion and became a great industrial center.

DETROIT AND VICINITY

DETROIT POPULATION 1,849,568

SCALE-ONE INCH EQUALS APPROX. 2½ MILES

Expressways

© 1959 By The H. M. Gousha Co.

The H. M. Gousha Co.

10-GG 207-5

DEW. Have you ever noticed the beads of water that form on a glass of cold lemonade on a summer day? This water is formed in the same way as the beads of water, called dew, that are found on cobwebs in the morning following a clear, cool night. Dew is the water that condenses from the air onto objects that are colder than air.

All air contains a certain amount of moisture. Warm air, however, holds much more water vapor than cold air. Therefore, when this warm air cools, it loses its moisture. Usually, it loses its moisture by forming clouds (or fog), which are millions of tiny droplets of water that collect on dust or salt particles. But under certain conditions the air deposits its moisture as dew.

Suppose that the day has been sunny. The sun has set, and the air is quite calm. The night is very clear. The air will cool slightly, but the earth, the trees, and the grass will lose heat even more rapidly than the air because solid objects are better radiators of heat than is air. The air is not cool enough to form clouds. But as it touches the colder objects, it cools on contact and deposits the burden of moisture it can no longer hold. In the morning we will probably discover clear skies, bright sunshine, and dew deposited over everything. See ATMOSPHERIC CONDENSATION; FROST; HOARFROST.

DEWEY, GEORGE (1837-1917), U.S. naval commander. Dewey is best known for his destruction of the Spanish squadron in Manila Bay during the Spanish-American War. As a result of this feat the United States became a naval power to be reckoned with in the Pacific Ocean.

George Dewey was born at Montpelier, Vt. He became a midshipman at the Naval Academy at Annapolis, Md., when he was 16 years old and was graduated fifth in his class. He received a commission in 1861 and served during the Civil War under David Farragut.

After the war he was given command of the *Narragansett*, which was assigned surveying duties in the Gulf of California. Dewey was made a captain in 1885. In 1889 he became head of the Navy Department's Bureau of Equipment, and in 1895 he was appointed head of the Board of Inspection and Survey, where he gained an intimate knowledge of the U.S. Navy. In 1897 Dewey was placed in charge of the Asiatic Squadron. War with Spain was declared in April, 1898, and

Courtesy U. S. Naval Academy Museum, Annapolis, Md.
Dewey was the first United States admiral.

Dewey sailed for Manila, with orders to capture the Spanish fleet.

Although the Spanish squadron in the Philippines was outmanned and outgunned by Dewey's fleet, it held a fine defensive position, with support from shore batteries. Dewey managed the entrance into the bay without mishap. He met the Spanish fleet anchored before Cavite. The battle began at 5:30 A.M., May 1, on a signal shot from Dewey's flagship *Olympia*. Two hours later Dewey disengaged his squadron. The Spanish flagship *Reina Cristina* exploded, and the *Castilla* (an old wooden ship) went down. About noon the battle resumed, and the *Don Antonio de Ulloa* sank. Dewey's *Petrel* cleaned up the small craft in the harbor, and the Spanish were finished. No American lives were lost in the action. The U.S. fleet remained until the arrival of troops under the command of Major General Wesley Merritt.

DEWEY, JOHN (1859-1952), American writer, philosopher, and educator. He was born in Burlington, Vt. At 15 he began to attend the University of Vermont, where he initially showed no exceptional promise. However, a textbook by Thomas H. Huxley, an able exponent of the ideas of Charles Darwin, stimulated his interest, and in his senior year Dewey earned the highest marks ever made at the university in philosophy.

Following his graduation Dewey began to write articles on philosophy. In 1882 he entered Johns Hopkins University, where his mind was further stimulated by the philosophical thought of Hegel. When Dewey had received his Ph.D., he went to the University of Michigan to teach. He also wrote a textbook on psychology, which he approached from the then novel standpoint of a natural science. In 1894 Dewey

was invited to head the department of philosophy, psychology, and education at the new University of Chicago. There he founded his famous experimental school, or laboratory school, to try out his ideas of education. In 1904 he resigned from the University of Chicago to accept a teaching post at Columbia University's Teachers College.

Dewey's ideas on education are expounded in *How We Think* and *Democracy and Education*. He felt that schools should stimulate a child's natural curiosity and teach him to work happily with his fellows. The Progressive Education Association was founded in 1919 to put these ideas into practice.

The philosophy of John Dewey was called instrumentalism. Instrumentalism meant that thought was guided toward definite ends and that the truth of ideas lay in their workability. He argued that human nature, influenced by institutions and customs, is not unchangeable. The task of philosophy, therefore, was to learn by the scientific method about the values that governed human conduct. This idea he presented in *The Quest for Certainty: A Study of the Relation of Knowledge and Action* (1929). In keeping with the dynamic doctrines of his philosophy John Dewey was active in many political and educational organizations. His work stirred many stimulating controversies on the proper aims of philosophy and education in a democracy.

DEW LINE (Distant Early Warning). See RADAR WARNING NETWORK.

DIABETES. Two diseases characterized by an excessive production of urine are called diabetes. Usually, however, when a person speaks of diabetes, he is referring to the disease characterized by sugar in the urine (diabetes mellitus), which is commoner than diabetes insipidus.

Diabetes insipidus is a relatively rare and chronic disease. It is marked by increased urination and great thirst. In this disease a hormone called pitressin, produced by the pituitary gland, is lacking. Persons with diabetes insipidus are treated by giving them this hormone. Usually hormone treatment cannot be discontinued.

Diabetes mellitus is a disease characterized by the presence of sugar in the urine (or in abnormal quantities in the blood) and an increased urinary flow. It is accompanied by increased thirst and appetite, loss of strength, and skin

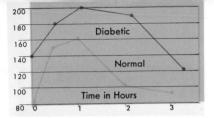

Diabetes mellitus may be diagnosed through the oral glucose-tolerance test. Patients' blood is tested for sugar content (in milligrams per 100 cubic centimeters) one-half, one, two, and three hours after sugar is given. Typical results are charted above.

disorders. Diabetes mellitus is a chronic ailment, apparently hereditary. It is believed to result from a hormonal imbalance (possible roles being played by the pituitary, adrenal, and thyroid glands) with a deficiency in insulin secretion by the pancreas.

The treatment of diabetes mellitus is based on aiding the body to utilize sugar and maintain the general health and nutrition. This is done by controlling the diet and by giving insulin. Because of the diabetic's tendency to get infections his observance of personal hygiene should be meticulous.

DIAGRAMMING, in the teaching of grammar, is a method of arranging the parts of a sentence so that those parts and their relationships may be seen more readily. In learning to diagram a sentence, a person should proceed slowly and should be sure he understands each step before he goes on to the next.

The first step in diagramming is to distinguish the complete subject and the complete predicate. Thus, in the sentence "The boy went to the library," it should be seen that "the boy" is the complete subject and "went to the library" is the complete predicate.

Now pick out the simple subject and the simple predicate. Place them on a single horizontal line separated by a vertical line that crosses the horizontal one. This is the skeleton of the sentence.

| boy | went |

Now place all modifiers under the words they modify. Adjectives and adverbs should be placed on slanting lines. For a prepositional phrase, place the object of the preposition on a horizontal line and place the preposition on a slanting line connecting the line under the object with the line under the word modified by the phrase.

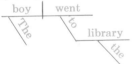

When the main verb in the predicate has a direct object, the object should follow the verb on the same line, separated from the verb by a vertical line that intersects but does not extend below the horizontal line. Notice that in the example "Open the door," the subject, *you*, is not stated and therefore is placed in parentheses.

| (you) | Open | door |

If the subject is compound, place the simple subjects on parallel lines. Place the conjunction on a vertical broken line that connects these lines.

Diagram a compound verb or a compound object similarly.

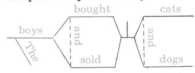

If the predicate verb is a linking verb, such as *is* or *seems*, separate the predicate noun or adjective from the verb by a slanting line that intersects but does not extend below the horizontal line.

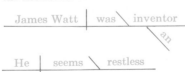

In a compound sentence each independent clause is diagrammed according to the principles for diagramming simple sentences, and the sentences are bracketed together, just as the simple subjects in a compound subject are. The conjunction is placed on a vertical broken line connecting the clauses.

In a complex sentence each clause is diagrammed as a simple sentence; a dependent clause is placed under the independent clause and connected to the word it modifies by a vertical broken line. The relative pronoun is placed on the broken line.

DIALECT. John Smith had studied the German language in high school. He knew it so well that he could converse without difficulty with people who had come from Germany. One year John accompanied his parents on a trip through Europe. Their first stop in Germany was in a farming village nestled away in forest-covered hills. John was eager to try out his knowledge of the language, but to his surprise he could understand no one. When John told of this problem, his father informed him that the village people spoke a dialect of German.

There are dialects of all the major languages. How are they formed? In the first place, language is always changing. New words appear in the language, and old words may disappear or be used in new ways. This movement, this change in language, is called drift by the linguist (the student of language). You probably do not notice the drift of your own language, because you drift right along with it, but your parents might be able to tell of expressions that were common in their youth that you might consider odd today.

Now if people who speak the same language are separated and do not communicate often with one another, their language may drift in different directions. You may understand people from England very well; yet, if you have ever seen an English motion picture, you may have noticed many different expressions and a different way of accenting words. Suppose that all communication between the United States and England had been cut off for hundreds of years. Then the peoples of the two countries might speak very differently; their languages would still be recognized as English, but they would be different enough to be dialects. See LANGUAGE FAMILY.

DIALOGUE, properly speaking, a conversation between two or more persons. The word *dialogue* also has a special meaning; it refers to a special type of conversation invented by the ancient Greeks.

Plato, one of the most famous Greek writers and philosophers, developed the art of the dialogue. Almost all his philosophical writings are in this form. The dialogue is especially effective in pointing up the merits and defects of various ideas. A speaker makes a point with clarity, and another speaker puts a piercing question or comment to the previous speech. As the dialogue continues, many intricate ideas can be developed.

Dialogue has been often used by thinkers because in it delicate and differing shades of meaning can, it seems, be more easily, convincingly, and movingly developed than in straight exposition.

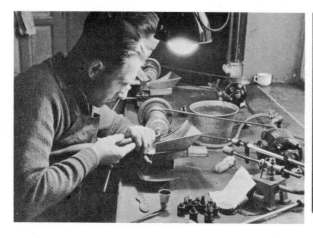

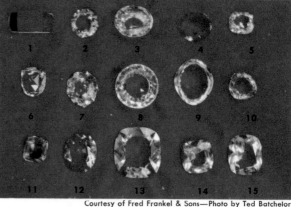

Courtesy of Fred Frankel & Sons—Photo by Ted Batchelor

A diamond cutter rounds or girdles two rough stones by rubbing one, held on a rod, against the other, fixed to a revolving shaft.

Famous diamonds in replica are: **1,** Shah; **2,** Pasha of Egypt; **3,** Orloff; **4,** Pigott; **5,** Polar Star; **6,** Sancy; **7,** Florentine; **8,** Great Mogul; **9,** Koh-i-noor (old cut); **10,** Nassak; **11,** Hope; **12,** Koh-i-noor (new cut); **13,** Jubilee; **14,** Regent; **15,** Star of the South.

A brilliant diamond is cut in nine stages. The rough stone, **1,** is sawed in two parts, **2.** Cutting of the larger part proceeds with rounding or girdling, **3.** Lopping begins, **4,** producing the first facet. Further lopping produces 4 main facets, **5,** and then 12, **6.** The main facets are finished, **7,** and brilliandeering, **8,** adds tiny star facets. The finished gem, **9,** has 58 facets.

DIAMOND AND DIAMOND MINING.

A diamond is a crystalline form of carbon developed by heat and pressure under natural conditions. No other known substance found in nature even approaches the diamond in hardness. Scientists believe that the hardness of the diamond is due to the compression of the carbon atoms during formation of the diamond.

Diamonds differ widely in color, which ranges from the clear, colorless type through the blues, yellows, and browns. Diamonds draw great quantities of light into their centers and, when they have been properly cut, send the light out again in sparkling brilliance. They also sep-

Almost all diamonds are mined in Africa.

arate light into the colors of the spectrum, and when turned slowly they send forth the familiar rainbow hues.

The diamond is mentioned in the Old Testament and was used to some degree by the Greeks and Romans. It is believed the first diamonds came from India. Borneo became the second producing area for diamonds, and in 1726 diamonds were found in Brazil. In 1867 the children of a poor Boer farmer named Jacobs picked up the first African diamond, which was valued at $2,500. During the next few years a few more were found, but it was not until 1871 that the great Kimberley district was opened up. Kimberley is the center of the African diamond area. The principal diamond mines of this area are Bulfontein, DeBeers, Jagersfontein, and Premier. There are several other mines in this area as well as in other places in Africa. There is a small diamond mine in Arkansas in the United States, and one in British Guiana, and in Australia.

Diamonds are found below the earth's surface and in the gravel of riverbeds. Below the surface layers is a deep and very thick layer of bluish-green rock. This layer, called blue ground, is where the diamonds are. It is mined and brought to the surface where it is spread out on "distributing floors" just outside the mining area. Big rollers then pound and crush the rock. It is put into large pans and washed while the pans spin rapidly, throwing the diamonds and other heavy minerals to the outer edge. A stream of water then washes away more dirt, and the diamonds are separated from the other minerals. This used to be done by handpicking, but now a vibrating greased surface is used. The diamonds stick to the grease while other material passes over it and is removed.

A list of several hundred famous diamonds could be made, each with a romantic and even fabulous history. The two largest cut diamonds in existence were originally part of the Cullinan, a stone that weighed over a pound found in the Transvaal in 1905. Over one hundred gems were cut from this rough monster, including the Star of Africa, which weighs 530.2 carats and is now mounted on the scepter of the queen of England, and another stone of 309 carats. The Koh-i-noor (Mound of Light) is an Indian gem of 190 carats, and it was known to exist several centuries ago. It belonged to various shahs and finally was taken by the English from Ranjit Singh, whose country (India) was declared under British domination in 1849. It was recut to 108.9 carats and placed in the queen's crown. Among the most famous diamonds of all time are the Great Mogul, the Orloff, the Shah, the

Sancy, the Vargas, the Jonker, the Nassak, and the Hope.

Approximately half of the diamonds mined have flaws or are of such quality as to be unfit for gems. These diamonds are widely used in industry, for example, for the manufacture of cutting tools for use in drilling and machine industries. In cutting stone, huge saws studded with diamonds are important tools. Diamonds are used also for cutting glass and for phonograph needles, dental drills, and delicate scales.

Artificial diamonds have been the goal of man for centuries; however, they never were produced satisfactorily until 1955. A process was developed in that year that produced small, yellow diamonds, made under tremendous pressures. These stones are usable as industrial diamonds. Artificial, or synthetic, diamonds produced in this manner are more costly than natural stones. See GEM; GEMCUTTING.

DIANA was the Roman goddess of hunting and the moon. She was the daughter of Jupiter and Latona and the twin sister of Apollo. In Greek mythology she was called Artemis.

Diana was a protector of women and youth. Whenever a woman died quickly and painlessly, it was said that Diana had killed her with her silver arrows. The goddess also was the guardian of wild animals, and she especially favored the deer and the bear. Roman hunters worshiped Diana by placing on her altars animals that they had killed.

Diana considered love a weakness and despised it. She was a goddess of grace and modesty, and she showed no mercy to those who disturbed her privacy. The hunter Actaeon once saw her bathing. Diana punished him by turning him into a stag. Actaeon's own dogs then chased and killed him.

This ancient design (below) depicts Diana.

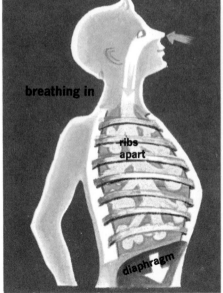

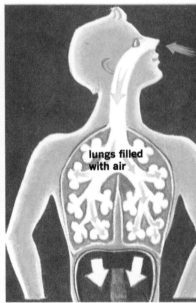

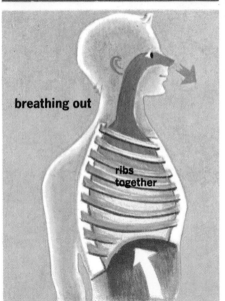

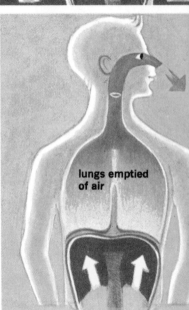

When the diaphragm contracts, its domed shape flattens. At the same time the intercostal muscles spread the ribs. The net effect is to increase the size of the thoracic cavity and draw air into the lungs. When the diaphragm and the intercostal muscles are relaxed, the thoracic cavity returns to its original size, and air is squeezed out of the lungs.

DIAPHRAGM, a muscular membrane that separates the thorax from the abdomen. Elliptical in shape, it is lined both above and below by serous membranes. The structure, sloping somewhat from right to left and downward, domes upward. The heart, on the thoracic side of the diaphragm, lightly rests on the apex of the dome, and the base of the lungs is located on either side. Three openings are present, providing for passage of the aorta, esophagus, and vena cava from the thoracic to the abdominal cavity. When a person breathes, the lowering of the diaphragm causes air to enter the lungs. During expiration the diaphragm returns to its former position. The diaphragm is controlled by the phrenic nerves.

In optics a diaphragm is any variable device or stop by which a portion of the light available may be excluded from a camera, telescope, or similar instrument.

DIARY, a day-to-day record of a person's thoughts and experiences. It is not usually intended for publication. Most diaries do not contain entries for each day of a given period, but the entries they do contain are written on the very day they refer to. If they are not, the transcription loses its value as an immediate and spontaneous expression of feelings. Since diaries are purely personal writings, they are as varied in character as are their authors. They may be aloof and reflective or absorbed in social and political events, concerned with domestic trivia or bursting with frank revelations of feelings ordinarily kept at bay.

Most surviving diaries have been written since 1600; earlier ones have been forgotten or left unpublished. Samuel Pepys, a 17th-century English civil servant, wrote one of the most amusing and interesting diaries on record. His comments on his wife, his household squabbles, and his adventures show the complete openness of a man who never intended his work to be read by others. Though not a person of powerful intelligence, Pepys's eyewitness accounts of political incidents of the day, such as Charles II's arrival in England at the Restoration, are written with a freshness and an eye for detail that a later historian could not possibly capture. Literary figures who write diaries for eventual publication are necessarily more guarded. Their attention turns more to general observations and reflections and less to affairs of the moment.

A diary of an archaeological expedition contains photographs of unearthed objects as well as a day-by-day written account. American School of Classical Studies, Athens, Greece

Famous political figures have expressed in their diaries opinions that had to be kept secret. The diary of Count Ciano, Italian minister of foreign affairs under Mussolini, is particularly interesting because it shows his growing antagonism toward Germany, Italy's ally during World War II. The *Diary of Anne Frank*, another personal chronicle from World War II, was written by an adolescent Jewish girl who lived in hiding during the German occupation of Amsterdam. The most ordinary details in the life of this high-spirited young girl, forced by menacing circumstance to introspection, take on a special intensity.

Photo, Brown Bros.

This statue honors Bartholomeu Dias and the navigator's greatest voyage of discovery.

DIAS, BARTHOLOMEU (1450?-1500), a noted Portuguese navigator, was born near Lisbon. He sailed with several vessels down the west coast of Africa and turned the southern point, which he called *Cabo Tormentoso* (Cape of Storms). Later the King of Portugal renamed it Cape of Good Hope. Dias sailed on several other voyages and accompanied Vasco da Gama on a voyage to the Cape Verde Islands. He also commanded a ship in Pedro Cabral's fleet headed toward Brazil. In 1500, nearing the coast of Brazil, the ship commanded by Dias foundered and was never seen again.

With Bartholomeu Dias' successful voyage to the Cape of Good Hope the Portuguese were one step closer to establishing a sea route to India. This long-sought goal was accomplished 10 years later by Vasco da Gama. The arrows on the map indicate the extent of Dias' voyage before he turned back.

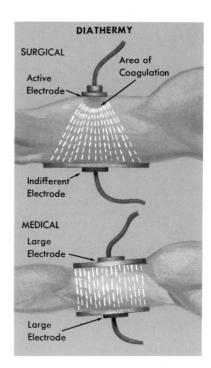

DIATHERMY

SURGICAL

Active Electrode

Area of Coagulation

Indifferent Electrode

MEDICAL

Large Electrode

Large Electrode

Diathermy may be used in two kinds of medical treatment. In surgical diathermy the active electrode concentrates high-frequency currents (broken lines) in one area, coagulating diseased tissue. Medical diathermy heats tissues for therapeutic effects.

DIATHERMY is the generation of heat in body tissues by the application to the tissues of a high-frequency electric current. Diathermy is used in the medical treatment of inflammations and injuries of the joints and muscles.

Electrodes are applied to the appropriate body part, and a high-frequency current or voltage is applied to the electrodes. Electric current is induced in the body tissues, and as this current flows through the resistance of the tissue, heat is produced.

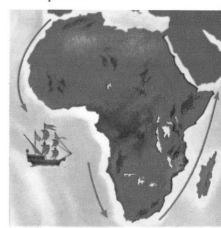

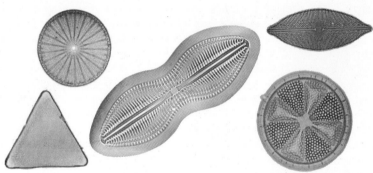

Above are diatoms in their natural habitat; at right are highly magnified individual specimens. These microscopic one-celled plants are food for fish and a basis for diatomaceous earth. The diatoms sink to the bottom of seas or lakes, where they form the diatomaceous ooze. Their skeletons eventually form the chalklike diatomaceous earth that is mined from the sites of ancient seas and lakes.

Courtesy of Bausch & Lomb Inc., Rochester 2, N. Y.

DIATOMACEOUS EARTH, a fine-textured grayish or white material composed essentially of silica. Diatomaceous earth is formed from the fossil remains of small plants called diatoms. Some of these plants lived eons ago, some lived during the recent Ice Age, and some deposits are forming now. Some deposits formed in marine environments and some in fresh-water lakes. Extensive deposits of diatomaceous earth are found in California, Washington, Nevada, Maryland, Virginia, New York, and many other places in the United States and throughout the world. Diatomaceous earth is used in filters, as insulating material, as a filler, and for various purposes by the building industry.

DÍAZ, PORFIRIO (1830-1915), Mexican general and statesman. He was born in the southern state of Oaxaca, of part-Indian ancestry. His father, an innkeeper, died when Porfirio was three and left a family of seven children. Porfirio started to study for the priesthood in the Roman Catholic Church but abandoned these studies at 16. A year later he walked most of the 250 miles to Mexico City, intending to enlist in the war against the United States, but he arrived after the treaty had been signed. Returning to his native town, he took up law, studying under Benito Juárez, then governor of Oaxaca. In 1854 he joined the liberals in their revolt against Santa Anna. After Santa Anna's overthrow Díaz fought under Juárez in the Three Years' War.

He further distinguished himself in the war against the French and Emperor Maximilian from 1862 to 1867, capturing Mexico City two days after Maximilian was shot.

After failing several times to become president, Díaz overthrew Lerdo de Tejada, successor to Juárez, and became provisional president in 1872. Elected president, he served from 1877 to 1880. After he was elected president again in 1884, he served seven consecutive terms until he was forced to abdicate in May, 1911, by the revolution led by Francisco Madero. Díaz died in exile in Paris.

Díaz' administration as president, generally known as the Age of Díaz, was marked by internal peace and material prosperity for the government. This prosperity was achieved principally through concessions to foreign capitalists. Díaz built up a strong central government through which he controlled elections and legislation. In general he allowed the conservative classes to regain most of their lost privileges at the expense of the lower classes. Social legislation was lacking; there was little improvement in the condition of the masses under the administration of Diaz.

DICE, small cubes of ivory, bone, wood, or metal used in games of chance and in board games, such as parcheesi, backgammon, and Monopoly. The name is really the plural form of the word *die*, which is now used only in such phrases as "the die is cast." The six sides of the

Dice have been used since antiquity.

dice are marked with black dots, with a different number on each side. The dots on any two opposite sides add up to seven. For the board games two dice are shaken together in a box and are thrown onto the board or table.

Dice have been found that date from as early as 3000 B.C., and dice games were very popular in ancient Egypt, Greece, Rome, and the Far East. The ancient dice found in Egyptian tombs are exactly like the ones used today.

CHARLES DICKENS

DICKENS, CHARLES (1812-1870), English novelist and satirist, was born in Portsmouth, the son of a minor naval functionary. He spent his early years in Kent, where he received an incomplete education. He then went to London. There his father and family spent time in the debtors' prison, and Charles was employed in a warehouse. After this period of struggle the boy attended a respectable private academy and was then apprenticed to a lawyer. Shortly thereafter he began reporting for various London newspapers. In 1833 he started his pen pictures of life with *Sketches by Boz*, which were so popular that his publishers immediately demanded more. *Pickwick Papers* was the result. Their success placed him in the front rank

George Cruikshank and Phiz (Hablot Browne) were two noted caricaturists whose work appeared in early editions of Dickens' novels. At the left is one of Cruikshank's illustrations for *Oliver Twist;* at the right is a Phiz illustration for *David Copperfield.*

of writers. He then published in monthly installments *Oliver Twist, Nicholas Nickleby, Old Curiosity Shop,* and *Barnaby Rudge.* A voyage to the United States, where he became a popular lecturer, gave him material for *American Notes* and *Martin Chuzzlewit.* During a sojourn in Italy he wrote the brief but ever-popular *A Christmas Carol.* It was followed by *Dombey and Son, David Copperfield, Bleak House,* and *A Tale of Two Cities.* Meanwhile Dickens continued to be active as an editor and a lecturer. Toward the end of his life he became interested in books of horror and mystery. *Great Expectations* was considered by many critics the best of his books from the standpoint of sheer artistry. *Edwin Drood* was left unfinished when he died, its mystery unsolved. He was influential in bringing to light the social injustices he found in 19th-century England and the United States. Upon his death he was buried in Westminster Abbey.

DICKINSON, EMILY (1830-1886), American poet, was born in Amherst, Mass. She was educated at Amherst Academy and spent one year at Mount Holyoke Female Seminary. Her father was a lawyer, and a student in his office, Benjamin Newton, encouraged her to write. Newton's early death left her bereft, and she turned for guidance to the clergyman Charles Wadsworth. After Wadsworth went to San Francisco, she made an almost complete withdrawal from society and devoted herself to writing poetry.

During her life only two of her poems were published and these without her permission. Only after her death were volumes of her work issued. In 1930 her work was issued in *Poems: Centenary Edition.* In 1945 other unpublished poems were issued in the volume *Bolts of Melody.* A three-volume scholarly edition with variant readings, *The Poems of Emily Dickinson,* was issued in 1955.

DICOTYLEDON, an angiosperm that has two cotyledons, or seed leaves. Cotyledons are small, leaflike structures that store and provide nutriments for a young seed plant. The cotyledons usually wither and fall off as soon as the young plant has

Two cotyledons are grown by the four-o'clock and the strawberry and pumpkin plants.

grown leaves and can manufacture food by means of photosynthesis.

Dicotyledons differ from monocotyledons in having two seed leaves instead of one. All angiosperms, or flowering plants, are either dicotyledons or monocotyledons. The dicotyledons include about 250 different families and more than 150,000 different species of flowering plants.

A few familiar dicotyledons are oak, elm, maple, willow, apple, peach, cherry, carnation, buttercup, poppy, daisy, sunflower, clover, cabbage, bean, pea, carrot, tomato, potato, turnip, cotton, flax, strawberry, and tobacco.

Besides possessing two cotyledons, dicotyledonous plants have other characteristics that distinguish them from monocotyledonous plants. The flowers of most dicotyledons have four or five sepals, petals, and stamens, or multiples thereof, whereas the flowers of most monocotyledons have three sepals, petals, and stamens, or multiples thereof. The leaves of most dicotyledons have veins that ramify to form a complex network, whereas the leaves of most monocotyledons have parallel veins. See COTYLEDON; MONOCOTYLEDON.

DICTATING MACHINE, a machine used in offices to record voices, usually in order that a typed copy of the recording may be made. Although ordinarily used by businessmen dictating letters, the dictating machine may also be used to make transcriptions of conversations, conferences, and telephone calls.

A complete dictating unit consists of a microphone, records, a recorder, and a transcriber. Microphones are available in hand and desk models. Some desk models have attachments that allow the businessman to turn the microphone on and off with his foot. The records are usually plastic belts, plastic disks, magnetic tape, or magnetic wire. Wax cylinders, at one time the only type of record used in dictating machines, are no longer widely used. Recorders are either small magnetic-tape or wire recorders or recorders similar to those used to make phonograph records. The transcriber is the machine used to play back the recording and is usually operated by a typist who types the content of the record as it is played.

Dictating machines have many advantages over dictation to stenographers. Businessmen can save time by dictating letters at their convenience instead of waiting for a stenographer, and the stenographer is left free for other work. Since the record can be replayed, the possibility of the typist's making an error is reduced. Businessmen take portable recorders on business trips and mail records to their secretaries for typing. Accurate records of important conferences can be made.

Dictating machines with as many as 20 microphones are now avail-

Courtesy of Dictaphone Corp.

A dictating machine aids this businessman.

able. Each microphone may be used by a different executive. The microphones are connected to the recording system by a complicated wiring system that is similar to a telephone switchboard.

DICTATORSHIP, a government in which the will of the state is regarded as above the will of the individuals it governs. The relationship of the dictatorial state to its citizens and to other states is one of force. Dictatorships may consist of a single individual, a royal family, an army, a political party, or a religious organization. At one time the term *dictatorship* was reserved for the emergency power given to one man in order to tide a nation over a period of stress. Thus, in the Roman Republic, dictatorial power was temporary. Mark Antony abolished the title "Dictator" in order to indicate the permanence of his rule. Monarchy was not necessarily a dictatorial institution, for the king was sometimes quite limited in his powers. Modern monarchies are often democratic. After World War I the term *dictatorship* came to be applied to all absolutist governments. The intention of modern dictatorships is to retain power permanently, to dominate democratic institutions such as the parliament, to nullify personal and property rights, and to monopolize political power.

Dictatorships arise from unstable political conditions. They may arise in nations used to constitutional government, in nations with no history of constitutionalism, or in nations that are chronically unstable (as were the Latin American countries after achieving independence from Spain). A dictatorship in some

ways unique is the Soviet Union's "dictatorship of the proletariat." See COMMUNISM.

Periods of stress, such as a war or an economic depression, may plant the seeds of a dictatorship in a constitutional republic. Wars make discipline necessary, and people find how easy it is to act under orders. Postwar conditions may present many difficulties, such as inflation, hunger, unemployment, debts and reparations, fear of minorities, and boundary disputes. Parliaments may find it impossible to act, and talented writers may begin to accuse democracy of failing to provide action, of corruption, and of failure to produce "great men." People lose faith in democratic machinery. Almost inevitably the "great man" appears who seems capable of bold, aggressive action. He may be a leader with charismatic (mystical) qualities that capture the imagination.

Lisl Steiner

Fidel Castro rose to power in Cuba in 1959.

Once in office, the dictator will retain his power by suppressing freedom of speech. His secret police will inspire fear and silence in those who might protest. Although the army may have helped him to power, the dictator may create his own elite guard, such as the Black Shirts of Mussolini. Even dictatorships need popular support, however. In modern totalitarianism it is no longer possible to "mind one's own business." The individual must strenuously believe in an ideology. Every facet of his life is controlled. (See FASCISM; NAZISM.) The dictator will sponsor flashy public-works projects, successful wars, and public ceremonies. Eventually, trapped by the legend in which he wraps himself, he may attempt the impossible and bring himself and his nation to destruction, as did Francisco Solano López in the Paraguayan War. (See PARAGUAYAN WAR.) Generally, dictatorships can only be displaced by violent uprisings. See DEMOCRACY.

DICTIONARY, a book of words listed in alphabetical order, with explanations of their spelling, pronunciation, etymology, meaning, and examples of usage. In addition to the familiar general dictionary, there are also specialized types—dictionaries of slang, dictionaries of dialects, or dictionaries of synonyms, for example, Roget's *Thesaurus*. There are also encyclopedic dictionaries, such as the *Oxford Classical Dictionary*, the *Dictionary of National Biography*, and many others covering different branches of the arts and sciences. Finally, there are foreign-language dictionaries, which give translations of words from a foreign language to the native tongue and vice versa. Such a work is Larousse's *French-English, English-French Dictionary*.

Rudimentary forms of the dictionary are evident in the most ancient civilizations, but the original of our own type was the Greek lexicon. These works were usually lists of special vocabularies, such as words and phrases from ancient stories, Homer's vocabulary, or barbarous phrases. The first English dictionaries, like those of the Greeks, were vocabulary lists of difficult, foreign, or new words.

In the 18th century, English lexicographers were influenced by the Italian and French academies that had been established to purify their languages. Samuel Johnson, the 18th-century poet and critic, wrote an English dictionary based on literary examples in an attempt to set a standard of proper usage. But a century later, the whole conception of the dictionary changed. It was now regarded as an inventory of words as they are and have been commonly used, rather than as an authority on good English. In 1884 Sir James Murray, Scottish lexicographer and philologist, published the first volume of his *New English Dictionary*, in which he illustrated the meanings of words with quotations taken from various sources and placed in historical sequence. The final volume of this work was published in 1935, the editorship having been shared by Henry Bradley and William Craigie.

Some time later, William Craigie wrote a historic dictionary of American English, but the most famous lexicographer in the United States was Noah Webster. He was the first to compile a dictionary of distinctly American words and usages. Later editions based on his original work are still widely used in America. The Merriam-Webster *Webster's*

surcingle 1218 surmounter

sur·cin·gle (sûr'sĭng'gəl), n. **1.** a girth for a horse or other animal, esp. a large girth passing over and keeping in place a blanket, pack, or the like. **2.** a girdle with which a garment, esp. a cassock, is fastened. [ME *surcingle*, t. OF: m. *surcengle*, f. *sur-* SUR-¹ + *cengle* (g. L *cingula* girdle]

sur·coat (sûr'kōt'), n. **1.** a garment worn over medieval armor, often embroidered with heraldic arms. **2.** an outer coat or garment. [ME *surcote*, t. OF. See SUR-¹, COAT]

sur·cu·lose (sûr'kyə lōs'), adj. *Bot.* producing suckers. [t. L: s. *surculōsus*]

surd (sûrd), adj. **1.** *Math.* (of a quantity) not capable of being expressed in rational numbers; irrational. **2.** *Phonet.* voiceless. —n. **3.** *Math.* a surd quantity. **4.** *Phonet.* a voiceless consonant. [t. L: s. *surdus* deaf, indistinct]

Surcoat,
13th century

sur·feit (sûr'fĭt), n. **1.** excess; an excessive amount. **2.** excess in eating or drinking. **3.** oppression or disorder of the system due to excessive eating or drinking. **4.** general disgust caused by excess or satiety. —v.t. **5.** to bring to a state of surfeit by excess of food or drink. **6.** to supply with anything to excess or satiety; satiate. —v.i. **7.** to eat or drink to excess; suffer from the effects of overfeeding. **8.** to indulge to excess in anything. [ME *sorfait*, t. OF: excess, prop. pp. of *sorfaire* overdo, f. *sor-* SUR-¹ + *faire* do (g. L *facere*)] —**sur'feit·er**, n.

surf fish, any of the small to medium-sized viviparous fishes constituting the family *Embiotocidae*, inhabiting the shallow waters of the Pacific coast of North America.

surf scoter, a large North American diving duck, *Melanitta perspicillata*, the adult male of which is black except for two white patches on the head.

surf·y (sûr'fĭ), adj. abounding with surf; forming or resembling surf.

surg., **1.** surgeon. **2.** surgery. **3.** surgical.

New Collegiate Dictionary is particularly suitable for students and for everyday use in the home.

HOW TO USE A DICTIONARY

The dictionary is probably the most valuable of all reference books. It gives information on matters of word form—such as spelling, division into syllables, inflectional forms, and abbreviations—on pronunciation, and on meaning. In introductory material and appendices it may give a large variety of other useful information.

As a student you should learn how to find and interpret quickly the information offered by a dictionary. Since entries are arranged in alphabetical order, you must know the alphabet well—not merely to be able to recite it, but to know immediately what letters a particular letter follows and precedes. A thumb index may save time, particularly in using a large dictionary. By using key words—the first and last words on a page, printed at the top of that page—you can avoid scanning each page. In order to interpret readily the information given, you should learn the signs and abbreviations used in dictionaries. Most important, you should develop the habit of consulting a dictionary; the value you gain from it will increase with practice in using it.

A dictionary entry begins with the vocabulary entry—the term or combination of terms to be defined—in boldface type, with the preferred spelling or form given first. When you look up a variant form of a word, you will usually be referred to the preferred spelling. Capitalization or hyphenation will be indicated in the vocabulary entry. Foreign words will be preceded by parallel bars; such words should be italicized in print.

Division into syllables is indicated in the vocabulary entry. The end of each syllable is marked by a centered period, an accent mark, or a hyphen; this is where you should divide a word at the end of a line, whether in handwriting, typing, or printing.

Inflectional forms, including the plural form of a noun, the past tense and participles of a verb, and the comparative and superlative of an adjective, are given only if they are irregular. Some dictionaries give only the endings for such forms. If no forms or endings are given, you may assume that a plural is formed by adding *s* or *es*, a past tense and past participle by adding *ed*, a present participle by adding *ing*, and a comparative and a superlative by adding *er* and *est*.

Abbreviations for a word may be found either in the dictionary entry or in a separate section devoted to abbreviations.

The pronunciation is given, in parentheses following the vocabulary entry, by respelling the word in a phonetic alphabet. This alphabet may be learned fairly easily; you may find it explained either in an introduction to the dictionary or at the bottom of each page. Stress in pronunciation is indicated by heavy and light accent marks. The word is again divided into syllables, this time according to pronunciation; you should remember that this division sometimes differs from that of printers' usage, which is given in the vocabulary entry and should be followed in dividing a word at the end of a line. When more than one pronunciation is given, the first is usually preferred.

In finding the meaning of a word, you should note carefully its part of speech. This is indicated by an abbreviation following the pronunciation. You should learn these abbreviations, which are usually explained in a list headed "Abbreviations Used in This Book."

The etymology, usually given in square brackets, will help you to understand a word through an appreciation of its history. Words in italics, whether English or foreign, are those from which the vocabulary entry is derived; meanings of these root words are given in roman type immediately following them. If a word in italics is foreign, the language is indicated by an abbreviation.

In the definition, meanings are numbered with Arabic numerals, while closely related meanings may be grouped after one numeral and numbered with letters. You should read all definitions of a word you look up, since there are no preferred meanings as there are preferred spellings or pronunciation; one meaning is as good as another unless it is marked *rare* or *obsolete*. Meanings are usually arranged, as far as possible, in the order of their historical development.

A cross-reference from a definition may invite you to see another entry or compare the meaning of another word. Another way of indicating related words is the presentation of synonyms and antonyms. These may be given merely as a list or with a full treatment of the distinctions of meanings between the words. Synonyms should be distinguished carefully from definitions: Synonyms are single words; definitions are explanations of meaning using several words.

Usage of a word may be indicated by a label, according to the field of knowledge, geographical area, or kind of usage in which the word occurs. Usage may also be clarified by use of quotations from literature. You should be careful not to confuse these quotations with definitions; the quotations are intended merely to illustrate how the word has been used.

Introductory material and appendices may be of value to the student who is familiar with them. A section of biographical names and a pronouncing gazetteer are frequent features. Lists of abbreviations and of signs used in various fields are often included in the appendices. There may also be dictionaries of rhymes, of synonyms and antonyms, and of given names. Guides to colleges and universities are also frequently included in dictionaries designed for students. Special sections on pronunciation, spelling and grammar, letterwriting, and the preparation of copy for the press are occasionally included, either as introductions or as appendices.

DIDEROT, DENIS (1713-1784), French philosopher and writer, born in Langres, director of the influential encyclopedic dictionary of knowledge the *Encyclopédie*. Diderot was well educated at Jesuit schools in Langres and Paris. When he left school, he made his living as a hack writer and occasional teacher so that he would have the time to study philosophy, mathematics, literature, art, and science.

Under Diderot's direction the *Encyclopédie* became a vast compendium of the thought and knowledge of his time. This systematic classification of all knowledge was noted for its skeptical attitude toward religion, its propagation of the scientific spirit, and its attempt to replace authority with reason in religious, political, and artistic matters. Diderot worked on the *Encyclopédie* for over 20 years, from about 1749 to 1772.

Diderot was not a great writer, but he was a bold thinker with an exceptionally fertile mind. He was at his animated best as a conversationalist. His numerous other writings included novels, plays, critical essays, and philosophical treatises. Also of interest are his letters to his friend Sophie Volland and to various prominent people of the time: Jean Jacques Rousseau, Friedrich Melchior von Grimm, Jean Le Rond d'Alembert (his associate until 1758 on the *Encyclopédie*), and Paul Henri Dietrich d'Holbach.

DIDO. See AENEAS.

DIDRIKSON, BABE (1912-1956), properly Mildred Didrikson Zaharias, American athlete, was born in Port Arthur, Tex. She began playng basketball at the age of 14. At 16 an insurance company hired her so she could play on its basketball team. Playing for the company, she was twice named as all-American women's basketball forward. As captain of the company's women's track team, she took second place in

UPI

"Babe" Didrikson was the only woman ever to compete against men in the Los Angeles Open Golf Tournament. In the opening round of the tournament, which was held at the Riviera Country Club, she shot a score of 76.

national standings. She also set eight southern and three national track and field records. She won 17 loving cups and 92 medals. In the 1932 Olympic Games at Los Angeles, Babe won the javelin throw and the 80-meter hurdle race. At this time she turned professional and became the only woman on an all-American basketball team. Then she became interested in golf. After spending three years learning the game, she won her first tournament in 1935. Later she turned professional and toured the United States and Australia.

DIECASTING is a method of producing castings in molds. Diecasting is used when large numbers of a particular casting are required. The die, made of steel, usually has two halves that are closed for casting and opened for removal of the finished casting. The mold is filled under pressure, which is maintained until the piece is solidified. Alloys of copper, aluminum, and zinc are most frequently used for this purpose. Diecasting allows for precise control of the size of a finished part, and the uniformity of thickness leads to less waste of material. Also, the accurate tolerance of the dies reduces the amount of machining required for the finished product. However, the cost of the equipment and the dies is relatively high, and this generally limits their use to mass production.

DIEFENBAKER, JOHN GEORGE (1895-   ), Canadian statesman and prime minister, was born in Ontario and studied at the University of Saskatchewan. After serving in World War I as a lieutenant, Diefenbaker took a law degree, was called to the bar, and opened a law office in Wakaw, Saskatchewan, where he was notably successful as a defense lawyer.

In 1929 Diefenbaker was made king's counsel. From 1936 to 1940 he was the Conservative party leader in Saskatchewan, and in 1940 he was elected to the Canadian House of Commons. In 1943 Diefenbaker was chairman of the first British Commonwealth Conference, and in 1946 he served as a delegate to the

National Film Board, Ottawa

John George Diefenbaker

Empire Parliamentary Association. He was a delegate to the United Nations in 1952, and in 1955, a delegate to the North Atlantic Treaty Organization. Diefenbaker became opposition leader in the Canadian House of Commons in 1956, and in 1957 he became the Canadian prime minister, heading the first Progressive Conservation government in 22 years. In 1958 he won an overwhelming victory over Lester Pearson. Under Diefenbaker Canada began its space program, and the St. Lawrence Seaway, one of the greatest of modern engineering feats, was opened.

DIESEL, RUDOLF (1858-1913), a German inventor, was born in Paris. He was educated in England and at the Polytechnic School in Munich, Germany. In 1893 he proposed a method of utilizing directly the energy created by the combustion of fuel oil. His first plan was unsuccessful, but it led to his invention of the diesel engine.

DIESEL ENGINE, a highly efficient internal-combustion engine in which air is compressed in the engine's cylinders to such a high degree that it is heated above the ignition point of the fuel. Oil is sprayed under pressure into the combustion chamber of the engine.

Like the gasoline engine the four-cycle diesel engine has four strokes with different functions. On the

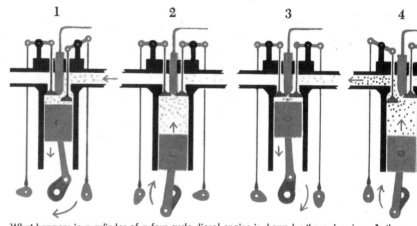

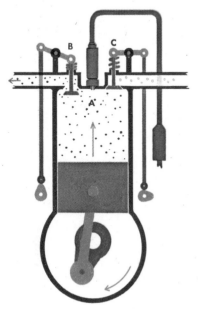

The cylinder of a diesel engine has three openings, including the fuel-injector nozzle, **A**; intake valve, **B**; exhaust valve, **C**.

What happens in a cylinder of a four-cycle diesel engine is shown by these drawings: **1,** the piston draws in fresh air; **2,** the piston compresses the air; **3,** fuel is injected into the cylinder and ignited by heat of the compressed air; **4,** the explosion pushes the piston down. The piston forces out exhaust gases. These four actions of the cycle are continuously repeated.

first, or intake, stroke of the piston air is drawn into the cylinder. On the second, or compression, stroke the air is compressed to pressures upward of 400 pounds per square inch. On the third, or power, stroke the heated air ignites the atomized fuel, and the reaction from this combustion pushes the piston downward to drive a crankshaft. On the fourth, or exhaust, stroke the burned gases are expelled through an exhaust valve. It is evident, then, that it is only on the third stroke that power is developed.

Unlike the gasoline engine, the two-cycle diesel engine is fully as popular as the four-cycle type. Starting with the firing stroke, the

fuel is injected near top dead center into the high-temperature compressed air, and the piston descends with impetus from the expanding mixture. A few degrees before bottom dead center the exhaust opens so that the burned mixture can escape. Shortly after the exhaust opens, the air intake opens, and fresh air is blown into the cylinder under several pounds of pressure. Shortly after the piston reaches the bottom of its stroke (dead center), all valves close, and the piston rises on the compression stroke to prepare for the firing stroke, as noted. The exhaust may be by valves in the cylinder head and ports uncovered by the piston, or both may be

A diesel locomotive may consist of several coupled units. This three-unit locomotive develops the power needed to pull a long freight train through mountainous country.

Union Pacific Colorphoto

controlled by ports uncovered by the piston.

The greatest problem that faced the builders of diesel engines was that of reducing weight. Because of the high compression necessary for the diesel engine's operation, stronger materials must be used in its construction than in other types of internal-combustion engines. However, progress in metallurgy was invaluable in furnishing lighter alloys to diesel-engine builders, and the weight was reduced. Diesel engines have come into widespread use in steamlined trains, trucks, and tractors, and in a few instances they have been successfully used in airplanes and automobiles. Diesel engines are important as prime movers in generating electricity, since they can be geared to generators in stationary powerplants, ships, and locomotives.

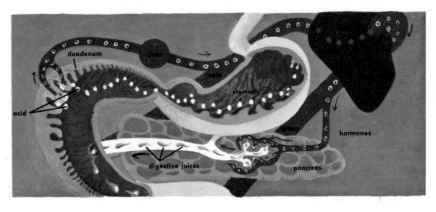

Digestion is controlled by many complex mechanisms, such as the one that governs the secretion of pancreatic juices. Acids from the stomach stimulate the walls of the duodenum, or upper small intestine, to release certain hormones into the bloodstream. Carried to the pancreas, the hormones cause pancreatic juices to be sent to the small intestine.

DIET. A modern diet is a selected quantity and type of food suitable to the needs of an individual. The basic needs of the body can be supplied by following a daily diet of the seven basic foods. See BASIC-SEVEN FOODS.

There is a wide variation in the number of Calories, or energy-units, required by individuals. The number depends upon the person's daily activities, size, age, and sex. Recommended daily allowances of Calories for boys and girls 13 to 15 years of age are 3,100 and 2,600 Calories repectively. About 3,600 Calories are recommended for boys of 16 to 19 years. Girls of 16 to 19 years need about 2,400 Calories a day.

Nutrients are substances essential in a diet designed to maintain good health. Some of the essential vitamins are vitamin A, the B vitamins (thiamine, riboflavin, niacin, and others), vitamin C (ascorbic acid), vitamin D, and vitamins E and K. Protein, carbohydrate and fat, and water are vital nutrients. Minerals such as iron, calcium, iodine, and many others are also nutrients. Recommended daily allowances of nutrients for boys of 13 to 15 years are 85 grams of protein, 1.4 grams of calcium, 15 milligrams of iron, 5,000 I.U.'s (International Units) of vitamin A, 1.6 milligrams of thiamine, 2.1 milligrams of riboflavin, 21 milligrams of niacin, 90 milligrams of vitamin C, and 400 I.U.'s of vitamin D. Girls of 13 to 19 years need slightly less of most nutrients than the amounts listed. Boys of 16 to 19 years need somewhat larger allowances of nutrients.

An adequate diet is one that supplies enough Calories and nutrients each day to maintain good nutrition in a healthy person. An adequate diet supplies more than the bare minimum of minerals, vitamins, and proteins. An adequate diet provides a margin of safety.

Persons with special health problems may need special diets. All special diets should be prescribed by a physician or a dietitian for the individual's needs.

Food fads and unsupervised reducing diets are commonly useless in improving health or reducing weight. At most, such diets can induce serious malnutrition.

DIGESTION is the process of converting food into materials for absorption and assimilation by the body. It is accomplished by the action of digestive juices that produce chemical changes in the food and break it down into simpler substances. Digestion takes place in the alimentary canal. It begins in the mouth with the grinding action of the teeth and the mixing of saliva with the food particles. In the act of swallowing, the food is passed to the esophagus. (See SWALLOWING.) The wall of the esophagus is lined with a muscular coat that contracts in waves to force the food into the stomach. The stomach is a large, elastic sac, which also has a muscular wall capable of churning and moving the food along. In addition, the stomach has a mucous membrane lining that secretes certain digestive juices. Secretion is stimulated by the presence of food in the stomach. By chemical action, the enzymes in the digestive juices break the food down into smaller particles. For example, pepsin, secreted in the upper part of the stomach, breaks down proteins. Here the food also assumes a liquid form before it passes into the first part of the small intestine, or duodenum. In the duodenum bile from the liver and juices from the pancreas continue the process of digestion. Fats and starches are broken down. Absorption of food materials into the bloodstream occurs in the small intestine by means of small blood vessels lining the intestinal wall. Proteins are absorbed in the form of amino acids, fats in the form of fatty acids, and carbohydrates in the form of simple sugars. By the time the contents reach the large intestine, most of the food materials have been fully digested and absorbed. During passage along the large intestine water is absorbed from the nondigestible material so that it is expelled from the body in semisolid form.

DIGITAL COMPUTER. See COMPUTER.

DIKE AND LEVEE, walls or embankments of masonry, earth, or timber, used to keep the sea or a river from overflowing an area of land. The dikes of Holland are famous examples of one kind of embankment. These dikes date from Roman times. Drusus, the Roman general who conquered Holland in 10 B.C., built an elaborate system of canals and dikes in the country. In the 10th and 11th centuries the archbishops of Bremen in Germany called upon the inhabitants to build dikes to protect the marshes around the city.

In the United States the walls of earth and sandbags that hold the Mississippi River within its banks are called levees. These extend for many miles along the banks below the mouth of the Ohio River.

DIKE AND SILL. A dike is a tabular body of intrusive igneous rock. It has two flat sides. A dike may be very long or very wide, but it is never very thick in comparison to its length or width. A dike has dimensions something like those of a sheet of cardboard. A dike does not follow the structures of the rocks surrounding it but cuts across them.

Most dikes were formed when small amounts of molten rock intruded solid rocks close to the earth's surface. Dike rocks are usually fine grained or porphyritic (one kind of mineral in the rock has much larger crystals than other kinds of minerals). A dike rock may be of any composition.

Dike rocks are often more resistant to erosion and weathering than the rocks surrounding them. Such dikes may project from surrounding rocks like walls. On a cliff face a dike looks like a ribbon of rock of different color or texture that cuts across other rocks.

Some dikes are exposed for only a few feet or yards on the earth's surface. Other dikes can be traced for miles. A dike may be only a fraction of an inch thick or several hundred feet thick. Most dikes are a few feet thick.

Sills are sheetlike bodies of intrusive rock that are similar to dikes but are parallel to the dominant structure of the surrounding rock. Sills, like dikes, are thin compared to their length and width. Sills may be large or small, thick or thin. Sill rocks of many different compositions have been found.

Dinosaurs are divided into two great orders: the Ornithischia, or "Bird Hips" (top, right); and the Saurischia, or "Reptile Hips" (right).

Sills are oftenest formed when molten rock invades layered sedimentary rocks. The molten rock spreads out where it finds the least resistance—in the divisions between sedimentary layers. Thus, thin, sheetlike intrusive bodies that follow the main sedimentary structure are formed.

Perhaps the most famous sill in the United States is the sill that forms The Palisades, a line of cliffs on the west bank of the Hudson River opposite New York. This sill is more than 900 feet thick in places. The sill is not horizontal but dips west. The layered sedimentary rocks in which the sill was intruded have been tilted. Because of its resistance to erosion the sill forms a series of high cliff faces extending for about 15 miles.

DINOSAUR, a general name for two orders of ancient, and now extinct, reptiles. One dinosaur group is the order Saurischia, meaning reptile-like pelvis, and the other is the order Ornithischia, meaning bird-like pelvis. All dinosaurs were not large. The earliest dinosaurs were of small or medium size, like modern lizards, and so were many of the later dinosaurs. The dinosaurs lived in the Mesozoic era.

Some of the early forms of the saurischians, or reptile-like dinosaurs, were small, but later forms became very large. The theropods were a group of saurischian dinosaurs that walked on their hindlegs and were flesh eating. Some theropods were very large, for example, the tyrannosaurs. (See TYRANNOSAUR.) Another reptile-like group

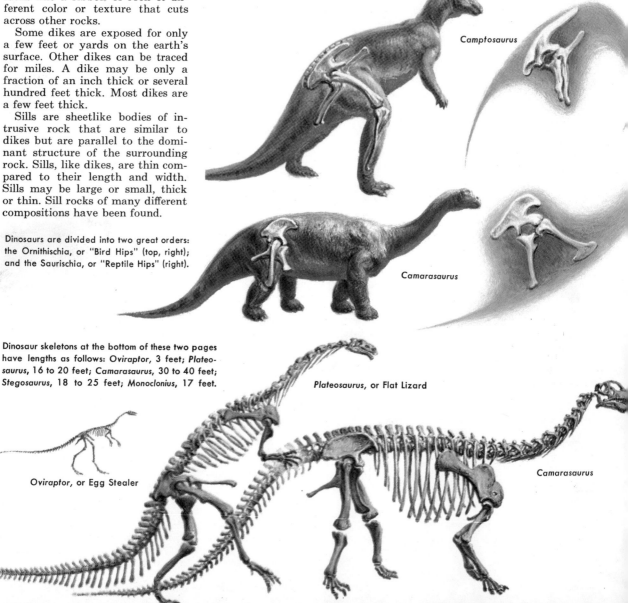

Camptosaurus

Camarasaurus

Dinosaur skeletons at the bottom of these two pages have lengths as follows: *Oviraptor*, 3 feet; *Plateosaurus*, 16 to 20 feet; *Camarasaurus*, 30 to 40 feet; *Stegosaurus*, 18 to 25 feet; *Monoclonius*, 17 feet.

Plateosaurus, or Flat Lizard

Oviraptor, or Egg Stealer

Camarasaurus

Brontosaurus' name means "Thunder Lizard."

Stegosaurus used his spiked tail for defense.

Proceratops was "first of the horn faces."

Iguanadon, or Lizard Tooth

Stegosaurus, or Covered Lizard

Monoclonius, or Single Horn

This dinosaur is *Oviraptor*, or Egg Stealer.

Triceratops' name means "Three-Horn-Face."

was the sauropods, the huge plant-eating dinosaurs that walked on four feet. These animals were mostly amphibious. The plants the sauropods fed on were abundant in swamps and lakes. Some of the sauropod dinosaurs were so large that it was difficult for them to move on land. The brontosaurs were amphibious sauropod dinosaurs. So was *Brachiosaurus*, the giant of all known dinosaurs. A *Brachiosaurus* weighed about 50 tons and was tall enough to have looked over the top of a three-story building.

The early ornithischians, or dinosaurs with birdlike pelves, were plant-eating animals that often walked on their hindlegs. One group of ornithischians was the duck-billed dinosaurs. (See DUCK-BILLED DINOSAUR.) Another group was the stegosaurs, a type of armored dinosaur. The stegosaurs had projecting plates or spines on their backs and walked on four feet. Another armored vegetarian group was the ankylosaurs. The ankylosaurs looked something like large armadillos and were cov-

ered with bony plates and spines. A fourth group of ornithischian dinosaurs was the horned dinosaurs, of which *Triceratops* is an example. *Triceratops* was a large quadruped plant-eating dinosaur with two long horns above his eyes and a third horn on his nose. *Triceratops* also had a bony neck frill for protection.

The dinosaurs became abundant shortly after the beginning of the Mesozoic era. However, at the end of the Mesozoic all dinosaurs became extinct. It is thought that changes in land forms, climate, and vegetation may have led to the extinction of the dinosaurs.

DIOGENES (412?-323? B.C.), a Greek Cynic philosopher, lived in both Corinth and Athens. He opposed nature to convention and emphasized self-sufficiency and shamelessness. For this last characteristic he was called *kynos* (dog); from this the word *cynic* was derived. Three legends are traditionally told of Diogenes: that he lived in a tub; that he once walked with a lantern through the streets searching for an honest man; and that his reply to Alexander the Great, when the king asked the philosopher what he wished, was: "Stand between me and the sun."

DIONYSUS. See BACCHUS.

DIPHTHERIA, a contagious disease, commoner among children than among adults. It causes severe toxic reactions and is often fatal. Diphtheria is known to be caused by a specific germ called the diphtheria bacillus.

The disease begins with malaise, a feeling of chilliness, loss of appetite, headache, and more or less fever. Soon the throat feels hot and painful, and the neck is stiff and tender. If seen early, the throat is red and swollen, but a false membrane of yellowish or grayish color quickly appears in spreading patches.

Scientists have succeeded in discovering a remedy that, injected into the veins of the patient, neutralizes the toxin produced by the diphtheria germ and is therefore called antitoxin. Diphtheria antitoxin is obtained from the blood of horses infected with diphtheria. Immunization may be secured without an attack of the disease by use of toxin-antitoxin, or toxoid. Also the degree of immunity (indicating absence of susceptibility to the disease) can be determined by a skin reaction, the Schick test.

DIPLOMACY, in international relations, the art of conducting political relations between nations. The word *diplomacy* came from the French, who have provided history with many great diplomats, Richelieu and Talleyrand to name only two. The task of diplomacy is a continuous one. There is no respite in the endeavor to resolve conflicts that arise between nations that have agreed to live more or less peacefully with one another. This last stipulation is important. For example, attempts to arrange diplomatic settlements with Nazi Germany led only to appeasement, for Hitler was bent on conquest.

Diplomacy is one of the elements of a nation's power. Its importance must not be overemphasized, but it is logical that a nation with a well-conceived and consistent foreign policy carried on by efficient diplomats will be more powerful thereby. It follows that one aim of diplomacy is to maintain and increase a nation's power. Given the destructiveness of modern warfare, most diplomats would agree that the best way to increase a nation's strength is to maintain peace among nations. To carry out the complicated tasks of diplomacy, the diplomat must make a number of difficult judgments. First, he must be able to appraise correctly the strength of his own nation. Francisco Solano López of Paraguay failed in this task when he fomented a hopeless war against Argentina, Brazil, and Uruguay in 1864. Second, the good diplomat must correctly appraise the power of other nations. Mussolini, who was a poor diplomat, did not do this when his armies invaded Greece in 1940 and were defeated. Finally, diplomats, having analyzed the elements of strength in their own and other nations, must devise the means whereby they may further the aims of their nation.

The various means used in diplomacy to adjust differences are direct negotiations between diplomats or heads of state, conferences or congresses between the diplomats of many nations, and international organizations. At one time diplomats could carry on much of their negotiation in secret, which was easier for the diplomat. Since the French and American revolutions, however, diplomats have become responsible to the public opinion of the nations they represent, and the ease of communication after the invention of the telegraph meant that the diplomat was always in contact with his home government—he was no longer a relatively free agent. See ALLIANCE; BALANCE OF POWER; DIPLOMAT; INTERNATIONAL LAW; INTERNATIONAL RELATIONS; TREATY; UNITED NATIONS.

DIPLOMAT, an official who represents his nation in another nation. A diplomat is a government employee who resides abroad.

The head of a diplomatic mission is called an ambassador. He is appointed by the president to be ambassador to Great Britain, to France, or to some other nation. Ambassadors are assisted in their duties by other career diplomats, specialists in various subjects, and military attachés.

You may have heard of the many receptions and other social functions that diplomats are said to attend. Actually, these functions are a chore to the conscientious diplomat. They mean that he will have to make out his reports at irregular times. These reports are the real job of the diplomat. They tell about the political and economic affairs in the nation to which he is sent. In order to discover facts for these reports, the diplomat must meet many people. He must know other diplomats and members of the party in power, members of opposition parties, and other leaders of the country.

Diplomats must be well educated. To enter the foreign service the young person who aspires to be a diplomat must take an examination that lasts an entire day. He must have a college education, a good command of English and at least one foreign language, and training in history, geography, economics, sociology, and political science. If he is admitted to the foreign service, he may take special courses in other subjects or languages.

Very early in its history the United States had two remarkable diplomats. Benjamin Franklin was appointed commissioner to France in 1776 by the Continental Congress. Franklin was one of the most remarkable men of his time. His scientific works were read all over Europe. He was very well liked in France. When he left France, there were enough portraits, busts, and medallions of him to make him one of the world's best known diplomats. He was replaced in France by Thomas Jefferson, another diplomat of many talents. When asked if he was sent to replace Franklin in Paris, Jefferson said, "No one can replace him, sir; I am only his successor." See STATE, UNITED STATES DEPARTMENT OF.

OCCUPATION: Diplomat (U.S. Foreign Service Officer)

NATURE OF WORK: Protecting and promoting the welfare and interests of the United States abroad

PERSONAL FACTORS—ABILITIES, SKILLS, APTITUDES: Traits needed are: a pleasant personality; integrity and sensitivity in dealing with people; an open, curious mind; quick thinking and good judgment; an interest in international affairs; and robust health.

EDUCATION AND SPECIAL TRAINING: A bachelor's degree in liberal arts with emphasis on social science studies and with some business administration is recommended. Training in a school offering bachelor of diplomacy courses is helpful but not essential. Applicant must be a United States citizen and at least 21 years old and must pass oral, written, and physical examinations. He must submit to a background investigation.

WORKING CONDITIONS:

1. **INCOME:**
   COMPARED WITH OTHER CAREERS WITH EQUAL TRAINING: High to low
   COMPARED WITH MOST OTHER CAREERS: High to average

2. **ENVIRONMENT:** Variable, in home-office departmental staff with regular hours or in foreign post with irregular hours and conditions

3. **OTHER:** Liberal travel, housing, and medical allowances for overseas posts; salaries and advancements on merit system; employment opportunities excellent for qualified applicants

RELATED CAREERS: Foreign Service Staff, Foreign Service Reserve, civil-service employee, government worker

WHERE TO FIND MORE INFORMATION: Employment Division, U.S. Department of State, Washington 25, D.C.

DIPPING NEEDLE. A dipping needle indicates the local vertical component of the earth's magnetic field. A dipping needle is a magnetic needle supported at its center of gravity so that it can swing freely in a vertical arc. A circular scale to show the angle of dip from the horizontal is fixed in the plane in which the needle rotates. To show the true local vertical component the plane in which the needle rotates must be parallel to the local compass direction.

Dipping needles are often used in prospecting for minerals having magnetic properties, such as iron, nickel, or cobalt. Since the magnetic field of the earth is distorted by the presence of a deposit of magnetic material, it is possible, by making many measurements over an area, to obtain an idea of the shape and size of the mineral deposit.

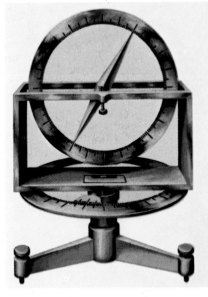

A dipping needle shows the angle between the earth's magnetic field and the horizontal.

DIRECT CURRENT, an electrical current that flows continuously in one direction, as compared with alternating current, which periodically reverses direction. It is usually abbreviated to DC. Direct current is produced by batteries, by generators, or by rectifying alternating current. The principal disadvantage of direct current is that it is not as easily converted from low voltage to the high voltage required for long-distance transmission of power as is alternating current.

A direct-current generator differs from an alternating-current generator chiefly in containing a commutator, which is a mechanical device to rectify the alternating current set up in a continuously rotating armature. The direct-current motor must also use a commutator. See ELECTRIC GENERATOR; ELECTRIC MOTOR.

Some electrical processes require the use of direct current, for example, electroplating or electrorefining. Storage batteries are charged with direct current. Small amounts of direct current are used in many electronic devices; there are tubes, rectifiers, and circuits available to produce this direct current as it is needed. See ALTERNATING CURRENT; ELECTROPLATING.

DIRIGIBLE, a rigid or semirigid gas balloon that is steerable. Three names are given to the same type of lighter-than-air craft; these are *dirigible*, *airship*, and *zeppelin*. The name *zeppelin* is used only for certain of these ships made in Germany. Dirigibles have a rigid, cigar-shaped framework, generally made of aluminum alloy, such as Duralumin, and divided structurally into several transverse compartments, most of which contain gas cells that supply the lifting power. The entire structure is covered with fabric or sheet aluminum or is wrapped with strips of aluminum. Airship motive power is supplied by gasoline or diesel engines mounted either within the framework of the dirigible or located in nacelles along the sides. Ingenious drive-shaft mechanisms transmit power to the large multi-bladed outboard propellers in dirigibles that have the engines mounted internally. Directional control is attained by horizontal and vertical fins projecting from the stern of the ship, by water ballast tanks at strategic positions, and by the use of the individual motors. Built into the lower front of the framework and protruding from it is the gondola,

When the German zeppelin *Hindenburg* exploded and burned on May 6, 1937, at Lakehurst, N.J., 36 people were killed.
UPI

This cutaway shows the interior construction of the U. S. Navy's *Shenandoah*. A metal framework covered with cotton fabric painted with aluminum was filled with helium gas. It was destroyed by a storm in 1925.

The dirigible built in 1852 by the French engineer Henri Giffard was steered by a small sail attached at the rear.

which contains accommodations for passengers and crew, freight, and observation and control rooms.

The first dirigible to be constructed was built by Henri Giffard, a French engineer, in 1852. It had a steam engine that aided its propulsion. In 1872 Paul Haenlein, a German engineer, flew the first dirigible powered by a gas engine. A metal dirigible was built in 1897 by David Schwarz, a Hungarian. It was powered by a Daimler engine. Because of leaking gas, it crashed after traveling several miles. Count Ferdinand von Zeppelin of Germany made his first flight in a rigid-frame airship in 1900. He reached a speed of 18 miles per hour and flew $3\frac{1}{2}$ miles before being forced down.

The first dirigible flight across the Atlantic Ocean was made in 1919 by the R-34, a British craft. The trip took 108 hours from Firth of Forth, Scotland, to Long Island, New York. In 1921 the first helium-filled balloon was developed by the U.S.

The Bettmann Archive

Navy. It was flown from Hampton Roads, Va., to Washington, D.C.

With the exception of a few ships, including the world-famous *Graf Zeppelin*, the majority of dirigibles have come to tragic ends. For the most part this has been due to explosions resulting from ignition of the highly flammable hydrogen gas that is used to raise many of the huge cigar-shaped bags. Hydrogen has a high rate of diffusion and readily escapes through porous materials, such as the gasbags of dirigibles, even though every precaution is taken to make the pores as minute as possible. Since hydrogen is the cheapest and most available of the lighter-than-air gases and one that furnishes more lift per unit volume than any other, it has been, despite its flammability, widely used in dirigibles. Many disasters have occurred, even to dirigibles using helium, a somewhat heavier gas than hydrogen but one that is nonflammable. Furthermore, helium is much more expensive than hydrogen, is less available, and possesses less lifting capacity than hydrogen; hence its use is greatly restricted. The causes of accidents in helium-inflated dirigibles are diverse and obscure; the greatest single factor appears to be adverse weather conditions. During the era of the dirigible a large number of the craft crashed, causing great loss of life and property.

DISARMAMENT means the complete or partial reduction of weapons by nations. In the past, the only successful disarmament has been that imposed upon the vanquished during war. And that has not always been successful.

Centuries before the birth of Christ, there was a state of "cold war" between mighty Rome and Carthage. Although they once had been allies, conflicts grew up between these cities and erupted into war. After the Second Punic War, Rome imposed disarmament on Carthage, making that city give up most of its ships and all of its elephants (the tanks of ancient armies). But Rome still feared the power of Carthage. After the Third Punic War, Rome imposed terrible terms of absolute disarmament on Carthage. The city was plundered and burned to the ground.

Voluntary disarmament, however, has not been so successful as the disarmament of the vanquished. Perhaps, we can learn why voluntary disarmament has not worked well among nations by looking at one of the rare instances in which it has worked. The best model of effective disarmament is the Rush-Bagot Agreement of 1817 between the United States and Great Britain. The agreement limited the number of warships on the Great Lakes. It worked because after 1817 relations between the United States and Great Britain were friendly. Warships on the Great Lakes were not necessary. Therefore, there was no arms race. The lesson to be learned is that disarmament between friendly powers is possible. Disarmament between hostile powers is not so easy. The weapons themselves do not cause wars. Wars are caused by conflicts that make weapons seem necessary.

After World War I efforts to limit armaments were to no avail. Disarmament, however, if only as a sign that relations between nations have finally become friendly, remained the hope of many people. This hope was expressed in 1941, early in World War II, by President Franklin D. Roosevelt and Winston Churchill in the eighth point of the Atlantic Charter: "Eight, they [the Allies] believe that all of the nations of the world, for realistic as well as spiritual reasons, must come to the abandonment of the use of force."

In 1952 the UN Disarmament Commission was established to explore ways of achieving disarmament, both of atomic weapons and conventional armaments. See INTERNATIONAL LAW; LEAGUE OF NATIONS; PACIFISM; UNITED NATIONS.

DISCUSSION, the interchange of ideas, varying in form from conversational exchange to formal, assigned speeches. In discussions the speakers express views about questions. The views of all speakers may be modified as the discussion progresses. For groups trying to make decisions discussions often clarify thinking. The participants in a discussion may include a leader, or chairman, and an audience as well as the speakers. The job of the leader in all discussions is to keep the discussion moving and perhaps to summarize the conclusions.

A discussion may take several forms. The type selected should be appropriate to the group and to the purpose of the discussion.

TYPES OF DISCUSSION

Informal discussion consists of free, unprepared speaking. Usually from 10 to 20 persons participate. Members speak from their seats without being called on by the chairman. The leader sees to it that the discussion runs smoothly and that the speakers know one another and the issues. An informal discussion may have two leaders, one of whom takes notes and summarizes the discussion at intervals.

A discussion consisting of a short speech followed by participation or questioning from the audience is called an open-forum discussion. The chairman keeps order and sees to it that no one individual dominates the discussion.

An informal discussion among speakers with different points of view as well as different information about a subject is called a roundtable discussion. Such a discussion rarely involves audience participation. The speakers interrupt one another at will. The purpose of the roundtable is to inform the public about a subject and about the views of various authorities on the subject. The chairman's job is to stimulate discussion by questions.

A panel discussion is similar to a roundtable discussion in that the speakers represent different points of view. However, a panel usually serves as a preliminary to a discussion in which an audience participates. The audience puts questions to individual speakers or to the entire panel. In a symposium each speaker in turn gives a fairly long, prepared speech. There is no interruption of any symposium speaker until all of the speakers have finished their presentations.

A panel in which the speakers' opinions are evenly divided may become a debate. See DEBATE.

PREPARATION FOR A GROUP DISCUSSION

The chairman as well as the speakers should be well prepared for a discussion. He should be acquainted with the subject. He should list beforehand important points that will come up. On a separate list he might list items of secondary importance for discussion if there is time.

The chairman should know something about the occupation and

field of study or interests of the participants. He often keeps back his own opinions, while encouraging the participants to express theirs. This is done to avoid dominating the discussion. The chairman should make all participants feel that their contributions are appreciated.

The chairman's job is to begin the discussion, to keep it moving, and to bring it to an end. Either he or a second person records the important points of a meeting and presents a final summary.

The chairman will find that there are various ways to begin. One way is to announce the subject and then to address the speakers at large or an individual speaker with a question. If the chairman is able to chat with several participants before the meeting, he may open the meeting by saying that he has just been discussing a certain topic with Mr. Blank and then call on Mr. Blank to speak.

The chairman must always keep the subject and purpose of the meeting in mind. It is up to him to forward the discussion with questions and contributions. He should summarize as seldom as possible.

If a topic becomes exhausted, the chairman should be able to lead the speakers to the next subject. The chairman should end the meeting before participants become repetitive or tired. At the end he will summarize the discussion and list the points that require action or more thought.

The dead man lying on a cart in a London street was the victim of an epidemic of bubonic plague that in 1348 ravaged England and most other European countries, killing millions of people. This epidemic could not be checked because people did not know that the disease, then called the Black Death, was transmitted by fleas that were carried by rats from one locality to another.

DISEASE, a state of lack of health; an illness; a sickness. Each specific disease is an abnormal process that has characteristic symptoms and follows a recognized course. Common examples of diseases are measles, mumps, chickenpox, scarlet fever, tuberculosis, pneumonia, anemia, arthritis, diabetes, and cancer.

Diseases may be classified according to cause. For example, infectious diseases are those caused by infection with plant and animal parasites (fungi, bacteria, viruses). Diseases may also be classified according to the organ or organ system affected. Some diseases affect the whole body. Others affect the skin and mucous membrane. There are also diseases of muscles and bones; of the respiratory system; of the cardiovascular system; of the blood-forming and lymphatic systems; of the digestive system; of the urogenital system; of the endocrine system; of the nervous system; and of the special sense organs (eye and ear).

The main symptoms of disease are comparatively few. Some of these symptoms are weakness and insensibility, disorders of breathing, disturbances in the circulation of the blood, digestive and nutritional disturbances, disorders of kidney function, disorders of blood-forming organs, and new growths.

Diagnosis of disease means discovery by the physician of all the factors — physical, environmental, and emotional—that contribute to the patient's illness. In making a diagnosis the physician first asks the patient for a history of his illness. The physician then performs a physical examination and orders laboratory tests. These tests may include chemical or microscopic examination of the blood and body wastes; X-ray examinations; basal metabolism test; electrocardiographic examination of the heart; and electroencephalographic examination of brain function. In correlating the history of the illness with the findings on physical examination and laboratory tests, the physician seeks to eliminate signs that are not significant from signs that point to possible causes. For example, many of the signs of the common cold in the first day or two of illness are similar to those of measles and chickenpox and also of meningitis.

The treatment of a disease is based on the discovery of the specific cause, if there is one, and then eliminating the cause. In some infectious diseases the specific germ causing the disease has been identified and a specific drug has been proved to destroy the organism without harm to the body. Treatment of such diseases is almost always successful. The same is true of diseases caused by improper diet, for example, beriberi or pellagra. Hormone treatment in such diseases as diabetes permits the patient to live a fairly normal life. Diseases that have no known specific cause and hence no specific treatment include high blood pressure and cancer.

Disease may be prevented if its specific cause is known. When the germ and mode of transmission of an infectious disease are known, it may be prevented by public health measures. Industrial diseases caused by known toxins, trauma, and chemical and physical irritants can be controlled by measures that have become standard in many industries. The prevention of nutritional diseases depends on adequate diet. More and more is being learned about the factor of stress and emotions in human illness. Such disease may be prevented by the establishment of healthy patterns of physical and mental activity. See MEDICINE.

DISH, a shallow, concave, usually round vessel generally used for serving food at the table. Fragments of dishes, among the most common of archaeological artifacts, provide the scientist with important clues to the level and character of past civilizations. During the classical periods of Greece and Rome dishes were generally made of pewter, silver, bronze, and earthenware. In China by the 7th century the art of making porcelain dishes, along with bronzes and paintings, was considered among the prized accomplishments of a Chinese nobleman. During the Middle Ages in Europe large silver dishes were used for decoration in the dining hall of the feudal castle. Food was brought to the table in large flat pewter dishes, called chargers. Portions were then doled out into smaller individual bowls. The lower classes ate out of trenchers—round or square pieces of wood with a rimmed, slightly sunken center. During the Renaissance highly decorated pottery dishes began to appear, especially in Spain, France, and Italy. Very often the coat of arms of the owner was painted in the center of each dish of a set. These dishes were usually used for display purposes only. By the end of the 17th century earthenware dishes had become popular throughout Europe. Chinese porcelain began to be imported during the later part of the 17th century. (See CHINA.) Soon European artisans began to turn out porcelain tea and coffee sets. Names such as Meissen and Wedgwood became well known throughout the civilized world. By the end of the 19th century table settings had become quite large, not only in size but in the number of pieces as well. The trend in recent years has been toward smaller settings of simpler, more functional design.

DISHWASHING

Dishwashing is a task that has been made easier in recent years by the automatic dishwasher. In many homes without an automatic dishwasher the kitchen sink is divided into two parts with a drainboard at one side. Dishes can be washed in one part of the sink, rinsed in the other, and placed on a rack on the drainboard to dry. With an undivided sink it is best to use one large pan for washing dishes and another for rinsing, although many people prefer to do the rinsing directly under the tap. Washing is easier if the dishes are first scraped. It is important that water for washing and rinsing be hot enough to destroy harmful bacteria. Begin by washing the glasses and the least soiled dishes, then the silverware and the remaining dishes, and finally the pots and pans. Wooden salad bowls and articles with wooden, bone, or plastic handles should be merely wiped off with a damp sponge. Aluminum ware should not be soaked in hot, soapy water for long periods of time. If necessary, use a fine abrasive cleaner on the highly polished surfaces of pots and pans. Steel or copper wool is suitable for use on rougher metal surfaces. Rinse the dishes in a separate pan or under the tap. If the rinse water is very hot, dishes may be left in the rack to dry. Otherwise, dry with a linen or cotton dish towel. Pots, pans, and silverware should always be wiped dry. Special care must be taken when washing fragile glassware and china. Temperature of the wash and rinse water should be about the same.

Lever Bros.

Courtesy of Whirlpool Corporation

A dishwasher automatically washes and rinses dishes and silverware. The housewife merely places the dirty dishes on the racks and removes the dishes after they have been washed.

DISHWASHER, a machine that washes, rinses, and dries dishes, silverware, and cooking utensils. The dishes are stacked in racks, and an electric motor forces hot water over them at high pressure. The dishes are washed with a detergent and rinsed, usually twice, with clear water. The temperature and pressure of the water are sufficient to remove all food particles and grease and kill all germs. Some dishwashers dry the dishes by circulating hot air around them; others open automatically and allow the dishes to dry more slowly at room temperature.

Dishwashers used in homes usually have two racks. In the kitchens of restaurants, hospitals, and other institutions where many dishes must be washed, dishwashers with several removable racks are used.

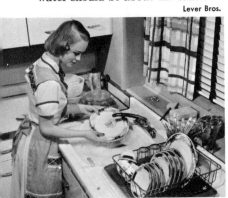

This housewife washes her dishes by a method approved by home economists. She rinses the soapy dishes in hot water and then lets them dry in the air without being wiped.

Use of these racks saves time by making it possible to perform three operations at once. While one rack is in the dishwasher, a second may be prepared for washing, and several more may be drying.

DISINFECTANT, an agent used to destroy germs that cause infections or enzymes that cause spoilage. Destruction of all living matter on any object is called sterilization. Destruction of disease-producing germs only is called disinfection.

An effective disinfectant should kill the germs it is used against. It must be chemically stable. It must not be harmful to animal tissues, yet it must penetrate deeply. It should also be a deodorant and a cleanser.

A disinfectant may kill by chemical or physical action. Heat, ultraviolet light, and X-rays are disinfectants. Common chemical disinfectants include carbolic acid, cresol, and mercuric chloride.

DISNEY

Disneyland transportation includes a skyway and a monorail (above).

A ride by stagecoach (above) across the cactus-strewn "desert" of Frontierland is a popular attraction at Disneyland.

This startlingly lifelike model of a bull elephant (below) contributes to the realism of the Adventureland "jungle."

The section of Disneyland known as Main Street, U.S.A., represents a small American town during the early 1900's. The oldtime train, stopped at the Main Street Station (above), tours the entire amusement park.

Behind the futuristically clad spaceman and spacegirl (below) is a tall, rocket-shaped pylon, a symbol of Tomorrowland.

DISNEY, WALT (1901-   ), in full Walter Elias Disney, American producer of animated cartoons, was born in Chicago. He studied at the Academy of Fine Arts in Chicago and served in World War I as an ambulance driver.

After a brief career as a commercial artist, Disney went to Hollywood to draw animated cartoons. He drew pictures in a series so that each drawing differed slightly from the one before it. When the pictures were photographed and projected on the screen in rapid succession, the figures appeared to be moving.

Among his early pictures were *Steamboat Willie*, starring a promising young actor named Mickey Mouse, and *The Skeleton Dance*, the first "Silly Symphony," produced in 1929. The latter was a forerunner of Disney's feature-length cartoon with classical music, *Fantasia*.

Disney's full-length motion pictures (some cartoons and some using live actors) included *Pinocchio*, *Snow White and the Seven Dwarfs*, *Dumbo*, *Cinderella*, *Peter Pan*, *20,000 Leagues Under the Sea*, and *Davy Crockett, King of the Wild Frontier*.

His nature series included *Seal Island*, *The Vanishing Prairie*, and *Secrets of Life*. In 1954 he began a television series "Disneyland," and a year later he opened an amusement park, also called Disneyland, near Los Angeles.

DISNEYLAND, a large amusement park at Anaheim, Calif., 22 miles southeast of Los Angeles. It was created and opened in 1955 by Walt Disney, the famous American motion picture producer. On 160 acres a wonderland of fairy tales and adventure was built. The main parts of the park are known as Tomorrowland, Fantasyland, Adventureland, and Frontierland.

In Tomorrowland the world of the future is represented by a monorail train, men in space suits, a huge rocket, a world clock, and modernistic buildings. Fantasyland has a large Sleeping Beauty Castle and other reproductions from fairy tales, as well as a 146-foot-high model of the Matterhorn, the famous mountain in Switzerland. Real cable cars carry passengers through tunnels in the mountain. Adventureland has such features as a trip through the jungle by boat, a submarine ride under the sea, and exotic Oriental and Latin bazaars. In Frontierland the old Wild West of the days of cowboys and Indians has been recreated. A frontier mine train takes people across the desert and through the underground Rainbow Caverns. Along the river runs the riverboat *Mark Twain*. Tom Sawyer Island is reached on Huckleberry Finn's raft.

The park has a hotel and 18 restaurants. Buses, trains, helicopters, and limousines arrive at Disneyland on regular schedules several times a day from various points in southern California.

DISRAELI, BENJAMIN (1804-1881), 1st earl of Beaconsfield, English statesman and author, was born in London. He was educated privately, never attending a public school or a university. In 1817 he was baptized into the Church of England.

Disraeli entered politics as a radical, but it was not until he stood as a Tory that he was elected to represent Maidstone in the House of Commons in 1837. In 1839 he married Mary Ann Evans Lewis, the widow of Wyndham Lewis, his former colleague from Maidstone. In 1841 he was sent to Parliament by Shrewsbury and in 1847 by Buckinghamshire. He held this seat until he entered the House of Lords.

About this time he became the leader of the Young England party, which upheld the crown and the aristocracy against the wealthy manufacturing classes and advocated measures to protect the working class from the evils of the factory system. In 1846 he was the chief

The British statesman Benjamin Disraeli was twice Queen Victoria's prime minister.

advocate of protection against the free-trade policy of Robert Peel.

Disraeli was chancellor of the exchequer in 1853, 1857-1858, and 1867. In 1868 he was prime minister and again from 1874 to 1880. His greatest feat as prime minister was the purchase from Egypt of the control of the Suez Canal for Great Britain in 1875. He was responsible for conferring the title of "Empress of India" on Queen Victoria in 1876. The same year he was raised to the peerage as earl of Beaconsfield. He took a prominent part in the Russian-Turkish question and the conclusion of the Treaty of Berlin (1878). Though Disraeli resigned office in 1880, he retained the leadership of his party.

Lord Beaconsfield was one of the most remarkable men of the 19th century. Endowed with great intellectual power, he had astonishing tenacity of purpose and remarkable tact. As a speaker he had few rivals; he was a master in wit, sarcasm, and epigram.

DISTANCE is the separation of things in space. The units that we use to measure distance range from tiny invisible units to the enormous units used by astronomers in describing the universe. (For a description of these units, see LENGTH.) Earth distances are measured scientifically by special methods of surveyors. (See SURVEYING.) This article will be concerned with perception of distance.

Usually we are so much aware of the objects we see that we forget that we also see distances at the same time. This sense of distance

or depth is enormously important in understanding our surroundings. Without it we would see only flat scenes of shape and color. However, we have a surprising number of ways of perceiving distance, and most of them have to do with our eyes. Some of the ways depend on using two eyes, and others work just as well with only one eye.

Binocular vision, or seeing an object through two eyes, is mainly responsible for our feeling of depth and solidity around us. Because the two eyes are a short distance apart, each sees an object from a slightly different angle. The right eye sees a little more of the right side of the object, the left eye a little more of the left side, and the brain puts the two images together into a single image. One image alone would lack the dimension of depth.

If the eyes are to combine two images when an object is at close range, tiny muscles attached to the eyeball must turn the eyes slightly inward. The sensation of this small effort, although it is usually unconscious, gives us another way of sensing whether we are seeing something near or far.

These two ways of sensing distance involve both eyes. The other ways are true for each eye alone. For instance, one shape will often partly block your view of another shape. If you already know what each shape should look like, you can tell which object is behind the other.

Another sense of distance comes from the fact that the same object looks smaller farther away. If you draw two lines from your eye, one to the top of an object and another to the bottom, the lines will spread wide apart when the object is close, but they will lie close together when it is distant. The angle between these lines determines the size of the image in the eye. The image gradually narrows as the object recedes. This effect is called linear perspective. See PERSPECTIVE.

Light and shading on objects, as well as the shadows cast by them, also contribute to a sense of distance. The air itself contributes to one sense of distance. Since it absorbs less blue light than light of other colors, we associate a faint blueness with distant scenes.

A last sense of distance, called parallax, depends on movement. When you ride through the country, a farmhouse in the distance seems to stay on a line with you, but the fenceposts near the road rush by in the opposite direction. Rapid movement is associated with nearness.

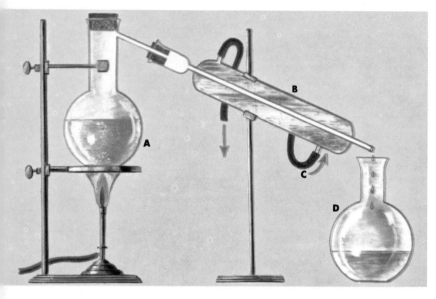

Distillation may be carried out with the simple still shown here. Liquid to be distilled is boiled in the distilling flask, **A**, and the vapors pass into the condenser, **B**. Ice water is kept flowing through the jacket, **C**, as indicated by the arrows. The ice water causes the vapors to condense, and relatively pure liquid drips into the receiving flask, **D**.

DISTILLATION is used to change a liquid into a vapor and the vapor back into a liquid. The purpose of distillation is to separate one liquid substance from another or to purify a liquid substance.

In distillation the liquid is heated in a closed vessel until it boils and becomes a vapor. The vapor then passes into another container where it is cooled and is thus converted into a liquid.

The separation of liquid substances by distillation is possible because almost every substance has a different boiling point. When a mixture is boiled during distillation, the liquid substance (in the mixture) with the lowest boiling point will turn into a vapor first. When all of this vapor has passed off, the temperature of the mixture will rise to the boiling point of the liquid with the next highest boiling point, and this liquid will pass into a vapor form. The same process will be repeated until all the liquids in the mixture have boiled away.

The conversion of a solid substance, such as iodine crystals, into a vapor and back into a solid is called sublimation. Destructive distillation is a term applied to the heating of such substances as coal, wood, bone, and petroleum until they decompose. This process yields products with properties different from the properties of the original substance. For example, coal gas is obtained from the destructive distillation of coal.

DISTRICT OF COLUMBIA. See WASHINGTON, D.C.

DIVINATION, the attempt to see things that are secret or are in the future. Such an attempt may range from crystal gazing to tossing a coin for "heads" or "tails." The practice of divination is found in all societies throughout the world. The motive behind divination is man's curiosity about the future, but the motive of the diviner may be avarice.

One of the most famous centers for divination was that of the Delphian oracle in ancient Greece. If a Greek desired advice from the god Apollo, he visited the oracle at Delphi. There a woman called the Pythia ate of the sacred laurel leaves, drank from the prophetic water of the subterranean Kassotis, and seated herself on a pedestal. In an ecstasy she gave an answer.

The Romans used to consult Virgil's *Aeneid* about the future. The *Aeneid* is a very exciting epic about the adventures of Aeneas after the fall of Troy. A Roman would choose a passage at random and interpret it to fit the future.

One interesting form of divination is crystal gazing. The practice is found all over the world: in Egypt, Polynesia, and Europe. It was practiced even among the Incas. The seer gazes at the large glass ball until it takes on a milky appearance (to the seer's eyes). Then, so it is said, the globe turns black. Images

appear to the seer. Some crystal gazers claim to see the past, the future, or present events happening in distant places.

DIVINE COMEDY, the greatest work of Italian literature and one of the greatest poems in any language, was written by Dante sometime between his exile from Florence in 1302 and his death in 1321. (See DANTE.) The poem, which is about 14,000 lines long, is in three parts: *Inferno*, *Purgatorio*, and *Paradiso*. Each part is divided into cantos; *Inferno* has 34 cantos, each of the others 33, so that the entire poem consists of 100 cantos. Dante uses a rhyme scheme of his own invention, called *terza rima*, whose three-line stanzas are interlocked by rhyming the second line of a stanza with the first and third lines of the following stanza.

In the *Comedy* the poet describes his visionary journey, guided by the Roman poet Virgil and his childhood sweetheart Beatrice Portinari, through Hell, Purgatory, and Paradise. The action begins on the Thursday before Easter, 1300. Dante is lost in a dark wood—symbolic of his state of total spiritual confusion—from which he is guided by the wisdom of Virgil. Virgil leads him through Hell, a funnel-shaped pit ending at the center of the earth, and through Purgatory, a seven-terraced mountain whose summit reaches to Heaven. Dante encounters many famous people and some of his own acquaintances both among the damned in Hell and among those purging themselves of their sins in Purgatory. At the summit of Purgatory Beatrice becomes Dante's guide and leads him through Heaven, where he learns the ultimate truths of theology and science as he moves toward the culmination of his journey, the direct apprehension of God.

Since Dante wanted his portrayal of a sinner's progress from confusion to salvation to reach the widest possible audience, he wrote it in Italian rather than in the Latin that had been the standard written language of medieval Europe for centuries. He entitled it simply *Commedia*, a work with a happy ending; the adjective *Divina* was added in the 16th century. The addition was justified, because Dante combined an understanding of all the human passions with a summary of the thought and knowledge of medieval Europe to produce an all-embracing vision of medieval man, of his universe, and of his Creator.

DIVING means entering the water, hands first, except in the case of some somersault dives, when the entry is made feet first. The dive may be performed from the pool side; from a starting block in racing; from a springboard, 1, 3, or 5 meters above the water; or from a firm board, 5 or 10 meters high.

The United States has a proud record in Olympic diving in both men's and women's sections. Although these performers are expert at all types of intricate movement, the basic principles of approach, takeoff, flight, and entry are the same for both simple and complex dives. Thus, to be a good diver one should learn the basic principles. Correct practice, interest, and helpful coaching will aid in the production of satisfying and first-class performance.

LEARNING TO DIVE

1. Sit on pool's edge, feet on the rail, knees wide apart. Place upper arms against ears, join thumbs, stretch arms, and look at the water. Allow hands to touch the water, look at your toes, and roll into the pool, hands first.

2. Repeat, but as roll starts, stretch legs. Have a friend in the water to take your hands. Always keep upper arms on ears; if the arms move, the head will also move. Learn to think of the head and arms as one.

3. Kneel on pool side, knees just over edge. Keep upper arms against ears, thumbs tightly joined. Keep jaw down, look at your knees, and roll over. Stretch hands forward, keep looking at knees. Practice from low and from high kneeling positions.

4. Stand, feet together, toes gripping edge. Keep upper arms against ears, thumbs crossed, arms perfectly straight. Bend knees forward and together, chest close to thighs. Drop gently into water, hands first. Try to keep feet on pool's edge as long as possible.

5. As above, but as hands are about to enter the water, stretch legs vigorously. Make sure water is entered hands first.

6. Stand, one leg bent, toes gripping edge. Raise other leg backward, about a foot from pool side. Lean body forward, hands and arms as formerly. Raise free leg farther back (or have a friend hold ankle of free leg), fall forward, and enter water hands first. For the first time the entry will be fairly deep (water should be from 4 to 5 feet in depth). When the whole body is in the water

Springboard diving is a very difficult sport, requiring exceptional body control, timing, balance, and agility. Below are only a few of the many kinds of fancy dives: The running islander, or half gainer, **1,** a forward jump into a backward-layout dive; the forward dive half twist, **2,** also known as the half-screw dive; the double backward somersault tucked, **3;** the running forward somersault layout, **4;** the forward piked somersault from a backward standing position, **5;** the backward dive piked, also known as the backward jackknife dive, **6.** Because of the danger of physical injury, the beginning diver should take lessons from an expert diving coach. He should refrain from attempting the more difficult dives until he has learned and mastered the fundamentals of good diving.

(and this is an important factor), the back of the hands should be turned toward the face. The body will then smoothly rise. Never turn hands upward until all of the body is in the water. This applies to all types of diving.

7. Stand, toes gripping pool's edge, body erect, hands high above head, upper arms against ears, thumbs locked, eyes looking across pool. Bend the knees a little, then spring upward and a little outward, guide the hands down (keeping jaw down, too), and enter the water close to pool side, hands first. It is helpful to imagine one is diving over a high wall. If there are lines on the bottom of the pool, aim to enter the water with the hands directed to a line. If this is done, the dive will be arched, never flat, and will be deep enough.

Later progress can be made by swinging the arms to get more elevation. Timing is an important factor in all diving, so learn to spring up to achieve a neat dive. From the springboard the hurdle step must be learned before a running dive can be successfully executed, and from a firm board the double-footed spring requires much practice. Again, there are various types of racing dives for the different strokes. Why not read about diving, see films, and then, if you are really interested, practice, practice, practice. The hard work will bring its own satisfaction in this graceful sport.

DIVING, UNDERWATER. See DEEP-SEA EXPLORING; SALVAGE, MARITIME.

DIVINING ROD, or dowsing rod, a metal or wooden rod supposed to be useful in finding underground water or mineral deposits. A familiar

To use a forked-twig divining rod the dowser holds it as shown, with the stem pointing up. Then he walks slowly over the ground. As he passes over water or oil or whatever, the stem is supposed to jerk downward.

form of divining rod is a forked hazel or peach twig used in a process often called water witching to locate sites for wells.

It is not known exactly when or where the practice began. Belief in superstitions was common even among educated people in the 16th century; and one such belief was in the sympathetic attraction of some substances for certain woods—for example, that silver attracted ash and water attracted hazel. Agricola's book on mining, published in 1556, describes this belief and gives the first published description of the divining rod. Agricola thought it pure superstition and warned against belief in it. In one form or another, however, it has been practiced all over the world.

Belief in the power of the divining rod seems to be certainly of superstitious origin, yet scientific investigation over many years has not clearly shown either that the practice has scientific merit or that it has not. Studies have shown that there are changes in heartbeat and nervous reactions with the action of the rod; and some dowsers have been very effective in finding water, minerals, and other things. But many dowsers have been shown to be frauds.

It is generally agreed that the rod has no mystical powers in itself and that it is probably only a convenience to the operator. The ancient Romans used divining rods of wood in some religious ceremonies, but this had nothing to do with finding water. Probably the name was adopted later through ignorance; the term *dowser* is considered preferable. Most exploration for oil and other minerals is done with methods using electronic apparatus and proved scientific principles.

DIVISION is a way of finding how many times one number is contained in another number. You can find this by repeated subtraction, much as you can solve a multiplication problem by repeated addition. For instance, to divide 21 by 3 you could subtract 3 from 21, 3 from what was left, and so on, until you reached 0. You would find, of course, that 3 subtracts 7 times from 21. But for larger problems repeated subtraction becomes impossibly time consuming. By learning division processes you can solve problems in large numbers easily. It is helpful to think of division as finding how many times one size fits into another size. Thinking of the previous prob-

lem in this way, you can say that 3 fits 7 times into 21.

The parts of a division problem have special names. The number you divide is called the dividend. You divide it by the divisor, and the result is the quotient. In the problem of dividing 21 by 3 the dividend is 21, the divisor is 3, and the quotient is 7.

Now suppose you divide 22 by 3. You will find that 3 fits 7 times into 22 but that this time there is 1 left over. This amount left over is called the remainder. In order to make it part of the quotient, you must write it as a fraction of the divisor. The remainder becomes the numerator of the fraction, and the divisor is its denominator. In the example the fraction is therefore $\frac{1}{3}$, and the complete quotient is $7\frac{1}{3}$.

DIX, DOROTHEA LYNDE (1802-1887), American humanitarian and reformer, was born in Hampden, Maine. At the age of 14 she became a schoolteacher in Worcester, Mass., and at 18 she opened a school for girls in Boston. She remained head of the school until ill health forced her to close it in 1836. Soon afterward she went to England to improve her condition, but she returned in 1837 a semi-invalid.

A trip to the East Cambridge (Mass.) House of Correction in 1841, during which she was alarmed by the treatment given its inmates, led her to undertake the cause for which she soon became famous—the reform of hospital and prison conditions. Evidence collected during an 18-months' tour of the jails, asylums, and almshouses of the state was presented to the public by means of letters to the press. Public indignation was followed by corrective legislation. In the years that followed, Dorothy Dix carried her campaign of reform to all parts of the United States and to Japan, Canada, Great Britain, and Italy as well, with positive results. During the American Civil War she served the Union as its first superintendent of women nurses. As a result of her labors of about 40 years, 32 new hospitals were established in the United States, and several were established in Europe and Japan.

DNA, or deoxyribonucleic acid, a chemical found prominently in the chromosomes of plant and animal cells and believed by many scientists to play an important role in heredity. Research with synthetic DNA has shown that this chemical may be effective in the treatment of cancer.

The pioneering work on DNA's role in heredity was done in the early 1950's by J. D. Watson, an American, and F. H. C. Crick, a Briton. It had been known for a number of years that DNA is an important constituent of chromosomes. From X-ray studies Watson and Crick decided the DNA molecule is composed of two long strands of atoms twisted together like the banisters of a spiral staircase. Connecting the strands, like steps in the staircase, are hundreds of groups of atoms, called bases, in pairs.

Watson and Crick theorized that DNA transmits hereditary information in the chromosome by means of a code in the arrangement of four kinds of bases along the DNA molecule. During mitosis, or cell division, the molecule duplicates itself, with the two strands unwinding and one of each pair of bases going to each new molecule. Thus DNA embodies properties of the somewhat hypothetical units long known as genes.

In 1956-1957 Jacques Benoit and Pierre Leroy, French biologists, succeeded in changing both the appearance and the heredity of ducks of one breed by injecting DNA from ducks of another breed. Later, at the Sloan-Kettering Institute for Cancer Research in New York, it was discovered that tumors can be created in mice by injecting the animals with DNA extracted from cancer-causing viruses. It was also discovered that synthetic DNA will interfere with the manufacture of natural DNA in the cell nucleus and thus slow down the growth of the cell. Scientists hoped to find synthetic types of DNA that would act specifically against the unruly growth of cancer cells.

DODGEBALL, a popular playground game for any number of players. The players divide into two groups. One group forms a circle, and the other group stands in scattered positions inside the circle. The object of the game is for the players forming the circle to try to hit the ones inside with a basketball while the others dodge about trying to avoid being hit. The players inside may run, stoop, jump, or do anything else except leave the circle. The last player remaining unhit is considered the winner. The two groups then change places and start a new game.

DODGSON, CHARLES LUTWIDGE. See CARROLL, LEWIS.

The dodo now exists only as a museum piece, reproduced from a few of its skeletal remains.

DODO, a large, heavy, clumsy bird that became extinct over 200 years ago. It was larger than a turkey and had a big head and a huge hooked bill. Its name comes from the Portuguese word *doudo*, meaning "stupid" or "silly." *Dodo* today describes a simple-minded person who is not aware of changes in conditions and ideas.

The dodos were pigeons that reached three of the Mascarene Islands in the Indian Ocean as flying birds. Since there were no predators on the islands, the birds lost the power of flight. They walked with a wobbly gait and were easily captured by the Portuguese mariners who discovered the island in the early 16th century. The dodos on Mauritius, one of the Mascarene Islands, became extinct by about 1681. Another species of dodo, also now extinct, lived on the island of Réunion, while a third species was exterminated on Rodrigues about 1730. In the 17th century live dodos were exhibited in Europe. Now the only traces are the remains found in various museums.

DOG, the most familiar and best loved of all animals. The dog may have been the first animal to be domesticated, for evidences of it appear in findings in caves that were inhabited by prehistoric men. The wild ancestor of the dog may have been the wolf. Some scientists think that the dog may have resulted from the interbreeding of the wolf, the jackal, and other unknown canines. The ancient Egyptians, Greeks, and Romans had several breeds of dogs. More types were bred during medieval and early modern times. Today there are dozens of different breeds. In the chart on the next page, 119 breeds of dogs are shown in four

groupings according to genealogy. In the following discussion dogs are arranged in other groupings according to the use made of their various abilities.

Dogs have done many tasks for man. They have herded his sheep and cattle, guarded his house and belongings, assisted him in hunting game, and pulled his carts or sleds. Dogs have always been highly valued as pets. Throughout the centuries men have developed various types of dogs, by means of selective breeding, to specialize in each of these various tasks.

HOUNDS

This classification includes a wide variety of dogs useful in hunting or sport but differing from the sporting dog in breeding, training, and so on. Some of the bigger breeds are the Irish wolfhound, borzoi, Scottish deerhound, greyhound, whippet, and Afghan hound. The Irish wolfhound, as its name indicates, was formerly used for hunting wolves and later for hunting deer and fox. Good male specimens should be at least 32 inches high and should weigh about 120 pounds. The borzoi has been bred for hunting on the cold steppeland of Asia. The Scottish deerhound has long, wiry hair and is somewhat smaller than the Irish wolfhound. The greyhound has a slight body and gives the impression it is all legs. It is used in racing at tracks. The whippet is similar to a greyhound in appearance but is much smaller; it is used for the same purposes. The Afghan hound has long hair and is similar to the greyhound. It is an ancient breed that generally weighs about 60 pounds and stands about 27 inches high. Most of these breeds that have been listed are descendants of the Egyptian greyhound through the saluki, which is similar to the Afghan.

The external anatomy of a dog is shown here.

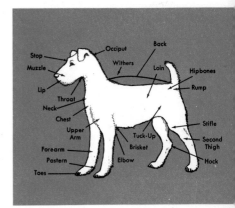

DOG GENEALOGY

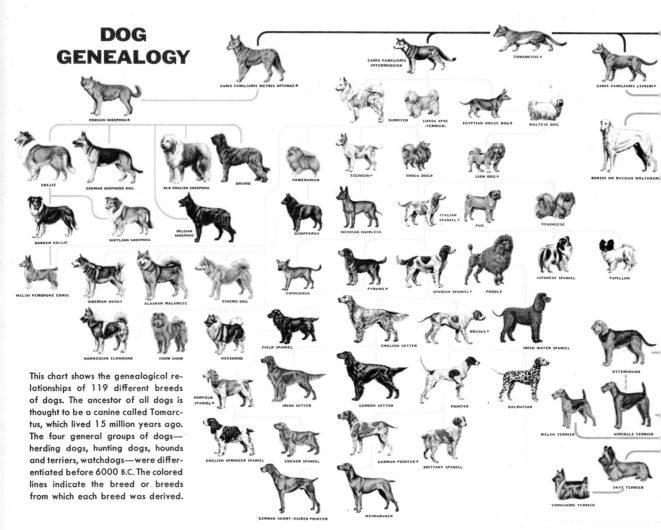

This chart shows the genealogical relationships of 119 different breeds of dogs. The ancestor of all dogs is thought to be a canine called Tomarctus, which lived 15 million years ago. The four general groups of dogs—herding dogs, hunting dogs, hounds and terriers, watchdogs—were differentiated before 6000 B.C. The colored lines indicate the breed or breeds from which each breed was derived.

Among other dogs belonging in this group are the basset, beagle, bloodhound, dachshund, foxhound, harrier, otterhound, and the Norwegian elkhound. The basset is a French breed used in rabbit hunting. It is short legged and long bodied and has a keen sense of smell. The beagle, a small trailing hound, is similar to the basset, but it has somewhat longer legs and shorter body. The bloodhound is one of the oldest of this group. It was used first for hunting bear and boar, but its speed being developed, it became useful in following human trails. For this function it is extraordinarily equipped, being able to follow an extremely faint trail. It is used in police work and in hunting missing persons. The dachshund is an ancient breed, drawings of it being found in ancient Egyptian art. The hindlegs are longer than the forelegs, both being very short in contrast to the long body. It is used, as are the beagle and basset, in rabbit

hunting. The foxhound is a descendant of one of the oldest types of hounds—the Talbot hound, which is now extinct. But as a separate, specialized breed its development is comparatively recent. Hunting the swift and elusive fox requires strongly developed qualities of scent, speed, and endurance; all are combined in the foxhound. It developed its present form about two centuries ago, and many packs have been kept free of all admixture from that time to the present. The foxhound is around 23 inches in height and weighs around 75 pounds. The harrier is a fine dog of mixed lineage, bred for hare hunting. It is descended from the Talbot hound, with admixture of the foxhound breed; since the foxhound was crossed with the breed rather late, there remain many harriers that are unmixed with the foxhound breedings. The otterhound has been bred for a difficult task; it is used in hunting otter, which fight savagely when

attacked. Since the otter lives in or near water most of the time, the otterhound must be a strong swimmer, hardy, and game; in sheer gameness the otterhound probably excels all other breeds. It is a large dog, about 25 inches high, and weighs up to 75 pounds. It has shaggy hair and an oily undercoat to protect it from water. The Norwegian elkhound is very closely related to the sled dogs, although it is bred to hunt elk, bear, and so on. It also resembles the sled dogs in appearance.

WORKING DOGS

Among the working dogs are the German shepherd, St. Bernard, Newfoundland, collie, old English sheepdog, great Dane, mastiff, Doberman pinscher, and giant schnauzer, along with the sled dogs. The German shepherd is the most famous of all dogs as war dog, Seeing Eye dog, and obedience contender. The St. Bernard and the

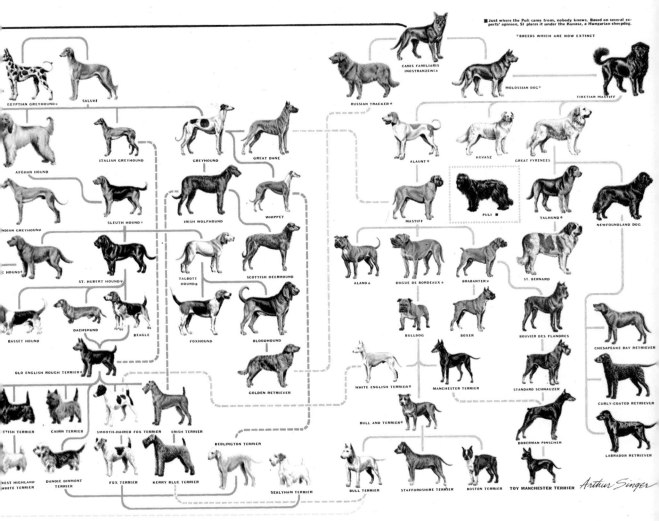

■ Just where the Puli came from, nobody knows. Based on several experts' opinion, SI places it under the Kuvasz, a Hungarian sheepdog.

*BREEDS WHICH ARE NOW EXTINCT

CANIS FAMILIARIS INOSTRANZEWI*
RUSSIAN TRACKER*
MOLOSSIAN DOG*
TIBETIAN MASTIFF

EGYPTIAN GREYHOUND*   SALUKI   ALAUNT*   KUVASZ   GREAT PYRENEES

AFGHAN HOUND   ITALIAN GREYHOUND   GREYHOUND   GREAT DANE   MASTIFF   PULI ■   TALHUND*   NEWFOUNDLAND DOG

INDIAN GREYHOUND   SLEUTH HOUND*   IRISH WOLFHOUND   WHIPPET   ALANO*   DOGUE DE BORDEAUX   BRABANTER*   ST. BERNARD

HOUND   ST. HUBERT HOUND*   TALBOTT HOUND*   SCOTTISH DEERHOUND   BULLDOG   BOXER   BOUVIER DES FLANDRES   CHESAPEAKE BAY RETRIEVER

BASSET HOUND   DACHSHUND   BEAGLE   FOXHOUND   BLOODHOUND   WHITE ENGLISH TERRIER*   MANCHESTER TERRIER   STANDARD SCHNAUZER   CURLY-COATED RETRIEVER

OLD ENGLISH ROUGH TERRIER*   GOLDEN RETRIEVER   BULL AND TERRIER*   LABRADOR RETRIEVER

TTISH TERRIER   CAIRN TERRIER   SMOOTH-HAIRED FOX TERRIER   IRISH TERRIER   DOBERMAN PINSCHER

BEDLINGTON TERRIER

WEST HIGHLAND WHITE TERRIER   DANDIE DINMONT TERRIER   FOX TERRIER   KERRY BLUE TERRIER   SEALYHAM TERRIER   BULL TERRIER   STAFFORDSHIRE TERRIER   BOSTON TERRIER   TOY MANCHESTER TERRIER   Arthur Singer

mastiff are the largest of the group as well as the largest of all dogs. There are two varieties of St. Bernards, the smooth and the long haired. They were originally developed at the Monastery of St. Bernard in the Alps, where they were used in rescuing lost travelers. They are almost 3 feet high and weigh as much as 150 pounds. Like the hounds, they have a well-developed sense of smell. They are very muscular and strong boned and have a large, heavy head. Similar to the St. Bernard in size and build is the Newfoundland, which developed from crossbreeding between the native dogs of the Indians and various importations, from Spain in particular. The Newfoundland is smaller than the St. Bernard, usually weighing around 100 pounds and standing about 27 inches high. It has a well-developed scent and is supposed to have been used in rescuing drowning persons; it is a strong swimmer and likes water. The color is usually

black or black and white. The collie is a well-known breed. It is a sheep dog, but because of its gentleness it is often kept as a pet. It is about 23 inches high and weighs around 55 pounds. Like the other sheepdogs, it has long hair, though there is also a smooth-haired variety. The old English sheepdog is remarkable for its extremely long hair, which almost covers its eyes. It is a heavy dog, and the coat is gray or gray and white. The great Dane is one of the largest of all dogs and is probably descended from the fighting dogs of classical times. These dogs were used in battle and in the arena. The great Dane, primarily a guard dog, is sometimes considered a descendant of the Molossian, or lion fighter, of Greece. It should average about 32 inches in height and weigh about 140 pounds. It is exceeded in size only by the mastiff. The mastiff is a rather large watchdog of ancient British origin. It weighs, on an average, about 160

to 175 pounds; and it stands almost 36 inches high. Though powerful and very dependable as a watchdog, the mastiff is gentle. It is solidly built, muscular, and well proportioned. The Doberman pinscher is a fine, medium-sized dog, beautifully colored and marked. It is a good watchdog and Seeing Eye dog. The giant schnauzer is also a good watchdog, large, strong, and reliable.

The sled dogs consist of the Alaskan Malamute, the Samoyed, and the Siberian Husky. These dogs are, on the whole, less domesticated than other dogs. They are a very hardy type, pulling heavy loads and enduring extreme cold. The Malamute is powerfully built and has a covering of warm, thick hair. The Samoyed is very similar to the Pomeranian, except that it is much larger, weighing as much as 60 pounds. It is white except for the nose. The Husky is smaller than the Malamute; it has a thick, furry coat and powerful frame.

SPORTING DOGS

These dogs are bred chiefly for hunting and sport. There are the setters, pointers, retrievers, and spaniels. The setter is found in three distinct breeds—the English, the Irish, and the Gordon. The English is the oldest; the Gordon setter was developed at the beginning of the last century. All setters have much in common; they have long heads, weigh around 50 pounds, and carry their tails horizontally. When a setter comes upon the quarry, he assumes a crouching position, points his nose in the exact direction of the hidden birds, and remains motionless until the hunter comes up. Pointers are represented by several different breeds and include the Dalmatian besides the true hunters. They have excellent noses and are very quiet in approaching the quarry. The pointer serves the same purpose as the setter; instead of crouching when indicating the direction of the hunted birds, he stands erect. The retriever is used in hunting birds over water or swamps. He has an excellent sense of scent and is a good swimmer. The five retriever breeds average 60 pounds and are more heavily built than pointers and setters; they have strong jaws, which enable them to carry dead or wounded game. The American breed is known as the Chesapeake Bay retriever, so called from the region where it was first developed. It is one of the finest retrievers, bred for use on rough, cold water. It can carry the largest birds, is a strong swimmer, and has a keen sense of smell.

Both cocker spaniel breeds—the English and the American—are hunters weighing from 20 to 30 pounds; they are square bodied and sturdy, with soft, thick hair. The field spaniel is larger, longer in back, and lower on the legs. The clumber is a large spaniel, weighing as much as 60 pounds or more. Though most spaniels bark a great deal when hunting, the clumber hunts without barking. The water spaniel, or Irish water spaniel, is an old breed and is used as a retriever. It is somewhat smaller than the clumber and bears a close resemblance to other spaniels.

NONSPORTING DOGS

This group includes among its nine breeds the bulldog, the poodle, the chow, and the schipperke. The bulldog is especially heavy set, muscular, and short legged. It is one of the best of the home protectors if only because of its ugly face. The poodle was formerly a retriever but is now used mostly as a pet. It has a fine curly coat of hair. The chow has a dense reddish coat and is powerfully built. The schipperke is somewhat small with a black coat.

TERRIERS

Terriers constitute a group of small and medium-sized breeds. The best known is the fox terrier, occurring in two varieties, wire haired and smooth. It is a fast dog and has the endurance necessary in hunting. It weighs about 20 pounds. Among others are the bull terrier, Sealyham, Welsh, Kerry blue, Irish, Scottish, Australian, and Airedale. The Airedale is the most recently developed of these breeds. It stands higher than the rest and weighs about 40 pounds. Terriers have been, and still are, used for killing rats. The Australian terrier is the smallest, being about 10 inches in height. Many of the terriers are kept as house pets because of their intelligence and versatility.

TOY DOGS

The toy dogs include 14 different breeds, among them the Chihuahua, English toy spaniel, miniature pinscher, Pekingese, Pomeranian, poodle (toy variety), Yorkshire, and the silky terrier. The English toy spaniels come in four varieties: King Charles, Blenheim, ruby, and Prince Charles, each characterized by its coloring. The smallest of the toys is the Maltese, which weighs from 2 to 6 pounds. Toy dogs as a group are the tiniest of all, but despite their size they rate as superior watchdogs.

TRAINING DOGS

The intelligence of dogs is surpassed only by that of monkeys and apes. Dogs can readily be trained to do many things. By the eighth week they can begin to learn simple exercises, such as walking on the leash.

"Sit" is one of the basic commands a dog should learn to obey. When he has learned this lesson well, the dog will remain seated as long as desired.

Sit!

Heel!

A properly trained dog walks at his master's heel, out of the way of master and other pedestrians. The dog should first be taught to heel while on the leash. After long and careful training the leash will not be needed.

The command "Down" is used to make the dog lie down full length. This exercise is easily taught once the dog has been thoroughly trained to sit. Sometimes this command is given by hand signal only.

Down!

The dog is commanded "Stay" in order to make him keep a sitting or lying position. The dog should stay in that position even when his master is out of sight for several minutes.

Stay!

UPI

Dogs of various breeds are being judged to ascertain the winners in this big dog show.

Dogs learn by associating spoken words and pleasurable or painful experiences with their own actions. For example, to train a dog to come when called, his master should place a morsel of food on the floor and then call "Come!" The dog, upon seeing and smelling the food, will come running and will bolt it down. At other times the master should pet his dog and speak kindly to him when he comes upon being called. The dog will soon associate these pleasurable rewards with his action of running to his master upon hearing the command "Come!" Then the dog will come automatically whenever he is called.

Never slap a dog when he fails to come, for that will only cause him to associate your spoken command with a painful experience. Then he will be afraid to obey. A dog should be scolded only after he has done something naughty, such as chewing a tablecloth or jumping onto the sofa. He then will associate the scolding tone of your voice with the forbidden action and will soon desist from it.

Dogs can be trained to obey any simple command by being rewarded when they obey properly. Most people want to restrain their dog from running all over the house and train him to remain in one place, as on a mat before the door. To do this the master should lead the dog to the doormat and, while pushing him to a sitting position, utter the command "Stay!" Hold the dog down for a minute; then give him a morsel of food. Repeat this procedure, but gradually lengthen the period of holding. Soon the dog, if properly rewarded, will learn to stay on the mat for ten minutes or more without being held. Eventually he should learn to stay for longer periods without being rewarded.

When being exhibited in shows dogs are judged for their ability to obey commands and to perform various tasks upon command. The commands, which are given by the judge, constitute what is called an obedience test. The judge may command a dog to stand up for examination, to walk some distance and then turn to the right or left, and to retrieve an object both over flat ground and over a hurdle. A dog must be scrupulously trained if he is to perform well in an obedience test and win a prize at a dog show.

The performance of trained hunting dogs is sometimes evaluated at hunting events called field trials. Trained setters, pointers, retrievers, and spaniels compete with each other in scenting, tracking, revealing, and retrieving game birds for their masters. All of their actions are observed by experts and judged by the criteria of skill, speed, and grace. The purpose of the field trial is to discover the most skillful hunting dogs and the actions that make them such so that other dogs can also be trained to become skillful hunters.

Trainers should always remember that the learning capacity of a dog is no greater than that of a child two or three years old. A dog must be trained with repetition and persistence until a simple task is mastered. Unless training is always tempered with patience and kindness, the dog will not be able to learn.

DOG RACING, a modern form of the ancient sport of coursing, in which dogs chase a mechanical rabbit around an oval racetrack. Coursing, in which fast dogs were used to run down wild game, was a popular sport in ancient Egypt. It was introduced into England over ten centuries ago. The English monarchs John and Elizabeth I are said to have been fond of coursing.

The first coursing races in the United States were held in Massachusetts. Whippets were used at first, but later the larger and stronger greyhounds became popular. In the early races the dogs raced after colored cloths that were waved just beyond the finish line. Then live rabbits were substituted, but the killing of the rabbits for the pleasure of gambling spectators drew public protest, and the practice was outlawed. In 1919 Oliver P. Smith invented the mechanical rabbit for use in dog racing, and the sport took its present form. Dog racing takes place at night. The course is from $\frac{3}{8}$ mile to 1 mile in length. The sport is legal in Arizona, Colorado, Florida, Montana, Massachusetts, North Carolina, Oregon, and South Dakota. Since Smith made his mechanical rabbit, more than 125,000 greyhounds have been bred for racing in this country. There are also dog-racing tracks in England, France, Ireland, and Italy and in some of the Latin American countries.

DOG SHOW, a competition to select the best dogs in their breeds. It is a big business, as well as a sport, in the United States. Some dog owners send or take their dogs all around the country during the show season and enter them in one show after another. Such dogs are not really household pets at all, but professional workers. Other owners, proud of their animals and believing them to be of championship caliber, show them occasionally when a competition is being held nearby.

The American Kennel Club (AKC) is the governing organization for shows in the United States. Dogs competing at shows under AKC rules must be registered or listed with this club. The AKC recognizes 114 breeds of dogs, which are classified for show purposes in six groups: sporting dogs, hounds, working dogs, terriers, toys, and nonsporting dogs. (See DOG.) Each breed is passed on by a judge licensed for that breed. Each breed is judged on a basis of its own standard, a word picture of the ideal specimen as drawn up by the sponsoring breed club and approved by the AKC. The standard describes the type of head, body, legs and feet, coat, color, tail, size, action, and temperament. After the winner of each breed has been selected, it competes in its group for best of group; then the group winners compete for the honor of best in the show.

The first dog show in the United States was held in New York City, May 8-10, 1877. It was so successful that the Westminster Kennel Club, sponsor of the show, decided to make it an annual affair, and it has been held each year since that time. It is now held in Madison Square Garden. The record number of dogs entered in an American show was 4,456 in the Morris and Essex Kennel Club, show of 1939.

There are kennel clubs in 16 European countries, 4 South American countries, Canada, Mexico, and several other parts of the world where Europeans have settled. Each of the clubs holds at least one major show annually.

DOGSLED. A dogsled is usually long, narrow, and close to the ground. Two is the smallest number of dogs used. As many as ten may be used for heavy loads. In northern Europe dogsleds are used for fishing and seal hunting on the ice. Most sled dogs are harnessed in files. However, the Eskimos harness the dogs side by side so that each dog pulls directly on the sled. It is probable that dogsleds were the first animal-drawn sleds used by man.

DOG STAR. See SIRIUS.

DOGWOOD, one of a genus of small and generally bushy deciduous trees and shrubs that have broad-bladed leaves and small flowers in loose or dense terminal heads. Fifteen different species of dogwood grow in the United States.

A familiar species is the flowering dogwood, which is native to eastern North America as far west as Illinois, eastern Kansas, and Texas. The flowering dogwood is never large, usually not more than 10 to 15 feet high, and it often grows in the shade of larger trees on the edge of woods or in open forests. It is also planted in parks and gardens. It has round limbs, a flat crown, and spreading branches with the branchlets curved up at the ends. In early spring dense clusters of small greenish flowers stand on very short stalks within a flower-like cup 3 to 4 inches wide, formed from four large, pink or white, deeply notched, leaflike bracts, which are so conspicuous as to give the tree its common name. The white-flowered variety is much more abundant than the pink, which seems less hardy. Clusters of waxy, bright-red berries, each about $\frac{1}{4}$ inch in diameter, follow the flowers. During autumn the leaves often turn to a brilliant scarlet hue.

These are flowers and leaves of the dogwood.

The doldrums are created when air at the Equator, heated by direct rays of the sun, rises. Sailing ships were often stranded here for weeks for lack of even a breeze.

DOLDRUMS, the equatorial belt of calms. The doldrums lie between the northeast trade winds of the Northern Hemisphere and the southeast trades of the Southern Hemisphere. They are generally just north of the Equator. But they tend to move north and south with the sun. In addition to the absence of sustained winds, the doldrums are also subject to heavy downpours, thunderstorms, and squalls. See WIND CIRCULATION.

The doldrums were once the terror of the captains of sailing vessels. Many terrible tales are told of ships that were becalmed for weeks in the doldrums, while the supplies of food and water diminished. The Ancient Mariner became stranded in the doldrums in the famous poem by Samuel Taylor Coleridge:

> Day after day, day after day,
> We stuck, nor breath nor motion;
> As idle as a painted ship
> Upon a painted ocean.

DOLLAR DIPLOMACY, a U.S. policy of encouraging U.S. financial ventures in China and the Caribbean area in order to prevent foreign domination and to maintain or increase U.S. political influence. The policy was begun by President William Howard Taft and his secretary of state, Philander C. Knox, but in the Caribbean, where it included the use of force, and consequently aroused the bitter resentment of most Latin American nations, it was a continuation and expansion of Theodore Roosevelt's Big Stick Diplomacy and of the aims expressed in his corollary to the Monroe Doctrine.

To preserve the Open Door Policy in China, the U.S. State Department in 1909 urged U.S. bankers to join Europeans in financing China's railways. As a result of the failure of later and similar State Department projects aimed at eliminating Russian and Japanese control of Manchuria, dollar diplomacy was abandoned in China in 1913.

Dollar diplomacy was far more important in the Caribbean, where protection of the approaches to the Panama Canal was at stake. To stabilize Haiti, the State Department encouraged U.S. bankers to invest in the Haitian National Bank. It also tried to arrange for U.S. bankers to assume debts owed the British by Honduras and indirectly supported the 1909 overthrow of a Nicaraguan dictator unfriendly to the United States. In 1911 Knox negotiated the Knox-Castrillo Treaty. By it New York bankers were to fill Nicaragua's empty treasury in return for payment from Nicaraguan customs collections, which were to be under U.S. management. When it appeared that Nicaragua might default on debts owed a British company, the substance of the treaty was carried out despite the treaty's rejection by the U.S. Senate. In 1912 Nicaraguan popular resentment of the arrangement resulted in a revolt. U.S. marines helped suppress it and remained in Nicaragua until 1933.

President Woodrow Wilson continued U.S. control of Nicaragua. In 1915 he ordered military occupation of Haiti, and in 1916 of the Dominican Republic in an effort to bring peace and good government to these chaotic countries as well as to protect the Panama Canal. U.S. troops remained in the Dominican Republic until 1924 and in Haiti until 1934.

DOLL FESTIVAL, a popular holiday in Japan, dedicated to girls and celebrated each year on March 3. In every household where there are daughters, the family collection of ceremonial dolls is brought out and displayed. These are special dolls that have been handed down as a family heritage from one generation to another. They are seen only on this day of the year, when they are placed in the best room of the house. The dolls are all dressed in ancient, colorful old costumes. Parents who can afford it buy a new set of dolls for a girl baby born since the preceding festival, and sometimes relatives and friends give gifts of dolls. The festival is celebrated to encourage family loyalty.

DOLLHOUSE, a small house used by girls when playing with their dolls. Dollhouses are built to look as much as possible like real houses. Dollhouses were rarely made before 1700, and it was not until the 19th century that these miniature houses were actually used as toys. The dollhouses of the 18th century were elaborate pieces of cabinetmaking used by adults for artistic display. In the mid-19th century many German ideas were introduced into England, and one of them was that girls should learn to be good housewives and mothers by playing with dolls and dollhouses. This play became popular and created a large demand for dollhouses and doll clothes, furniture, and utensils. The wish for dollhouses spread quickly to the United States, where over the years the houses have become more and more realistic. Many famous people, including Queen Victoria, have kept elaborate dollhouses as a hobby.

DOLLS AND DOLLMAKING. Dolls have been favorite playthings since the beginning of history. Dolls of clay and of jointed wood have been found in the ruins of Egyptian houses dating from about 2000 B.C. The wooden ones could be made to move their arms and legs by pulling strings. Greek and Roman children played with dolls made of clay and of wire and rag. During the Middle Ages girls played with clay dolls, and their brothers had toy horses and knights. In 16th-century and 17th-century France, dolls made of pulp, wood, clay, wax, and other materials were popular. One young prince received as a gift a complete set of hunters, hounds, and animals to be hunted—all in miniature. His sister was given a furnished doll's kitchen and a miniature poultry yard. Modern dolls are made of a variety of materials, including plastic that feels like flesh. The most realistic dolls have hair made of Saran fibers, which have the appearance and texture of real hair and can be washed with shampoo. These dolls will also walk, talk, cry, and eat. Some dolls are dressed in colorful costumes representing a particular nationality. Many women, and children too, make their own dolls with patterns or complete kits that can be bought in a store.

At the right is shown a Hopi katcina, a wooden doll carved, painted, and decorated to represent one of the vast number of spirits, also called katcinas, that are worshiped by Hopis and other Pueblo Indians.

DOLOMITE is a calcium magnesium carbonate mineral closely related to calcite. (See CALCITE.) Dolomite crystals often have curved faces and a flesh-pink color. However, most individual dolomite crystals are too small to be seen without magnification. Dolomite is transparent or translucent. It can be easily scratched with a steel knife.

Dolomite is also a rock name. Dolomite is very similar to limestone in appearance but is made up of dolomite rather than of calcite. Dolomite does not effervesce, or bubble, readily in cold dilute hydrochloric acid as does limestone. In the western and middle-western United States dolomite is found in thick beds with areas of many square miles. Large masses of dolomite are also found in the Tyrol in Europe.

Dolomite is used as an ornamental stone and as a building stone. It is also used in making certain cements and in the preparation of refractory linings of basic steel converters.

Any rock is called dolomite that is made up chiefly of the mineral dolomite. Note crystals in this specimen, found in Mexico.

The exquisite Japanese doll shown immediately below is an example of dollmaking at its finest. Such a work of art belongs in a museum rather than in a child's playroom. The three dolls at the lower right date from the Victorian era, as their costumes suggest.

Laura Gilpin

Robert H. Bradley

Photographed at the Museum of the City of New York

The bottle-nosed dolphin, which can leap high above the water, inhabits the Atlantic Ocean.

DOLPHIN, an aquatic mammal that is related to the whale and the porpoise. Most dolphins are smaller than whales, the species called the common dolphin being about 7 feet long. Although dolphins and porpoises are of similar size, the muzzle of the dolphin is shaped like a beak, whereas that of the porpoise is rounded. Dolphins inhabit all of the world's seas but are most abundant in tropical and temperate waters. They often swim up large rivers.

Although dolphins resemble fish, they are really mammals that breathe air through lungs, bear their young alive, and suckle them with milk from mammary glands. The dolphin's forelimbs are modified into flippers, which superficially resemble fish fins. Dolphins swim by moving their tail; they steer and balance themselves with their flippers. Hind limbs are missing.

Some dolphins swim fast enough to overtake and pass ships traveling at 16 knots an hour. Groups of them often swim alongside ships for miles. They frequently leap high out of the water and appear to be engaging in frolicsome play.

The name dolphin is also applied to a marine fish found mainly in warm seas. Ranging in length to 6 feet, the dolphin fish has a blunt head and a dorsal fin that extends from the top of the head to the base of the tail. It is among the fastest swimming fish.

DOLPHIN, THE (constellation). See DELPHINUS.

DOMESTICATED ANIMAL. Animals were first domesticated by prehistoric men. Their domestication began so long ago that the wild ancestors of many of our common domesticated animals have never been identified with certainty. Anthropologists think that the dog was the first mammal to be domesticated and that its domestication began more than 10,000 years ago. Their conclusion is based on the presence of gnawed bones in caves inhabited by prehistoric men more than 10,000 years ago. Anthropologists think that these bones may have been gnawed by dogs or other doglike animals and that these canines were perhaps more or less domesticated. The wild ancestors of the dog are thought to be the wolf, the jackal, and possibly the fox.

The cat, horse, cow, hog, and sheep also have been domesticated for so long that their wild ancestors are not known for certain. The wild ancestor of the domesticated cat is thought to be some species of wild cat like the one that still survives in some parts of Europe and Egypt.

Some domesticated animals (below) are not as familiar as the hog (right). The reindeer is the domesticated descendant of the wild caribou. The domesticated water buffalo of India is used to plow muddy rice fields. The domesticated yak, whose wild ancestor was an Asiatic relative of the bison, is used as a beast of burden in Tibet.

The wild ancestor of the horse has become extinct since the domestication of that animal began. The wild horses that now exist in some parts of the world are believed to be descended from domesticated ones that escaped from captivity. The wild ancestor of European cattle may be the aurochs, or urus, an oxlike animal that once inhabited the forests of Germany and other parts of Europe but that now is extinct. The hog is thought to be descended from wild boars that still live in parts of Europe and Asia. Domesticated sheep may be descended from wild ones similar to those that still frequent parts of southern Europe and Asia. For thousands of years the camel has been domesticated as a beast of burden in the deserts of North Africa, Asia Minor, and other parts of Asia.

The wild ancestor of the chicken was a pheasant-like fowl that inhabited the jungles of India. The domestication of the turkey began during the colonization of North America. Its wild ancestor was native to Mexico.

Reindeer

Dromedary

Water Buffalo

Horse

Cow

Dog

Indian Elephant

DOMINICAN REPUBLIC, a country occupying the eastern two-thirds of the West Indian island of Hispaniola. It was the former Spanish colony of Santo Domingo. The city of Santo Domingo, now called Ciudad Trujillo, is the oldest existing city in the Americas. For a long time it was the center of Spanish power in the New World and served as the base for the expeditions that set out to conquer the new continent. Ciudad Trujillo is the Dominican Republic's capital, its largest city, and its chief seaport. The republic's area is about 19,000 square miles. It has about 3,000,000 people.

The surface of the country is generally mountainous, with extensive desert stretches in the extreme southwestern areas. The forested ranges run east and west. Pico Trujillo in the central range reaches 10,300 feet, the highest point in the West Indies. Fertile valleys abound in the central and eastern regions. The principal farming area lies in the north-central section of the country in the Cibao Valley, known as La Vega Real in its eastern part. The rapid rivers of the Dominican Republic are more important for irrigation than for shipping. Numerous bays indent the coastline.

Climate and rainfall vary considerably. Warm weather prevails the whole year. Although the country lies in the tropics, summer temperatures remain comfortable because of the constant northeast trade winds. In the mountain areas cooler weather is encountered. Rain falls mostly from May through October. Rainfall is heavy in the northeast and scanty in the west, where irrigation is necessary for successful farming. Huricanes are a problem in late summer and autumn. Ciudad Trujillo was practically destroyed in 1930 by the country's worst hurricane.

The Dominican Republic is basically an agricultural country. Agricultural products account for nearly all its exports. Sugarcane is the leading crop and supplies the chief export. Coffee, cacao, tobacco, and bananas are other important export crops. The United Kingdom is the leading buyer of Dominican sugar. Most of the coffee, cacao, and bananas go to the United States.

The Dominican people are mainly mulattoes, descendants of Spanish colonists and Negro slaves. There are small groups of Negroes and white persons. Spanish is the national language. Roman Catholicism is the principal religion.

Dominican Inf. Ctr.

This huge sugar mill is one of many found in the Dominican Republic.

Dominican Inf. Ctr.

A 10-mile block of almost solid salt stands in the dry southwest of the Dominican Republic.

Dominican Inf. Ctr.

This old cathedral in Ciudad Trujillo was begun around 1514. In the church's nave rest the remains of Christopher Columbus.

The republic's flag and coat of arms

Christopher Columbus discovered the island of Hispaniola in 1492. His brother Bartholomew founded the city of Santo Domingo in 1496. In the 17th century the French came to the western part of the island, now the republic of Haiti, and for a time controlled the whole island. After the Dominicans declared their independence from Spain in 1821, they were conquered by the Haitians. The Haitians were not driven out until 1844.

For many years afterward the republic suffered from revolutions and civil wars. It even returned to Spanish rule for a short time because of these troubles. On account of the country's huge debt, it seemed that the European nations would step in to collect. So the United States in 1905 took charge of customs receipts, and after a few years the debt was greatly reduced. From 1916 to 1924 U.S. Marines occupied the country. From 1930 to his assassination in 1961, Trujillo was dictator. For detailed map, see Cuba.

DOMINICAN REPUBLIC

Area: 19,332 sq. mi.
Population: 3,000,000
Capital: Ciudad Trujillo
Largest cities: Ciudad Trujillo, Santiago
Highest mountain peak: Pico Trujillo (10,300 feet)
Chief river: Yaque del Norte
Chief lake: Enriquillo
Climate: Warm throughout the year —cooler in mountains—rainfall heaviest in east
National flag: Four alternating sections of blue and red, separated by white cross—coat of arms in center of cross
National anthem: *Quisqueyanos valientes* (Valiant Quisqueyans)
Form of government: Republic
Unit of currency: Peso
Language: Spanish
Chief religion: Roman Catholic
Chief economic activity: Agriculture
Chief crops: Sugarcane, cacao, coffee, tobacco, bananas, rice
Chief exports: Sugar, coffee, cacao, tobacco
Chief imports: Machinery and vehicles, foodstuffs, petroleum products, textiles, iron and steel, electrical equipment

DOMINOES, a game, usually for two persons, played with 28 rectangular pieces of wood, ivory, bone, or other material. Each piece is black with white indented dots on one side. The face is divided into halves by a center line. There are several different forms of the game, and the number of pieces distributed to each player depends on the form that is to be played. After each player has received the proper number of dominoes, the remainder are placed face down as a reserve.

When one player leads by laying down a domino, the next player must follow by placing beside it another domino that has on at least one half of it the same number of dots as are on the first one. The players continue in turn to lay down matching pieces until a player has played all of his dominoes. The first player to do this wins the game. If a player cannot play a matching piece, he must draw one from the reserve. Among the various forms of dominoes are the block game, draw game, Sebastopol, and domino pool.

DONATELLO (1386?-1466), a famous Italian sculptor, whose real name was Donato di Betto Bardi. He worked at sculpture in Florence at the same time Ghiberti, Brunelleschi, and other great artists were working there. With Brunelleschi he went to Rome to study ancient sculpture and felt the influence of the antique style very strongly. He became one of the greatest artists of his day and had an enormous influence over all Italy. His first great works were studies of St. Peter and St. Mark in the church of San Michele, or St. Michael, Florence. In the same church is his famous statue of St. George. He made many beautiful monuments, bronze statues of Mary Magdalen and of John the Baptist, reliefs of many saints and other religious subjects, and a famous equestrian statue of Gattamelata, which stands at Padua. This was the first great portrait of a general on horseback since the time of the Romans, and nothing like it was produced for many years except the statue of Colleoni, in Venice, by Donatello's pupil Verrocchio. Donatello also made a beautiful gallery for the organ in the Cathedral of Florence, with figures of children dancing and playing.

Donatello valued greatly the critical comments of his Florentine contemporaries, for he felt they aided his growth as an artist. His work had a powerful influence not only on Verocchio but also on such artists as Masaccio, Pollaiuolo, and Desiderio da Settignano.

DONIZETTI, GAETANO (1797-1848), Italian composer, was born in Bergamo. During his relatively short lifetime he composed sixty-five operas, three or four of which are still prominent fixtures in the world's repertory. He was a student at the Naples conservatory and at the Liceo Filarmonico in Bologna, but because of parental opposition to his musical career he enlisted in the Austrian army. In his spare time he completed his first opera in 1818, and his fourth, which was produced at Rome in 1822, won him a release from his military service.

Donizetti's first notable opera, *Anna Bolena*, was performed in 1830 and brought him fame throughout Europe. After this, he wrote his most famous operas—*Elsir d'Amore* in 1832, *Lucia di Lammermoor* in 1835, *La Favorita* and *The Daughter of the Regiment* in 1840, and what is generally considered his masterpiece, *Don Pasquale*, in 1843.

DONKEY, an animal closely related to the horse. It looks much like the horse but is smaller and has longer ears, a somewhat rougher and shaggier coat, and a less bushy tail. The donkey brays instead of neighing like the horse. The donkey is also known as the ass or jackass.

John Strohm

In Karachi, Pakistan, small carts are pulled by teams of two donkeys.

Wild donkeys are found in the dry regions of Asia and in northeastern Africa. They are usually shy and wary and are very difficult to approach. They have been hunted in Asia since ancient times. The donkey was known to the ancient Egyptians before the horse and probably was first caught and tamed in the valley of the Nile. In many countries the donkey is the principal beast of burden. Ancient Romans did much to improve the donkey by selective breeding, and the Arabs still continue efforts in that direction. In the United States donkeys are often used to father mules. The mule is the offspring of the male donkey and the female horse, or mare. See Mule.

DONNE, JOHN (1573-1631), English poet, was born in London. He was educated at Oxford, Cambridge, and Lincoln's Inn. He served with Robert Devereux, the earl of Essex, on expeditions to Cadiz and the Azores. Appointed secretary to Sir Thomas Egerton, Donne alienated his superior in 1601 by marrying Anne More, a 16-year-old girl. Sir George More, the bride's father, had Donne imprisoned for awhile in 1602. Upon his release Donne had a difficult time reestablishing himself and was long dependent upon patrons. In 1615 Donne was ordained an Anglican priest, and in 1621 he was made dean of St. Paul's Cathedral, an office which he held until his death in 1631.

As a poet Donne is generally recognized as the greatest of the metaphysical poets, a school that in 17th-century England produced a body of poetry that was passionate and logical. Donne, like George Herbert and Henry Vaughan, used such devices common to modern poets as wit, irony, and ambiguity. Among his best poems were "An Anatomie of the World," "The Progresse of the Soule," "The Canonization," "The Ecstasie," and "Hymn to God the Father." In addition to his work as a poet Donne was a great religious writer in prose. His *Essays in Divinity, Devotions,* and his sermons were notable for their imagery.

DON QUIXOTE, a novel by Cervantes, is generally considered the greatest work in Spanish literature and one of the greatest novels. Cervantes began the work about 1602 and published Part I in 1605, and Part II in 1615. See CERVANTES.

Don Quixote is the record of the adventures of a would-be knight and his too-sane squire, Sancho Panza. The Don has read too many chivalric romances and, his mind unhinged, sets off to lead the life of a knight errant. (See KNIGHTHOOD AND CHIVALRY.) He acquires a set of rusty armor, a remnant of a horse (whom he christens Rosinante), and a lady for whom to perform heroic deeds (actually a peasant girl whom he renames Dulcinea del Toboso). After having been knighted by an innkeeper (whom he believes to be the lord of a castle) and experiencing several other misguided adventures, the Don acquires his faithful squire Sancho Panza, a shrewd, earthy realist, who accompanies him on the remainder of his adventures. Don Quixote is finally defeated in combat by a friend (disguised as a knight),

The drawing below of Don Quixote and his horse Rosinante was made by the famous German book illustrator Hans Meid.

who requires that the Don refrain from knighthood for a year. Brokenhearted and humiliated, the Don retires to his home village and shortly dies.

When he began to write *Don Quixote,* Cervantes apparently had little more in mind than making fun of the chivalric code. As he progressed, however, the story of the wandering knight and his squire took on greater meaning, until *Don Quixote* became one of those rare works that has application to all mankind. Like many other works of such magnitude, it has several levels of meaning. Among the simpler, widely favored comments on the novel is that the wanderings of the Don and his squire are a kind of pilgrimage through life, and that Don Quixote and Sancho Panza represent "the two elements of human nature: soul and sense, poetry and prose." One has too much imagination, the other has none; one sees things as they ought to be, the other as they are. Each complements the other, and Cervantes'—and the reader's—sympathy is with each.

DOPPLER'S PRINCIPLE. When an approaching train blows its whistle or when a fast car sounds its horn, the pitch of the sound is higher as the object comes toward you than it is when the object passes and goes away from you. The cause of this phenomenon was first determined by an Austrian physicist, Christian Doppler, in 1842, and it is often called the Doppler effect. Doppler's principle states that any source of wave motion (sound or light) approaching an observer will appear to that observer to have a greater frequency than wave motion moving away from the observer.

Sound, of course, travels in waves. When the source of sound is approaching, each wave sent out by the source has a shorter distance to travel than the one before it, and each one reaches the listener a little sooner than it would have if the source had not been moving. The waves therefore are more closely spaced and have a higher frequency. As the train or car goes away, each wave starts a little farther away, and each one is longer than it would ordinarily be; the pitch is lowered.

The same thing happens with any other wave motion. The change in color of a light source is not large enough to notice unless the source is moving at very great speed. The stars move at very high speeds, and a star moving away from the earth will therefore appear redder than if

Doppler's principle is illustrated by the way in which sound waves are crowded together in front and spread out behind the whistle of a moving train. The whistle sounds higher pitched to someone in front of the train than to someone behind it. A person standing near the track would hear a definite lowering of pitch as the train passed him.

it were approaching. An apparent change in the position of a fixed line in the spectrum will indicate the direction and speed of the star. The same thing happens with radio waves. See SPECTRUM.

DOSTOEVSKI, FĒDOR (1821-1881), Russian novelist, was born in Moscow, the son of a surgeon. He studied at the Academy of Military Engineering at St. Petersburg (now Leningrad) and was commissioned an officer in 1841, a commission he resigned to devote himself to writing. He lived in poverty for the next few years, supporting himself chiefly by translating the French novelist Balzac. In 1846 his first novel, *Poor Folk,* was published; it won him a certain amount of attention but brought him very little money.

Dostoevski was closely connected with various radicals of the period and with them was arrested and imprisoned in 1849. After eight months of imprisonment he was told that he was to be executed. At the last minute, as he was being led before a firing squad, his sentence was commuted to four years of hard labor and four years of army service. This unnerving experience and the hard years in Siberia that followed ruined his health—he suffered the rest of his life from epilepsy—and radically altered his outlook on life.

Dostoevski returned to European Russia in 1859 and almost immediately began writing again. In addition to writing novels he edited the periodicals *Time, The Epoch,* and *A Writer's Diary.* His reputation steadily increased, and after the publication in 1861 of *Notes from the House of the Dead,* a record of his Siberian experiences, he was recognized as one of Russia's most important writers. That Dostoevski was acutely aware of man's inherent cruelty

Fëdor Dostoevski, a Russian novelist, was the creator of some of the most memorable characters in all world literature; they are noted for their psychological complexity.

and that he was profoundly compassionate toward all forms of human suffering is evident in even his earliest works, but the psychological and philosophical penetration of his greatest work first appeared in his middle years in the short novel *Notes from Underground.* It was followed by the four great novels of his maturity—*Crime and Punishment, The Idiot, The Possessed* (also translated as *The Devils*) and his masterpiece *The Brothers Karamazov.*

Dostoevski, unquestionably one of the great novelists, is today looked upon by many as one of the first modern writers. His novels are disliked by many, but their terrifying power cannot be denied. His work is distinguished not by its plot construction, which is usually very involved and highly melodramatic, nor by his writing style, which is often coarse and wordy, but rather by his uncanny insight into the previously unexplored depths of the human mind. He is outstanding for his acute observations of what is irrational in man, and in his analyses of neurotic complexes and unconscious urges in these novels he foreshadowed and influenced much of the thought and literature of the 20th century.

In a double-star system, the principal star, **A**, and the companion star, **C**, revolve about a common center of gravity, **E**. The more-massive principal star lies closer to the center of gravity and moves only to point **B**, while the companion moves to point **D**.

DOUBLE BASS, the bass member of the violin family. (See VIOLIN.) It averages about 6 feet in length and ordinarily has four strings, although sometimes a fifth string is added. It is played standing up.

The double bass is descended from a similar instrument called the contrabass, which first appeared in orchestras late in the 17th century. It was not widely used, however, until after 1806, when Beethoven used it in his Fourth Symphony. The double bass is the only member of the violin family used extensively by jazz musicians, who ordinarily dispense with bowing and instead pluck the strings.

DOUBLE STAR. Some stars are a single point of light to the naked eye, but seen through a telescope they turn out to be two separate stars. Stars like this were noticed soon after the telescope was invented, but most people assumed that the stars were far apart and only accidentally in the same direction from earth. For some of these stars this explanation was correct. No gravitational attraction connects them, and they are called optical double stars to distinguish them from other types.

The important type of double star was discovered in 1803 when William Herschel noticed that the two stars of the double star Castor were revolving around each other. Over 40,000 such double stars have since been found. They are often known as binary stars.

Sometimes a third star circles a binary star, or two binary stars circle each other. Castor is now known to be a group of three binary stars connected by gravitation. They are so close together that they appear as one star to the naked eye. These stars are called multiple systems.

Alpha Centauri, the closest star to the sun, is a multiple system of

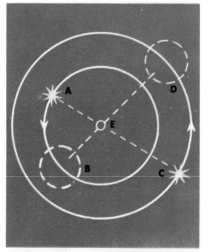

three stars. Two of them form a binary star and revolve around each other in about 80 years no farther apart than the sun and its outer planets, while a third star circles them at a great distance. (See ALPHA CENTAURI.) In another binary the two stars revolve around each other in the shortest known period of 1.7 years about as far apart as the earth and the sun.

In some binary stars one star is so dim it is invisible through the telescope. We know it as a binary star because the brighter star follows a wavy path through space as it and the dimmer one revolve around each other.

If both stars happen to revolve in a common plane with the earth, the dimmer star will periodically pass in front of the bright one and cut off some or all of its light. This eclipsing effect is noticeable even when both stars are visible, since the star in front will still block off light from the one behind. These stars are called eclipsing binaries. Algol is a famous example of this type. See ALGOL.

Some binary stars are so far away that we cannot separate them even with the strongest telescope. We cannot see their path as a wavy motion, and their light does not vary. They are identifiable as binaries by the spectroscope, which shows that the lines of their spectrum oscillate periodically. This type of binary star is called a spectroscopic binary; those visible in a telescope as separate stars are visual binaries.

Astronomers have learned much about stars in general from the study of binary systems. They are able to compute the masses of many binaries and the diameters of their stars, and from eclipsing binaries they are able to prove the rotation of individual stars.

DOUGHNUT, a fried cake, usually with a hole in the center. Twisted doughnuts with no hole are called crullers. Bismarcks are doughnuts filled with jelly. Other varieties of doughnuts are sugared or covered with flavored frostings.

Something resembling a doughnut, at least a cake with a hole in it, has been found among the remains of Indians in the Southwest. Crullers and other types of doughnuts were brought to America by the Dutch settlers in the 17th century. According to folklore, the first real doughnut with a hole in it was made for a sea captain who got indigestion from the uncooked insides of his fried cakes.

Stephen Arnold Douglas

DOUGLAS, STEPHEN ARNOLD
(1813-1861), noted U.S. senator, was born in Brandon, Vt. As a boy he was apprenticed to two cabinetmakers, and later he studied at Canandaigua Academy in New York. He studied law and was admitted to practice in Jacksonville, Ill., in 1834, the year he was elected attorney general of the state. He was a member of the legislature in 1835, secretary of state in 1840, and a judge of the state Supreme Court in 1841. He served in the House of Representatives from 1843 to 1847 and in the Senate from 1847 until his death. In the lower house he advocated the annexation of Texas and of Oregon, and he favored the war with Mexico. In the Senate he opposed the ratification of the Clayton-Bulwer Treaty and declared himself in favor of the acquisition of Cuba. On the question of slavery he maintained that the people of each territory should decide whether it should be a free or a slave state. This was known as the doctrine of popular, or squatter, sovereignty. In 1860 he received the regular Democratic nomination for the presidency, the seceding delegates nominating John C. Breckinridge. Douglas obtained 12 electoral votes and 1,375,157 popular votes as against 180 electoral votes and 1,866,352 popular votes cast for Lincoln, to whom, in the early days of the Civil War, Douglas gave support.

DOVE. See PIGEONS AND DOVES.

DOVER, capital of the state of Delaware, on the St. Jones River, 40 miles south of Wilmington. The population in 1960 was 7,250.

Dover is the marketing, processing, and shipping center for a rich farming and fruitgrowing region. It has canneries and factories making rubber products, hosiery, and paints. A U.S. Air Force base employs large numbers of the people of the city. Part of the state Capitol dates from 1722. Dover was settled in 1683 and became the capital of Delaware in 1777.

DOYLE, SIR ARTHUR CONAN (1859-1930), English author, was born in Edinburgh, Scotland. He was educated at several Jesuit schools and at the University of Edinburgh, where he took a degree in medicine. He attempted to establish a medical practice at Southsea; to supplement his meager income he began writing light fiction. Within a short time he was such a popular success that he abandoned medicine and devoted the rest of his life to writing.

Doyle wrote several science-fiction adventure stories and some excellent historical novels, including *Micah Clarke*, *The White Company*, and *Sir Nigel*. He hoped to be remembered by these books, but they have been completely overshadowed by his writings about Sherlock Holmes, a detective with amazing powers of scientific analysis, whom Doyle introduced in 1887 in his first work of fiction, *A Study in Scarlet*. Holmes almost immediately became the most popular fictional character in the world. The public demanded more Sherlock Holmes stories, and Doyle turned them out in abundance. They include the longer works *The Sign of the Four*, *The Hound of the Baskervilles*, *The Valley of Fear*, and *The Last Bow*. There were also several collections of shorter stories: *The Adventures of Sherlock Holmes*, *Memoirs of Sherlock Holmes*, *The Return of Sherlock*

Sir Arthur Conan Doyle created the famous fictional English detective Sherlock Holmes and his assistant, Dr. Watson.

Holmes, and *The Case Book of Sherlock Holmes*. Doyle at one time attempted to end the series by ending a story with Holmes' death, but later he was forced to resurrect him. Before Doyle's death Sherlock Holmes had become the most famous character in all English literature, and more has been written about him than about any other character except Hamlet.

DRACO, or the Dragon, is a large constellation visible all year from midnorthern latitudes. It winds in a long S-shaped curve among several other constellations. The star at the end of the Dragon's tail is between the Pole Star and the pointer stars of the Big Dipper. From there the constellation parallels the handle of the Big Dipper, turns away in a curve around Ursa Minor (the Little Dipper) toward Cepheus, then turns back in the direction of Hercules. It ends in a small quadrangle of four stars that represent the Dragon's head.

The third star from the end of the Dragon's tail is especially interesting, because it was the so-called North Star several thousand years ago. Since then the direction of the earth's axis has changed until the axis now points to Polaris, our present North Star.

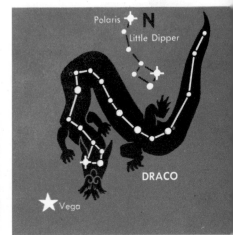

Draco, the Dragon, according to one legend, was the monster guarding the golden apples in the Garden of Hesperides. Hercules slew the beast after a desperate battle and took away the apples. According to another legend, Draco was the guardian of a sacred spring. Ordered to get water from the spring, the Thracian hero Cadmus slew the monster.

DRAFT (conscription). See MILITARY TRAINING AND SERVICE.

DRAGON, THE (constellation). See DRACO.

GREEN DARNER
2.6″

TEN-SPOT
DRAGONFLY
2.0″

nymph

BLACKWING
DAMSELFLY 1.3″

cast
skin

arrowhead

DRAGON BOAT FESTIVAL, a holiday formerly celebrated in China in June or July. It was observed by regattas and other boating sports. A big feature of the celebrations was the races between long, graceful, dragon-shaped boats. The Communist government of China abolished many of the traditional festivals and substituted others.

DRAGONFLY, a large iridescent-winged insect. It develops through incomplete metamorphosis directly from aquatic nymph into aerial adult. The adult is noted for its swift flight and its voracious preying on other insects. It has inspired a great amount of poetry and popular folklore.

The dragonfly is a very ancient insect, and it is primitive in many ways. Its peculiar kind of life cycle —incomplete metamorphosis—is shared only with a small group of insects, including the mayfly and stonefly. The nymphs, which inhabit fresh waters, are grotesque and rapacious creatures. They breathe oxygen from the water by means of tracheal gills. These minute, flat gills are located in an enlargement of the nymph's thin-walled lower intestine. The nymph expands and contracts this chamber to suck in fresh water containing oxygen. The chamber also serves for a unique kind of jet propulsion; the nymph sends itself forward by forcefully expelling water through its rectum.

Among the commonest species of dragonfly in North America are the green darner and the ten-spot dragonfly. The damselfly is not a dragonfly, but it belongs to a very closely related suborder of insects. The dragonfly lays its eggs on water plants or in water, and the nymphs develop in water. After several growing stages the nymphs leave the water. The skin splits, and the adult emerges.

The dragonfly is represented by more than 2,500 species, distributed all over the earth. The adult's abdomen is long, slender, and segmented. Its broad head is freely attached to the thorax, enabling the dragonfly to rotate its head and look in all directions. Its large, projecting eyes are very keen, aiding the dragonfly in hunting other insects and in avoiding its enemies.

Its ability for swift, darting, long-sustained flight probably qualifies the dragonfly as the strongest flier among the insects. It consumes great numbers of mosquitoes, flies, gnats, and other small insects; it scoops up these insects in a basket formed by its legs as it flies through the air.

The dragonfly is probably more celebrated in poetry than any other insect. Many superstitions have grown up around it: It is the devil's-darning-needle, which sews up the ears of bad boys, and the snake feeder, which ministers to the needs of snakes.

DRAINAGE. Natural drainage is the removal of excess water from land surfaces and soils by the action of gravity. The excess surface water is carried by streams and rivers to lakes and oceans. Streams and rivers form surface drainage patterns. Ground-water movements drain surplus water in the soil and rocks of the earth into rivers, lakes, and oceans. See GROUND WATER.

The surface drainage pattern of an area is controlled by the climate, the types and arrangements of rocks beneath the land surface, the soil, and the land forms and relief. The geological and climatic history of an area may also affect its drainage pattern. An area that is drained by one master stream and its tributaries is called a drainage basin.

Deserts have distinct drainage patterns. Desert streams, because the rainfall is so light and infrequent, are often intermittent—at times the streambeds are dry and carry no surface water. Streams, when they do flow, do not join larger

DRAINAGE

streams but end in stagnant pools or disappear in mudflats. The pools and flats, often called playas, are in low enclosed land basins. Such a system is called interior drainage.

In drainage basins that have abundant rainfall and one type of underlying rock, the streams form a branching, irregular pattern called a dendritic stream pattern. When the drainage basin contains rocks of different resistances to water erosion, the streams follow the rocks that are least resistant. If the resistant and nonresistant rocks are in parallel strips, the main streams are parallel to each other.

If the rocks beneath the drainage basin are limestone, the basin may have few surface streams. The limestone contains many caves and underground passages. Surface streams plunge into openings of the caves and passages. Such an area is called a karst region.

The rapidity with which rain that falls on land surfaces can drain into streams and lakes depends on the soil present and the land relief. Water drains more rapidly in areas of high relief. Sandy, loose soils transmit water rapidly. Clay soils and tightly packed soils do not transmit water well.

The great ice sheets that covered northern Europe, Asia, and North America during much of the Pleistocene greatly affected the drainage patterns of the areas they overrode. Areas that were glaciated often have many lakes, ponds, and swamps. Many lakes and swamps are isolated and are not drained by a stream. No efficient surface drainage pattern is in operation. The glaciers completely disrupted the preglacial drainage patterns, and too little time has elapsed since the retreat of the glaciers for new drainage patterns to become fully established.

Russ Kinne

Typical of glaciated areas in its drainage pattern is the Christian River area, Alaska.

The natural drainage system of North America is mapped at right. There are no river systems in two large areas shown on this map—the Great Basin in the western United States and a similar area in Mexico. Rainfall is scant in these areas. Drainage is very rapid on bare mountain slopes, such as the slopes of the Cascade Mountains (below) in Washington. Here water from melting snows on Mt. Chiwawa drains into Lyman Lake, which occupies a glacial basin.
Bob & Ira Spring

DRAKE, SIR FRANCIS (1540?-1596), an English navigator, was born in Tavistock, in Devonshire. He served as a sailor in a coasting vessel and afterward joined Sir John Hawkins in his last expedition against the Spaniards in 1567. He lost nearly all he possessed in that unfortunate enterprise.

Drake then gathered a number of adventurers around him and fitted out a vessel, in which he made two successful voyages to the West Indies in 1570 and 1571. Next year, with two small ships, he again sailed for the Spanish Main, captured the cities of Nombre de Dios and Vera Cruz, and took home much treasure. In 1577 Drake made another expedition to the Spanish Main, having this time command of five ships. On this, the most famous of his voyages, Drake passed through the Strait of Magellan and later lost all his ships but the *Golden Hind* in storms. He worked his way up the South American coast, plundered ports, and captured Spanish treasure ships. He then steered straight across the Indian Ocean, rounded the Cape of Good Hope, and arrived at Plymouth, England, Sept. 26, 1580.

Queen Elizabeth I showed her favor to Drake by knighting him aboard his own ship. Five years afterward Drake was again attacking the Spaniards in the Cape Verde Islands and in the West Indies. In 1587 he made a raid on the Bay of Cadiz, where the Spanish Armada was gathered, and destroyed 33 ships. In 1588 he commanded a division of the English fleet that defeated the Spanish Armada. In 1593 he represented Plymouth in Parliament. His later expeditions to the Spanish West Indies and Panama were not successful. He died aboard his ship off Portobello (now in Panama).

Francis Drake is here shown being knighted by Queen Elizabeth I in honor of his voyage around the world. She had hesitated to knight him because of Spanish protests about his damage to their shipping.

DRAMA originated probably among savage tribes in the dance at religious festivals or in mimetic action for purposes of showing how a certain feat was accomplished on a given occasion—the hunting exploit of some member of a tribe, for example.

ANCIENT DRAMA

Among the Egyptians of about 2000 B.C. drama existed in religious ceremonies for the worship of Osiris. There are some evidences of drama in the Book of Job and in the Song of Solomon, where occasionally there appear to be parts for two speakers. But the drama as it is known today, in distinct forms of tragedy and comedy, originated in Greece in the festivals of Dionysus in the 6th and 5th centuries B.C., where poetry, a dithyrambic ode with song and dance, was presented by a leader and a chorus. In the dramatic contests under Pisistratus the dithyramb developed into drama. The earliest Greek dramatic production of which there is an extant record is the tragedy contest won by Thespis of Icaria about 534 B.C. Following Thespis Greek tragedy reached its highest peak in the plays of Aeschylus, Sophocles, and Euripides. Aeschylus added a second, and Sophocles a third, actor to the leader-chorus drama, and these actors in various masks and costumes took various parts. Aeschylus' *Suppliants* is the earliest Greek drama that has survived. He wrote also the famous *Oresteia* trilogy, consisting of the *Agamemnon*, the *Choephoroe*, and the *Eumenides*. Aeschylus' characters are heroic, superhuman; his style is lofty, magnificent. Sophocles' characters are idealized but true to life, though life furnishes no such models. His plots are models of skill; his language, the perfection of Attic Greek. Only 7 of his 120 plays have come down to us, among them *Oedipus Tyrannus*, *Antigone*, and *Electra*. Euripides in the *Trojan Women*, *Hippolytus*, and *Medea* humanized tragedy with characters that were drawn from the daily life of his time, with more natural situations, and with more intense human emotions.

Greek comedy originated in the joyous side of the Dionysiac processions as tragedy grew out of their solemn features. The first actual

Ministry of Inf., Greece

The theater at Epidaurus, Greece, built in the 4th century B.C., is noted for its fine acoustics. Performances of ancient Greek tragedies are still given in it every year.

producers of comedy at Athens were Cratinus, Eupolis, and Aristophanes, representatives of the Old Comedy. The subject matter of their plays was coarsely satirical. The chorus, dressed sometimes in fantastic costumes, as in *The Birds*, *The Wasps*, and *The Frogs* of Aristophanes, gave utterance to some of the most exquisitely beautiful lyric song in Greek literature and, again, to some of the most scurrilous abuse ever heaped upon a public character. The comic poets of the 5th century B.C. did not hesitate to bring upon the scene by name and in character the best known men of their day, including the notorious demagogue Cleon, the great general Lamachus, Socrates, and even Pericles. The spirit of personal abuse became intolerable to the Athenians, sobered after the Peloponnesian Wars, and was prohibited. Thus arose the comedy of manners, the society play, represented by Philemon, Menander, Diphilus, and many others.

Greek drama was introduced into Rome in the 3d century B.C. and in the hands of Roman playwrights did not develop far beyond the Greek models. The works of the earlier tragic poets of Rome have all perished. The only Roman writer of tragedy whose plays, ten in number, have survived was Seneca (about 4 B.C.—A.D. 65). All but one, the *Octavia*, are based on the great Greek tragedies, such as *Agamemnon*, *Troades*, *Hercules*, and *Medea*. Two producers of Latin comedy, however, were outstanding: Plautus, who wrote the *Captivi*, *Miles Gloriosus*, *Trinummus*, and 17 more that are preserved, and Terence, who wrote *Andria*, *Adelphi*, and four others.

MEDIEVAL DRAMA

Modern Western drama originated in the trope inserted in the Introit of the mass in the medieval church, with the intention of picturing for the unschooled people the events in a great Bible episode, which they could not understand in the Latin reading. The first of these is the Easter trope, the *Quem quaeritis*, so named for the introductory words. The characters are the three Marys (choir boys with covered heads), who have come to the tomb of Christ, and the angel who guards the tomb. A whole cycle of Easter plays developed from this first *Quem quaeritis* trope, and the subjects were taken from the Scriptures. From the custom of enacting the Nativity trope at Christmas, cycles of Christmas plays developed. The English *Second Shepherd's Play* (15th century) is one of this type.

Gradually there developed three kinds of medieval play. The mystery play was based on the Holy Scriptures. In France, but not in England, it is to be distinguished from the miracle play, which dealt with the life of a saint or a miracle of the Virgin. In England both these forms were termed miracles. The morality play came later; in it the chief characters represented abstract qualities, such as Vice, Mankind, or Death, and the tone was generally philosophical. The moralities contained little humor. The most famous example is the English *Everyman* (15th century), which has often been revived in the 20th century.

As plays were moved into the churchyard, then into the streets and marketplaces, and finally came under the control of guilds, elements of humor and realism began to creep into the drama. One of the first comic characters was the Devil. From his clowning it was but a short step to purely secular drama, which dealt with everyday characters—the lawyer, the merchant, the student, the young wife, and the old foolish husband. The first truly secular plays were the French *Maistre Pierre Pathelin* (1470, anonymous) and Pierre Gringore's *Play of the Prince of Fools* (1511).

RENAISSANCE DRAMA

With the rediscovery of classical literature during the Renaissance the Greek and Roman dramatists were imitated first in Italy and, later, with the spread of humanism, in France, Germany, and England. In the early 16th century the Italian Lodovico Ariosto produced *La Lena*, a picture of social life in Ferrara. Machiavelli and Pietro Aretino also wrote comedies of manners in which a certain refinement of structure was reminiscent of the early Greeks. Other stage performances, particularly the court spectacles, were meaningless, but the *commedia dell'arte* was original and lifelike. It was unwritten impromptu drama, produced on platforms in the streets by strolling players. Masks and costumes, conventionalized with time, told the audience what to expect of the characters, all of whom were popular types, used again and again: the Captain and Pantaloon, for instance. Even the court became interested in the *commedia dell'arte*, and its vogue spread throughout Europe.

Drama in Spain in the 16th century was much like that in Italy except that the swaggering Captain overshadowed Harlequin. Lope de Vega and Pedro Calderón de la Barca were the chief Spanish dramatists, with Tirso de Molina and Ruiz de Alarcón y Mendoza ranking next. Lope de Vega produced tragedies, comedies, and religious plays.

The most brilliant 16th-century drama was the English, chiefly because, in the reign of Elizabeth I, drama was the source of entertainment for all classes of people. All of the medieval and Renaissance types of drama were produced. Latin comedies, like those of Terence and Plautus (*Ralph Roister Doister*), and tragedies, like those of Seneca (*Gorboduc* was the first), were performed in the universities and at court. The Italian and Spanish dramas were imitated by Thomas Kyd and Christopher Marlowe. Polemic plays grew out of the moralities. Pastoral idyllic comedies were written by Francis Beaumont and John Fletcher in partnership. Domestic dramas were written by Thomas Heywood (*A Woman Killed with Kindness*) and by Thomas Dekker (*The Shoemaker's Holiday*); and terrifying melodramas, by John Webster (*The Duchess of Malfi*). Lesser figures were John Lyly, George Peele, Robert Greene, George Chapman, John Marston, and James Shirley.

The greatest dramatists were Marlowe, Jonson, and Shakespeare. Marlowe was the most gifted of the

The above drawing is from a 1486 edition of Terence's plays. It shows the so-called bathing-box stage developed in Italy during the Renaissance for the performance of classical drama. This stage had a platform on which the actors stood and a rear façade of curtained entrances that were supposed to lead to the houses of the characters.

The picture below shows the staging of the *Passion of Valenciennes* in the Middle Ages. Liturgical drama was performed on a stage set with decorated platforms called mansions, each representing a separate and distinct locality. The space around them was called the platea.

Photo, Henri Paul

The scene above is from a modern production of Molière's *The Forced Marriage*, which was first performed in Paris in 1664. This play is not one of the playwright's best comedies. Molière's best works include *The Imaginary Invalid*, *Tartuffe*, and *The Misanthrope*.

At the right is a scene from a production of *Waiting for Godot* by Irish playwright Samuel Beckett; it is one of the best plays of the modern theater. Originally written in French, this play was first performed at the Théâtre de Babylone in Paris in 1952.

university wits. He introduced blank verse into drama and produced the first play that approached a psychological study. His *Tamburlaine* was a tragedy of a man influenced by the lust for power. Ben Jonson's Senecan tragedies were an utter failure; he was the slave to the classical tradition—the unities, the bombast, the wooden characterization of the noble, inhuman great. His humorous dramas, *Bartholomew, Fair* and *Every Man out of His Humour*, on the other hand, are lively comedies with satirical, exaggerated character types. Shakespeare, of course, was the genius of the age, having the best qualities of the other dramatists. He improved blank verse, made dialogue more natural, and created individual characters and put them in human situations. Among his best comedies are *As You Like It, The Merchant of Venice, Twelfth Night,* and *The Tempest.* His great tragedies include *Hamlet, King Lear, Othello,* and *Macbeth.* He is the only Elizabethan dramatist still widely produced.

DRAMA OF THE
17TH, 18TH, AND 19TH CENTURIES

In England the casual charm that characterized Elizabethan drama died out under the Puritan regime and did not return until near the end of the 18th century. The theaters, closed during the Civil War and the Commonwealth period (1642-1660), reopened under Charles I to produce the sophisticated, witty, coarse comedies of William Wycherley, George Farquhar, Thomas Shadwell, and William Congreve and the bombastic, spectacular, heroic tragedies of John Dryden and Thomas Otway. The church finally put a stop to the former; after the Stuart reigns ended, English comedy became maudlin and sentimental, and tragedy became stiff and dull. In the middle of the 18th century the theater was briefly revived by the comedy of manners of Oliver Goldsmith and Richard Brinsley Sheridan.

French drama emerged in the 17th century from its medieval and religious shackles with the classical tragedies of Pierre Corneille and Jean Racine and the superb comedies of Molière. Corneille's masterpiece, *Le Cid*, was produced in 1636. Thirty years later Racine produced *Andromaque*, which was followed by *Iphigénie*, and *Phèdre*. Racine was less austere than Corneille, but both raised French tragedy to its greatest heights. Molière was the greatest dramatist of the period. He satirized most of the foibles of the society of his day in such plays as *The School for Husbands, The School for Wives, The Doctor in Spite of Himself,* and *Tartuffe.* His *The Misanthrope, The Miser,* and *The Bourgeois Gentleman* were excellent character studies.

German drama came to maturity much more slowly than did the Romance and English dramas. Before the middle of the 18th century the only playwright of note was Hans Sachs (16th century), who wrote both formal comedies and tragedies and popular carnival plays. Although English players introduced Marlowe and Shakespeare to Germany at the end of the 16th century, theatrical performances soon degenerated into improvised farce, featuring certain stock characters, without, however, the merits of the *commedia dell'arte.* Johann Christoph Gottsched and Caroline Neuber attempted to reform the German theater during the years following 1727, but not a great deal was accomplished until Gotthold Ephraim Lessing urged that a national theater be established. It produced the first great German plays, his *Minna von Barnhelm* (1767) and *Emilia Galotti* (1772). The great dramatists of the German classical period were Goethe, with *Egmont, Iphigenie auf Tauris,* and *Faust,* and Schiller, with *The Robbers, Wallenstein, Maria Stuart,* and *Wilhelm Tell.* Drama after Friedrich Gottlieb Klopstock, Christoph Martin Wieland, and Friedrich von Klinger declined into sentimental melodrama with the plays of August von Kotzebue.

The popular 18th-century drama in France was the farcical comedy of Pierre Caron de Beaumarchais; in England, the comedy of manners and the domestic drama. In the 19th century romantic drama flourished throughout Europe. Idealized, historical, or sentimental characters figured in complex plots of adventure and triumphant love. René de Pixérécourt, in France, shares with Kotzebue credit for the invention of melodrama. Various types of romantic drama—melodrama, the historical play, the fantasy play—

flourished in Italy with Alessandro Manzoni; in Russia with Mikhail Lermontov, Alexander Pushkin, and Alexei Tolstoi; in the United States with William Dunlap, John Howard Payne, and Robert Montgomery Bird; in Germany with Christian Grabbe, Heinrich von Kleist, Ludwig Tieck, Karl Gutzkow, and Georg Büchner; in Austria with Franz Grillparzer, Johann Nestroy, and Ferdinand Raimund; in France with Victor Hugo, Alfred de Musset, Alexandre Dumas *père*, Alfred de Vigny, and Edmond Rostand; and in Great Britain with Edward Bulwer-Lytton and Dion Boucicault. In the latter part of the 19th century more sophisticated social dramas came from Eugène Scribe, Victorien Sardou, Emile Augier, and Alexandre Dumas *fils* in France; Henry Arthur Jones, Arthur Wing Pinero, and James M. Barrie in England; and from Gabriele D'Annunzio in Italy. Meanwhile realism and naturalism entered drama in the plays of Friedrich Hebbel, Emile Zola, Henry Becque, Nikolai Gogol, Alexander Ostrovski, and Ivan Turgenev, but the real liberating influence was Henrik Ibsen in Norway. His serious social dramas included *A Doll's House, Ghosts,* and *Hedda Gabler;* his *Peer Gynt* and *The Master Builder* marked the entrance of symbolism into modern drama.

MODERN DRAMA

Ibsen's influence on modern drama was immense. The production

Below is Sidney Poitier in a scene from the play *A Raisin In the Sun.* The play, written by Lorraine Hansberry, deals with the problems and aspirations of a Negro family living on Chicago's South Side.
Freidman-Abeles

of his work throughout Europe stimulated a great burst of dramatic activity everywhere. The last two decades of the 19th century and the first half of the 20th century witnessed a great variety of trends. There was a brief revival of romantic fantasy in France; symbolism was carried to great extremes; expressionism appeared in Germany after World War I; comedy was rejuvenated in England and the United States; French impressionism made a small showing in the theater; and poetic drama reached new heights in England, Ireland, France, Spain, and the United States. From the time of Ibsen the greatest dramatists in the major countries included August Strindberg in Sweden; Gerhart Hauptmann and Bertolt Brecht in Germany; Luigi Pirandello in Italy; José Echegaray y Eizaguirres, Jacinto Benavente y Martínez, and Federico García Lorca in Spain; Paul Claudel, Jean Giraudoux, Jean-Paul Sartre, Jean Anouilh, and Albert Camus in France; William Butler Yeats, John Millington Synge, and Sean O'Casey in Ireland; Anton Chekhov in Russia; George Bernard Shaw, Oscar Wilde, John Galsworthy, and T. S. Eliot in England; and Eugene O'Neill and Tennessee Williams in America.

Many other notable dramatists wrote plays that were well received when they were produced. Among these were Pär Lagerkvist in Sweden; Arthur Schnitzler, Frank Wedekind, Hugo von Hofmannstal, Georg Kaiser, and Ernst Toller in Germany and Austria; Karel Čapek in Czechoslovakia; Ferenc Molnár in Hungary; Maurice Maeterlinck in Belgium; Eugène Brieux, Jean Cocteau, Eugène Ionesco, and Samuel Beckett in France; Maxim Gorky in Russia; John Masefield, Somerset Maugham, Christopher Fry, and John Osborne in England; and Maxwell Anderson, Thornton Wilder, Sidney Howard, Elmer Rice, Clifford Odets, S. N. Behrman, Philip Barry, Robert Sherwood, Lillian Hellman, James Thurber, Arthur Miller, and William Inge in the United States.

In the Orient several forms of drama that are greatly different from those of western Europe have developed.

This encyclopedia contains separate entries on many of the dramatists mentioned here. See COMEDY; THEATER; TRAGEDY.

DRAPERY. See CURTAINS AND DRAPERIES.

DRAWBRIDGE, a movable bridge over a river or canal. The three kinds of drawbridge are the swing bridge, the bascule bridge, and the vertical lift bridge. All are operated by either hydraulic or electric power.

A swing bridge turns sideways. The pivot on which it turns may be either in the middle or on or near the bank of the river. If the pivot is in the middle, two spans of the bridge turn; they are of equal length, and their weights balance each other. If the pivot is on or near the bank, only one span turns; its weight must be balanced by a counterweight.

A bascule bridge is raised in the center. The raising mechanism is ordinarily aided by weights, which are usually underground but may be built into the superstructure of the bridge.

A vertical lift bridge is one in which the entire movable part spanning the channel is lifted rather than tilted as in the bascule bridge.

Castles had drawbridges across their moats.

DRAWING, the art of representing an object or scene on a flat surface, such as paper. It is through the use of line and light and shade that the artist is able to render lifelike figures and objects. The illusion of nearness or distance is achieved by means of perspective and foreshortening. Depending on the medium used, drawings may be black and white or colored. Drawing may be done with metal point or pen; pencil, crayon, chalk, or charcoal; or brush.

Metal point is rarely used for drawing nowadays, although it was popular during the Renaissance. It was used for sketches later finished in ink or chalk or elaborated in oil paintings. Pen-and-ink drawings are often confined to pure outlines; an appearance of relief or projection is given by thickening the lines on the shadow side. Many artists also use pen and ink for detailed drawings.

This completed still life, showing familiar objects painted and arranged in a pleasing manner, is based upon a series of drawings in charcoal pencil.

First the outlines of the objects are sketched. Note the importance of the relative sizes and shapes of the objects for a good pictorial composition.

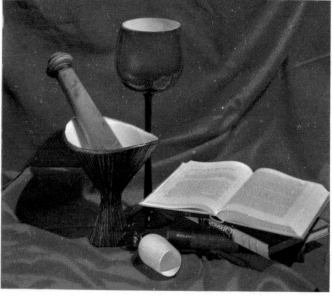

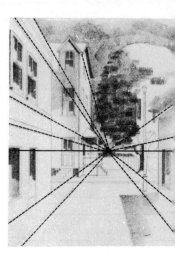

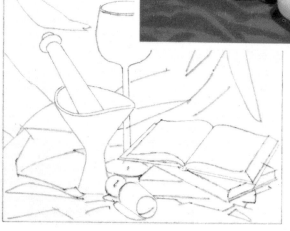

In this drawing the street and the houses appear to converge to a vanishing point on the horizon as they recede into the distance. The apparent diminution of objects when they are seen from a distance is called foreshortening.

In this drawing, which is the exact replica of the one above it, the same linear perspective is achieved without the plotting of horizon lines and vanishing point. Beginners should use the lines to learn the proper distances.

When the gray half-tones have been completed, dark shadows are introduced that accent the three-dimensional quality of the forms and make them appear more solid and truer to life.

Next the objects's three-dimensional forms are built up by contrasts of light and shade. This tone-building process can be done in different ways, such as rubbing in charcoal with a thumb.

These drawings show an easy method that can be used in either reducing or magnifying the size of a picture. The network of squares framing the picture is the grid.

Graphite pencils, because of their varying degrees of hardness or softness, can be used for almost any type of drawing, from a rough sketch to an accurate mechanical drawing. Chalk and crayon of various colors are commonly used for drawings with large masses and broad outlines. Charcoal, being a cheap substance and easily rubbed off, is a good medium for quick, rough sketches. However, many Italian Renaissance painters used charcoal to make full-scale designs, called cartoons, for a projected work, such as fresco, oil painting, or tapestry.

Drawings made with a brush are known as watercolors or wash drawings. There is also a form of brush drawing in which the subject is first outlined with the pen, and the shading is laid on afterward or washed in with the brush. Some artists have even made line drawings in this medium by using the point of the brush. See MECHANICAL DRAWING.

DREAMING. When we see things during sleep and seem to be looking at a fantastic play, we are dreaming. Dreams are often so real that they seem to be a strange part of our waking life, and sometimes when we wake up we can hardly believe we have been dreaming. It is no wonder that primitive people thought that spirits visited them during sleep to give them messages, and that these messages would give a person clues as to the future. Ancient priests and physicians would interpret dreams to help the person who sought their advice at a temple.

A complete explanation for dreaming is still to be given. However, scientists think that dreams are a form of communication from the unconscious mind of the dreamer. During dreaming, unconscious impulses reach the level of consciousness. What one sees in a dream is symbolic, and dreams are supposed to give a person gratification of wishes that he cannot gratify during his waking life.

Dream books, which supposedly give clues to the meaning of dreams, may be used for entertainment but should not be taken seriously.

DREDGING, the removal and disposal of submerged mud, sand, and rocks by means of a powered bucket, screw, or suction pipe swung from the frame of a barge and let down through the water to the bottom of the area to be cleared. Dredges are specialized types of excavation machines to cut and deepen channels, keep canals and rivers open for navigation, and excavate valuable material (such as gold-bearing sands) from streams. Dredges are designed and built according to the nature of the material to be removed and according to the depth at which it lies.

A ladder dredge contains a narrow steel framework up to 50 feet long, one end of which is fastened to the barge with a pivot. An endless belt on which excavating buckets are fastened runs around the length of the ladder.

When the ladder with its endless belt of buckets is let down, the empty buckets descend on the lower side of the ladder, scoop up a load of spoil, rise on the upper surface of the ladder, and as they reach the top of the ladder, dump their loads into a tank on the barge. In digging the Suez Canal, where submerged rock had to be removed with the sand, a vertical rock-crushing tower built into the dredge extended down into the water so that the drills broke off the rock just ahead of the bite of the buckets.

The hydraulic, or suction, dredge is essentially a large steel pipe lowered from the barge to the bed of sand, soft clay, or silt. At the end of the pipe is generally a powerful rotary cutting head to chew up the material.

The dipper dredge, widely used in the Panama Canal, is a floating excavator with a 40-foot or 50-foot steel arm actuated by geared rods and steel ropes. On the end of the arm is a huge steel bucket, the cutting edge of which is a set of steel teeth. The teeth bite deep into the muck, loosen it, and slide it into the bucket.

The grab dredge for working in deep water suspends from steel ropes a spherical clamshell bucket or orangepeel bucket, the jaws of

This dredge is depositing spoil on a riverbank as it clears a waterway for shipping.

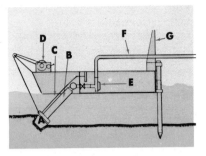

The parts of a suction dredge are the cutting head, **A**, the suction pipe, **B**, the drive pole, **C**, the windlass, **D**, the pump, **E**, the rinsing tube, **F**, and the tube support, **G**.

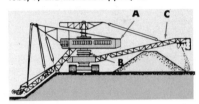

Above is a ladder dredge. Indicated are the rotating control cabin, **A**, the stationary base, **B**, and the conveyor arm, **C**. The ladder dredge does placer mining for gold.

which open from the top. The open jaws are dropped onto the rocks and mud, bite in deeply, and close; the load is then pulled to the surface, where it is dumped by opening the jaws.

Dredging includes not only the excavation of spoil but also its disposal. Self-propelled dredges for operating where ship traffic is heavy load themselves with hundreds of tons of spoil and then steam out to sea to dump it. This type of dredge sometimes has propellers both fore and aft so that it does not have to turn around. Other dredges pour or dump the spoil into barges whose bottoms open up when the barge is towed out to the dumping area. Still other dredges use a floating pipeline to pour forth the spoil onto levees and fields. The inhabitants of The Netherlands have built a large part of their country in this way.

Except for the self-propelled types dredges are moved in their work with mooring chains attached to deck winches. Often the dredge is held in place with movable posts, or spuds, that stick in the bottom; and the cutter is pivoted in an arc.

For oceanographic explorations dredge buckets of steel and canvas are let down to catch samples of marine life, mud and rocks, and sand on the floor of the ocean and also to sample marine life at various depths. These dredges are like those used to gather oysters.

DRED SCOTT DECISION. On Mar. 6, 1857, the Supreme Court of the United States ruled that Dred Scott, a Negro, was to remain a slave because a slave or the descendant of a slave was not, and could not possibly become, a citizen of a state or of the United States.

This ruling gave constitutional validity to the desire of the slave-holding South to extend slavery into the territories. Dred Scott was originally a slave in Missouri, a slave-holding state; but his master, an army surgeon, took him to the free state of Illinois, where slavery was prohibited by the Ordinance of 1787, and to the Wisconsin Territory, where slavery was prohibited by the Missouri Compromise. Ultimately, Dred Scott was brought back to Missouri. There he was persuaded to bring suit for his freedom on the ground that he had lived in free territory for years.

The Supreme Court also maintained that Congress had no constitutional right to forbid slavery north of 36°30', the line designated in the Missouri Compromise. The Republicans of the North, including Abraham Lincoln, were opposed to the decision of the Supreme Court. The Dred Scott decision increased the distrust that the southern and northern sections of the United States had for each other. A few years later this distrust was one of the factors that led to the Civil War.

DRESSER, a chest of drawers. In the United States the dresser is usually in the bedroom, for the storage of clothes, and has a mirror over it. In England the dresser is in the dining room, for the storage and display of china and utensils. Dressers have a peculiar significance in history in that they evolved from the strong chests of the Middle Ages, when fighting and marching were a part of everyday family life. But as wealthy people settled down, drawers were added to chests in order to simplify the problems of storage.

The heavy, tall-back, oak dresser was eventually replaced in the homes of the wealthy by the long, walnut side table. The dresser remained, however, an important piece of furniture in the country cottage. The Welsh dresser, which was developed in the 18th century, became popular throughout the world. It was made with a recessed superstructure of shelves for display purposes; its sideboard section usually had a row of three drawers above a row of three cupboard doors.

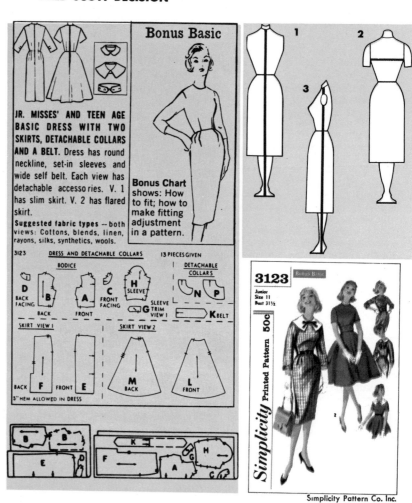

Complete dress patterns are available to the home dressmaker. Left and below are patterns for the various dress parts. Below them is a diagram indicating how the patterns should be placed on the dress material for cutting. How the garment should fit is shown at the upper right. Unless the garment is bias cut, the center front and back grainlines, **1**, of the material should be perpendicular to the floor; bustline and crosswise back grainlines, **2**, should be parallel to the floor; and shoulder and underarm seams, **3**, should form a vertical line from shoulder to floor. Completed dresses are modeled at the lower right.

DRESSMAKING, a type of handicraft that requires cutting out pieces of fabric according to a pattern, fitting and assembling the parts, and then sewing them together to make a dress or similar garment. To choose a fabric for a dress, you must, of course, consider the qualities of different cloths. For example, stiff cloths cannot be made to drape. Some cloths fray easily at the edges and require special seam finishes. Pleats flatten out in springy materials.

Some women have models constructed of their figures, and they use these in making their own clothes. However, the paper pattern in standard sizes is commoner nowadays. It comes complete with directions for each step of the dressmaking process.

There are some general rules that should always be observed in dressmaking. Before cutting the fabric, pin the main parts of the pattern together and fit them to the right side of your figure, so as to make necessary alterations at the outset. These alterations can then be copied for the left side. You will save time in the long run if you make a simple muslin dress with your figure adjustments sewn in, since standard sizes and patterns do not allow for individual irregularities. The muslin dress, fitted to your particular figure, can then be used as a pattern for the other dresses you may make.

After you have made the alterations, press the material and pin the main parts of the altered pattern to it. Cut the pieces carefully to ensure a good fit. With tailor's chalk, copy the required pattern marks on the material. To complete the garment, follow the directions given on the instruction sheet that accompanies the pattern.

OCCUPATION: Dressmaker

PERSONAL FACTORS—ABILITIES, SKILLS, APTITUDES: Eye for fashion and clothing construction, imagination, accuracy, and patience with detail are needed as well as a pleasing personality to deal with the public.

EDUCATION AND SPECIAL TRAINING: A trade-school or vocational-school course is helpful although not essential. Short courses in design and technical training are needed for specialization.

WORKING CONDITIONS:

1. **INCOME:**
   COMPARED WITH OTHER CAREERS WITH EQUAL TRAINING: Average
   COMPARED WITH MOST OTHER CAREERS: Average

2. **ENVIRONMENT:** Variable—factory, alteration department of exclusive shop, or own shop

3. **OTHER:** Hours possibly irregular; work tedious

RELATED CAREERS: Dress designer, tailor, theatrical-costume designer, teacher in vocational school

WHERE TO FIND MORE INFORMATION: Nearest city or state vocational or trade school

---

DREYFUS CASE, a French political and military scandal that began with the arrest of Captain Alfred Dreyfus, a French Jewish army officer, in 1894, on false charges of treason and ended with the reversal of his conviction in 1906. The Dreyfus case not only involved anti-Semitism but also threatened the existence of the Third Republic.

In 1894 Dreyfus was convicted by court-martial of giving French military secrets to Germany. The crime was really committed by Major Marie Charles Esterhazy. In 1896 Colonel Georges Picquart of French military intelligence discovered evidence of Esterhazy's guilt. Though the army tried to suppress the evidence, news of it leaked out and forced a military trial of Esterhazy. At this point the Dreyfus affair began to be a contest for supremacy in France between elements that reflected divisions—present almost from the beginning of the republic, in 1870—over the form of government and the relation of state to church. Some army officers forged evidence to strengthen

the case against Dreyfus and discredit Picquart. As a result of these forgeries the court-martial acquitted Esterhazy. The French novelist Emile Zola then published an exposé of the forgers and the military court. The exposé, entitled *J'accuse,* eventually resulted in a second military trial for Dreyfus in 1899. The court, unwilling even in the face of evidence to admit the army could be wrong, again found Dreyfus guilty but with "extenuating circumstances." Dreyfus was then pardoned. Seven years later the French Supreme Court threw out the verdict, and Dreyfus and Picquart were reinstated in the army.

DRILL, a tool that bores holes in metal, wood, or other hard material. It has cutting edges on one end and is rapidly rotated to make a cylindrical hole in the material that is being bored. The forms, which vary according to the material in which

Cal-Pictures

The rotary table of an oil-drilling rig (above) turns a long steel pipe with a bit on the end. Special muds are pumped down the pipe to flush rock cuttings to the surface.

it is to work, include the awl, auger, gimlet, and brace and bit. Drills may be electrically powered or operated by hand.

The drill press is an electric drill mounted on a supporting frame. The drill is lowered into the material, which rests on a platform and is held in place by a vise.

Drills designed for especially hard materials have cutting edges of very hard, black diamonds, or carbonados. Percussive drills, which chip rather than bore, are sometimes used in drilling stone.

Drilling wood with a brace and bit or a hand drill can be done easily and accurately if a few simple rules are followed.

An electric hand drill is one of the handyman's most valuable tools. With the proper bits, it may be used for drilling holes in masonry as well as in wood and metal.

The truck-mounted rotary drill below is used in drilling water wells. The heavy steel mast is raised from vertical to horizontal position behind the truck during operation. The drill is powered by a hydraulic motor.

Courtesy of Schramm, Inc.

Tighten the wood in a vise. Make a mark where the hole will be. As you begin boring, check the angle of the bit to the wood with a try square or a square block. This should be repeated twice after the hole is started.

If the bit squeaks, remove it and clean the shavings from the grooves. If it becomes hot, allow it to cool before you resume drilling.

If possible, use a vise to hold the wood. If a vise is not available, put a piece of scrap wood under the piece you are working on. This will prevent you from drilling holes in workbenches and floors or damaging the point of the bit on metal or concrete. See BRACE AND BIT.

DRIVE-IN THEATER, a type of outdoor motion picture theater with a large screen and an area reserved for motorists who watch the film from their automobiles. These theaters, starting as a form of novelty entertainment in the southern states, became increasingly popular after World War II. The first ones had a screen, a sloped amphitheater where automobiles could be parked, and loudspeakers serving the general area. They showed older or less popular films and at first attracted couples out for a drive.

Drive-in theaters, showing the latest films, have mushroomed throughout the United States and have even begun to take hold abroad. A factor in their popularity is that the whole family, including small children, can go to the movies together. The present-day drive-in

USDA

holds from 200 to 2,000 automobiles. Most theater areas are located on a stretch of open land close to a town. They are pie-shaped strips of ground, formed in a series of ramps that permit each row of motorists to see over the automobiles in front. Speaker units can be hooked inside the automobiles to amplify the sound. At Loew's drive-in theater in Rome, the viewer may listen to a film in either English or Italian by pressing a button on his speaker.

There are about 5,000 drive-in theaters in the United States, and the industry is expected to continue expanding. These theaters bring in more than 20 percent of moving picture box-office earnings, and about half of this amount comes from food and snacks served on the grounds. In many areas drive-ins show films the year round and provide special heaters for cold weather.

DROMEDARY. See CAMEL.

At left is a South Dakota farm showing how soil drifted in the Dust Bowl in 1935.

Below is the same farm after a soil-holding crop was planted to prevent drifting.

USDA

DROUGHT, in general, is an unusually long period of dry weather or a period of insufficient rainfall. It is difficult to define exactly because of the variety of factors responsible for drought. These factors include wind movement and direction, soil characteristics, temperature of the region, and evaporation and cloudiness. Drought can also be considered in relation to crop loss; when there is not enough rainfall in a region, crops suffer. Droughts during the late 1930's and mid-1950's in the western United States and Canada were unusually severe. Drought usually revisits regions again and again. See DESERT; DUST BOWL.

Below is a drug-producing center in an Egyptian temple of 1500 B.C. A temple priest, the physician of that time, dictates a prescription to a scribe. These prescriptions contained such ingredients as animal fats and herbs. A collection of 800 such prescriptions, known as the Papyrus Ebers, has survived until the present time.

Courtesy of and ©1957 Parke, Davis & Co.

Below is Ernest F. Fourneau in a laboratory of the Institut Pasteur in Paris. A pioneer research scientist, he developed many drugs now used to combat disease. Modern drugs are often purified extracts of the herbs used medicinally in ancient times. Serpentine, a high-blood-pressure medicine, is such an example.

Courtesy of and ©1957 Parke, Davis & Co.

DRUG. Any substance used to treat or prevent sickness in man or other animals is a drug. Men have always used parts of plants and animals and mineral substances as drugs. Men probably first got the idea of using plants as drugs from seeing sick animals eat certain herbs and berries.

Some drugs used by ancient people are still used. Opium is one of these drugs. Iron was given by the ancient Chinese for anemia, and it is still used for the same purpose. However, some drugs used by ancient people are certainly not highly regarded now. Among these are moonstones and crocodile fat.

About 100 years ago chemists first learned how to break down substances into their elementary parts. From that time they have been able to tell the specific material in a plant or animal substance that makes it useful as a drug. And they have also been able to make drugs by combining chemicals. Such drugs are called synthetic drugs.

Doctors now use far fewer drugs than ever before. Also, most of these drugs have proved valuable in the treatment and prevention of sickness. The main kinds of drugs are those that fight infections, those that make a person unconscious for a surgical operation (anesthetics), those that relieve pain, and those that supply substances that the body needs (vitamins, hormones).

The U.S. government has passed a law, known as the Federal Food, Drug, and Cosmetic Act, that protects the users of drugs from impure or dangerous drugs. All drugs that meet legal standards are listed in the *United States Pharmacopoeia*, the *National Formulary*, or *New and Nonofficial Remedies*. Drugs that are protected by patents, trademarks, secrecy, or monopoly are generally considered to be nonofficial, that is, they are not listed in the official publications of drugs that meet legal standards. Such drugs are called proprietary drugs or patent medicines.

DRUM, a musical instrument, consisting of a hollow, round body of wood or metal, with a head of tightly stretched skin or membrane, which is struck with a stick or a pair of sticks or—as in African drums and tom-toms—is rubbed hard or patted with the hand. The stretched skin is called the head of the drum.

The drum is one of the most ancient of instruments and has always been used by primitive peoples. The ancient Egyptians used it, and all over Africa, even today, it is a means of transmitting news across rivers and jungles by its sound. It is supposed to have been adopted from the Mohammedans by the Crusaders and so brought to Europe from the East.

There are three principal types in use for military and orchestral purposes. The snare drum (sometimes called the side drum because the drummer wears it hanging by his side), gets its name from the snares, or strings, stretched across its lower head. The deep, wooden, barrel-shaped snare drum, seen largely in military pictures of a century ago, has been replaced by a shallower kind made of brass. The bass drum is beaten on both heads and is much larger and makes a deeper sound than the snare drum. The kettledrum is made of thin copper or brass and is shaped like a half sphere, so that it has only one head. See KETTLEDRUM; PERCUSSION INSTRUMENT.

DRY CELL, an electric cell, or battery, in which the electrolyte is a jelly-like substance rather than a liquid. The commonest form of dry cell is the flashlight battery. Strictly speaking, this type of cell is not dry. If there were not some water, the electric current would not flow. The electrolyte is, however, nonspillable. Since this battery is completely portable, this property is a distinct advantage. Usually a dry cell has a positive electrode of carbon forming a center rod through the cell. The negative electrode, made of zinc, is shaped like a small can in order to contain the electrolyte and carbon rod. The electrolyte is a sal ammoniac paste with certain other chemicals added. As current is drawn from the cell, hydrogen collects on the carbon rod. This combines with oxygen from one of the chemicals to form water. If a large current is drawn from the battery, too much hydrogen forms around the carbon rod, and the cell stops working. As the battery rests, the hydrogen leaves the carbon rod, and the cell's potential power is restored. See BATTERY; ELECTRIC CELL.

Below is a picture of Henry H. Rusby in the jungles of Peru, about 1886. Rusby made one of the first scientific botanical explorations of South America. In a trip across the continent he collected 45,000 specimens of native plants. He, and others like him, have found many plants useful as drug sources.

Courtesy of and ©1957 Parke, Davis & Co.

Courtesy of and ©1951 Parke, Davis & Co.

The interior of a modern drug-manufacturing plant is shown above. Drug production requires extreme precautions in sanitation. Some drugs developed by the growth of micro-organisms are produced in sealed, sterile rooms, which no one enters. The cultures are grown and handled by remote-control methods.

DRYCLEANING is a clothes-cleaning process in which liquids other than water are used. In this process the oily or fatty substances that hold dirt in or on fabrics are dissolved by the drycleaning fluid, or solvent, so that the dirt may be easily washed away. Special drycleaning detergents are often used to add to the efficiency of the solvent.

Although drycleaning processes vary, all have several basic steps. The first step is cleaning. The clothes are placed in a machine resembling a washing machine. As the garments are agitated, solvent is circulated through the machine by a pump-and-filter system. Rinsing with clear solvent may follow. The next step is extraction, during which the solvent is pressed from the fabric. Extraction is followed by drying the fabric in a current of warm air. The next step, called spotting, is the removal of stains. Because each type of stain needs special treatment, spotting requires special equipment, chemicals, skill, and experience. The final step is finishing, which includes steam pressing, ironing, or steam-air forming.

Most fabrics can be drycleaned because drycleaning solvents, unlike water, do not cause fabrics to shrink or wrinkle. A few textiles cannot be drycleaned because they soften in the solvent. These textiles include rubberized fabrics, artificial leathers, and some plastic materials.

Because drycleaning solvents either yield poisonous fumes or are highly flammable, drycleaning without proper equipment is extremely dangerous and should never be attempted at home.

DRYCLEANING FLUID. See Carbon Tetrachloride.

DRYDEN, JOHN (1631-1700), English poet, critic, and dramatist, was born at Aldwincle, Northamptonshire. He studied at Westminster and Trinity College, Cambridge. Dryden's early work of note includes "Heroic Stanzas" on the death of Oliver Cromwell and "Astraea Redux" on the restoration of Charles II. His early plays, *The Wild Gallant* and *The Rival Ladies*, are of less interest.

In 1665 appeared Dryden's heroic play *The Indian Emperor* and in 1667 "Annus Mirabilis," a poem of the war between England and the Dutch Republic and of the London fire of 1666. In 1668 he was made poet laureate and two years later historiographer. Dryden's best plays

appeared during the next ten years. These include *Almanzor and Almahide, or the Conquest of Granada, Aurengzebe, Marriage à la Mode,* and *All for Love.* Dryden's best critical work, *Essay of Dramatic Poesy,* appeared in 1668.

About the year 1680 Dryden began writing the brilliant satires in verse for which he is so well known. "Absalom and Achitophel" appeared in 1681, and in the following year "The Medal," "MacFlecknoe," and "Religio Laici" were published. In 1687 "The Hind and the Panther" was printed. Because of conflicts with the crown Dryden was deprived of his laureateship and a government post in 1688. He was consequently compelled to do translations in the last years of his life. His famous translation of Virgil appeared in 1697. Among Dryden's other notable poems are "Ode to the Memory of Mrs. Anne Killigrew" and "Ode for St. Cecilia's Day." He was buried in Westminster Abbey.

DRY ICE, trade name for solidified carbon dioxide, a substance created by freezing the gas used in making carbonated beverages. It resembles snow, though it will not melt but evaporates to a dry gas, losing as little as 2 percent of its weight per day if properly insulated. It maintains itself at a temperature of 109° F. below zero.

Since Dry Ice expands to 690 times its volume when it is allowed to sublimate (evaporate), the great pressure developed in this way has led to its use by California forest rangers in fighting forest fires in mountainous country. Its cost is but a few cents a pound.

The manufacture of Dry Ice is based on the principle that highly compressed substances will lose heat, or drop in temperature, when they are allowed to expand rapidly.

Solid carbon dioxide is obtained by compressing the gas until it liquefies. This compression is accomplished by pumping the gas into a cylinder. The tube from the pump to the cylinder and the cylinder itself are kept cool by running water. The liquid carbon dioxide in the cylinder is then allowed to evaporate rapidly through a small opening, from which it is sprayed into an insulated container. In the container Dry Ice is formed in a snow-like fashion. See Carbon Dioxide.

DUBLIN is the capital of Ireland. It is a seaport on the island's east coast, on Dublin Bay at the mouth of the Liffey River, which divides the city into two nearly equal parts. Besides being the nation's capital, it is also the center of Irish culture. Dublin is linked with the interior of the country by the Royal and the Grand canals, and the city is the connecting center for the four railways of Ireland. It has more than 500,000 people.

Dublin's Phoenix Park is one of the largest and most attractive in Europe. It contains the residence of the president of Ireland, the U.S. Legation, the headquarters of the civic guard, and a number of gardens. One of the largest breweries in the world is located in Dublin. The city's manufactures include poplin, linen, and food and tobacco products. There are iron foundries and woodworking establishments.

Dublin Castle is perhaps the most notable of the public buildings. It was built in the 13th century and stands on an elevation in the southern side of the city. The Bank of Ireland, formerly Parliament House, is another of its noteworthy public buildings. Others are the Court of Justice buildings, which face College Green, and Leinster House, the present seat of the Parliament. Churches include St. Patrick's and

O'Connell Bridge, the chief bridge across the Liffey River, leads on to one of Dublin's busiest main streets. Double-decker buses line the street.

Sheridan H. Garth

Christ Church cathedrals, both Protestant, and the Metropolitan Pro-Cathedral, the chief Catholic church in Dublin.

There are many hospitals and other charitable institutions. The city's educational, literary, artistic, and scientific institutions include Trinity College (whose library contains the famous 7th-century *Book of Kells*), the National University of Ireland, the Abbey Theatre, the National Gallery of Art, the Municipal Art Gallery, and the National Museum.

Dublin was occupied by the Danes in the 9th century, but they were driven out in 1170 by the Anglo-Normans. Two years later Henry II gave the city to the men of Bristol and made it the center of the English-held part of Ireland. Dublin was attacked often. It was besieged by Edward Bruce in the 14th century, and in 1647 it surrendered to the Parliamentarians. James II held his last parliament in Dublin in 1689. Civil uprisings against the British marked the city's history throughout the 19th century. In 1916 it was the center of the rebellion that ended in the founding of the Irish Free State in 1922.

DU BOIS, WILLIAM E. B. (1868-), American Negro leader, writer, and educator, was born in Great Barrington, Mass. He attended Harvard University, where he received an A.B., an A.M., and in 1895 a Ph.D. In 1910 Du Bois began a long association with the National Association for the Advancement of Colored People, editing the magazine *Crisis* for them until 1933. In that year Du Bois became head of the department of sociology at Atlanta University and stayed there until 1944. Among the writings of Du Bois are *The Philadelphia Negro*, *The Souls of Black Folk*, *Black Reconstruction*, and *Black Folk: Then and Now*.

DUBOS, RENE (1901-), in full René Jules Dubos, French-American bacteriologist and internationally famous microbiologist, was born in St.-Brice, Seine-et-Oise, France.

He attended an agronomy school in Paris, where he majored in science. After receiving his degree, Dubos sailed for the United States and enrolled in Rutgers University. Later he became the university's instructor in bacteriology and a research assistant in soil microbiology.

In 1939 Dubos discovered the drug tyrothricin, which he took from soil bacteria. He found it was effec-

The duck-billed dinosaur, which lived somewhere between 70 million and 100 million years ago, is so named because its broad, flat, toothless beak was presumably covered with a bill somewhat like that of a duck. The forefeet of this dinosaur were webbed.

tive in destroying certain types of pneumococci. Dubos further found that tyrothricin contained two chemicals. One chemical, tyrocidine, had no effect in destroying germs. The other, gramicidin, Dubos suggested would be useful in treating such infections as boils, carbuncles, and ulcers.

In 1946 Dubos discovered a new method of cultivating tuberculosis bacilli. They could be grown in large quantities by simply adding a household detergent to the culture medium. Dubos served as a member of the Rockefeller Institute for Medical Research in New York and a professor of tropical medicine at Harvard Medical School.

DUCK-BILLED DINOSAUR. The duck-billed dinosaurs belonged to the order Ornithischia, or "birdlike pelvis" dinosaurs. They lived during the Cretaceous in many parts of the world.

Duck-billed dinosaurs were quite large. They walked on their hindlegs. Duck-billed dinosaurs had a horny sheath on the front part of the jaw. Such a "duck bill" was an efficient device for cutting off or ripping up the plants on which these dinosaurs fed.

The duck-billed dinosaurs probably lived near streams or shallow lakes and were probably amphibious. A few impressions of duck-billed dinosaur remains have been found in rocks. The impressions of the limbs show that these dinosaurs had webbed feet.

Many duck-billed dinosaurs had peculiar enlargements of the bones of the nasal region. Some forms had bony crests like a rooster comb. Some had horn-shaped projections of bony material. One form had a long, thin, backward-projecting crest that contained a pair of tubes connected to the nose and throat. Possibly this animal stored air in the tubes for use when it was feeding under water.

DUCKS, GEESE, SWANS, three of the major types of waterfowl. Because of their similarity in behavior and structure they comprise a single bird family. They are found worldwide but especially in the Northern Hemisphere. Fossils date from the Eocene period.

These three types have many common characteristics. They have short legs, a straight bill, and dense plumage with heavy down, which is often used as nest lining or as cover for temporarily unattended eggs. Eggs are of uniform color; clutches are large, often from 10 to 20. Young birds are covered with down when hatched and can swim when about a day old. Many adult birds shed their wing quills simultaneously during their primary molt following the breeding season, and

SIZE AND IDENTIFYING MARKS OF COMMON NORTH AMERICAN DUCKS, GEESE, AND SWANS

DUCKS

Common Name	Length in inches	Wingspread in inches	Summer plumage of male (female often different)
Bufflehead	13-15	22-24	Large white head patch; white sides
Green-winged teal	13-15	23-24	Green patch on head and wing; dark body; white shoulder mark
Ruddy	13-16	22-23	Rufous body; white cheeks
Blue-winged teal	15-16	24	Blue wing patch; white face crescent
Ring-necked	15-18	27-30	Black head, chest, and back; white mark before wing
Cinnamon teal	16-17	24-25	Rufous body; blue wing patch
Lesser scaup	16-18	27-28	Blue bill; black head and chest; short white wing stripe
Hooded merganser	17-19	25-26	White crest; dark sides
Wood	17-20	24-29	High coloring; distinctive face pattern
Shoveler	17-21	31-35	Chestnut sides; shovel bill
Common (or American) scoter	17-21	32-33	Black body; orange on bill
Greater scaup	18-20	30-31	Blue bill; black head and chest; long white wing stripe
American widgeon (baldpate)	18-22	32-35	Brown body; gray head; white crown
Goldeneye	18-23	28-31	Black and white; round white spot before eye
Redhead	18-23	32-33	Gray back; rufous head; black chest
Fulvous tree	19-21	36	Tawny body; light side stripe
Surf scoter	19-22	32-33	Black body; white head patches
Gadwall	19-22	34-35	Gray body; black rump
White-winged scoter	20-23	37-38	Black body; white wing patch
Canvasback	20-24	33-35	White body; rusty head; sloping head profile
Red-breasted merganser	20-25	33-35	Dark crested head; white collar; rusty breast
Old squaw (male)	21-23	28-30	Bold brown-and-white pattern; needle tail
King eider	21-24	36	Dark rear parts; white fore parts
Black	21-25	36	Dark body; paler head; white wing linings
Common (or American) merganser	21-27	36-39	Long white body; black back; dark uncrested head
Common (or American) eider	22-26	41	White back; black below
Mallard	22-28	36-40	Green head; white neck ring; ruddy breast; white tail
Pintail (male)	26-30	34-36	Needle tail; brown head; white breast; white point on side of neck and head

GEESE AND SWANS

Canada goose	22-42	43-66	Gray-brown body; black head and neck; white cheek-and-chin patch
Brant	24-30	45-52	Dark head, neck, and chest; small white patch on neck
Snow goose	23-30	58	White; black wingtips
Blue goose	25-30	54	Dark body; white head and neck
White-fronted goose	27-30	58-60	Dark body; white at base of bill
Whistling swan	48-54	72-84	White body; black bill; straight neck; yellow spot before eye
Mute swan	58	60	White; curved neck; orange knobbed bill
Trumpeter swan	65	100	White; black bill; no yellow spot before eye

Whistling Swan

Blue Goose (juvenile)

White-Fronted Goose

White-Fronted Goose (juvenile)

Canada Goose

Black Brant

Hutchins' Goose

Wingspread is measured with wings outspread.

To measure its length the bird is laid

Ross's Goose

Mallard

American Goldeneye

Ring-Necked Duck

White-Cheeked Pintail

Mallard & Pintail Hybrid

Trumpeter Swan

Bufflehead Duck (female)

Mute Swan

Green-Winged Teal

Pintail

Shoveler

Eurasian Widgeon

Ruddy Duck

Muscovy Duck

White-Faced Tree Duck

Garganey Teal

Torrent Duck

Mallard

Baikal Teal

Flightless Steamer Duck

Cinnamon Teal

Common Teal

Canvasback

Steller's Eider

Surf Scoter

Ruddy Shelduck

Barrow's Goldeneye

Harlequin Duck

Common Shelduck

Greater Scaup

Old Squaw

for several weeks the birds are flightless while new quills are growing. Another common habit is using the bill to distribute among the feathers a waterproof dressing from an oil gland near the base of the tail.

Other characteristics mark many though not all of these three types. Usually they are found in flocks. Many of them are omnivorous. Many of the species breed in the northern regions, where the nests are often close together on marshy ground. To start their flight, geese, swans, and some ducks run on the water. Speeds of 45 to 50 miles per hours are common; speeds up to 75 miles per hour occur, particularly if the bird has been frightened. Most of these waterfowl migrate in stringy lines or V-shaped formations and change leaders in flight.

Some differences appear. Swans are larger than geese; geese generally are larger than ducks. Swans have the longest necks; ducks, the shortest. After breeding, geese and swans go to their winter homes in family groups; in these the pair bond is strong, often lasting for life. Ducks, however, pair for only a few days, a season, or a few seasons; with some ducks promiscuity is the rule. The plumage of geese and swans is the same for both sexes; male and female ducks, however, usually look very different.

North America has three swans—the mute, the trumpeter, and the whistling. The graceful mute swan, often seen floating on park ponds, also lives wild in some areas; this is an Old World species that has been introduced and naturalized in the eastern United States. The huge trumpeter swans, once near extinction, are now increasing in numbers; they are protected in the Yellowstone Park area and in northern Canada. Whistling swans nest in Canada and winter in some parts of the United States.

Common North American geese include the familiar Canada goose, often called the honker; the brant; the blue goose; the snow goose; and the white-fronted goose. The emperor goose and Ross's goose appear in restricted sections.

North American ducks are often classified as diving ducks or surface-feeding ducks. Diving ducks, also called bay ducks, sea ducks, and divers, are often found on seas and oceans but also occur on inland water. They dive for their food. Before taking flight they patter along the surface of the water. They include such well-known species as the goldeneye, scaup, bufflehead,

ring-necked, redhead, canvasback, old squaw, eiders, and scoters. Special diving ducks are the ruddy duck and the three species of mergansers. Mergansers are fisheaters and have slender, serrated bills to hold their slippery prey.

Surface-feeding ducks, also called marsh ducks, pond ducks, and dabblers, are usually found on creeks and inland pools. They feed in shallow water by tipping up with feet and rump in the air and head and neck held downward to pluck food from the bottom. When taking flight they spring up from the surface of the water. These ducks include the mallard, black, pintail, gadwall, teal, widgeon, shoveler, and wood duck. The fulvous tree duck, a gooselike duck of the Gulf coast, is a dabbler and is often classed with the surface-feeding ducks.

John Foster Dulles   UPI

DU FAY, CHARLES (1698-1739), born at Paris, was a French scientist of the 18th century who made several fundamental discoveries about the nature of electricity.

He began his experiments by rubbing glass rods and pieces of sealing wax with dry silk in order to charge them with electricity. Upon placing two charged glass rods together, he found that they would automatically move away from each other. However, when a charged glass rod and a piece of charged sealing wax were brought close together, they would automatically move into contact. Two pieces of charged sealing wax, when brought close together, would automatically move apart. From these and other experiments Du Fay concluded that there must be two distinct kinds of electricity —positive and negative. He then formulated a fundamental law of electricity, which is that like charges repel each other and unlike charges attract each other.

He next discovered that all solid

objects and liquids could be charged with electricity and that wet thread conducted electricity better than dry thread. He later found that substances, such as copper wire, that were good conductors of electricity could be electrically charged by friction only with difficulty. He also found that poor conductors were much more readily charged by friction.

DULLES, JOHN FOSTER (1888-1959), the 53d U.S. secretary of state. Dulles' interest in diplomacy dated from the Hague Peace Conference of 1907, which he attended with his grandfather John W. Foster. Dulles formulated the foreign policy of the United States from 1953 until his death.

John Foster Dulles was one of five children of Allen M. Dulles, a Presbyterian minister. He was graduated as valedictorian of his class at Princeton in 1908, studied international law at the Sorbonne in Paris, and received a law degree from George Washington University. Dulles entered the firm of Sullivan and Cromwell, New York specialists in international law. At the Peace Conference in 1919 Dulles served on the Supreme Economic Council and on the Reparations Commission.

Dulles was always a Republican in politics. He was Thomas E. Dewey's foreign-policy adviser in the presidential campaign of 1944. He shared in the organization of the United Nations and was made a delegate to the UN in 1946. In 1951 Dulles negotiated the peace treaty with Japan.

President Eisenhower's first cabinet appointment in 1952 was that of Dulles as secretary of state. Dulles immediately made a goodwill tour of the Middle East, India, and Europe, and his stay in office was characterized by such vigorous personal diplomacy. It soon became evident that the liberation policy espoused during the presidential campaign did not entail the use of force; thus the foreign policy pursued by Dulles resembled the previous containment policy. Dulles believed that the United States had a mission in the world to promote the spread of free institutions. He felt that the social and economic base of democracy in the West was ever widened by means of peaceful change, whereas under communism the ruling class tried to suppress change. Until the inevitable changes occurred to produce a broadened participation in the Communist government, according to Dulles, the nations of the West would be menaced by the ambitions of a party aspiring to world domination. Therefore Dulles believed that the United States had to protect itself by means of collective security (which had to be regional considering the frequent paralysis of the United Nations), the strengthening of world institutions, military might, and efforts to reduce the danger of surprise attack. Military, technical, and economic aid to foreign nations was necessary to assure this collective security.

Dulles had many critics, which was natural in his difficult and responsible position. The liberation policy was criticized by those who thought that it would be pursued with the use of force or would arouse false hopes on the part of nations under a Communist government. Dulles' reliance on the United States "great capacity to retaliate against aggression" was criticized by those who were afraid that the United States might unleash an atomic war. The trade restrictions against the Communist nations and the threats to cut off aid if these restrictions were not honored were criticized by Western powers dependent on foreign trade. Some critics also felt that Dulles was not responsive enough to changes in the international situation.

DULUTH, a city and port in northeastern Minnesota, on Lake Superior at the mouth of the St. Louis River, 140 miles northeast of St. Paul. In 1960 its population was 106,884. It is one of the most important inland ports in the United States. There are extensive dock facilities for the shipment of iron ore, lumber, wheat, and manufactured products. The harbor is protected by two sandbars called Minnesota Point and Wisconsin Point. An aerial-lift bridge connects Minnesota Point with the mainland. The city manufactures lumber products, textiles, machinery, iron and steel products, and processed foods. It has a branch of the state university and the College of St. Scholastica. Points of interest include the Skyline Parkway, a scenic route above the city, the zoological gardens, and Jay Cooke State Park southwest of the city.

The city derives its name from Sieur Duluth, a French officer, who visited the site while trading with the Indians in Wisconsin in 1679. The first permanent settlement was made in 1853. For many years it was important as a lumber-shipping

center. The discovery of iron ore in the nearby Mesabi and Vermilion ranges in the 1890's caused Duluth to become one of the world's greatest shipping points of iron ore. Since that time many mills, foundries, and factories have been established.

Lick Observatory

The Dumbbell Nebula is one of the best known of the planetary nebulae. It may be seen in the constellation Vulpecula. In a low-power telescope this nebula resembles a dumbbell, but its actual shape is more that of a hollow, spherical shell.

DUMAS, ALEXANDRE, the name of two French literary figures. Dumas *père* (1802-1870), French novelist and dramatist, was born in Villers-Cotterêts. In 1823 he went to Paris and obtained an assistant secretaryship from the Duke of Orleans.

His first writing successes came in the theater. Politically, Dumas was an ardent republican and strongly supported the 1848 revolution. In 1860 he fought with Garibaldi for Italian independence.

Turning his attention to the novel, he wrote historical romances and adventure stories. Among his 300 works, some with collaborators, are *The Count of Monte Cristo, The Three Musketeers, Twenty Years After, Le Vicomte de Bragelonne* (part of which was translated into English as *The Man in the Iron Mask*), *The Knight of Maison Rouge,* and *The Black Tulip.*

Dumas *fils* (1824-1895), French dramatist and novelist and the son of Dumas *père*, was born in Paris. Educated by his father, Dumas *fils* spent his early life writing poetry. He had his first success with the novel *The Lady of the Camellias.* Later, in dramatic form, it was known as *Camille* and was the basis for Verdi's opera *La Traviata.*

Alexandre Dumas, père
Courtesy of The Metropolitan Museum of Art,
Dick Fund, 1917

The plays of Dumas *fils* showed a deep concern for social and moral problems. Among his best known plays are *The Demimonde, The Question of Money, The Natural Son, The Prodigal Father,* and *The Ideas of Madam Aubray.*

DUMBBELL NEBULA, a huge envelope of gas, illuminated by a small star at its center, located in the constellation Vulpecula between Sagitta and Cygnus. The nebula is a planetary type and is known scientifically as Messier 27. (See NEBULA.) The gas is expanding outward at a distance many thousands of times farther from the central star than the earth is from the sun. The nebula is not visible to the naked eye.

DUNANT, JEAN HENRI (1828-1910), Swiss philanthropist and founder of the Red Cross movement, was born in Geneva. He conceived the idea of founding a society for aiding wounded soldiers while he was visiting the scene of the Battle of Solferino in Italy.

Returning to Geneva, he wrote *Souvenir de Solferino.* He gave lectures advocating relief in war before the Society of Public Utility. His efforts led to the formation of a conference that resulted in the Geneva Convention of 1864. It founded the International Red Cross.

With Frédérick Passy, he was awarded the first Nobel peace prize in 1901.

DUNCAN, ISADORA (1878-1927), American dancer who tried to raise her profession to the level of a creative art, was born in San Francisco into an artistic but poor family. She started dancing at the age of six. Later she and her sister devised a new dance form in which there were no formal or set movements and steps. Performances were given in flowing gowns and with bare feet. She performed without success in Chicago, but in New York she starred in the Augustin Daly company for two years.

She next toured England, where she spent much of her time studying Greek art in the British Museum. The actress Mrs. Patrick Campbell introduced her to influential people on the Continent. She appeared in London and Paris and became an artistic sensation.

Joining another dance company, she played in such cities as Budapest, Vienna, and Berlin. She spent a year in Athens, where she built a temple of dancing on a hill outside the city. In 1904 she opened a dancing school outside Berlin. In 1915 she returned to the United States. Later she made more attempts at establishing schools in Paris, Athens, and Moscow. She wrote an autobiography entitled *My Life*. In 1927 she was accidentally killed in an automobile when the long scarf she was wearing caught in the wheels.

DUPLICATING MACHINE, a machine that reproduces a drawing, map, plan, document, or other object in actual size or enlarged or reduced. Duplicating is done in various ways: by using carbon paper in a typewriter, by cutting a stencil, by using transfer paper, and by photocopying. A typewriter is used as a duplicator when only a few copies are required. In stenciling, a stencil is cut on a typewriter or by an electronic machine that can make a stencil from drawings, photographs, or printed material. It is then transferred to a mimeograph machine, where ink is forced through the cuts onto the paper. For representing lines and figures a stylus is used to cut the stencil.

The hectograph makes use of transfer paper and aniline ink. The machine consists of a frame and a gelatinous plate. The ink is put on the paper by typing or by drawing, and the paper is then placed on the plate to transfer the ink. Each copy is then produced by pressing a piece of paper to the gelatinous plate.

Photocopying, in its broad sense, involves a variety of machines and reproduction processes. Microfilming copies records and documents directly onto film. Drawings, tracings, and documents are copied by blueprint, brownprint, diazotype, and other processes. Machines have also been devised that copy records without the need for developing solutions and washings.

DU PONT, complete name Du Pont de Nemours, a French-American family prominent since the latter part of the 18th century in U.S. industrial, financial, and political life.

Pierre Samuel Du Pont de Nemours (1739-1817), French economist and statesman, was born in Paris. In 1783 the Comte de Vergennes authorized him to help draft the treaty by which England formally recognized the independence of the United States and an economic treaty that France and England signed in 1786. As inspector general of commerce and manufactures and as a councilor of state, Du Pont helped to encourage French industry. He was twice president of the National Assembly and always supported moderate principles. Under Robespierre he was imprisoned and escaped the guillotine only by the death of that tyrant. In 1799 Du Pont came to the United States, but in 1802 he returned to France. He did not take office, notwithstanding the offers made by Napoleon. After Napoleon's return from Elba, Du Pont rejoined his sons in the United States. Following François Quesnay in economics, he expanded his master's theories in his *Physiocratie* in 1768.

Eleuthère Irénée Du Pont (1771-1834), a U.S. manufacturer and son of Pierre Samuel Du Pont de Nemours, was born in Paris. Early in his life his tastes turned toward scientific pursuits. He was placed in the royal powder works at Essonnes to acquire a practical knowledge of the manufacture of gunpowder.

He remained there until the French Revolution broke out. He then was called to take charge of his father's printing and publishing house. He came to the United States in 1799. Soon after his arrival, he discovered through accidental circumstances the bad quality of gunpowder in America.

He revisited the Essonnes mills in 1801 to procure plans, models, and machinery and returned to the United States. Soon afterward he erected his first powder works near Wilmington, Del. The firm has become internationally known and has supplied vast quantities of explosives to the U.S. government since the War of 1812.

Victor Marie Du Pont (1767-1827), brother of Eleuthère Du Pont, was born in Paris. He came to the United States as a member of the French legation and later settled in New York. He established one branch of the family.

In 1903 the E. I. Du Pont de

Courtesy of Du Pont

Eleuthère Irénée Du Pont founded the firm that is internationally famous.

Nemours Powder Company was formed to consolidate about 100 firms in which Du Pont held major interests. This combine was broken up by a U.S. government antitrust prosecution that resulted, in 1913, in the formation of the Hercules Powder Company and the Atlas Powder Company.

The present E. I. Du Pont de Nemours and Company was organized in 1915.

The Albrecht Dürer House (foreground) in Nuremberg, Germany, was the home of Dürer from 1509 to 1528. The Gothic house and its original contents are fully preserved.
Robert J. Bezucha

"A Gathering of Soldiers," an engraving by Albrecht Dürer

DÜRER, ALBRECHT

DÜRER, ALBRECHT (1471-1528), German painter and engraver, born in Nuremberg. His father, a skilled goldsmith, instructed him in that art, and Michel Wohlgemuth, then the best painter in Nuremberg, became his teacher. In 1505 he went to Venice for further study. Pro-

This is a self-portrait by Albrecht Dürer. Dürer was a painter of great vitality.

New York Public Library

found application, great facility in the mechanical part of his art, and a remarkable talent of imitation were the characteristics of Dürer and enabled him to exert a great influence on the character of German art. His notable paintings included "The Four Apostles" and the portrait of Hieronymus Holtzschuher. Among his best engravings in copper were his "Melancholy" and "The Knight, Death and the Devil." Among his best woodcuts were two entitled "Large Passion" and "Small Passion."

DURHAM REPORT, a series of recommendations made by the Durham Commission, of which John Lambton, Lord Durham was chairman, to the British Parliament in 1839 on the organization of the British colonies in Canada. The Canadians had been dissatisfied with the rule of appointed governors and councils who paid no attention to the will of the people as expressed by their elected assemblies. These dissatisfactions led in 1837 to open revolts by small groups in the two provinces of Upper Canada (now Ontario) and Lower Canada (now Quebec). In his report (called *A Report on the Affairs of British North America*) the English statesman called for a union of the two provinces under one parliament and for an executive who would rule according to the will of the majority

of the legislature, except on subjects reserved for control by the imperial government. These two recommendations—union of the two provinces and responsible government—were only part of the long report, but they were the major points. The union was accomplished by an act of Parliament in 1840. However, responsible government was not granted in full until 1849. Lord Durham, like an increasing number of British leaders in the 1840's, realized that the old policy of repression would no longer work, and that the British Empire could only be held together on a voluntary basis of consent by the people of the colonies. It was thus an important milestone in the development of the British Commonwealth of Nations.

DUSE, ELEONORA (1859-1924), Italian actress, was born in a third-class railway carriage between Venice and Vigevano. As a child she suffered many hardships because of the constant traveling of her theatrical parents. When she was 14, her mother died. Duse's first performance came at the age of 14 in the play *Romeo and Juliet.* However, she went unrecognized until 1885, when her restrained, simple but forceful stage technique began to attract attention. She played a wide variety of parts with great success. After appearing in Cesare Rossi's company, in which she made a triumphant tour throughout Italy, she scored in Dumas' *Lady of the Camellias* in 1892. She introduced many of Gabriele D'Annunzio's plays to American audiences. He was the Italian poet and dramatist with whom she had a romance of some years' duration. She appeared in all the principal countries of Europe and America. Her last appearance was in Henrik Ibsen's *The Lady from the Sea* at New York's Metropolitan Opera House.

DUST. In weather and climate, dust includes all the tiny, solid particles suspended in the atmosphere. Scientists have made rough guesses as to the amount of dust in the atmosphere. They think that if all the tiny particles were collected into a cube, the cube would be about 600 feet on each side. This atmospheric dust has many sources. It comes from volcanic eruptions, ocean spray, blowing soil, sandstorms, plant pollen, bacteria, smoke and ashes of forest fires, smoke from industrial districts, and motor exhaust fumes from automobiles.

Sometimes atmospheric dust joins

with fog to create smog. Smog can be very dangerous, for it can contain poisonous gases. See SMOG.

Dust is not useless in nature's scheme. If it were not for dust, we would have little rain; water condenses from clouds and gathers on these tiny dust particles to form clouds. Finally, some of these water particles grow to become raindrops. Each drop of rain that falls contains a tiny dust particle. Dust intercepts some of the heat coming from the sun. It also plays a part in creating the colors of sunrise and sunset. See RAIN.

Dust particles are shown magnified 24,000 times in this photomicrograph.

Natl. Inst. of Health

DUST BOWL, a region of drought and duststorms that covered over 100 counties, especially in Texas, New Mexico, Oklahoma, Kansas, and Colorado. The Dust Bowl was settled largely during World War I. At that time it was profitable to farm land in areas that had never been used before because they were too dry. The rainfall during this period was also better than usual. The district yielded rich harvests of wheat. But in 1933 and the following years a series of terrible droughts were followed by duststorms. Dust swept over the area again and again in black clouds that covered the sun. At dawn the dust-filled skies held a sun that shone blood red.

Some farmers and their families tried to hold out against the conditions in the Dust Bowl. The stubborn spirit of those who remained there was captured by Woody Guthrie in his Dust Bowl Ballads:

"That old dry spell
Killed my crops, boys,
But it can't kill me, Lord,
It can't kill me."

Other people fled to other parts of the nation. About one million Dust-Bowl refugees filled the roads during the worst years. They pushed baby buggies filled with their few belongings, while their children trudged behind. Or they piled their families into rickety jalopies and drove over U.S. Highway 66 to California. There they worked at near-starvation wages, if they were lucky enough to get work.

In the meantime the government began to attack the problem of the Dust Bowl. Belts of trees were planted to allay the force of the wind and to stop erosion. The Department of Agriculture made studies of dry-land farming to help those who remained in the Dust Bowl. Irrigation works and reservoirs were built, and families were aided by grants of money from the Farm Security Administration. See DROUGHT; DUSTSTORM.

DUST EXPLOSION. A dust explosion is the rapid combustion of finely divided oxidizable material mixed with air. Smaller particles of a material, such as dust particles, are more chemically active than larger particles of the same material because of the greater surface area per unit of mass. A 1-ounce solid cube of zinc is not combustible under ordinary conditions. One ounce of fine zinc dust distributed in 1 cubic foot of air is an extremely combustible and explosive mixture. In general, the higher the concentration of dust particles, the smaller the size of the particles, and the more readily oxidizable the material, the more readily an explosion will occur.

Dusts of some metals, coal dust, grain dust, flour dust, plastic dusts, and other organic dusts are easily ignited, and they explode with con-

Photo by Soil Conservation Service—USDA

siderable force. Explosions may be set off by a small flame, sparks from electrical equipment, static electricity, or friction sparks. Dust explosions in confined spaces may cause severe damage because of the high pressures developed by the expanding gas-dust mixture. Dust explosions can be prevented by good ventilation and by eliminating equipment that may give off sparks or flames.

DUSTSTORM, a violent wind moving across a dry, sandy or dusty region. The wind sweeps up powdery soil in great quantities and carries it high into the air in a whirling cloud that darkens the whole atmosphere. At the height of such storms it is often so dark that electric lights must be turned on at midday. The dust cloud extends upward sometimes as high

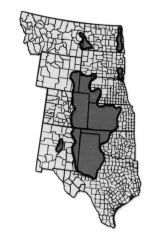

The vast Dust Bowl and other major areas that have been damaged by wind erosion are outlined on this map of the Great Plains.

Winds laden with dust were of frequent occurence in the Dust Bowl in the 1930's.

as 10,000 feet. Such storms are frequent in dry desert regions like the Sahara, also on the plains of Iraq, of northwestern India, of northern China, and of the United States. In the summer of 1934 dust from storms over the Great Plains was collected in Washington, D.C., and in New York City. Such a dustfall may be extremely heavy, saturating snow and rain and coating all exposed surfaces. On Mar. 9, 1918, 13 tons per square inch was deposited at Madison, Wis., by a snowstorm. All the snow that fell had a yellow tint.

DUTCH, a language spoken by more than nine million persons, most of whom live within the boundaries of The Netherlands. It is one of the Germanic languages, as is English. Actually it is the most northwestern of Low German dialects and can be traced back only to the mid-13th century. Through extensive trade and shipping and the close proximity of The Netherlands to France, Germany, and England, these countries have influenced modern Dutch and have been influenced by it. Afrikaans is a variant of the Dutch language and is spoken by more than 1,500,000 persons of European descent in the Union of South Africa. See GERMANIC LANGUAGES.

DUTCH EAST INDIA COMPANY, organized in 1602, was one of several companies formed by European nations to trade with the East, chiefly in spices. Through it the Dutch erected the foundation of their later empire. Although establishing an empire in the East Indies was the company's principal achievement, in 1652 Cape Town, in South Africa, was founded, and five years later free farmers were permitted to colonize the Cape area.

In the East the Dutch company had to contend with the Portuguese, who were already established in the Malaya Peninsula. After the Portuguese decline and the winning of Dutch independence from Spanish rule the vigor of Dutch expansion increased, with the British East India Company as the chief opposing force. This was so particularly in Java and the Moluccas. This rivalry was ended in favor of the Dutch in the second quarter of the 17th century. Throughout the 17th and 18th centuries the company extended its power over Java and established trading posts in most countries east of the Gulf of Suez.

Toward the end of the 18th century the reassertion of British inter-

ests in the Orient—particularly in the Indies—and the unwieldly management of the Dutch company combined to break down the system that had been built up. The excuse for reorganization was offered by the French occupation of the Dutch Republic in 1795, and in 1796 the Dutch East India Company was liquidated. Its territories, however, were taken over by the Dutch government. These territories formed the basis of the Netherlands East Indies (now the Republic of Indonesia) and the Boer colonies of South Africa (now the Union of South Africa). See BOER WAR; IMPERIALISM; INDONESIA.

DUTCH EAST INDIES. See INDONESIA.

DUTCH GUIANA. See GUIANAS, THE.

DUTROCHET, RENE (1776-1847), a French physiologist and botanist of the early 19th century who made important discoveries about the vital processes of plants. The son of a wealthy French nobleman, Dutrochet was born 13 years before the French Revolution of 1789. Since his father was an officer in one of the king's regiments, the family estates were confiscated during the revolution, and young René was compelled to enter a profession in order to earn a living. After studying medicine, he served briefly as physician to the king of Spain. He then devoted his life to research and study in plant and animal physiology.

It had previously been discovered that plants absorb carbon dioxide from the air and convert it into their

own tissues. Dutrochet discovered from his experiments that sunlight is necessary for this conversion and that the conversion occurs only in those parts of a plant that contain the green pigment called chlorophyll. Other scientists discovered later that the chlorophyll in plants utilizes energy from sunlight to convert carbon dioxide and water into carbohydrates contained in the plant tissues. This process came to be known as photosynthesis. Dutrochet was the first person to detect some of the most important stages in photosynthesis.

Antonin Dvořák

DVOŘÁK, ANTONIN (1841-1904), a music composer, was born in Mühlhausen, Bohemia (now Milevsko, Czechoslovakia). His father, a butcher, intended him for his own trade, but the boy showed so much musical ability that he was permitted to study the organ. In 1888 his setting of the *Stabat Mater* gave

Courtesy of the South African Tourist Corporation
With the founding of Cape Town the Dutch East India Company gained a foothold in Africa.

Courtesy of American Cyanamid Company, Organic Chemicals Division

In colonial times wool was dyed blue by using indigo, an extract then obtained from plants.

him great reputation. Among his other works are a cantata, *The Spectre's Bride*, an oratorio, *St. Ludmilla*, and operas, symphonies, concertos, songs, and dances. In 1892 he came to New York as director of the Conservatory of Music. While in the United States he wrote a symphony entitled "From the New World." In 1895 he returned to Prague. He was called to the Austrian House of Peers, awarded many decorations and honors. He died in Prague when he was 63 years old. His melody entitled "Humoresque" is widely known.

DWARF, a human being much below the ordinary size of man. Miniature plants may also be called dwarfs. An example is the dwarf marigold.

Dwarfs that are of normal proportions despite their tiny size are often called midgets. Dwarfs of odd shape with large heads and long arms are among the quaint creatures of folklore and story. Pygmies, or races of men of dwarfish stature, can be found in many parts of the world, mainly in Africa and Asia. The best known of modern dwarfs were Charles Sherwood Stratton, or, as he was popularly called, General Tom Thumb, and his wife. When fully grown, Tom Thumb was 40 inches high and weighed about 70 pounds.

Human dwarfs simply fail to grow. The reason is poor functioning of a body gland, the pituitary, which causes growth.

DYE AND DYEING were known to prehistoric men. This was revealed by remnants of cloth found in tombs of the Swiss lake dwellers and in the tombs of Egypt and Mesopotamia. These people used indigo and woad to dye cloth blue. The Minoans in Crete found a shellfish that could be used to produce a bright red. The men of Tyre used another shellfish to dye cloth a rich purple. The Aztecs of South America discovered a female insect that could be treated to produce a brilliant red dye. This dye, cochineal, was, like gold, demanded of the enslaved Aztecs by the Spaniards. Brazil, or brazilwood, was first used in India to produce a red dye, and when it was found in South America, the name was applied to the country. The Indians of eastern North America used bloodroot and roots of barberry to dye their bodies red and yellow. Until the middle of the 19th century almost all dyes were extracted from animal or vegetable material.

In 1856 the dye industry of the world was completely revolutionized by the accidental discovery in England of mauve, a purple c tracted from aniline th refined from coal Sir William F sistant tc gust u

national financial arrangements, the dye industry remained in Germany until World War I, when the United States government confiscated and sold the German patents for public use.

Dyeing of some manmade fibers is done in the solution stage, with the result that an almost infinite variety of patterns can be woven into the cloth with no possibility of the colors' running.

DYNAMITE is a blasting explosive first made by absorbing nitroglycerin in a porous clay, kieselguhr. It was patented by Alfred Nobel in 1867. It is much safer to handle than the sensitive liquid nitroglycerin and has come into wide use for blasting in mining, road building, and so forth. It was found that by substituting a flammable material, such as woodpulp, for the inert kieselguhr and adding sodium nitrate and/or ammonium nitrate a considerably more powerful explosive could be made. This is one of the types of dynamite in wide use in the United States today. Antifreeze materials, such as nitrotoluene, are also added to dynamite to prevent freezing.

Nobel also originated blasting gelatin, a strong explosive gel of nitrocellulose (up to 12 percent) and nitroglycerin. Gelatin dynamites are essentially mixtures of dynamite and blasting gelatin, made by substituting some nitrocellulose for part of the woodpulp. Guncotton is now also used in some dynamites.

DYNAMO, or dynamoelectric machine, is any machine for changing mechanical energy into electrical energy or for changing electrical energy into mechanical energy. The word *dynamo* is not often used today; when it is used it means generator of electrical current fro mechanical power. See ELECT GENERATOR; ELE   TOR

DYSENTER
ber of int
there
of

E is the fifth letter of the English alphabet and most cognate alphabets. In chemistry E is the symbol for einsteinium, an artificial element discovered in 1952. In music E is the symbol for a tone and key. The lowercase italic E (e) is used in mathematics to denote the base of natural logarithms, approximately equal to 2.718.

EAGLE. The strength, dignity, and grandeur of the eagle have given it the worldwide rank of king of birds, and its likeness is to be found on the flags, coins, and coats of arms of many nations. Its feathers have been used as ornaments by American Indians. No other wild creature has so often been used as a symbol. During the past 5,000 or 6,000 years it has represented such diverse things as power, conquest, independence, freedom, truth, and immortality.

There are many species of large birds to which the name eagle is applied; these all belong to the hawk family. In America there are two species—the bald eagle (the national emblem of the United States) and the golden eagle. Both have a wingspread of about 7 feet.

The adult bald eagle is easily recognized by its white head and tail. The young bald eagle is dark all over. The bald eagle is a member of the group known as sea eagles. It prefers the vicinity of lakes, streams, or the ocean, where it feeds on dead or dying fish. Not a skilled fisher-

The golden eagle, below, builds its large, bulky nest on a high, inaccessible cliff.

man itself, it often robs the ospreys by forcing them to drop their catch of fish. Occasionally the eagle may take crippled ducks or other small animals, but stories that the eagle carries away children are false. An eagle's nest is built in the main crotch of a huge tree and is often of unbelievable size. Nests 10 feet deep and 6 or 8 feet across are not unusual. A ton or more of sticks occasionally goes into such a nest.

The golden eagle ranges over half the land in the world. It is primarily a mountain bird, and in the United States it is most frequently found in the western states. It is a dark bird with an inconspicuous glint of gold on its head. It is faster than the bald eagle and lives by catching rabbits and other live animals.

The bald eagle, below, is the U.S. emblem.

EAGLE, THE (constellation). See AQUILA.

EAR. The human ear is the organ of hearing. It consists of three principal parts: the outer ear, the middle ear, and the inner ear. The outer ear protrudes from the side of the head and forms a canal into the skull. It collects sounds and directs them inward to the eardrum. The middle ear contains three small bones that link the eardrum with the inner ear. It is also connected

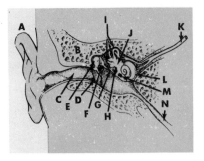

Principal parts of the human ear include the visible outer ear, **A.** Other parts are enclosed by bones, **B.** The external ear canal, **C,** leads to the eardrum, **D.** Movements of this membrane are transmitted through the hammer, **E,** anvil, **F,** stirrup, **G,** and oval window, **H,** into the fluid of the cochlea, **L.** A membrane over the round window, **M,** stretches to let the fluid move. The acoustic nerve is at **K.** The semicircular canals, **I,** and the vestibule, **J,** are the chief centers of the sense of balance. The eustacian tube, **N,** leads to the throat.

with the throat by means of the eustachian tube. The inner ear is a cavity that contains fluid. The essential hearing mechanism (in the fluid of the inner ear) is the cochlea, which is spiral shaped and contains a membrane, the organ of Corti, which has thousands of nerve endings leading to the brain. In hearing, sound waves of air move the drum membrane, which vibrates the small bones of the middle ear. One of these, the stirrup, causes movement of fluid in the inner ear. The movement of the fluid causes vibrations that stimulate the organ of Corti, which sends impulses to the brain.

Infection and damage to the ear can be carried not only from the outside through the ear canal, but from the throat through the eustachian tubes, which normally have the function of equalizing the pressure inside and outside the eardrums. Earache is a pain in the ear. Young people seem to be much more inclined to have earache than older people. Sometimes the pain is caused by enlarged tonsils or adenoids, by a cold, or by something wrong with a tooth. Young people also have a tendency to have ear infections, which can cause very severe pain and which, unless properly treated, could lead to a condition called mastoiditis. Because the hearing could be affected, earache should be treated by a doctor.

EARP, WYATT (1848-1929), U.S. frontier marshal and gunfighter and one of the most famous law officers in the world, was born in Monmouth, Ill. For a time he was a buffalo hunter in Kansas. In 1873, at the age of 25, he became the marshal of Ellsworth, Kan. A year later the townspeople of Wichita, Kan., elected him marshal of one of the toughest cattle towns in the country.

In 1876 Earp went to Dodge City, Kan., where he encountered numerous outlaws and supposedly engaged in more than 100 gun battles.

In 1879 Earp and his three brothers, James, Morgan, and Virgil, went to Tombstone in the Arizona Territory. They intended to start a stage line between Tombstone and Tucson; however, two lines were already in operation. Earp instead became the peace officer of the community.

In 1881 at the O.K. Corral in Tombstone the Earp brothers and Doc Holliday battled to the death with the Clanton brothers, the McLowery brothers, and Billy Claiborne. Three men were killed, and

two Earp brothers were wounded. Virgil recovered, but three months later he was shot from ambush. Morgan, also wounded in the famous corral fight, was later shot and killed while playing a game of pool.

Wyatt and his brother James became partners in the Oriental, a gambling casino in Tombstone. In 1882 Earp left Arizona Territory and went to live in Colorado. Because the sheriff of Tombstone tried to arrest him for the killing of his brother Morgan's slayer, Earp went to the Klondike region in the Yukon, where he remained several years. He returned to spend his remaining years in Los Angeles.

EARTH, the planet we live on, a spinning sphere of rock and iron about 8,000 miles through and 25,000 miles around. It is one of the sun's nine principal planets, all of which are traveling at high speeds through space. They are held in circular paths around the sun by the sun's gravitational attraction. These paths, called orbits, are millions of miles apart, and compared with such distances the planets themselves are only tiny specks.

The earth's orbit is about 93,000,000 miles out from the sun, past the first two planets, Mercury and Venus. Over 10,000 earths set side by side would be needed to equal such a distance. But compared with many of the planets the earth is rather close to the sun. All the first four planets—Mercury, Venus, Earth, and Mars—are relatively close to each other and close to the sun. They lie in a band only one-half to one and one-half times the earth's distance from the sun. The five outer planets are scattered through a band five to forty times the earth's distance from the sun, across literally billions of miles. From some of these planets the earth would lie so close to the sun that it could not be seen because of the sun's glare.

The earth seems very large to us, but it is one of the smaller planets. The inner four planets have diameters of 3,000 to 8,000 miles, compared with outer planets' diameters of 31,000 to 89,000 miles (excepting Pluto). Jupiter, the largest, would hold over 1,000 earths with ease.

Geologists believe that the diagram at left is a good picture of a cross section of the earth. The mantle would consist of solid rock. The core might consist of a liquid outer layer and an inner solid layer, both composed of iron and nickle.

From space the earth would look like this.

The shape of the earth's orbit is not quite a perfect circle: It is slightly elliptical. This means that the earth is sometimes closer to the sun than at other times. It is farthest in July at 94,500,000 miles and nearest in January at 91,500,000 miles. These points are called aphelion and perihelion. See APHELION AND PERIHELION.

The earth travels in its orbit at about $18\frac{1}{2}$ miles per second, which is over 66,000 miles per hour. In going once around the sun it covers nearly 600,000,000 miles.

The earth spins from west to east, making one complete spin in 23 hours and 56 minutes. Its axis of spin is not exactly vertical to the plane of the earth's orbit but is tipped about $23\frac{1}{2}$ degrees, or about one-fourth of the way over to horizontal. The direction of this tip stays almost the same, so in part of the orbit (summer) the North Pole is tipped toward the sun, while in the opposite part (winter) it is tipped away from the sun. This change causes our seasons. See SEASON.

However, the axis of spin does move slightly. Its angle stays the same, but its direction swings ever so slowly in a circle, making a complete circle in 26,000 years. This motion is called precession. See PRECESSION.

The earth is heavier for its size than any of the other planets. It is $5\frac{1}{2}$ times denser than water. The other three inner planets are only somewhat less dense, but the very large outer planets are about the same density as water.

The total material of the earth would amount to about 6,600 billion billion tons if it were weighed at the earth's surface. This is called its mass. The pressure of this material increases toward the inside of the earth to about 25,000 tons per

crust 4 to 30 miles

mantle 1,800 miles

core 2,200 x 2

liquid core

solid core

square inch at the center. The study of earthquake waves indicates that the interior of the earth is divided into layers of different material at different densities. The outer crust of granite and basalt extends down about 20 miles. Below the crust to a depth of about 1,800 miles lies a mixture of minerals, probably consisting of silicates of magnesium and iron. This region and the crust together make up the mantle. The rest of the interior, called the core, is from two to four times as dense as the mantle. The outer part of the core shows some evidence of being in a liquid state. The very dense inner core is apparently solid. The material of the core is probably a mixture of iron and nickel.

The strength of gravity at the earth's surface is not too different from its strength at the surface of the other planets, except for Jupiter, where it is over twice as strong, and for Mercury and Mars, where it is only about half as strong. The attractive force of the earth will pull back any object hurled outward at a speed of less than 7 miles per second (25,000 miles per hour), a speed called the escape velocity. See ESCAPE VELOCITY.

The origin of the earth is part of the story of how the solar system was formed. See SOLAR SYSTEM.

EARTH, HISTORY OF. The history of the earth is the story of the shaping of the continents and the ocean basins and of climatic changes. It is the story of the formation and destruction of mountain chains, plains, lowland areas, and seas. The history of the earth is the story of such a long time and includes so many events that it is impossible to summarize that history here. Some of the kinds of events that took place and are taking place can be de-

scribed, and a few examples can be mentioned.

No one knows exactly how old the earth is, or exactly how it came into being. (See EARTH; SOLAR SYSTEM.) The oldest known records of earth events are in the most ancient rocks yet found. Rocks have been discovered that are more than two and a half billion years old. It is possible to determine the age of some ancient rocks by radioactive dating. (See RADIOACTIVE DATING.) But there is evidence that the oldest rocks yet found are not the oldest rocks that exist or have existed on the earth.

The continents, mountains, plains, seas, and climates of the earth are, and always have been, constantly changing. At most times and in most regions the change is extremely slow. But a few small events are rapid, such as earthquakes. Anybody who has been in an earthquake knows the earth is indeed changing and active.

At times in the past great basins have accumulated sediments several miles thick. The sediments have been transformed to solid rocks of many kinds. Often the rocks in such basins have been compressed, folded, broken, and thrust over each other to form great mountain chains. As soon as the rocks were elevated, weathering began decomposing the rocks; and erosion by running water, wind, glacier ice, and ocean waves and currents began carrying pieces of rock away. Many great mountain chains of the past have been worn down to low hills in this way. Sometimes one mountain chain has gone through several cycles of elevation and erosion. The Appalachians of the eastern United States are old mountains that have undergone several cycles of elevation and erosion. The cycle of accumulating sediment, transforming it to rock,

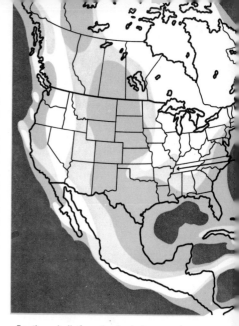

Fossil seashells from the shaded areas above show geologists the site of ancient seas. Darker areas were covered longest.

and elevating the rock as a mountain range takes a long time—some mountain chains have been built gradually over hundreds of millions of years.

Rocks are being folded, compressed, broken, and elevated as mountain chains in many parts of the world today. Such a process subjects the rocks deep within the earth to tremendous pressures. Occasionally some rocks break or slip because of the pressures, and an earthquake or a series of earthquakes results. From time to time large earthquakes take place in Japan, the western United States, the western coastal regions of South America, and the lands surrounding the Mediterranean Sea. In all these places mountains are being formed and elevated.

Vast amounts of sediments that will probably become the rocks in future mountains are accumulating

New data indicate that the earth has the shape of a pear, as shown at left. This would alter a molten-interior theory, shown at right.

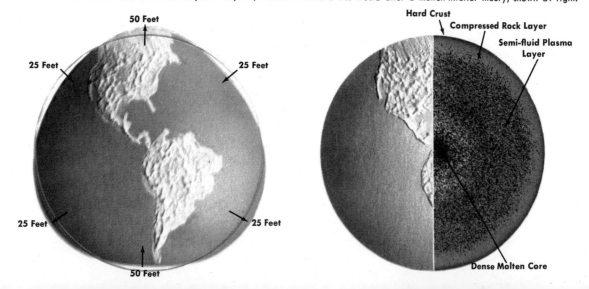

50 Feet

25 Feet · 25 Feet

25 Feet · 25 Feet

50 Feet

Hard Crust
Compressed Rock Layer
Semi-fluid Plasma Layer
Dense Molten Core

in places today. The Gulf of Mexico and the East China Sea are such great sedimentary basins.

A volcanic eruption is a small event in the earth's history that a person can watch. Volcanoes existed in the most ancient times of which we have a record. Throughout the history of the earth there have always been some active volcanoes. Sometimes there were many and sometimes fewer. We are living in an age of unusually great volcanic activity. Volcanoes are often concentrated near places where mountain-building processes are taking place. Japan, for example, has famous volcanoes. So does the western region of South America.

Most geologic events are not sudden and spectacular like earthquakes and volcanic eruptions. They are very gradual and very slow. For example, the area around the Great Lakes is gradually rising and tilting toward the southwest. Parts of northern Europe are also being uplifted. During the most recent glacial epoch, called the Pleistocene, these northern areas were depressed by the weight of the very large and thick continental glaciers. Now that the great glaciers have melted, the land is rising at the rate of a fraction of an inch to a few inches a century. Many slow rises and subsidences of land areas have taken place in the earth's history. Most of these

changes had no connection with glaciation. As areas subsided, shorelines on shallow coasts were greatly changed. Large lowland areas were flooded. At many times in the past large parts of the present land areas of continents were under shallow seas. When the land rose, the shallow seas were drained.

Changes of climate have played their part in earth's history. For long periods of time the earth's climate was more uniform than it is now. Tropical and subtropical animals and plants lived all over the world. Present climates are greatly affected by the recent continental glaciations. In fact, we are still living in a glacial age. Perhaps we are living at the very end of the age, but we may be in a warm interval in the middle of the age, and the glaciers have receded only temporarily.

The Pleistocene continental glaciations of the near past were not unique; the earth has experienced such glaciations several times in the distant past. These glaciations occurred in places that may seem surprising to us, because we think in terms of our present climate. In both the Pre-Cambrian and the Permian, areas in Australia, southern Africa, and the Indian Peninsula were glaciated. (See GEOLOGIC TIME SCALE.) There is evidence that areas in the Northern Hemisphere were also glaciated at these times.

EARTH, MEASUREMENT OF. The ancient Greeks were the first to discover that the earth was a sphere. They also made the first scientific attempts to measure it. Men like Anaximenes, Pythagoras, and Aristotle saw a proof of the shape of the earth in the fact that the hull of a ship moving away from the shore goes out of sight before the masts and sails. They also observed the shadow of the earth on the face of the moon during eclipses of the moon and saw that it was a round shape.

In the 3d century B.C. Eratosthenes, a Greek mathematician in Alexandria, using a method of measurement still in use, estimated the circumference of the earth with remarkable accuracy.

It was not until 1774 that the first measurement of the weight of the earth was made. In that year Nevil Maskelyne, the astronomer royal of England, set up two stations on a mountain in Scotland and determined the earth's weight by a process of comparison between the mountain and the earth. He first measured the gravitational force of the mountain. Then, by comparing the gravitational force of the mountain with that of the earth, he found the earth's weight. Measurements of the earth since then have used improved techniques and tools to obtain more and more exact results.

Distribution of earthquakes during the past 50 years shows that earthquakes tend to occur in zones. These zones follow lines of weakness in the earth's crust. In some areas underground forces may be so finely balanced that a storm may touch off an earthquake.

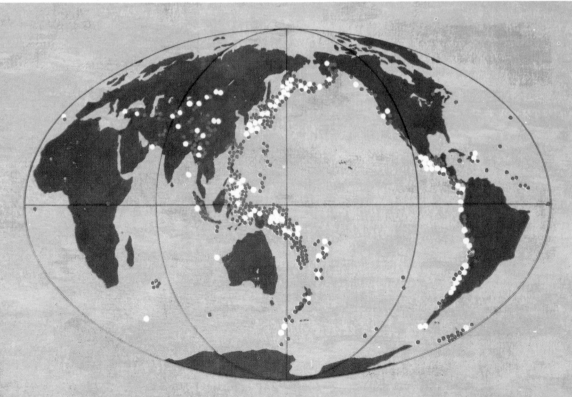

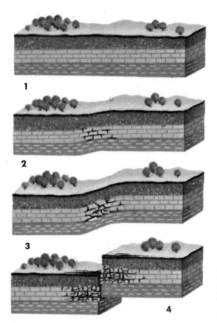

Earthquakes occur, it is believed, when rock strata break, then vibrate before settling in a new position. The earthquake occurs between stages **3** and **4** in these drawings.

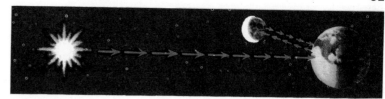

Earthshine is only a small part of all the sunlight reflected by the earth. Only a fraction of this reflected light hits the moon. Of this fraction, only 7 percent is reflected back into space by the moon. And only a small part of this light reaches the earth again.

EARTHQUAKE, a shaking of the earth's crust, caused by natural forces. Earthquakes are the result of rocks breaking suddenly after having been subjected to great forces that bend and distort them. Earthquakes are caused by faulting—the movement of one block of the earth's crust past another block. Most earthquakes originate 5 to 20 miles below the earth's surface; a few, as deep as several hundred miles.

Earthquake shocks vary in strength, from small ones that can be recorded only on very sensitive instruments to great destructive shocks like the disastrous Assam earthquake of 1897. At that time 150,000 square miles of northeastern India were affected. In that huge area all buildings, railroads, and bridges were completely destroyed. In some places the land was pushed up, and new cliffs 35 feet high were formed. In other places the land sank, and lakes were quickly formed in the hollows. In Tokyo the terrible earthquake of 1923 did only a small part of the damage. The greatest cause of destruction was fire that broke out in the light wooden dwellings from upset stoves and braziers.

Because of the frequency of earthquakes in certain areas a special kind of architecture has been developed. Buildings are constructed on rollers so that the structure is free to move backward and forward when a movement of the earth occurs. Some buildings have floating foundations.

EARTHSHINE. The earth reflects sunlight even more brightly than does the moon. If you were on the moon, the "full" earth would look 13 times larger than a full moon. The earth reflects more light per square mile than the moon does, so full earthlight would actually be about 50 times brighter than full moonlight. Some of this bright earthlight shining on the moon reflects back to the earth, giving a faint illumination to the shadow side of the moon. This twice-reflected sunlight we call earthshine.

EARTHWORM, a large terrestrial worm of the phylum Annelida that inhabits moist clay soil. Unlike the unsegmented flatworms and roundworms, the body of the earthworm and of other annelid worms is composed of many ringlike segments, or somites, that are essentially alike in shape and size. Some earthworms attain a length of 12 inches and a width of $\frac{3}{8}$ inch. Their segments number between 115 and 200. Although the earthworm has no distinct brain, it has in its anterior end a concentration of nerve bodies that functions as a simple brain. Although it lacks eyes, its skin contains numerous sensitive nerve endings that inform it of the conditions of its environment. A ventral nerve cord extends from these anterior nerve bodies to the last segment. The earthworm has five pairs of contracting blood vessels, or hearts, that pump red blood through a system of closed arteries, capillaries, and veins to all parts of the body.

Earthworms are most numerous in moist, clay soil that is rich in humus. They inhabit such soil in almost every region of the world. They cannot live in soil that is too dry, too sandy, or too deficient in humus. An earthworm burrows through light topsoil by wedging its anterior end forward through the soil particles and then by swelling its pharynx to force them outward. To burrow through heavier, deeper soil, the earthworm swallows the soil, passes it through its digestive tract, and eliminates it. The worm can then crawl through the vacant places

from which it has eaten the soil. Earthworms live near the surface of the soil when it is moist and warm. During periods of summer drought they retire to a depth of 6 feet or more, where the soil is more moist. During winter they go below the frostline and remain inactive. During the day earthworms remain beneath the soil's surface. At night they thrust the anterior two-thirds of their body above the surface to seek food and to explore. However, the posterior end of the body remains firmly attached beneath the surface so that the worm can quickly withdraw to safety if danger threatens. Sometimes the worms crawl about the surface.

1. The segmentation of the earthworm is discernible. **2.** A lateral view of the anterior end shows the minute, bristle-like setae, **2A**. **3.** The ventral view of the anterior end shows the mouth, **3A**. **4.** This internal view shows the thin partitions called septa, **4A**; a segment, **4B**; the body cavity, **4C**; and the digestive tract, **4D**. **5.** This internal view shows the pharynx, **5A**; esophagus, **5B**; calciferous glands, **5C**; crop, **5D**; gizzard, **5E**; intestine, **5F**; blood vessels, **5G**; hearts, **5H**; and seminal vesicles, **5I**.

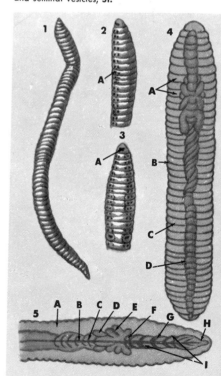

Visitors to Jesus' tomb on Easter morning were told by an angel that Jesus had arisen.

EASTER, the English name for the oldest and most important festival in the Christian church, celebrating the Resurrection of Jesus Christ. The date of Easter is not fixed: It comes on the Sunday following the first full moon after the vernal equinox (March 21). The word *Easter* comes from the old Anglo-Saxon word *Eostre*, or *Ostâra*, the name of the Anglo-Saxon goddess of spring. The month that corresponds to our April was dedicated to her and was called *Eostur-monath*. Many curious customs have been practiced at the Easter season, most of them beginning as pagan customs that were taken over by Christianity. The Easter fire, lit on the tops of mountains all over Europe, was one of the most interesting of these customs. It symbolized the victory of spring over winter. The early Christian church adopted the practice and gave it a Christian meaning. This was the origin of the new fire, kindled with a flint on Holy Saturday and symbolizing the Resurrection of Jesus Christ, who is called the Light of the World.

In many countries it is still customary to give hard-boiled dyed eggs to youngsters on Easter. Eggs were symbols of renewed life in all the ancient lands before the beginning of Christianity. In Christian countries the Easter egg was used as a symbol of the Resurrection of Jesus Christ as early as the 13th century.

Egg rolling is also an old custom connected with Easter. The eggs are hard boiled and colored with dye. The custom was widespread in Europe and America and is still practiced in some places. Large numbers of people gathered on a grassy hill and rolled the eggs down the slope. Those that were unbroken supposedly brought good luck to the owners during the coming year. It is still the custom for the president of the United States to invite large numbers of children to roll Easter eggs on the White House lawn each year.

Distribution of cakes among the poor every Easter Sunday is also practiced in certain parts of England. In the mountainous country of Tyrol, in Austria, children are given eggs for their singing of Easter hymns and guitar playing. Probably of pagan origin are the customs of "lifting" and "sprinkling." On Easter Monday in some countries young men roam the streets looking for girls they can lift or sprinkle with perfume or water. The next day, the girls go about in the same manner.

Easter is the central event in a series of religious holidays. Ash Wednesday, the seventh Wednesday before Easter, is the first day of Lent. Holy Week, the week before Easter, includes Palm Sunday Maundy Thursday, Good Friday, and Holy Saturday, all of which are observed by religious ceremonies. See GOOD FRIDAY; LENT.

EASTER ISLAND, an isolated island in the Pacific Ocean about 2,350 miles west of Chile and belonging to that country. It is roughly triangular in shape, 15 miles long and 11 miles wide, with an area of 45 square miles and a population of about 500. There is an extinct volcano at each corner of the triangle, the highest being Mt. Rano Raraku (1,765 feet). The soil is fertile, and the Polynesian natives raise tobacco, sugarcane, taro roots, yams, and tropical fruit. The only vegetation on the island is grass, which provides grazing for sheep and cattle of a Chilean company. The only communication between Easter Island and the rest of the world is radio contact and a ship sent once a year from Chile.

Easter Island has long been famous for the huge statues scattered all over the land, carved from volcanic rock, and the inscriptions engraved on small stones. The origin of the carvings is wrapped in mystery, and many theories have been

How the prehistoric statues on Easter Island were moved into position remains a mystery.

put forward to explain them. No one knows who the people were who made the statues and inscriptions or when they were made. The figures represent the upper portion of human figures and stand 30 to 40 feet high and weigh between 5 and 8 tons.

The island was named on Easter Day, 1722, by the Dutch navigator Roggeveen. Several nations claimed it before Chile took possession in 1888. At the time of Roggeveen's visit the native population was between 2,000 and 3,000. European diseases later killed large numbers of the people, and between 1860 and 1870 slave traders from Peru carried off most of the able-bodied men to work on plantations and in the mines, where most of them died.

EASTERN ORTHODOX CHURCH, a group of churches that had their origin in 1054, when the Greek (or Eastern) Catholics separated from the Roman (or Western) Catholics. This break in relations, known as the Great Schism, has continued.

From the beginning Christians in the eastern half of the Roman Empire used the Greek instead of the Latin language in their divine services, and their ceremonies were different from the liturgy practiced in the West. The Easterners also developed attitudes of thought and worship that were different from those of Westerners. Even more important was the close relationship that developed between the Byzantine emperors, residing in Constantinople, and the Eastern Orthodox Church. The Eastern Orthodox Church remained more dependent on the support of the state than did the Roman Catholic Church of the West. While the Christians of what is now Italy, Spain, France, and northern Africa looked to the bishop of Rome as their leader, the eastern Christians grouped themselves around the patriarchs of Constantinople, Alexandria, Antioch, and Jerusalem.

During the 9th century there was a great dispute between the patriarch of Constantinople and the bishop of Rome. Each claimed to be the head of all Christians. The question remained undecided, but the differences between the Christians of the East and the West continued to increase. Finally, in 1054 Michael Caerularius, patriarch of Constantinople, broke relations with the bishop of Rome. The Eastern Orthodox Church has always refused to accept the headship, or primacy, of the bishop of Rome.

The Eastern Orthodox Church has a patriarch in almost every country where Christians follow the eastern rite, and he governs the church with the aid of a synod (assembly of churchmen) independent of the patriarch of Constantinople. Moreover, there are many different bodies within the Eastern Orthodox Church.

Principal groups are the Russian, Albanian, Bulgarian, Greek, Romanian, Serbian, and Syrian.

Nearly all the European and Asiatic bodies of the Eastern Orthodox Church have branches in America. For political reasons, the American branches of the Russian and Ukranian Orthodox churches have proclaimed themselves independent from the patriarch of Moscow.

EAST INDIA COMPANY, the name given to various European companies chartered to trade in the East Indies, India, and China. The companies flourished between the early 17th century and the mid-19th century. The most prominent of them, the British East India Company, was in effect the ruler of British India from about the mid-18th century until the Sepoy Mutiny (1857-1858). (See BRITISH EAST INDIA COMPANY; SEPOY MUTINY.) Also of importance was the Dutch East India Company, which developed areas in the East Indies that later became part of the Dutch Empire as the Netherlands East Indies. (See DUTCH EAST INDIA COMPANY.) Another of the major trading companies was that formed by the French. See FRENCH EAST INDIA COMPANY.

EAST INDIES, a name given to the group of islands lying between Australia and Asia. In the 15th century this region was called simply India or the Indies. Columbus thought that he had reached it when he discovered America. Later, when it was found that America was not India, the newly found region was called the West Indies. The name East Indies was given to Asiatic India and the nearby islands. Later the term was restricted to the islands of the Malay Archipelago. Most of these islands are now part of the Republic of Indonesia.

EATING HABITS are influenced by environment—climate and the availability of water and of plants and animals to serve as food—and by customs whose origins may be remote. Our ways of eating, as well as the implements we use, are by no means universal.

The nomadic Arabs eat what they can transport and find in the desert. Dates from oases, goat's or camel's milk, goat's cheese, rice, and a bit of meat at times may constitute the only meal of the day. These nomads sit close together and eat with their fingers, partaking from a common bowl. The Arabian nomads have a longstanding tradition of democracy and hospitality. Rich and poor eat similar food. Visitors are always offered coffee and invited to share the common meal.

Another group of people with an

A workman's noonday meal is by necessity simple, for it must consist of items that can be carried conveniently to the job. These workmen (right) in Naples, Italy, eat a lunch of bread and wine.

A young citizen of South Vietnam, below, is seen eating his meal in the accepted oriental manner. Chopsticks are manipulated in the right hand, while the bowl is held close to the mouth with the left. Individual bowls are filled from a common container.
John Strohm

Max Tatch—Shostal

King ibn-Saud of Saudi Arabia, below, sits at the head of the banquet table. Guests help themselves from large bowls.
John Strohm

ancient civilization who eat with their hands are the people of India. They are trained to use only the tips of the fingers of the right hand to touch food. Banana leaves are the only utensils required. They are plentiful and are disposable. In India people wash their hands and mouths before and after eating. In Indian villages there has been no mass use of plates, forks, and knives. Furthermore, servants bring water for washing and clean up after people when they eat. As the economic situation changes in India, eating habits may change also. In many industrialized parts of India people now eat with forks and knives.

In Mexican villages and in other rural areas in Latin America the tortilla is sometimes used as an eating utensil in place of the fork or spoon. This custom is disappearing in urban areas.

Among peoples organized in clans or similar social groupings each group may maintain a special relationship with a special plant or animal that is called a totem. (See TOTEM.) In East Africa each clan of the Baganda people has two totems, and the clan is named after one—for example, Lion clan, Leopard clan, or Mushroom clan. The people may not eat the totem for which their clan is named. This refraining from eating certain food is called a food taboo. Food taboos are found in many parts of the world. Often the original reason for the taboo is no longer known and gives rise to myths and speculations. Temporary food taboos, imposed in Polynesia during times of scarcity, were also of economic advantage.

In the United States we find many variations in eating habits. Sometimes these habits are prescribed by religious groups. Sometimes people have particular eating habits because of their ideas about health or morality.

Thus, eating habits vary widely. Like other customs, they arise out of the environment where they are practiced. There is a close relation between eating habits and ways of living; when these ways change, many eating habits change also. See ETIQUETTE.

EBONY, a kind of wood. One of the sources of this wood is the black Macassar ebony, a large tree that ranges from India to the East Indies. Several other species furnish ebony, but this species is the most important. Its very hard, heavy, intensely black heartwood takes a fine

FAMILY TREE OF SPINY-SKINNED ANIMALS

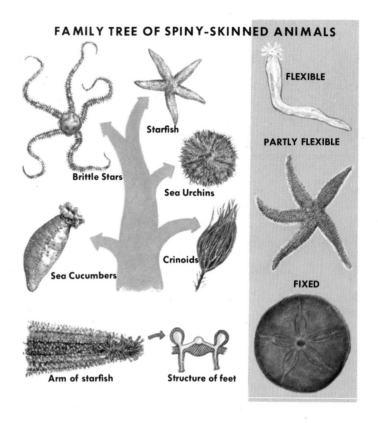

Sea cucumbers and some other echinoderms superficially resemble plants more than animals.

polish and is much used as a veneer wood for furniture. To manufacture this product, a thin layer of ebony is glued onto less expensive wood. Ebony is also used for making scientific instruments, piano keys, and knife handles. The fact that only the heartwood yields the black ebony makes it expensive. There is ebony of other colors, for example, the streaked, dark-red wood of the American ebony, but it is less valuable. Some furniture called ebony is really made from cherry wood stained black. The American and the Japanese persimmon belong to the ebony family.

Ebony has been used since ancient times. The records of ancient Egypt tell of bringing heavy logs of ebony to the king's palace, and ebony is mentioned in the Old Testament.

ECHINODERM, a marine invertebrate that belongs to the spiny-skinned phylum Echinodermata. Echinoderms have neither head nor brain. The adults are radially symmetrical. In radial symmetry the organs of an animal are arranged around a central body axis so that a line extending outward in any direction from this axis would intersect similar organs.

Some echinoderms, including starfish, have projecting arms, or rays, that number either five or multiples of five up to fifty. Other echinoderms, such as the sea cucumber and the sea lily, superficially resemble plants more than animals. Sea urchins have rounded, oblong bodies covered with long, movable spines. The sand dollars are disk-shaped with short spines.

Echinoderms have a hard skeleton of joined plates composed of calcium carbonate. The short, blunt spines covering the surface of the starfish are extensions of this skeleton.

Echinoderms are the only animals to possess a water vascular system consisting of interconnecting canals through which sea water circulates. In starfish these canals extend into numerous tube feet that cover the undersides of the arms. Locomotion, the primary purpose of the water vascular system, is accomplished in the starfish by the contraction of the tube feet as the water flows through them. Echinoderms also obtain minute food particles from sea water in the vascular system.

The circulatory system is separate from the water vascular system. Oxygen is obtained through gill-like structures on the surface of the body.

The phylum Echinodermata is the only exclusively marine-animal phylum. Echinoderms inhabit the sea from its shore to a depth of more than 12,000 feet. Some can swim; others can only crawl along the bottom; a few remain permanently attached to the bottom or to rocks.

Echinoderms are the only invertebrates in which complex organs and organ systems exist in conjunction with radial symmetry. See STARFISH.

The moon makes one complete circle around the earth about every 28 days. The moon's path is slightly tilted from the plane of the earth's path around the sun, so the moon usually misses the earth's shadow. But occasionally it does pass through the shadow, and we see an eclipse.

The dark shadow of the earth is called the umbra. However, the earth also has a partial shadow, called the penumbra, that surrounds the umbra. In this partial shadow only part of the sun's light is blocked off by the earth. If you

passes completely into the umbra, it is in total eclipse. If only part of it passes through the umbra, it is in partial eclipse. If it passes only through the penumbra, it is in penumbral eclipse.

Even during a total eclipse the moon is still faintly visible because a small amount of light is bent around the earth by its atmosphere. This light is red because the atmosphere absorbs the other colors of light, just as it absorbs them at sunrise and sunset, when the sun's rays slant through long distances of atmosphere.

ECHO.
Sound bounces off a surface just as a ball bounces off a surface. When the sound bounces off the surface, it is heard again. This repetition of sound is called an echo.

The waves of sound on meeting the surface are turned back on their course according to the same laws that hold for the reflection of light. In order for an echo to come back to where the sound originated, the reflection of the sound (like the bounce of a ball) must be direct. Otherwise the echo may be heard, not by the person who made the sound, but by somebody else.

Echoes in buildings interfere with the good conduction of sounds. Out of doors woods, rocks, and mountains produce natural echoes; some localities have become famous for their echoes.

ECLIPSE OF THE MOON.
On the side of the earth away from the sun a long black shadow extends deep into space. This is the earth's own shadow. As the earth speeds around the sun, this shadow sweeps along beside the earth, always pointing away from the sun. Anywhere inside this shadow the sun is totally hidden behind the dark bulk of the earth. What we call night is really just this shadow side of the earth. When the moon passes through this shadow, we say it is in eclipse.

were on the moon as it entered the penumbra, you would see the dark disk of the earth gradually cover the sun. Finally the sun would be completely covered, and you would be in the full shadow of the earth. Watching the same event from the earth, you would see the moon dim slightly as it entered the penumbra, where part of the sun's light still shines on the moon. Then you would see a black, disk-shaped shadow move across the moon as it entered the umbra, where no light from the sun reaches. If the moon

The diagram below shows the cause of a lunar eclipse. The moon in the position shown here is in total eclipse, for it is completely immersed in the umbra. The moon in this picture appears to have a coppery glow. This is the result of red or orange rays of the sun that are bent by the atmosphere into the cone of the earth's shadow.

ECLIPSE OF THE SUN.
Sometimes when the moon is between us and the sun, its shadow crosses the earth. The shadow is too small to cover all the earth, but if you are in an area where the shadow falls, you will see the sun gradually disappear behind the dark, round shape of the moon. This is called an eclipse of the sun.

The moon completes an elliptical path round the earth about every 28 days. Since it must regularly pass between us and the sun, you might expect an eclipse of the sun every 28 days. But for several reasons eclipses do not occur that often.

One reason is that the moon's shadow is only rarely long enough to reach the earth. The cone shape of the shadow tapers to a point usually a few thousand miles short of the earth. However, during part of the year the earth is farther from

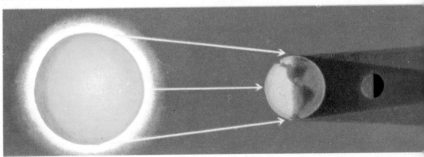

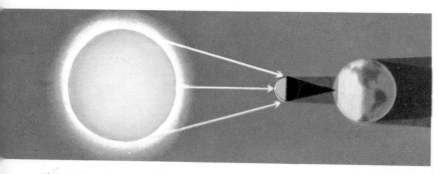

Above is shown the cause of a solar eclipse. Few areas on the earth's surface experience a total eclipse of the sun, but the sun is partially eclipsed in the penumbral belt.

the sun than at other times, and this greater distance causes the moon's shadow to lengthen. Also, the moon is not always the same distance from the earth. At its closest point it may be several thousand miles closer than its average distance. When the moon's shadow is longest, and when the moon is closest to the earth, the tip of the shadow reaches the earth and covers a circle 167 miles in diameter at its maximum size.

However, another motion of the moon may still keep the shadow from falling on the earth. The moon's orbit is tilted from the plane of the earth's orbit, so the moon is sometimes above the earth's plane and at other times below it. If the moon passes between the earth and the sun either above or below the earth's plane, the moon's shadow will fall above or below the earth and will not cause an eclipse. Only if the moon is crossing the earth's plane while passing between the sun and the earth can its shadow fall on the earth.

ECOLOGY, the biological science that studies the mutual relationships that exist among animals, plants, and their biological and physical environments. Ecology is not primarily concerned with animals and plants as isolated organisms. The primary focus of ecology is the influences that the animals and plants of a particular geographic region exert upon one another and the influences exerted upon both by their climate and other aspects of their physical environment. The

geographic regions include temperate forests, tropical jungles, prairies, deserts, arctic tundras, mountaintops, seashores, oceans, fresh-water lakes, and rivers or streams.

The animals and plants that are native to any of these regions influence one another in many ways. Plants constitute food for herbivorous, or plant-eating, animals and provide materials from which some animals construct their shelters. These herbivorous animals in turn serve as food for predatory carnivorous animals. They all eventually die, decay, and serve as food for other plants. Animals of different species occasionally form mutually beneficial associations, which are termed symbiotic. For example, certain birds of Africa ride on the backs of rhinoceroses or of cattle and eat the ticks that infest their skins. The birds thus obtain food, and the beasts benefit by being relieved of irritating pests. Forest trees provide the shade that is necessary for the growth of certain shrubs and herbs and keep the forest floor moist by preventing evaporation. They also constitute a support for vines. Parasitic fungi harm other plants by growing upon them and eating them. Dead, decaying plants

African tickbirds ride on the back of a rhinoceros and eat ticks that irritate its skin.

SEQUENCE OF FOOD AND FEEDERS

Man

Big Fish

Small Fish

Small Animal Life

Small Plant Life

fertilize the soil so that other plants can grow luxuriantly from it.

Ecologists study these and the many other complex relationships that exist among the animals and plants that are native to any particular region. They also study rainfall, temperature, intensity of sunlight, humidity, length of growing season, severity of winter, and other climatic factors that affect the plants and animals of a particular region. The other physical environmental factors that affect plants and animals and that are studied by ecologists include topography, soil content, and drainage.

The science of ecology has some some important practical applications. For instance, a knowledge of ecology is necessary for the conservation of forests and wildlife.

ECONOMICS. The word *economics* comes from two Greek words meaning "house" and "to manage." This gives a good idea of what economics is about, although *house* is nowadays interpreted broadly to mean not only "household" in the literal, or narrow, sense, but also "business firm," "government," and "nation." That is, the general field of economics is considered to have the subfields of household (consumer) economics, business economics, government economics (public finance), and national economics. Some scholars, in fact, interpret *house* to mean the whole world, and their subfield is called international economics.

Economics deals with man's efforts to wrest a living from his environment. It observes the ways people act or behave in this struggle and endeavors to discover principles or laws that explain their behavior. If reliable principles can actually be discovered, they serve as a basis for predicting people's behavior in any given set of circumstances. (This is called the scientific aspect.) They may even be used as a reason for trying to change people's behavior by changing the circumstances. (This is called the policy aspect.) For example, economists have long observed that, for most things, the lower the price of a thing the more of it people will buy. This is the law of demand. From this law or principle it is possible to make the scientific prediction that if everything else stayed the same, a seller would sell more if his price were lower. Furthermore, a seller might institute the policy of lowering his price in the expectation of increasing his sales. It is very important, of course, that all other things stay the same, but often they do not. His competitors, for instance, may lower their prices still more, in which case his policy may not result in the increased sales he expected. In fact, his sales will very likely show a decrease.

The most widespread interest today is in national economics and in government economics, or public finance. Whether or not the material welfare of society and of individuals would be improved by increasing government control of the processes of production and distribution, for example, is a subject of never-ending economic research, study, and debate. See CAPITALISM; COMMUNISM; SOCIALISM.

ECSC. See EUROPEAN COAL AND STEEL COMMUNITY.

Ernst Baumann—Birnback

Because much of Ecuador is mountainous, slopes as high as 10,000 feet are used for growing grains and potatoes for local consumption. Much of the highland area is covered with grass, on which cattle graze.

ECUADOR is a republic in northwestern South America. The Equator (which in Spanish is *ecuador*) crosses the northern part and gives the country its name. It is an underdeveloped land, divided in its climate, landscape, and culture. Quito, located at an elevation of some 9,000 feet in the Andes, is Ecuador's capital. Guayaquil, the country's principal seaport, is the largest city. Ecuador covers more than 100,000 square miles, but its exact size is not known. The people number about 4,000,000.

Two parallel ranges of the Andes Mountains, topped by lofty volcanoes, cross the country from north to south, dividing it into three regions. Ridges cross between the two ranges to form basins that contain Quito and other important towns. The highest of the volcanic peaks is Chimborazo, which rises almost 4 miles above sea level. Cotopaxi is considered the highest active volcano in the world.

Along the Pacific coast is a plain that slopes gradually from the mountains. Although it is generally flat, there are a few chains of low hills. East of the Andes is a rainy, heavily forested and sparsely inhabited lowland cut by a network of rivers that drain into the Amazon.

Although located on the Equator,

Ecuador's coat of arms consists of an oval shield resting on fasces and topped by a condor with outspread wings.

Tom Hollyman—Photo Researchers

Ecuador has a climate that is greatly changed by the high altitudes in the mountains and by the cold Humboldt Current along the Pacific coast. Except in the eastern lowlands, the year is divided into rainy and dry seasons. The climate in the east is hot and rainy all year. Throughout the country temperatures change very little from month to month. Although the lowlands are hot, the highlands are cool.

Ecuador's chief exports are bananas, coffee, and cacao. Rice is produced both for home use and export. These money crops are grown in the coastal region. In the highlands, wheat, corn, barley, potatoes, and other subsistence crops are raised for local use. Straw hats, commonly called panama hats, are woven in many homes. They are an important export item. Foreign trade is principally with the United States.

The country's rugged terrain makes highway and railroad construction difficult and costly. In much of the coastal region, rivers are the only means of transportation during the rainy season.

Ecuador's tropical forests are immense, covering the entire eastern lowland and the northern part of the coastal lowland. But the forests are only partly exploited. Among their leading products are balsa wood, prized for its lightness; vegetable ivory (for buttons) from the tagua palm; and mangrove bark, which yields leather-tanning materials. Ecuador is the world's chief source of balsa wood. Of the various minerals that are found in the republic, petroleum and gold are the most important.

The people of Ecuador are largely pure-blooded Indians, who cling to their old-fashioned way of life and

Ecuador is a land of great volcanic activity. The Ecuadorean Andes contain some 30 active volcanoes, among them some of the largest in the world. At night the clouds around their lofty summits are lighted by the reflection of molten lava in their craters. The highest peak exceeds 20,000 feet.

The ancient *quena*, a native flute made of clay or bamboo, is still played by Ecuador's Quechua Indians. The Quechuas are descendants of the Incas. Their music is based on a five-note scale.

Fujihira—Monkmeyer

have little national feeling. Most of the population lives in the Andean highlands. There is a large group of persons of mixed Indian and Spanish descent, known as mestizos. People of unmixed European ancestry are comparatively few. Negroes and mulattoes live on the Pacific coast. The country's official language is Spanish. Roman Catholicism is the main religion. Of the few people who live in the eastern forests, the most interesting are the Jívaro Indians, who shrink the heads of slain enemies.

Sections of the region that is now Ecuador were part of the great Inca Empire at the time of the Spanish conquest in the 16th century. Quito was taken in 1534. The region became part of the Viceroyalty of Peru and later of the Viceroyalty of New Granada. The movement for independence from Spain, which began in 1809, was successful in 1822. For a time Ecuador, with Colombia and Venezuela, formed a union known as the republic of Greater Colombia. Ecuador and Venezuela left the union in 1830 and became separate republics. The history of independent Ecuador has been marked by dictatorship and revolt. For detailed map, see PERU.

ECUADOR

Area: More than 100,000 sq. mi.
Population: 4,000,000
Capital: Quito
Largest cities: Guayaquil, Quito, Cuenca
Highest mountain peak: Chimborazo (more than 20,500 feet)
Chief rivers: Guayas, Esmeraldas
Climate: Cool in highlands, hot in lowlands—little change throughout the year—seasonal rainfall—heavy year-round rain in east
National flag: Top half yellow, bottom half two horizontal stripes blue and red—coat of arms in center
National anthem: *Salve! oh patria!* (Hail! Oh, Fatherland!)
Form of government: Republic
Unit of currency: Sucre
Languages: Spanish, Quechua
Chief religion: Roman Catholic
Chief economic activity: Agriculture
Chief crops: Bananas, cacao, coffee, rice, sugarcane, cotton, wheat, corn, barley, fruits, potatoes
Chief minerals: Petroleum, gold
Chief exports: Bananas, cacao, coffee
Chief imports: Machinery and vehicles, minerals, glassware, pottery, metal and nonmetal manufactures, textiles, wheat and other foodstuffs, chemicals

EDERLE, GERTRUDE CAROLINE
(1908-   ), U.S. champion swimmer, was born in New York. At the age of 14 she held the American long-distance swimming championship for women as well as the record for 150 yards.

She dreamed she would one day swim the English Channel, and she was the first woman to do so when, on Aug. 6, 1926, she swam from Cape Gris-Nez in France to the English coast at Dover in 14 hours and 31 minutes. There had been only five previous channel swimmers, all men, but her time broke the record by more than two hours. Not until almost 25 years later did another woman swim the Channel in a shorter time. (In 1950 Florence Chadwick swam it in 13 hours and 20 minutes.)

EDINBURGH,
the capital of Scotland and one of the finest, as well as most ancient, cities in Great Britain. It lies on a series of hills on the southern shore of the Firth of Forth, surrounded on all sides by lofty hills except on the north, where the ground slopes gently toward the Firth of Forth. The New Town, on rising ground in the north, consists of wide streets, squares, and gardens. The houses, all built of a beautiful white stone found in the neighborhood, are comparatively modern and remarkably handsome. In the Old Town the most famous public building is the castle, which is on top of a high, steep hill.

Holyrood Palace stands on a lower street leading to the castle. No part of the present palace is older than the time of James IV (1500), while the greater part of it dates only from the reign of Charles II (late 17th century). Next to the palace are the ruins of the church belonging to the Abbey of Holyrood (founded in 1128 by David I). Edinburgh has a large number of important cultural institutions, among which are the Royal Institution, the National Gallery of Scotland, the Royal Scottish Museum, the Episcopal Cathedral of St. Mary, and St. Giles Church. The city is a leading educational center; the University of Edinburgh is world-famous for its college of medicine.

The chief industries of Edinburgh are printing, bookbinding, tanning, brewing, whisky distilling, and the manufacture of machinery and paper.

Edinburgh grew from a military post established by King Edwin of Northumbria in the 7th century. The castle was built in the 12th century. In 1437 Edinburgh replaced Perth as the capital of Scotland, and thereafter its size and importance increased.

EDISON, THOMAS ALVA
(1847-1931), an American inventor, was born in Milan, Ohio. He had little education, and when he was quite young, he became a newsboy on a railroad. Becoming interested in chemistry, he fitted up a small laboratory in one of the cars, where he tried experiments; but one day he nearly set fire to the train, and the conductor kicked out the whole apparatus. He then got some old type and printed a little newspaper of his own, which he sold on the trains. He then learned telegraphy from the telegraph operators along the line and got a position in a telegraph office. But he tried so many experiments and attempted so many things thought to be impossible that his employers were often impatient.

For five years he led a wandering life as a "tramp operator," often out of a job but working hard on his ideas for inventions. At 21 years of age he devised a "stock quotation" printing apparatus, and for this and other inventions useful in brokers' offices he got $40,000. With this money he started, in Newark, N.J., a laboratory and factory employing about 300 men, where he sometimes had as many as 50 inventions in various stages of development at one time. But before he was 30 years old, his health failed, and he gave up his factory for a laboratory at Menlo Park, N.J. In 1886 he built an immense plant at Orange, N.J.

One of Edison's first inventions was a method of sending several telegraphic messages over the same wire. In inventing the incandescent electric light, he is said to have given light to the world. He also made many improvements in the telephone. The invention in which he took the greatest pride, however, was the phonograph. He succeeded in 1913 in making "talking" motion pictures, but the invention was not perfected at that time. One of the most important of his inventions was a cheap storage battery for streetcars and automobiles.

When the 50th anniversary of his invention of the incandescent light was commemorated in 1929, many honors were accorded him.

Edison conducts the first successful incandescent lamp experiment (below). A replica of the lamp itself is shown at the left.
Gen. Elec. Co.

Smithsonian Institution

Thomas A. Edison, Inc.

Edison poses with his newly completed first phonograph (below).

Many editors are engaged in the preparation for publication of literature for young people. Editors of children's storybooks must know what children like to read about, be able to write simply enough for children to understand, and be able to select pictures that children will find interesting.

EDITOR, in the most general sense, anyone who prepares the manuscript of another for publication. His job is to revise, correct, and organize the parts of a printed work or to supply explanatory notes. An editor may also be the director of a newspaper, a magazine, or a book company. This kind of editor establishes policies, examines contributions, and supervises the departments under him. In a more specific sense an editor is one who manages a particular department in publishing: for example, the sports editor of a newspaper, the poetry editor of a magazine, or the science editor of a textbook company. A member of the regular staff of a newspaper who writes for the leader column or page is also called an editor. His article, or editorial, expresses the newspaper's official opinion.

Book editors not only correct manuscripts and suggest revisions, but they also interview writers to arrange for payment of royalties, date of publication, number of copies to be printed, and other matters of publication. Magazine editors formulate policies for writing and printing and purchase manuscripts

and supervise their editing. Periodically they also write editorials and special articles. The editorial staff of both the book company and the magazine is divided into different departments. Each of these departments is under the direction of a department editor.

On a newspaper the editor in chief directs the entire newspaper policy according to the wishes of the owner. He hires the various department heads within the newspaper and writes editorials. Under him is the managing editor, who coordinates and approves the copy of the writing departments. The managing ed-

---

OCCUPATION: Editor

NATURE OF WORK: Supervising all phases of publications for the owners

PERSONAL FACTORS—ABILITIES, SKILLS, APTITUDES. A good knowledge of English, a knack for writing concisely, an interest in people and their activities, accuracy, patience, integrity, and some business management are all essential.

EDUCATION AND SPECIAL TRAINING: Usually a college degree in journalism is desirable although not required. Additional courses that are helpful are commercial studies, art, and social science, or a particularly specialized field of study.

WORKING CONDITIONS:

1. **INCOME:**
   COMPARED WITH OTHER CAREERS WITH EQUAL TRAINING: Average
   COMPARED WITH MOST OTHER CAREERS: Average to low

2. **ENVIRONMENT:** Variable—a noisy newspaper office or a quiet editorial office; usually indoor work with regular hours

3. **OTHER:** Usual industrial benefits; good opportunities for qualified personnel

RELATED CAREERS: Freelance writer; copywriter

WHERE TO FIND MORE INFORMATION: National Editorial Association, 222 North Michigan Avenue, Chicago 1, Ill.

---

itor also writes and edits copy and examines the final makeup of news editions, changing them to meet emergencies. He meets periodically with the owner's representatives to discuss newspaper policies and contents. The editorial department heads are responsible for the copy written in each of their news areas. They also write copy themselves but do not contribute to the editorial page of the newspaper.

OCCUPATION: Editorial Assistant

NATURE OF WORK: Assisting in various phases of production of a publication

PERSONAL FACTORS—ABILITIES, SKILLS, APTITUDES: An interest in publishing and in written communication, accuracy, and a working knowledge of English are needed.

EDUCATION AND SPECIAL TRAINING: A bachelor's degree in liberal arts, with training in English and journalism, is desirable. On-the-job training in the mechanics of publishing and printing is usual, with manual office skills essential.

WORKING CONDITIONS:

1. **INCOME:**
   COMPARED WITH OTHER CAREERS WITH EQUAL TRAINING: Average
   COMPARED WITH MOST OTHER CAREERS: Low to average

2. **ENVIRONMENT:** Indoor work in publishing-house office; quiet research or more active production

3. **OTHER:** Jack-of-all-trades; regular hours with usual benefits; good opportunities for qualified personnel

RELATED CAREERS: Copy editor, proofreader

WHERE TO FIND MORE INFORMATION: National Editorial Association, 222 North Michigan Avenue, Chicago 1, Ill.

Newspapers employ large staffs of editorial writers. Each editor specializes in a particular field: politics, sports, science, dramatic criticism, and so on.
Milwaukee Journal Photo

Children are learning to read at an outside school in India. In primary schools the aim is to provide general education through the three R's, geography, and hygiene.

Public education was discussed in theory by Aristotle, but it did not become a reality for 2,000 years—until after the French Revolution.

Johann Pestalozzi (1746-1827) was a Swiss who introduced new methods in education.

EDUCATION, the development of faculties by teaching, has always existed among men. Education of a sort even exists among animals. Mother cats, for example, educate their kittens in the ways of the household. The first examples of formal education are found in ancient Egypt, where the main subjects were writing, ethics, philosophy, etiquette, and gymnastics. On the other side of the world schools were established in China by the 23d century B.C. After the time of Confucius education consisted of memorizing and imitating sacred writings. The purpose of education was to train men for public office.

The modern idea of educating the individual developed in ancient Greece. The subjects taught in Athenian schools included poetry, music, reading, writing, drama, history, oratory, science, and gymnastics. The Athenian schoolboy started off to school early in the morning. Behind him walked an attendant carrying a lyre and writing tablets containing accounts of the adventures of the Greek heroes. In the morning the schoolboy worked hard at his books and exercised by hurling the javelin, and at noon he attended a class in wrestling. In the afternoon, following a bath and a meal, the boy returned to school to study the ancient heroes and their ideas on justice, truth, and beauty. When school was over, the young Athenian was ready to dine and to go to bed. He never had any weekends, for the weekend had not yet been invented. The school closed its doors only on feast days. When he was 16 years old, the schoolboy entered a state institution, where he practiced gymnastics and sharpened his mind in discussions with adults. The Greek ideal in education was "a sound mind in a sound body."

The Romans borrowed their ideas on education from the Greeks, but they tied education more closely to everyday affairs. Roman schoolboys entered a school of rhetoric (public speaking) when they were 15 years old. Public speaking was valuable in a society that had no newspapers.

In the early Middle Ages the best schools were those established by the monasteries. Teaching was concentrated at first on ethics and discipline, for the barbarian peoples who had conquered Rome were still uncivilized. But by the 12th century great universities, such as that at Paris, had been founded. Education was based on the thinking of men like Thomas Aquinas and Peter Abelard. The universities brought together boys of 14 to men of 40 years of age from all over Europe. They supported themselves by begging or by working at odd jobs. If a student was lucky, he might be given food from a professor's table or even some hand-me-down clothes. The subjects taught were theology, medicine, law, and the arts. Schools were also established by institutions to aid the poor and by guilds, but in these only practical, everyday knowledge was taught.

As a result of the Renaissance, education became more and more a state interest. The first state schools developed in Prussia at the end of the 18th century. The first public high school in the United States was established at Boston in 1821. In the United States one of education's purposes was the teaching of democracy. These new state schools were also influenced by the Industrial Revolution. To subjects like mathematics, natural science, literature and languages, social science, and history were added agriculture, commerce, and technical subjects.

Although modern education is based on that of the 17th, 18th, and 19th centuries, it is presented to students differently. Education in those centuries meant monotonous memorizing. Discipline was extremely strict. An engraving of a late 18th-century German school shows a cheerless school in which two children are standing with their legs clamped together, two are being switched, and two others are wearing dunce caps. The engraving suggests that no one seemed to learn much by this procedure. A German schoolmaster of the period listed "1,115,800 raps on the head" administered by him in his years of teaching. This system of education was changed by people like Johann Pestalozzi; Friedrich Froebel, who founded the first kindergarten; Maria Montessori; and John Dewey, the American philosopher. Not all the suggestions of these reformers were practical, but the general direction of their ideas was correct because they had a great liking for their students. See EXAMINATION; SCHOLARSHIP; SCHOOL; UNIVERSITY AND COLLEGE.

EEC. See EUROPEAN ECONOMIC COMMUNITY.

EEL. The common American eel is a long-bodied, slippery, snakelike fish found in rivers that empty into the Atlantic Ocean and the Gulf of Mexico. The eel has a pointed head and tail; it has long dorsal and anal fins but no pelvic fins. The color is olive and olive brown. The scales are deeply embedded in the skin. Eels are said to eat anything, living or dead, including small fish. They grow slowly and reach sexual maturity at ages ranging from 8 to 15 years. The females mature at a size of 2 to 3½ feet and the males at 1 to 1½ feet. The eel is a popular food fish in Europe but not in America.

All eels, including those living hundreds of miles inland, go out to sea to spawn. After spawning, they die. By towing fine-mesh nets back and forth in many parts of the Atlantic Ocean Johannes Schmidt, a Danish scientist, showed that the smallest baby eels were found in the Sargasso Sea southeast of Bermuda, and he concluded that this region was the principal spawning ground. The young eel in its larval stage is called a leptocephalus. It is very thin from side to side and is transparent. It changes into the eel shape at about 2½ inches while still in the ocean. It reaches the mouth of a fresh-water stream when about a year old, then moves up the stream, where it remains until mature.

Other species of eels, related to the American and European eels, live only in salt water. The conger eel, found on both sides of the Atlantic Ocean, reaches a length of 5 or 6 feet.

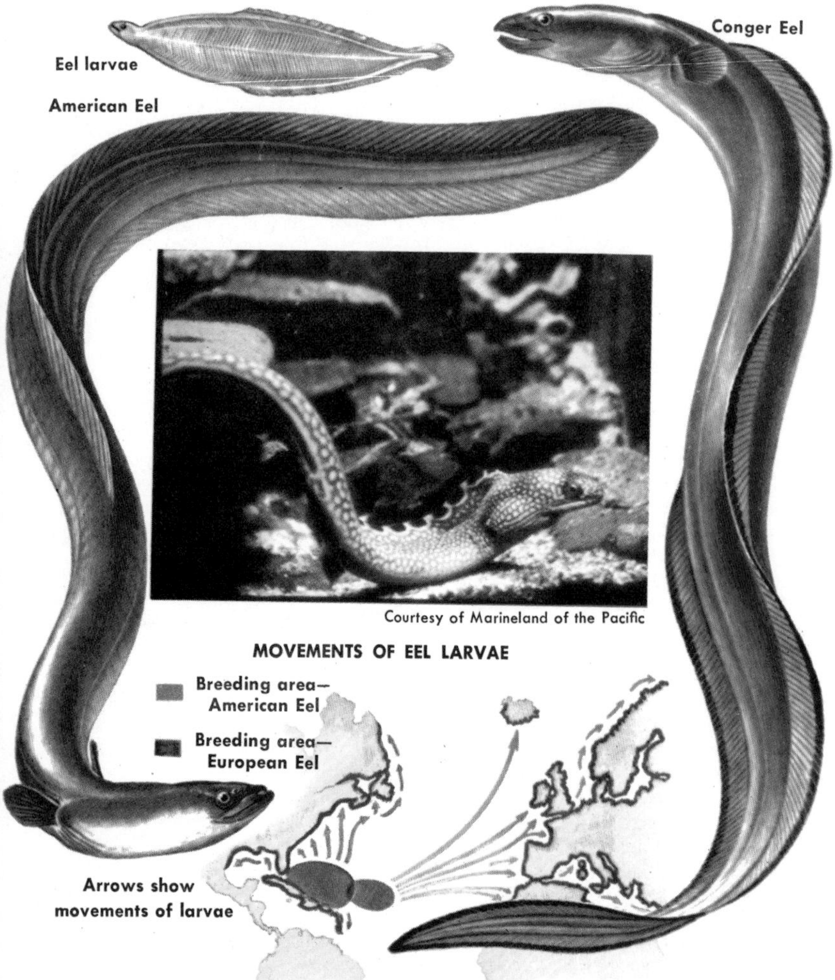

EGG. Eggs are laid by birds, most reptiles, amphibians, fishes, snails, insects, and many other invertebrates. Two primitive mammals, the

Bluebird Hummingbird House Wren Meadowlark Robin Barn Swallow Blue Jay Sparrow Hawk

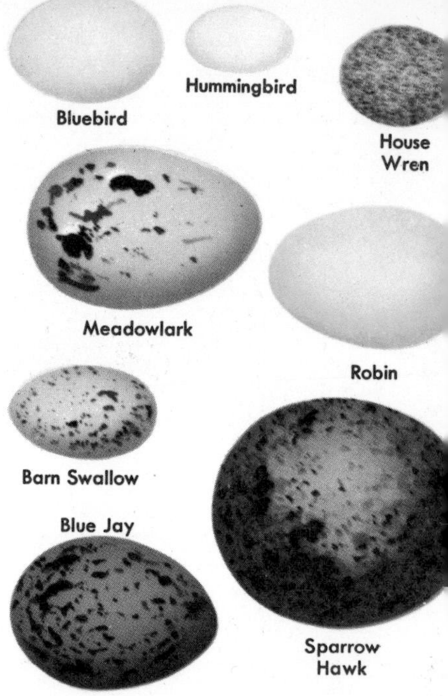

The colored eggs of birds are enclosed in a thin, brittle, limy shell. In most species of birds one or both parents sit on the eggs to warm them so that the embryos can grow.

The moray eel (center) has strong jaws and sharp teeth for seizing small fish. Moray eels usually inhabit the vicinity of coral reefs in tropical seas. The map shows the breeding areas of American and European eels in the western Atlantic. After the larval eels have hatched, they swim across the ocean to North America or Europe and then swim up streams.

Eel larvae
American Eel
Conger Eel

Courtesy of Marineland of the Pacific

MOVEMENTS OF EEL LARVAE

Breeding area— American Eel
Breeding area— European Eel
Arrows show movements of larvae

duck-billed platypus and the spiny anteater, or echidna, also lay eggs. A bird's egg is covered with a thin, lime shell. Inside of this is the white, which encloses the yolk. The yolk and the white furnish food and water for the embryonic bird while it is in the shell. An empty space in the larger end of the shell contains air for the bird. See EGG CELL.

The eggs of reptiles are usually rather large and are covered with a thick, tough, parchment-like shell. Within the shell is a membrane called the amnion; it encloses the yolk and the white. The eggs are laid in warm, sandy places, in dunghills, or on heaps of vegetable matter and are left to be hatched by the heat of the sun or the warmth from decay.

The eggs of fish are contained in little sacs called the roe, or spawn, which sometimes contain thousands or even millions of eggs. The spawn is sometimes laid on seaweed or on beds of sand or gravel that are near the seashore.

The eggs of insects are of different shapes and are generally white, yellow, or green. They are almost always laid near or on the objects on which the young will feed when hatched. Thus the fleshfly lays its eggs in meat; the cheese fly, in cheese; and the tumblebug, in a ball of dung, which it rolls away into a safe place. The mosquito lays its eggs in a floating, boat-shaped mass on the surface of quiet pools.

EGG CELL. Many animals begin life from an egg cell. We know that birds hatch from eggs; mammals, even human beings, also come from eggs. However, mammalian eggs are different from hens' eggs. The female mammal does not lay her eggs for later hatching. They remain in her body, where the embryonic mammals are nourished and grow until they are mature enough to be born.

Biologists apply the term "egg cell" to a tiny cell that forms within the ovary of female mammals, birds, reptiles, and other animals. Another biological term for the egg cell is *ovum*. In birds the egg leaves the ovary and enters the egg tube, where a large ring of yolk is formed around it. The yolk will later serve as food for the embryonic bird while it is growing within the egg. Since the mammalian egg has scarcely any yolk because of its extremely small size, the developing mammalian embryo must obtain food from its mother's bloodstream through a tube called the umbilical cord.

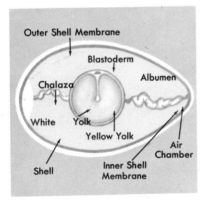

The egg cell of a bird consists of only the blastoderm and the yolk. The other parts of the egg are added after the egg cell leaves the ovary. The living portion, the blastoderm, a small disk on the surface of the yolk, grows through cell division. The yolk nourishes the developing embryo, while the albumen serves to suspend the egg cell and to give the embryo a watery environment.

When the egg has matured, it is discharged from the ovary and is moved down a tube called the oviduct. Certain glands in the oviducts of birds and reptiles secrete egg white, which surrounds the yolk and which later also serves as food for the growing embryo within the egg. Other glands in the oviduct secrete material for the shells that enclose bird and reptile eggs.

The egg cells of most female animals must be fertilized, or united with a sperm cell from the male parent, before they will develop into an embryo. After fertilization the eggs of birds and of some reptiles remain in the oviduct for awhile before they are laid. Mammalians eggs, after fertilization, stay in the mother's body, where the embryo develops for a long time before being born.

Egg-laying animals may be classified according to how their eggs develop. Oviparous animals, such as birds, lay eggs that hatch outside the mother's body. Viviparous animals, such as mammals, bear living offspring that have developed inside the mother's body and have been nourished by her bloodstream. Ovoviviparous animals, such as reptiles, produce eggs that hatch within the mother's body but are not nourished by her bloodstream.

EGGPLANT, an annual plant bearing a fruit that is a large, oval, white or dark-purple berry, 6 to 10 inches long, used as a table vegetable. The plant is a branching herb, several feet high. The eggplant belongs to the nightshade family and is closely related to the potato plant. It is a native of India but is widely grown in warm countries. The white varieties find little favor with American housewives.

The eggplant may be broiled, boiled, escalloped, baked with highly seasoned stuffing, or sliced and fried. In Syria it is a common food and is served in many ways. It is said to be regarded as evidence of a Syrian housewife's laziness or incapability if, during the eggplant season, she complains that she does not know what to have for dinner.

Varieties of eggplant have been developed that can be grown where the climate is comparatively cool and the growing season is short. Eggplants are attacked by a number of plant diseases and insect enemies.

The eggplant is probably so named because it is shaped somewhat like an egg. Most eggplants are dark purple, but some are white, yellow, or striped. The eggplant belongs to the same genus as the Irish potato plant and the deadly nightshade.

EGG PRODUCTS, as distinguished from fresh eggs in shells, are dried whole eggs, dried yolks, dried albumen, frozen whole eggs, frozen yolks, frozen albumen, and cold-storage eggs in shells. Of the 55 billion eggs a year produced in the United States about 44 billion go directly to consumers' kitchens. The other 11 billion go into egg products.

The egg-products industry arises from the seasonal nature of egg production and from the needs of food and candy manufacturers. Egg production is generally so heavy in March, April, and May that the market cannot absorb the output at profitable prices. The surplus goes into egg products, which are generally consumed before the end of the following winter.

During the spring months about one-eighth of the eggs go into cold storage. Supplies in the fall and early winter are usually short. Therefore, many spring-laid eggs are stored for fall and winter use. They are held at 30° F. and 85 percent relative humidity. To further reduce quality losses in storage, carbon dioxide or other gases such as phenol derivatives and ozone, are added to the holding room. Storage eggs are also treated with an odorless, colorless, tasteless oil, such as mineral oil, prior to storage to help preserve their original quality.

Eggs quick frozen at −40° F. are increasing in popularity among cake and candy manufacturers. The frozen eggs (in the form of yolk, albumen, or whole) are convenient and are stable over long periods; they may even be frozen twice. Frozen eggs come in 10-pound and 30-pound cans. Ice-cream and mayonnaise manufacturers use the frozen yolks, and candy manufacturers use the whites.

Eggs are dried by spraying under 3,500 pounds per square inch into an airblast of 320° F. About 98 percent of the water is removed. Dried eggs do not keep as well as frozen eggs. Dried eggs, however, are still popular in the food industries; in the production of soap, photographic supplies, glue, and artists' paints; and in food for turtles, birds, and goldfish.

Speed in handling and strict sanitary precautions are essential in the preparation of liquid egg to be frozen or dried.

EGRET. See HERONS, EGRETS, BITTERNS.

EGYPT. See UNITED ARAB REPUBLIC.

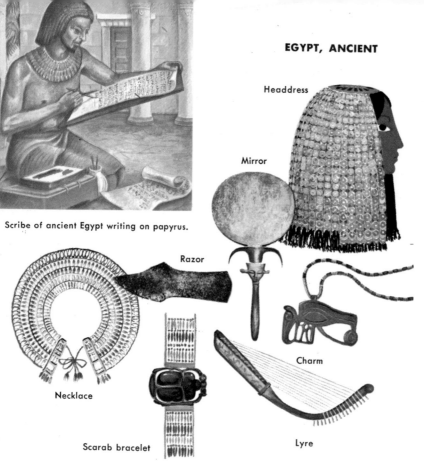

Scribe of ancient Egypt writing on papyrus.

Headdress

Mirror

Razor

Necklace

Scarab bracelet

Charm

Lyre

Memphis

Thebes

Abu Simel

Pyramids and temple cities of Egypt (above), which line the Nile River, honor various kings and Egypt's animal-headed gods. The ornaments (left) are from the New Egyptian Empire. The Egyptians were noted for their beautiful work in gold and enamel.

EGYPT, ANCIENT. This was once the most powerful kingdom in the world. In many parts are still to be seen wonderful ruins of temples and other great buildings, which show that the country was rich and far advanced in the arts at an early period.

When the migrations of peoples into the Nile Valley began is not known, but it is probable that the first settlers were Hamites from eastern Africa. The ancient Egyptian civilization developed at the same time as the civilizations in the

The Temple of Ammon at Karnak is one of the world's most imposing religious monuments.

Sabena-Belgian World Airways

Tigris and Euphrates valleys of Mesopotamia. By the dawn of recorded history the Nile Valley had been organized into the kingdom of Upper Egypt; and the Nile delta, the kingdom of Lower Egypt. The latter kingdom adopted the 365-day calendar about 3,000 B.C. and thus gave the world the first definitely established date in recorded history. The two kingdoms were ultimately united, and the history of Egypt as a nation began.

The history of ancient Egypt is revealed by archaeological remains, since the Egyptians left no recorded and chronological history as such. The Nile Valley is a great museum of temples and tombs that the ancient Egyptians built and the dry climate preserved. Historic records consist of hieroglyphics carved upon these temples and tombs. Hieroglyphics show evidence of the ancient Egyptian language, which was predominant in the Mediterranean Basin between 2000 B.C. and 500 B.C. Now a dead language, Egyptian is closely related to a group of living languages in North Africa called Berber and to the Cushitic and Chad languages of Africa. Scholars believe that Coptic, now a liturgical language is derived from ancient Egyptian.

This history of Egypt is traditionally divided into the periods covered by 26 ruling dynasties of Pharaohs. Internally, ancient Egypt had a relatively peaceful history, although there were periods of chaos caused by conflict among the Pharaoh, the nobles, and the priests. Externally, Egypt was always under the threat of invasion from the Nubians of the south, the Libyans of the west, and the Asiatics of the east. Although not warlike by nature, the ancient Egyptians had to carry on frequent wars.

About 1680 B.C. Egypt was conquered by the Semitic Hyksos. The Hyksos were expelled, but their period of rule had brought about some fundamental changes in Egyptian life by the introduction of improved irrigation implements and the horse and the camel.

Persia ended the independence of Egypt by an invasion in 525 B.C. Alexander the Great invaded Egypt in 332 B.C., and upon his death in 323 B.C. Egypt became a Hellenistic kingdom ruled by the Ptolemaic Dynasty. Cleopatra VII, the last ruler, committed suicide after failing to consolidate her power, and Egypt became a Roman province in 30 B.C. In the 7th century it came under the rule of the Arabs.

EGYPTIAN ARCHITECTURE. In ancient Egypt pyramids and temples were dedicated to a Pharaoh or a particular god. A religion dominated by the ritual of the dead naturally found expression in the building of mausoleums. Ancient Egypt, during a period known as the Old Kingdom, was ruled by the Pharaohs, kings regarded as immortal. Before the Pharaoh's death a vast tomb was built to house his body and soul, as well as equipment for his future life. The form for this tomb, or pyramid, developed gradually through a piling up of low, flat structures known as mastabas. After the steps formed by the layers of mastabas had been filled in and the apex placed over the top, the pyramidal form was perfected.

The pyramid contained an underground burial chamber; this and the galleries around it were faced in stone. Low reliefs cut in the stone showed scenes of Egyptian life—in agriculture, the arts, and industry, at the hunt, during banquets—all intended as offerings to the Pharaoh in his new life.

The pyramid had a chapel used for performing rites to the deceased and for storing his food and ceremonial vessels. A nearby temple of smaller size served as an elaborate entrance to the tomb.

In the Middle Period and Empire of Egypt the emphasis in religion shifted from the divine Pharaoh to the god Osiris. Temples rather than

An ancient Egyptian wall painting inside a pyramid shows workers pulling heavy stone blocks to be used for a pyramid. The Egyptians used thousands of workers to move tremendous weights. The enormous blocks were dragged up long earthen ramps and pushed into place by armies of workers.

tombs were the principal monuments. They were built in cliffs along the east riverbank of the Nile, separate from the tombs of the Pharaohs. In dedicating these temples to the gods, Egyptian kings provided themselves with a place for worshiping a patron deity during their lives and also assured themselves of a mortuary chapel after death. The basic design of these sumptuous temples was rectangular. The façade, or pylon, at the entrance had a huge doorway that opened into a roofless court surrounded by a colonnade. Here the people gathered for worship. Beyond this court was a roofed hall, or hypostyle, which led to a dark and secluded inner sanctum. Only the priests and Pharaoh were admitted here.

Approaching the temple was an avenue with a row of stone animals on each side. Beyond these figures were two high obelisks, and in front of these, just before the pylon, stood two colossal statues of the Pharaoh. Inside the temple, on the walls and columns, were decorative stone reliefs similar to those of the pyramids of the Old Kingdom.

EHRLICH, PAUL (1854-1915), a German scientist, first showed that a chemical could be made that would be a specific cure for a specific infectious disease. This was the beginning of chemotherapy.

Ehrlich was born in Silesia. Although he was educated to become a doctor, he was also interested in research, particularly in research in chemistry. By combining these interests he made a number of important discoveries. The most famous was his discovery of arsphenamine as a specific remedy for syphilis. He also proposed a theory, called the side-chain theory, that explained the mechanism of immunization. For this work he was given the Nobel prize in medicine in 1908.

The famous Great Sphinx, with its pyramid on the left, was built in ancient Egypt nearly 5,000 years ago. It signified the omnipotence of the Pharaoh, whom it represented. The Sphinx, with its lion's body and man's head, is about 75 feet high and over 160 feet long.

Courtesy of TWA—Trans World Airlines

Thomas E. Bachorz

The Eiffel Tower is in the Champs de Mars.

EIFFEL TOWER, the famous steel structure in Paris, designed by the French engineer Gustave Eiffel. The tower was erected for the Paris Exposition of 1889. Though not as tall as the Empire State Building in New York, it reaches to a height of nearly 1,000 feet. From the corners of its base rise four curving supports of open, interlaced ironwork that unite in a single shaft much farther up. At the top of the tower are a huge clock and thermometer; these are lighted at night.

The cost of the Eiffel Tower was more than $1,000,000, most of which was paid by the builders themselves. Granted a 20-year lease to the tower, Eiffel and Company made up its investment during the first year of operation. Millions of persons have ascended the Eiffel Tower since it was built. It affords a view of more than 50 miles.

EINSTEIN, ALBERT (1879-1955), a famous mathematician and physicist who developed the theory of relativity. (See RELATIVITY, THEORY OF.) Born in southern Germany at Ulm, he was the son of a fairly wealthy engineer and businessman. When the family business failed, the Einsteins moved to Milan, Italy, but left young Albert behind in school at Munich, Germany. He purposely did poorly in his examinations and thus managed to get permission to rejoin his family in Milan.

For six months Einstein taught himself calculus and higher mathematics. Then he was admitted to the Polytechnic Academy in Zurich,

Switzerland, where he studied mathematics and physics. In 1902, while working toward his doctorate at the University of Zurich, he began work on a series of five papers. Published in 1905, when Einstein was only 26 years old, these papers were destined to revolutionize physics and to make Einstein world renowned. The first of the papers proposed his now famous special theory of relativity. Another, describing his work on the photoelectric effect, provided a proof for Max Planck's quantum theory. (See QUANTUM THEORY.) For his work described in this paper Einstein was to win the 1921 Nobel prize in physics.

At 30 years of age he became a professor of physics at the University of Zurich and within five years attained the position of director of the Kaiser Wilhelm Institute of Physics in Berlin. In 1916 he published the general theory of relativity. In 1933 the Nazis forced him to leave Germany. He came to the United States and was appointed to the Institute for Advanced Study at Princeton University. In 1940 he became a U.S. citizen. Einstein announced his unified-field theory in 1953 and renounced the quantum theory, which was still held by most physicists.

In 1939 he wrote an important letter to President Franklin D. Roosevelt pointing out the possibilities of atomic warfare. Although the successful explosion of the atomic bomb was a spectacular verification of his theories of relativity, Einstein claimed that his role in the release of atomic energy was only indirect.

He was a philosopher as well as a scientist, and he devoted himself to many humanitarian causes. He was dedicated to achieving peace through world government.

Albert Einstein

EISENHOWER, DWIGHT DAVID (1890-   ), American general and 34th president of the United States, was born Oct. 14, 1890, at Denison, Tex., and spent his boyhood years in Abilene, Kan. A West Point graduate in 1915, he was a tactical instructor during World War I. In World War II Eisenhower was placed in charge of the European theater of operations in 1942, and as such he commanded the surprise invasion of French North Africa in November, 1942. In June, 1944, his forces successfully invaded Normandy in France. Eisenhower was promoted to the rank of general of the army in December, 1944.

Eisenhower returned to the United States in 1945 to serve as chief of staff through 1948. Then he became president of Columbia University but in 1950 took a leave of

Dwight David Eisenhower

absence to become chief of the integrated forces of the North Atlantic Treaty Organization. He was mentioned as a possible presidential candidate in 1948. He was elected president in 1952.

After his inauguration Eisenhower embarked on a middle-of-the-road policy. It was designed to be friendly to business, to quiet Cold War fears, and to reduce taxes and spending while maintaining a powerful defense force.

One of Eisenhower's biggest problems was how to conduct an efficient loyalty and security program, designed to rid the government of employees who might give state secrets to foreign powers, without violating civil rights.

During President Eisenhower's first term the fighting in Korea ended; the Supreme Court declared segregation in the public schools to be unconstitutional; and the SEATO

(Southeast Asia Treaty Organization) pact was signed. Friction between the U.S.S.R. and the Western powers over the unification of Germany and over disarmament and the tension generated by the Cold War resulted in a summit conference in 1955 at Geneva, Switzerland, which President Eisenhower attended.

The President's health became a major campaign issue after a heart attack in 1955 and an ileitis operation in 1956. He recovered quickly both times and was reelected by a large majority in 1956.

He was immediately beset by numerous international problems. Among these were the Soviet suppression of the Hungarian revolt and the invasion of Egypt by Israel, Great Britain, and France. U.S. opposition to the latter action resulted in temporary strain on U.S. relations with those three countries, especially with Great Britain. The problems that caused the Geneva Conference in 1955 remained unsolved, and tension was further sharpened in 1958 by Soviet demands for the immediate end of foreign occupation of Germany. Therefore the president invited Soviet premier Nikita Khrushchev to visit the United States and to confer with him. Khrushchev came in September, 1959, and for a while tension was much reduced. It increased sharply in May, 1960, when the Summit Conference at Paris collapsed owing to Khrushchev's demand that Eisenhower apologize for sending a U-2 spying plane over the U.S.S.R. The Soviets had shot down the plane earlier that month. President Eisenhower had already announced the suspension of such flights.

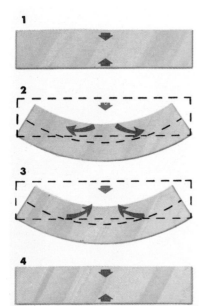

1

2

3

4

Elder leaves and berries are shown above.

Important domestic problems during Eisenhower's second and last term were the economic recession during 1957 and 1958, when unemployment increased sharply, and the selling of influence by a few important government employees, notably Sherman Adams, special assistant to the president.

ELASTICITY is that property of an object or substance that tends to return it to its original shape or condition when it has been deformed by an outside force or pressure. Chewing gum, putty, and lead have almost no elasticity. When they are pressed or are pulled out of shape, they do not return to their original forms. Air has great elasticity. If it is compressed and then allowed to return to its original pressure, it returns exactly to its original volume. According to Hooke's law, the extent of the deformation of an elastic body is proportional to the quantity of the deforming force up to a point. When the deforming stress (force per unit area of a cross section) exceeds a certain value, called the elastic limit, for a solid substance, the deformed body will no longer fully return to its original state when the external force is removed. Most solid substances are elastic; some others are plastic; others are brittle.

Most people consider rubber, such as a rubber band, to be highly elastic. When a rubber band is stretched and then released, it snaps back to its original form. Actually, because engineers consider elasticity in terms of the elastic limit of a substance, steel is far more elastic than rubber; its elasticity is demonstrated in the many steel springs in use.

Elasticity in a solid beam is produced by internal forces, or stresses. These forces, indicated by arrows, are in equilibrium when no external forces act on the beam. Force applied to the beam bends it, **2**, but equal and opposite forces act, **3**, to return the beam to a state of equilibrium, **4**.

ELDER, or elderberry, a common shrub bearing large, flat clusters of tiny cream-white flowers, which produce small purplish-black berries. It is usually 5 to 10 feet tall and grows in large, spreading clumps. The woody stems are light colored and are filled with soft white pith. The leaves are dark green and smooth on the upper side and light green and hairy on the underside. The flowers appear in June and July, and the berries ripen in August and September. The berries are edible and are used for pies, preserves, and jellies. The juice of the berries is a bright crimson.

There are several other species of elder, including the red-berried elder, which is shorter and more straggling in growth, and whose berries are not edible.

The elders belong to the honeysuckle family. The common tree known as the box elder is a member of the maple family and is not related to the elders.

ELEANOR OF AQUITAINE (about 1122-1204), also known as Eleanor of Guienne, was the queen of both France and England. She came into her inheritance upon the death of her father, William X, duke of Aquitaine, in 1137. That same year she married Louis of France, who later became Louis VII. Accustomed to the gay and luxurious life of Provence, she found the austere French court very little to her liking and spent much of her time in Aquitaine. The marriage was annulled in 1152 by mutual consent on the pretext that the couple was too closely related in blood.

A few months later Eleanor married Henry of Anjou, who soon after succeeded to the throne of England as Henry II. This marriage was purely political, and it set in motion a series of wars between France and England because it gave England a claim to part of Aquitaine.

Eleanor supported her two sons, Richard and John, in their revolt of 1173 against their father. During the last years of the reign she was kept in honorable captivity. She broke up a conspiracy between John and Philip II of France to seize Richard's throne and divide his lands while he was on the Third Crusade. She later reconciled the brothers and helped John succeed to the throne instead of her grandson Arthur of Brittany. Both in Aquitaine and in England Eleanor was a patron of learning, and literary men of the time were attracted to her court.

Democratic National Committee

On election day people express their preferences for candidates and political issues.

ELECTION CAMPAIGN

ELECTION CAMPAIGN includes all those things the candidate for public office does and all that others do for him in order to obtain the votes of the people. One of the most important parts of campaigning is speechmaking. Speeches either tell the voters what the candidate will do for them or attack rival candidates. Candidates and their supporters speak in auditoriums, over radio and television, at factory gates to workers, and on the city streets from sound trucks. However, candidates will often stand on the streets, introduce themselves to people, shake their hands, and kiss babies to win approval. Campaign posters are a vital part of election campaigns as are buttons bearing the candidate's name. Sometimes these buttons carry campaign slogans, as for instance the slogan "I Like Ike," which appeared on President Eisenhower's campaign buttons. The newspapers play an important part in an election campaign. If they approve of a candidate, they urge their readers to vote for him, keep his name in the news, and report his activities favorably. One of the basic activities of an election campaign is canvassing—visiting each house and apartment in a neighborhood to find out how many voters will vote for your candidate and trying to persuade undecided voters to vote for him.

Election campaigns in the past were far more colorful than they are now. They included parades, fireworks, and political songs. Debates between opposing candidates were more common than they are today; the Lincoln-Douglas debates were part of the 1858 senatorial campaign in Illinois.

Radio and television time, posters and buttons—all the elements of an election campaign—are very expensive. A presidential campaign usually costs millions of dollars. The political parties raise the money mainly from voluntary contributions. The parties also organize the campaigns.

ELECTORAL COLLEGE, in the United States, the body of men popularly elected in each state and the District of Columbia to cast the vote of the people for president and vice president. In over half of the states the presidential short ballot is used, and the names of the candidates for the electoral college are omitted. A vote for a presidential candidate automatically gives a vote to the electors in the state who will vote for that man. In other states the electors' names appear on the ballot, where they are voted for as a group or individually according to state law. Each party in each state holds a caucus or convention where it nominates the electors who will vote for the party's candidates. All 51 electoral colleges meet at the same time in their respective state capitals and separately ballot for the president and vice president. The colleges meet on the Monday after the second Wednesday in December in a presidential-election year.

ELECTRIC APPLIANCE, an apparatus that performs at least part of a task by using electricity. Most electrical appliances do work. Some appliances do work by means of moving parts; others provide heat. Some do both.

Most households have some electrical appliances. Some common ones are electric stoves, electric clocks, fans, toasters, mixers, shavers, vacuum cleaners, and water heaters.

All household appliances that provide heat work on the same principle. They contain a heating element. The element consists of strips or wires of metal that offer resistance to the flow of electric current. When current passes through the metal and meets with resistance, heat is generated.

An electric iron has a heating element inside near the soleplate the surface used for ironing. When the cord of the iron is connected to an electrical outlet, the heating element becomes hot, and heat is conducted throughout the soleplate. The temperature control of an automatic iron is provided by a thermostat. (See THERMOSTAT.) The upper part of the iron and the handle are kept cool by insulation between them and the heating element and the soleplate. Several types of irons are in use. The dry iron is the com-

Kitchen electrical appliances are generally divided into two groups: There are those that do some type of cooking by heat and those that perform work by chopping or mixing.

Courtesy of Hamilton Beach

Toaster

Fry Pan

Food Mixer

Food Converter

Can Opener

Blender

Saucepan

monest. Steam irons have internal chambers for heating water until steam is produced. The steam is emitted through openings in the soleplate. Lightweight irons with collapsible handles are called travel irons.

Another appliance that uses electric current to produce heat is the toaster. Most toasters are automatic and toast two slices of bread in one operation. Such a toaster has three heating elements and spaces between the elements for bread slices. The elements consist of wires wound about sheets of mica, which act as insulators. When current flows through the wires, heat is produced. The heat is radiated to the bread slices and toasts them. Automatic toasters have a thermostat to control the temperature and a timer to turn the current off at the proper moment. When the current is off, the bread pops up from the toaster.

Appliances that have moving parts to perform tasks contain electric motors. An electric motor converts electric power into mechanical power. A household electric fan is a good example of an appliance that has moving parts.

When the cord of a fan is connected to an electrical outlet, current flows to the motor. Certain motor parts rotate rapidly and turn a shaft. The fan blades are connected to the shaft, so they turn rapidly. The faces of the fan blades push air from them as they move. Soon a flow of air is set up.

ELECTRIC BELL AND BUZZER, devices that make noises by using electromagnets. Turning an electromagnet on and off causes a hammer to strike a bell or other object. At the same time, it is the movement of the hammer that causes the electromagnet to turn on and off. See ELECTROMAGNET.

Both bells and buzzers operate on the same principle. They differ only by having hammers that strike different objects. In an electric bell the hammer strikes a bell. In a buzzer the object struck may be anything hard that does not ring, but instead produces a rapid series of clicks or a buzzing sound.

An electric bell is one of the simplest of electric devices. When the button is pushed, the electromagnet attracts the armature and makes the hammer strike the bell. Meanwhile, the circuit is broken at the contact screw. A spring snaps armature and hammer back to their original position. The circuit is again completed at the contact screw, and the process repeats.

Electric bells and buzzers operate on 6 to 18 volts of either direct or alternating current. They may be powered by batteries or by current from an ordinary household lighting circuit. If the standard electric current is used, however, a transformer must first reduce the voltage from 110 volts to 6 to 18 volts. The small transformers used for this purpose are called bellringing transformers, or simply bellringers. See TRANSFORMER.

Because they are easily and inexpensively installed, electric bells and buzzers are widely used as signals. We are all familiar with them used as doorbells and school bells and in telephones, electric alarm clocks, and fire and burglary alarm systems.

ELECTRIC CELL. An electric cell is a device that changes chemical energy into electric energy. The necessary parts of an electric cell are a vessel to hold an electrolyte solution and electrodes, which usually react with the solution. These electrodes are connected with an external circuit.

There are two basic types of electric cells. A primary cell produces electrical energy from chemical energy. A secondary cell stores electrical energy as chemical energy. A storage battery is a secondary cell.

The first successful electric cell was built by an Italian physicist, Alessandro Volta, in 1800. His was the first cell to deliver a continuous current of electricity, and simple primary cells are called voltaic cells in his honor. See BATTERY; DRY CELL; STORAGE BATTERY.

ELECTRIC EEL. See ELECTRIC FISH.

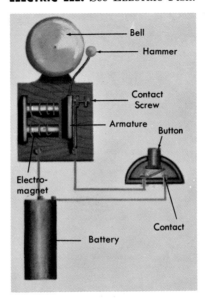

ELECTRIC EYE. Other names for an electric eye are phototube and photoelectric cell. An electric eye is sensitive to light—as an eye is sensitive—and sets up an electric current when light strikes it.

The electric eye may be a vacuum tube, a gas-filled tube, or a solid-state device. The important part of the tube is a light-sensitive plate. This plate is coated with a metal such as cesium or potassium. When such metals are hit by light, electrons are released by the energy carried by the light.

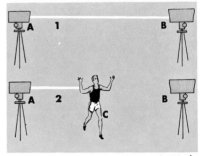

Electric eyes often operate an electrical device when the beam of light is broken.

In the electric eye, the light-sensitive part is the negative terminal, or cathode. In front of it is the positive terminal, or anode, such as a wire. An electric field in the photoelectric cell carries the released electrons from the cathode to the anode, and a photoelectric current is set up. The current varies with the amount of light the electric eye receives, and the current is maintained as long as the beam of light is unbroken. Because the current is weak, it has to be stepped up, or amplified.

There are a great many uses for the electric eye. A familiar one is the automatic door opener. In industry the interruption of the beam of light to an electric eye is all that is needed to control machines. The electric eye is also the basis of television, sound motion pictures, radio-photography, and computing machines. In addition to electric eyes that are sensitive to visible light, there are electric eyes that are sensitive to infrared light and ultraviolet light.

ELECTRIC FISH, fish equipped with electric organs that can give off electric shocks. Some of the best known electric fish are the torpedo, or electric ray, an ocean fish found all over the world; the electric catfish, found in the Nile and other fresh waters in Africa; and the electric eel, found in some of the fresh waters of Central America and

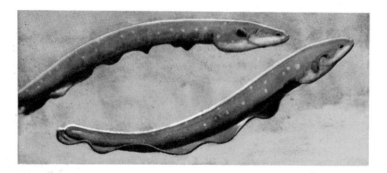

The shock of the electric eel is sometimes strong enough to stun a human being. With its electricity this eel stuns small fish so that it can eat them.

South America. The torpedo reaches a length of as much as 5 feet, the catfish 4 feet, the eel 6 feet.

The strongest electric currents measured from these fish are 550 volts for the eel, 350 for the catfish, and 220 for the torpedo. The strongest shocks are felt when contact with electric fish is made with the fish out of water.

Shocks are given off as needed for stunning small fish, which are then easily caught and eaten. They are also given off in defense, that is, for scaring off enemies. The strength of the current can be regulated so that the shock may be weak or strong. The shock received from the torpedo has been described as disagreeable, painful, and numbing; the shock from the electric eel, as vigorous, causing powerful muscular contractions; the shock from the catfish, as sharp and stinging but of short duration. The strongest shocks are considered somewhat dangerous.

The electric organs resemble a storage battery, both in their construction of tiny plates and in their tendency to "run down" if used too much over a short space of time. The plates that make up the electric organs are modified muscle cells. Each cell is supplied with blood vessels and nerves. It has been found that an electric eel is capable of giving off shocks of decreasing power for an hour; then it may require a two-hour rest before another strong shock can be given. The ability of electric fish to release powerful electric currents without injuring themselves, while stunning other fish, is not yet clearly understood.

ELECTRIC GENERATOR. Over a century ago Michael Faraday in London discovered that a magnetic field could be employed to generate electricity. Faraday arranged a copper disk so that it revolved between the poles of a large steel magnet, and from the disk he obtained an elec-

tric current. While Faraday's design was not practical, it was from his idea that the electric generator was developed.

The essential parts of a small electric generator are a field magnet, an armature, and sliprings and brushes. The field magnet is a permanent magnet. (In most power-producing generators it is an electromagnet.) The armature rotates between the poles of the magnet and produces a current that is carried off through the sliprings and brushes. Some source of mechanical power is needed to turn the armature; this power, for example, may be obtained from waterpower or steam.

The electric current obtained when sliprings are used on the armature is alternating current. To get direct current the sliprings are replaced with a device called a commutator. This is made of two half rings with a brush resting on each.

Actually, most electric power is

The rotation of an armature between the poles of a magnet is shown below. An alternating current, bottom, is formed when sliprings transfer the generated current.

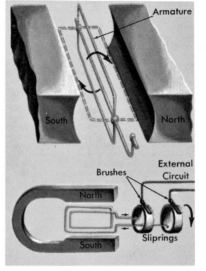

generated as alternating current and is transmitted in this form. When direct current is needed, it is produced by rectifiers or converters. An example of a direct-current generator is the automobile generator.

ELECTRIC HEATING is the production of heat in a body or at a particular spot by means of electrical resistance, electrical induction, or the electric arc. Resistance heating is used in domestic electric appliances. Inductance and arc heating are often used in industrial ovens, furnaces, and welders. See INDUCTANCE.

Resistance heating is used in such home appliances as electric stoves and ovens, toasters, clothes irons, electric blankets, and portable heaters. The amount of heat produced in resistance heating is proportional to the resistance of the wire or coil through which current is flowing and to the square of the current. If a current of I amperes flows through a wire with a resistance of R ohms for t seconds, the electrical energy converted into heat is I^2Rt watt-seconds.

In the metal industries the electric furnace is much used in the melting and alloying of metals. Electric furnaces may be either induction or arc furnaces. The induction furnace consists of a refractory crucible surrounded by coils for carrying current. High-frequency alternating current is used. Heat is produced in the metal in the crucible by eddy currents induced by the changing electric field of the coils. The molten metal is violently stirred by the eddy currents. The arc furnace has carbon or graphite electrodes that extend into the interior of the furnace. When current is applied, an electric arc that is immensely hot is formed between the electrodes. The metal in the furnace is rapidly melted.

An electric arc is used to produce heat in arc welding. See WELDING.

ELECTRICITY is one of the modern world's most important sources of energy. In addition to lighting homes, schools, offices, and factories and furnishing the power supply for home appliances from toasters to high-fidelity sets, electricity is used to run much of our industrial machinery. Our trains, airplanes, and automobiles could not operate without using electricity; nor without it would we have telephones, elevators, television, and many of the other conveniences and necessities of life in the United States today.

Armstrong Cork Co.

Above is a view of the electrical powerplant whose processes are shown at left. Coal in the hopper drops to a pulverizer, from which it is blown into the boiler. Water in tubes at the top becomes steam that turns the turbine-generators at the right. The steam, now condensed to water, returns through cylindrical heaters to the boilers.

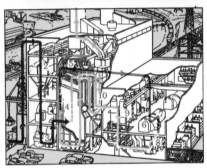

COAL   GASES   WATER   STEAM

Electric phenomena have been known to man since at least 600 B.C., when the Greek philosopher Thales observed that rubbing a piece of amber causes the amber to attract certain substances to its surface. In 1600 William Gilbert added several substances to the list of those that can be electrically charged. Kleist in 1745 devised the Leyden jar, the first known method of storing electrical charges. Benjamin Franklin introduced the terms *positive* and *negative* to electricity and in 1752 proved, in his famous kite experiment, that lightning and electricity are the same thing.

In 1800 Alessandro Volta announced his discovery that a continuous electric current may be produced by what he called an electric pile, the forerunner of the modern battery. Other important contributors to our knowledge of electricity were Charles de Coulomb, Luigi Galvani, H. C. Oersted, André Ampère, and Georg Ohm. In addition to his many important discoveries concerning the nature and behavior of electricity, Michael

Faraday in 1831 demonstrated the first electric generator. After Thomas Edison's invention of the incandescent light bulb in 1879 commercial production of electricity became profitable, and the first electric power stations were established. Since then innumerable discoveries and inventions have given electricity the position of great importance that it now occupies in every aspect of our lives.

Electricity cannot be seen or heard. It is invisible, and it has no weight. Scientists have yet to determine fully the nature of electricity. What is known or assumed about electricity is directly connected with scientists' theories about the fundamental nature of matter, or the atomic theory. See ATOM.

ELECTRIC CHARGES

One type of particle in an atom is the electron. Each electron in an atom has a very small mass ($\frac{1}{1,845}$ the mass of a hydrogen atom) and one negative electric charge. All electrons, no matter of what substance they are a part, are the same. All electrical phenomena are the result of the movement, gain, loss, or storage of electrons.

Under certain conditions an atom has just enough electrons to balance

its positive electrical charges. The positive and negative charges cancel each other in effect, and the total atom has no charge with respect to other atoms. However, ways have been found to remove electrons from, or add electrons to, atoms. When the effects of the positive and negative charges do not cancel each other because there are too many or too few electrons, the atom is electrically charged and is called an ion. An atom that has lost electrons is positively charged. It repels other positive ions, but it attracts negative ions. The negative ions have, of course, a surplus of electrons. Objects that are negatively charged have ions with a surplus of electrons. Positively charged objects have ions with a deficit of electrons.

Under certain conditions electrons transfer themselves from one substance to another and produce electrically charged objects. For example, when glass is rubbed with silk, some electrons transfer themselves from the glass to the silk. Because the glass now has a deficiency of electrons, it is said to have a positive charge. So long as the silk and the glass are not brought into contact with each other, they will retain their respective charges. However, if they are allowed to touch, the surplus of electrons on the silk will move to the glass and neutralize the charges on the two bodies.

An electrically charged body is surrounded by a field of force, called an electrostatic field. Any electric charge that enters the field of force is attracted or repelled.

Conductors and Insulators. In some substances the force holding some of the electrons to the atoms is not very large. Electrons can be easily dislodged from atoms to travel through the substance. Such substances are conductors. If an electric force is applied to a conductor, electrons migrate through the conductor.

Insulators are substances in which all the electrons are very strongly attached to atoms. Even a very strong electrical force cannot make an electron leave its atom and travel through the substance.

Metals are all good conductors as compared with other substances. Carbon, electrolytes (substances that transfer electric charges by the movement of ions), and gases under low pressure are also used as conductors. Conductors are a medium for the migration of electric charges. Electrical wires are conductors that electrons can travel in easily.

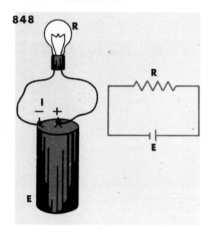

A simple electric circuit has one source and one load: E stands for potential, I, for current, and R, for resistance of the load.

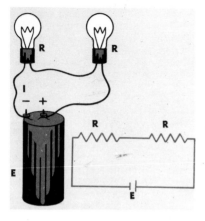

A circuit that is connected so that all of the current must flow through each of two loads is called a series circuit.

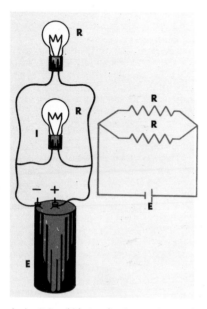

A circuit in which two loads are connected so that the current divides and flows part through each load is a parallel circuit.

Insulators are used to prevent electric charges from traveling to certain places. Usually, insulators are placed around conductors to keep charges from escaping to other conductors. Plastics, gases at ordinary pressures (such as air), ceramics, glass, mica, porcelain, rubber, and waxes all serve as effective insulators.

Electrostatic Induction. An uncharged conductor can be charged by placing it in a field of force of a charged body. Suppose there is a positively charged body and that an uncharged conductor is brought close to it but does not touch it. The uncharged conductor has an equal number of positive and negative charges. However, the negative charges of the conductor are attracted to the end of the conductor near the positively charged body. The end of the conductor away from the charged body now has a deficit of negative charges (electrons) and is positively charged. If the positive end of the conductor is connected by a wire to the earth, electrons will flow up the wire and neutralize the positive charges. The electrons at the other end of the conductor are held in place by the attraction of the positive body. If the wire is now taken away, the conductor has a total excess of electrons and is negatively charged. It has become charged by electrostatic induction.

Electric Condensers. A device for collecting negative and positive electric charges is a condenser. An example of a simple condenser is a Leyden jar. (See LEYDEN JAR.) It is a glass jar with metal coatings on part of the inside and part of the outside. If negative charges are conveyed to the coating inside the jar, the outer coating becomes positively charged by electrostatic induction. The outer coating of the jar touches a conductor so electrons can flow to the earth. The glass between the coatings keeps the opposite charges apart, but the force of attraction between the charges acts through the glass. Because the positive and negative charges are so close together, it is possible to concentrate a great many charges on each surface. The inner negatively charged surface is connected by a chain to a metal knob outside the jar. To discharge the condenser a conductor is put in contact with the outside coating and brought near the knob. An intense electrical discharge—a spark—takes place.

All condensers consist of two or more conductors with insulators between conductors. One of the con-

ductors is usually connected to the earth. Some condensers are metal plates with glass between the plates. Many condensers used in electrical equipment are a series of metal sheets separated by mica, paper, or air. All the sheets that are positively charged are connected to each other, and all the negatively charged sheets are connected. A variable condenser has many conductor plates that can be moved past each other. If small areas of positive and negative plates are near each other, the capacity of the capacitor to accumulate charges is small. If large areas of positive and negative plates are near each other, the capacity of the capacitor is increased. Capacitors are often called condensers.

MOVEMENT OF ELECTRIC CHARGES

Difference of Potential, or Voltage. Suppose there is a sphere with an excess of electrons so that it is negatively charged. If more electrons are to be brought to the sphere, work must be done to overcome the repulsion of the electrons and the sphere for each other. The greater the excess of electrons on the sphere, the more work is necessary to bring electrons to the sphere. If a sphere had a deficiency of electrons, work would have to be done to remove electrons from the sphere. If an electric charge is placed in the field of force near a charged body and is allowed to take the path it chooses, it performs work. Whenever work is required to move a charge from one body to another, or whenever work is done by a charge moving itself from one body to another, there is said to be a difference of potential between the two bodies. The work expended in moving the charge, or the work the charge does in moving, is a measure of this difference in potential, or voltage.

Electric Current. Electric currents are the result of moving electrons. Most electric currents are produced by streams of electrons moving through metal conductors. Electric current is usually measured in amperes. An ampere is a measure of the rate of flow of electrons. If a quantity of electrons called a coulomb flows past a certain place in a wire in 1 second, there is a current of 1 ampere.

In a metal wire there are a large number of electrons that can be easily made to move from one place to another. But to make the electrons move, there must be a difference in electrical pressure between the two ends of the wire. This differ-

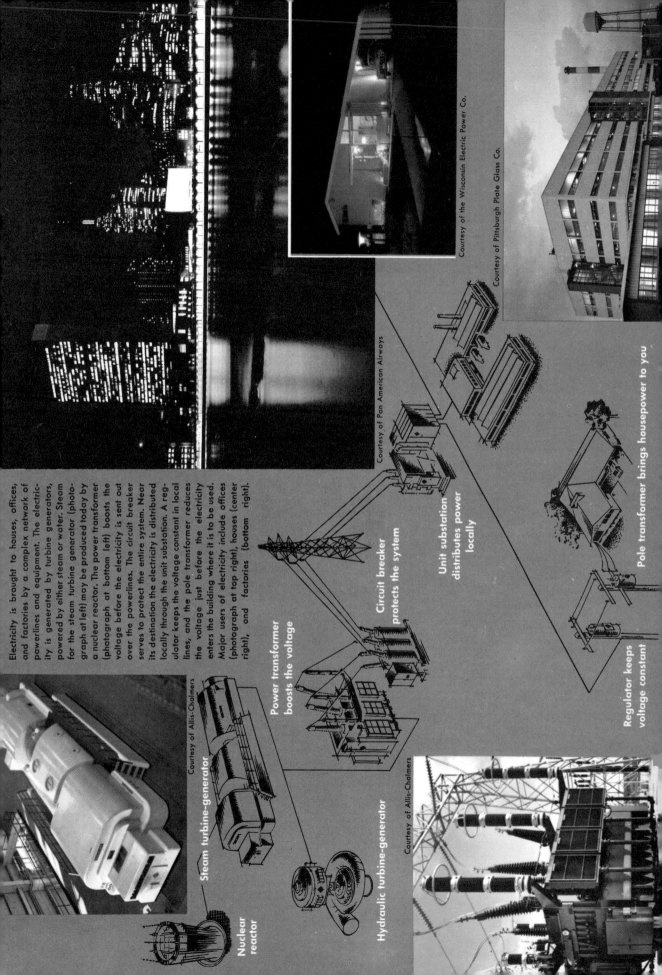

Electricity is brought to houses, offices, and factories by a complex network of powerlines and equipment. The electricity is generated by turbine generators, powered by either steam or water. Steam for the steam turbine generator (photograph at left) may be produced today by a nuclear reactor. The power transformer (photograph at bottom left) boosts the voltage before the electricity is sent out over the powerlines. The circuit breaker serves to protect the entire system. Near its destination the electricity is distributed locally through the unit substation. A regulator keeps the voltage constant in local lines, and the pole transformer reduces the voltage just before the electricity enters the building where it is to be used. Major users of electricity include offices (photograph at top right), houses (center right), and factories (bottom right).

Courtesy of the Wisconsin Electric Power Co.

Courtesy of Pittsburgh Plate Glass Co.

Courtesy of Pan American Airways

Courtesy of Allis-Chalmers

Courtesy of Allis-Chalmers

Steam turbine-generator

Nuclear reactor

Power transformer boosts the voltage

Hydraulic turbine-generator

Circuit breaker protects the system

Unit substation distributes power locally

Regulator keeps voltage constant

Pole transformer brings housepower to you

ence in electrical pressures is a difference in potential, or voltage. To have a difference in potential, one end of the wire must be more negative than the other end. Then electrons will flow from the more negative end, where there is an excess of electrons, to the more positive end, where there is a deficiency of electrons. Until quite recently it was the convention (set up before electrons were discovered) to say that an electric current traveled from the positive to the negative end of a wire. It really happens the other way.

Resistance and Ohm's Law. Electrical resistance is the property of a material that opposes the flow of an electric current. Resistance is measured in ohms, 1 ohm being equal to the amount of resistance through which 1 ampere of current will flow when the difference of potential is 1 volt.

The resistance of a conductor to current depends on the material, the length, and the cross-sectional area of the conductor. Some materials, insulators, have very high resistances. They have so much resistance that practically no current can flow through them. Among the conductors, some have more resistance than others. When a substance has little resistance, it has a high conductivity. The resistance of a conductor is proportional to its length. If one wire is twice as long as a second wire of the same material and cross-sectional area, the first wire will have twice as much resistance as the second wire. The resistance of a wire is inversely proportional to its cross-sectional area. Suppose two round wires of the same material and length have different cross-sectional areas. The wire with the greater area has the less resistance. The resistances of most substances increase as their temperatures increase. Carbon conductors and electrolytes are exceptions. They have less resistance as their temperatures increase.

Ohm's law states the relation between the amounts of current, voltage, and resistance in an electric circuit. The law states that the current in a circuit is equal to the potential difference of the circuit divided by the total resistance in the circuit. The current is measured in amperes, the potential difference in volts, and the resistance in ohms. Or

$$\text{current} = \frac{\text{voltage}}{\text{resistance}}$$

In electrical equipment of many kinds, devices called resistors are used. These are small units of known resistance. Resistors are introduced into an electric circuit so that with a set voltage a certain current may flow in the circuit.

Simple Electric Circuits. An electric circuit is a closed path for the flow of electrons. An electrical power source builds up a high pressure of free electrons at its negative terminal. In an electric circuit these electrons flow from the negative terminal, through an external conductor such as copper wire, to the positive terminal of the power source, where the pressure of electrons is low. The electrons then flow through the power source to the negative terminal and complete the electric circuit. The energy that builds up the pressure of electrons at the negative terminal may be chemical, as in a dry cell or a storage battery, or it may be mechanical, as in an electric generator.

When a resistance such as a light bulb or a toaster is connected as part of the external conducting path, it converts part of the energy of the electron flow into light or heat. See ELECTRIC WIRING.

PRACTICAL UNITS OF ELECTRICITY

The coulomb, the unit of quantity, is the basic practical unit of charge. One coulomb is the amount of electricity that will deposit 0.001118 grams of silver in 1 second. See ELECTROPLATING.

The ampere is the unit of current. One ampere equals the flow of 1 coulomb per second. It is the current produced by an electromotive force of 1 volt acting through a resistance of 1 ohm.

The ohm is the unit of resistance to electricity. The mercury ohm is defined as the resistance of a column of mercury 106.3 centimeters long and having a mass of 14.4521 grams and of constant cross section, measurements to be made at 0° C.

The volt is the unit of potential difference. One volt is the amount of potential difference that will make a current of 1 ampere flow against a resistance of 1 ohm.

The watt is the unit of power. One watt is the product of a current of 1 ampere at a potential difference of 1 volt.

The kilowatt-hour is the unit used in business to measure electrical energy. Since a kilowatt is 1,000 watts, a kilowatt-hour means the amount of energy delivered in one hour when the rate of using energy is 1,000 watts.

Various instruments are used to measure these units.

ELECTRIC LIGHT. The ordinary electric light bulb is an incandescent lamp. One standard incandescent lamp was invented by Thomas Edison in 1879. By this invention he is said to have given light to the world.

In the electric light bulb a fine wire with a high melting point is sealed in a glass bulb and is heated to a white heat by an electric current. So that the wire will not oxidize rapidly (burn up) when it gets this hot, electric light bulbs are usually filled with nitrogen and

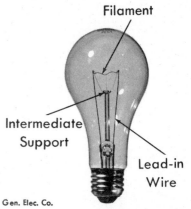

Gen. Elec. Co.

The lead-in wires in an electric-light bulb carry current to the tungsten filament. The filament is held in place by the intermediate support, which is made of glass.

argon; in other words, the oxygen that would support oxidation is eliminated. In the first electric light bulbs, a high vacuum was produced for the same purpose.

The filament in the electric light bulb is made of tungsten wire. The bulbs are classified on the basis of the power input required. Measured in watts, the standard sizes are 25, 30, 40, 60, 100, 200, 500, 750, and 1,000. The average life of a bulb is 1,000 hours or more.

ELECTRIC MOTOR. An electric motor converts electrical energy into mechanical energy. It is related to the electric generator, which converts mechanical energy into electrical energy. See ELECTRIC GENERATOR.

In principle, an electric motor is an electromagnet arranged to rotate between the poles of a magnetic field. The electromagnet rotates on its axis because its N and S poles are alternately attracted and repelled by the S and N poles of the magnetic field. Alternating current makes the electromagnet keep turning. It does so by changing the N pole of the electromagnet to an S pole and the S pole to an N pole

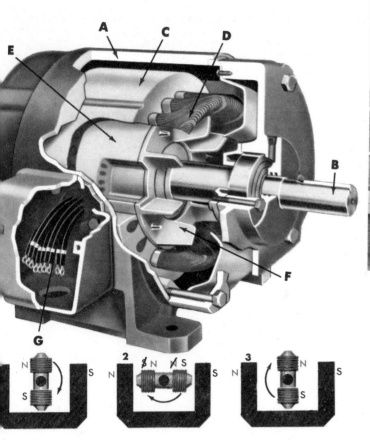

The electric motor shown in the cutaway drawing at above left is a three-phase squirrel-cage induction motor. Parts include motor frame, **A**; rotor shaft, **B**; epoxy-encapsulated stator, **C**; stator windings, **D**; rotor cage, **E**; fan, **F**; and leads to stator windings, **G**. A large motor of the same type is seen installed above. The drawings at left show how an electric motor works. **1.** Poles of a fixed magnetic field attract opposite poles of a pivoted electromagnet, making the electromagnet turn. **2.** Poles of the electromagnet are automatically reversed. **3.** The process repeats, so that the electromagnet rotates continuously.

many times per second, that is, it reverses the polarity of the electromagnet. The N and S poles of the magnetic field remain the same. As the N pole of the electromagnet becomes an S pole, it is repelled by the S pole of the magnetic field; at the same time, the S pole becomes an N pole and is repelled by the N pole of the magnetic field. The rotating electromagnet moves around until the new S pole comes opposite the N pole of the magnetic field. Then the current reverses again, the polarity changes, and the rotating electromagnet moves around once more. By attaching a belt to a shaft on the rotating electromagnet, we get mechanical energy that can be used to drive other machines.

Many common types of electric motors are operated by direct current, which is converted into alternating current within the motor by the action of the commutator.

Electric motors are the most compact sources of power anywhere available. They are used for almost every conceivable purpose in the manufacture of goods, in mining, in building, and elsewhere.

ELECTRIC POWER. The electric power in a circuit is the rate of supplying electric energy, or the rate of doing work. Electricity does work in a circuit whenever it lights a lamp, heats a stove, or turns a motor. Electric energy is thus transformed into other forms of energy, such as heat or motion.

The power, P, supplied to an electric circuit is the product of the potential difference of the whole circuit, E, times the current, I.

$$P = EI$$

The current is measured in amperes; the potential difference, in volts; and electric power, in watts.

1 watt = 1 ampere $\times$ 1 volt

The power available varies as either the voltage or the current is increased or decreased. A small current at a high voltage does not supply much power. A large current at a low voltage does not supply much power either.

Because all electric circuits offer some resistance, and electrical devices that convert electric energy to heat energy have a high resistance, it is often convenient to use the following relation in thinking about power. R, the resistance, is in ohms.

$$P = I^2R$$

Ohm's law states that the potential difference is 1 volt across a resistance of 1 ohm when the current is 1 ampere. Or, $E = IR$. If $E = IR$ and $P = EI$, then $P = EI = IRI = I^2R$.

When a flow of electricity encounters resistance in a conductor, some electrical energy is transformed to heat. Joule's law of heating states that the amount of energy transformed to heat is proportional to the resistance, the length of time of the flow, and the square of the current.

Large amounts of electricity are often sent through long-distance transmission lines from electric powerplants to cities. The energy losses from heating during transmission could be serious if the conducting wires carried large currents, because loss is proportional to the square of the current. However, since $P = EI$, the same amount of power can be transmitted by sending a small current at a high voltage. So all long-distance lines that transmit large amounts of energy do so at high voltages, usually around 100,000 volts. A transformer (or a series of transformers) at the powerplant increases the voltage and decreases the current that is supplied by the generators. Other transformers near cities decrease the voltage so that the electrical energy can be safely transmitted through heavily populated areas. Where the power lines enter houses or factories, transformers reduce the voltage to that for which electric motors and appliances are designed.

When a family pays the electric bill, they pay for the amount of electrical energy they have used. A

device to determine and record the energy used is the recording watt-meter, or the watt-hour meter. A recording wattmeter is connected to the wires that supply electricity from the main transmission lines. The current and voltage are continuously measured by the rate at which the armature turns in a little motor in the meter. The amount of electric energy used is recorded on dials on the meter.

ELECTRIC RAILROAD.

An electric railroad is composed of wires and rails arranged to form a complete electrical circuit. Electricity is sent through the circuit from a stationary power source. Locomotives and other vehicles that have electric motors supplied by the electricity in the circuit run on the tracks of an electric railroad.

Rail transportation powered by electricity has been and is used for many purposes. In the United States the majority of electric railroads are subways, elevated railroads, streetcar lines, and suburban train lines. Some medium-distance railroad lines in the eastern United States are electrified. A few sections of railroad through long tunnels and over steep mountains in the western United States have been electrified. Nearly all the railroads of Switzerland are electric. A large number of the railroads of Italy and Sweden are electric. Other countries that have many electric railroads are Great Britain, France, Germany, Norway, Spain, Brazil, Argentina, Chile, Mexico, Australia, and Japan. See ELEVATED RAILROAD; RAILROAD; STREETCAR; SUBWAY.

For moving medium-distance freight or passenger trains on electric railroads, electric locomotives are used. Subway trains, elevated trains, and suburban electric trains usually have an electric motor or motors in each car. A self-moving car is called a rail car or a multiple-unit rail car.

In electric locomotives and rail cars the electric motors provide the traction, or pulling power, of the train. Electric motors convert electricity into mechanical motion. Motors in electric locomotives and rail cars may be built to operate on either alternating current or direct current. Motors operating on direct current are more powerful and efficient than alternating-current motors. Alternating-current motors are simpler to operate and simpler to start. Direct-current motors must be brought up to operation at full voltage and full speed through a se-

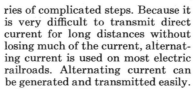
This electric train traveling through the Cascade Mountains uses a catenary electrical system. An electric locomotive has the highest power-to-weight ratio of all types. In mountainous terrain one crew can operate two or more locomotives by linking the electrical control circuits.

Courtesy of the Milwaukee Road

ries of complicated steps. Because it is very difficult to transmit direct current for long distances without losing much of the current, alternating current is used on most electric railroads. Alternating current can be generated and transmitted easily.

Until recently most large electric locomotives used alternating-current traction motors. Some electric locomotives convert alternating current to direct current in the locomotive. One type of locomotive has alternating-current motors to drive direct-current generators, which supply direct current to the traction motors. Locomotives of this type are used to haul very heavy trains up steep grades. Another sort of electric locomotive uses very large tubes filled with low-pressure mercury vapor to convert alternating current to direct current. The tubes are called ignitron tubes. The locomotives are called ignitron rectifier locomotives.

Many electric locomotives are equipped for regenerative braking. Such locomotives have traction motors that can act as generators when the locomotive and the train it is pulling are going downhill. The energy of the rolling train is used to move the parts of the generators; but since the parts of the generators have resistance to being moved, the train is slowed or braked. Regenerative braking is very helpful in controlling heavy trains going downhill on steep grades. See ELECTRIC GENERATOR.

All electric locomotives and rail cars are equipped with various resistors, transformers, and electrical control equipment. Electric locomotives have several motors to turn each axle and pair of wheels.

Electric rail cars function like locomotives, but they have fewer motors. Each car may have only one or a few motors. However, all the motors can be connected so that they can operate together and can be controlled from one place.

Electric current is supplied to electric locomotives or rail cars from overhead wires or from a third rail. An overhead wire system is called a catenary system. A locomotive or rail car picks up current from over-

head wires through shoes that slide along the underside of the wires. The shoes are supported by a retractable structure of rods and levers called a pantograph. A third rail to carry electric current is placed beside the rails the locomotives and cars run on. Locomotives and rail cars use pickup shoes that extend from their understructures to tap the current in the third rail. The third rail is usually enclosed by wooden guards so that careless people and children cannot touch it and receive shocks.

Third-rail systems use direct current and have voltages up to 800 volts. A third rail cannot carry large voltages because it cannot be sufficiently insulated. If large voltages are sent through a third rail, much of the electricity escapes to the ground and is lost. Overhead wires, or catenary systems, can be used to supply either alternating current or direct current. Overhead wires are able to carry low or high voltages.

Some electric railroads have their own powerplants to generate electricity to send through the overhead wires or third rail. Some electric railroad companies buy electricity from city or private powerplants. After an electric current has gone through a train's motors, the current goes to the rails the train runs on. These rails carry a large current, but they carry it at zero voltage with respect to the ground. A person who touches the rails will not receive a shock.

Between 1890 and 1920 electric railroads replaced some steam railroad lines near cities, and many electric street railroads, subways, elevated lines, and interurban electric railroads were built in the United States. After 1920 few new interurban lines were built in the United States, and many that had been built went out of business. As automobiles became popular and convenient, people did not need short-distance electric railroads for transportation. At present few electric railroads are being built in the United States, and some are discontinuing service. In Europe, Africa, and Asia, however, many electric railroads are being built.

Electric railroads are expensive to build. However, electric railroads can handle a greater volume of traffic on one track than can steam or diesel-electric railroads, because electric trains can maintain a higher average speed. Electric locomotives can accelerate or stop quickly and are capable of pulling very heavy loads for short distances. Electric multiple-unit rail cars can accelerate and stop even more quickly than electric locomotives. Electric railroads are useful in cities because electric locomotives do not give off smoke or gas.

ELECTRIC SHOCK, an injury or violent reaction resulting from contact with an electric current. If the voltage is high, the shock will cause serious injury, loss of consciousness, and sometimes even death. The loss of consciousness will usually prevent the person touching the high-voltage conductor from disengaging himself, and so the length of time that the electricity is passing through his body is increased. In such a situation the power should be immediately cut off and the person removed from the electrical conductor. If the power supply cannot be cut off, the unconscious person should be quickly dragged away from the electrical conductor, using great care not to touch his body. If his body is touched while he is being removed, the rescuer may also get an electric shock. Artificial respiration, just as it is used in cases of drowning, should be applied to the unconscious person. Fortunately most electric shocks that people get are not serious, because they usually come from house currents that are less than 120 volts.

ELECTRIC SIGN. An electric sign is any sign in which words or pictures are formed by electric lights. Electric signs are used to advertise theaters, restaurants, stores and shops, commercial products, and services.

Electric signs may have incandescent filament bulbs, fluorescent lamps, or vapor lamps. (See ELECTRIC LIGHT; FLUORESCENT LAMP; NEON LIGHT.) If incandescent bulbs are used, they are spaced and arranged in the form of letters or pictures. Vapor lamps and fluorescent lamps, which are long thin tubes, may be made with curves and bends to spell words or to form pictures. Many colors of fluorescent lighting are used in advertising displays. Neon lights are often used in electric signs.

The effect of motion may be pro-duced in signs by switching the electric lights off and on in patterns. A device called a motograph spells out messages word by word in moving patterns of lights. A flasher is another device for creating the illusion of motion in signs. The flasher is a drum that has many electric switches and contacts arranged on it. The drum is driven by a motor. As the drum revolves, patterns of lights in the sign are turned off and on rapidly in a regular order.

Large electric signs may contain several thousand incandescent lamps, or thousands of feet of fluorescent lamps, and miles of electric wiring. Such signs are expensive both to build and to operate.

ELECTRIC TOOL. As distinguished from an electrically powered machine such as a lathe, an electric tool is powered with a self-contained electric motor and is manipulated by hand. There are innumerable electric tools for home, workshop, and farm with more being devised and improved every year.

Common electric tools for the workshop are saws, drills, sanders, polishers, and even electric planes. The circular saw has a two-horsepower motor that turns a 7½-inch blade 4,200 revolutions per minute. The saw cuts out automatically when overloaded. A saber saw moving at 2,700 strokes a minute combines eight saws in one: rip, crosscut, coping, jig, band, scroll, keyhole, and hack. It will cut wood, plastic, plywood, wallboard, leather, metal, and hard rubber. There is a general-purpose motor with a basic frame, which can be attached to sanders, polishers, routers, and planes. With the perfection of the portable independent electric generator, electric tools are now made for cutting down trees in the forest with both chain and reciprocating saws. In orchards, electric limb trimmers cut swiftly and neatly. Electric paint sprayers are popular for covering large outside surfaces such as barn walls, machinery, and even fenceposts. Hogpens and chickenhouses can be quickly disinfected and whitewashed with an electric paint sprayer.

Most of these tools have been developed during the past 30 years. The small electric motor was perfected by Nikola Tesla about 1889 and first used on an electric fan. But as late as 1910, water-driven vacuum cleaners, which attached to the faucet in the kitchen sink, were still sold. Between 1909 and 1917 electric vacuum cleaners became popular. From then on the fractional horsepower electric motor was applied to many kinds of tools that had been hand powered.

ELECTRIC WIRING in homes consists of service entrance wires, a main switch and fuse or a main circuit breaker, a branch circuit box, wires that are electrical conductors and that form circuits in various parts of the house, and switches, outlets, and lighting fixtures.

Except in a few districts in large cities, electrical energy for homes is carried by alternating current. The service entrance wires carry electricity from the local transmission lines to the home. A transformer that steps down voltage is located where the service entrance wires branch off from a high-voltage transmission line. The service wires carry 230 and 115 volts. Most homes that use alternating current have three service entrance wires. A wiring system is used so that some branch circuits operate at 115 volts and some at 230 volts. Lights and small appliances operate at 115 volts. Large appliances, such as electric ranges, water heaters, and clothes dryers, operate at 230 volts. If a home has only two service entrance wires, the branch circuits operate only at 115 volts. The size of the service entrance wires determines the amount of electricity that

Courtesy of Skil Corporation

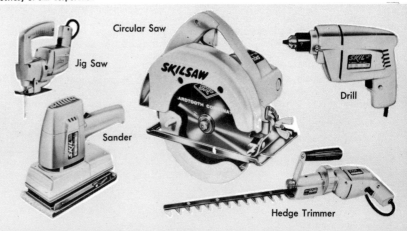

Jig Saw
Circular Saw
SKILSAW
Drill
Sander
Hedge Trimmer

can be channeled into the home at any one time. The larger the wires, the more electricity can be brought in.

Just inside the home is the main switch and fuse or the main circuit breaker. This equipment makes it possible to disconnect the house wiring from the service entrance wires when necessary. The main fuse or circuit breaker automatically disconnects the house wiring when an overload occurs. See CIRCUIT BREAKER; FUSE.

After electricity has passed the main switch and fuse or the circuit breaker, it goes to a branch circuit box. A number of circuits of different capacities are routed from the circuit box through the house. For each circuit there is a fuse or a circuit breaker in the circuit box. If an electrical overload occurs in a circuit, the proper fuse blows or the proper circuit breaker disconnects the circuit.

Wires conducting electricity are made of solid copper. Larger wires are able to conduct more electricity than smaller wires. Wire sizes are numbered according to a system called the American wire gauge (A.W.G.). The smaller the number, the larger the wire. Branch circuits are usually made of No. 14 or No. 12 wire. Service entrance wires are much larger. Wires are insulated by rubber, heat-resistant plastics, or asbestos. Wires are often enclosed by protective coverings called conduits.

Switches connect and disconnect circuits and parts of circuits. The parts of circuits include lights and electrical outlets. The switch most used in home wiring is the single-pole toggle switch. It connects or disconnects just one wire of a circuit. A double-pole switch controls two separate wires of a circuit simultaneously. Two three-way switches are used to control one light from two locations.

Convenience outlets are devices by which electrical equipment can be connected to a circuit. The piece of equipment usually has a cord and a pronged plug that fits into the outlet. Most outlets have two slots for plug prongs. Each slot is connected to a different point in a circuit. Some outlets have a third slot that is connected to a ground. Outlets for electric ranges have three slots connected to a three-wire circuit capable of supplying 230 volts instead of the usual 115.

ELECTROCARDIOGRAPH. See HEART DISEASE.

ELECTROCHEMISTRY is the study of the relation of chemical change and electrical energy. Chemical change may result in electrical energy, as in batteries and electric cells. Electric direct current applied to chemicals may result in chemical changes, as in electrolysis. See ELECTRIC CELL; ELECTROLYSIS.

Two types of conductors relay electricity in electrochemical reactions. One is the metallic, or electronic, conductor, in which electric current is carried by a flow of electrons from atom to atom. Metals, alloys, carbon and graphite, and a few other solids are electronic conductors. The other type of conductor is ionic, or electrolytic. Ionic compounds dissociate in liquid solution into negatively and positively charged ions, which carry the current. Some molecular compounds, when put in water, break up into ions. In electrolytic conduction there is a transfer of matter, the ions, from one place to another. Acids, bases, and salts in solution and some fused compounds are electrolytic conductors.

In the 1880's Arrhenius formulated a theory on which modern theories of electrolytic (ionic) dissociation are based. Arrhenius' theory was that the molecules of electrolytic compounds dissociate into ions spontaneously when the compounds are dissolved in water. It is now known that some electrolytic compounds are not made up of molecules at all, but of groups of ions.

Some molecular compounds dissociate only slightly in solution and are called weak electrolytes. Weak electrolytes have small conductivity —they transmit a small amount of electric current. Strong electrolytes are those compounds that dissociate completely and are able to transmit large currents.

When two different electronic, or metallic, conductors are placed in an electrolytic solution under certain conditions and are connected outside the electrolyte, an electric current is produced. See BATTERY.

When a direct current is forced through an electrolyte, electrolysis takes place.

ELECTRODE, a general term used in electricity to indicate the conductor by which electricity enters or leaves a vacuum tube, an electric arc, or the electrolyte in a battery. The positive electrode is called the anode, and the negative electrode is called the cathode. In a vacuum tube, such as a radio tube, elec-

tricity passes from one electrode (the cathode) to the other electrode (the anode) through space that contains so slight a trace of gas that it is almost a vacuum. There is no conductor between the two electrodes, so the electrons between the electrodes are moving freely in the space. They can only be directed and controlled by either electromagnetic or electrostatic fields. In the ordinary electron tube they are controlled by electrostatic fields. Once the electrons pass into the receiving electrode, their path again follows a conducting wire. Electrodes are made of many materials and in widely different shapes and sizes.

ELECTROLYSIS, the chemical action that results when an electric current is passed through an electrolyte (a substance, usually a solution, that conducts electricity by the transfer of ions). The products of the chemical action appear at the electrodes where the current enters and leaves the substance.

In electrolysis, two electrodes (an anode and a cathode) are placed in an electrolyte. The molecules of the electrolyte are ionized. This means that they decompose into two or more particles called ions. Each of the ions bears a charge of electricity. The ions that have a positive charge migrate toward the negative electrode (the cathode), and the ions that have a negative charge migrate toward the positive electrode (the anode). At the electrodes the ions give up their electric charges.

For example, when current flows through a solution of copper sulfate (the electrolyte) in which there are electrodes of copper, the copper sulfate is broken down into metallic copper, which is deposited on the

Electrolysis breaks water down into hydrogen and oxygen. A little sulfuric acid must be added to make the water a semiconductor. Hydrogen collects at the negative electrode and hydrogen at the positive electrode.

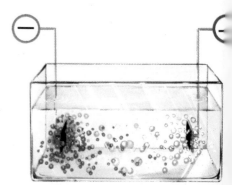

cathode in the form of a copper plate. The coating of an object with a thin layer of some metal by this process of electrolysis is called electroplating. See ELECTROPLATING.

Damaging electrolysis can occur in buried pipes in damp soil. The electric current that causes the destructive pitting of the pipes escapes from light or traction circuits.

A simple electromagnet may be made by coiling a piece of wire and passing a current through it. A soft iron rod inside the coil increases the pull of the magnet. The arrows indicate the direction of electron flow.

ELECTROMAGNET. When an electric current is passed through a coil of wire wound around a piece of soft iron, the iron becomes a temporary magnet. By increasing the number of turns of wire and the number of amperes of electricity flowing in the coil, the strength of the electromagnet can be increased as needed. However, the strength of an electromagnet is limited, in the practical sense, by the saturation of the iron when the number of ampere turns is high. The soft iron of the core allows the magnet to lose practically all of its magnetism when the current is turned off.

Because its strength can be controlled, because it can be made much stronger than a permanent magnet, and because it readily loses its magnetism, the electromagnet has many uses. The electromagnet (or the principle of electromagnetism) is part of nearly every electric machine. It is used in the telephone, telegraph, and electric bell, electric measuring instruments, as well as in electric motors, generators, and transformers. Very powerful electromagnets are often used as magnetic hoists to move masses of scrap iron. To unload, the electric current is simply disconnected.

ELECTROMAGNETIC SPECTRUM, the array of wavelengths of all the types of electromagnetic radiation. Their relationships are indicated in the chart.

Electric and magnetic effects can be transmitted through space as well as through solids, liquids, and gases. There are many kinds of these electromagnetic waves. Light, radio waves, X-rays, and cosmic rays are all electromagnetic waves. All travel at the same speed, but the waves have different lengths and frequencies. Increasing the frequency results in shorter waves, while decreasing the frequency produces longer waves. See COSMIC RAY; X-RAY.

ELECTROMAGNETISM deals with the magnetic effects of moving electric charges and the induction of electric currents by changing magnetic fields. Magnetism and electricity are related phenomena.

A wire through which an electric current is flowing is surrounded by a magnetic field. The lines of force in the field are circular, with the wire at the center. (See MAGNET AND MAGNETISM.) The direction of the magnetic force around the wire, clockwise or counterclockwise, depends on the direction of electron flow in the wire. A simple way to remember how to determine the direction of magnetic force is the left-hand rule. Grip the wire with your left hand, with the thumb pointing in the direction of electron flow. The other four fingers will point in the direction of the magnetic force.

The intensity of the magnetic field, represented by the number of lines of force in an area, decreases away from the wire. The intensity of the field also depends on the magnitude of the current in the wire.

When a coil of wire carries a current, the lines of force in the resulting magnetic field are arranged very much as if the coil were a bar magnet. One end of the coil acts as the N pole and the other end as the S pole. Lines of force leave the N pole and loop around the coil to the S pole. Then the lines of force extend straight down the inside of the coil to return to the N pole. The direction of magnetic force depends on the direction of electron flow in

The electromagnetic spectrum contains all electromagnetic waves, ranging from low-frequency electric currents to high-frequency rays that originate in interstellar space. Visible light is an extremely narrow band falling midway within this range.

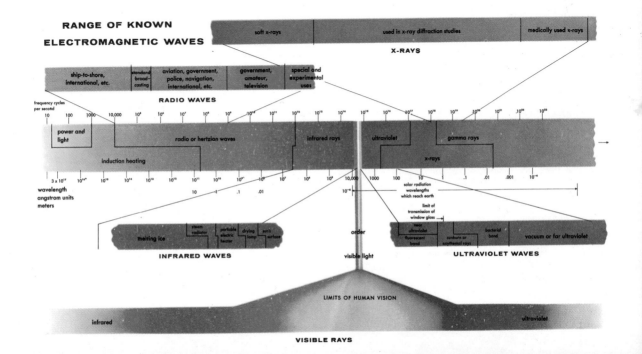

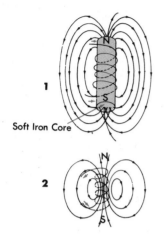

This drawing shows electromagnetic lines of force around an electromagnet with a soft-iron core, **1**, and around a simple coil, **2**.

the coil. The relation can be stated in another simple rule. Hold the coil in your left hand and curve the fingers, except the thumb, to point in the direction of electron flow. Hold your thumb parallel to the axis of the coil. The thumb will point toward the N pole of the coil.

The magnetic properties of current-carrying coils are used in several devices for measuring electricity. See GALVANOMETER; VOLTMETER.

Electromagnetic induction is a method of producing a flow of electrons in a conducting circuit. Suppose there is a coil of wire and that the ends of the wire are joined to form a complete circuit. If a bar magnet is moved in and out of the coil, a current is induced in the coil while the magnet is in motion. If the magnet is stationary, no current is induced. In other words, if the number of lines of magnetic force that pass through the coil is changing, a current is induced. The effect is the same whether the magnet is moved through the coil or the coil is moved past the magnet.

When a current is induced, electrons flow. The changing magnetic field produces a force that makes the electrons in the wire move. That force is called the electromotive force, or E.M.F.

As soon as a magnet moves toward a coil, some current is induced in the coil. The coil immediately has its own magnetic effect. If the N pole of the moving magnet is approaching one end of the coil, that end of the coil acts as an N pole and repels the bar magnet. If the motion of the magnet is reversed, the magnetic effect of the coil is reversed, and the end of the coil near the N pole of the magnet

acts as an S pole. The S pole of the coil will attract the N pole of the magnet, and work must be done to move the magnet away. The induction of current always requires work. Lenz's law states that an induced current always flows in such a direction that its magnetic effects oppose the motion of the magnetic field that is inducing the current.

Electric generators convert mechanical energy to electrical energy by electromagnetic induction. See ELECTRIC GENERATOR.

Any current-carrying wire that is not parallel to the lines of force in a magnetic field has a tendency to move. The wire tends to move across the lines of force.

Suppose a wire, running toward and away from the observer, is brought into a magnetic field in which the lines of force are directed from left to right. The wire, of course, has its own magnetic field. If the electron flow in the wire is toward the observer, the lines of force of the original magnetic field above the wire and the lines of force in the wire's magnetic field above the wire are in the same direction and add. Below the wire the lines of force in the large field oppose the lines of force about the wire and are subtracted. There are then more lines of force above the wire than below it. The intensity of a magnetic field is indicated by the number of lines of force in an area. The wire will move from the region of greater intensity to the region of lesser intensity. This principle applies to current-carrying coils as well as to straight wires. Electric motors operate by using this principle. See ELECTRIC MOTOR.

ELECTROMOTIVE FORCE

is a measure of the tendency of a charged body to move, and hence a current to flow, from one place to another. The electromotive force acting between two points is defined as the work done when a unit charge is moved from one point to another. Electromotive force is commonly measured in volts.

It is often helpful to draw an analogy with the action of gravity. When an object is moved from a place of low gravitational potential to one of high gravitational potential (from a low to a high place), work must be done. If the object is released, it will fall back down of its own accord, and it can be made to do useful work in the process, such as driving a clock mechanism.

Similarly, if work is needed to move a charge from point A to point

B, then if it is permitted to do so, the charge will move of its own accord back to point A again. The resulting current (which is merely a collection of moving electrical charges) can be used to do useful work, such as heating a filament or running a motor. We say that point B is at a higher potential than point A, and this potential difference is the electromotive force.

An electric generator is simply a device that uses mechanical work to move charges from a low potential to a high potential, ready to do useful work. A storage battery has terminals at different potentials, so that when a circuit is completed between the terminals, current will flow and useful work will be done. Most batteries, including the common flashlight cell, use chemical action to produce the potential difference, or electromotive force.

An electromotive force results when zinc atoms from the cathode of this electric cell go into solution and leave electrons behind.

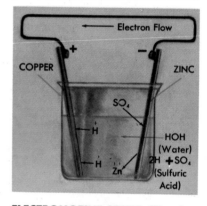

ELECTROMOTIVE SERIES.

The electromotive series of metals is a list of metals in the order of their decreasing electropositivity. The more electropositive a metal is, the more readily it gives up electrons and becomes a positive ion.

The electromotive series of metals is also a list of the decreasing potentials generated by different metals in equilibrium solutions with their ions. Hydrogen in equilibrium solution with its ions is used as a standard. The greater the separation in the list of two metals, and therefore the greater the difference in potentials between the metals, the greater the electromotive force that will be generated by the two metals in an electric cell. (See ELECTRIC CELL.) Zinc and copper in equilibrium solution with their ions in an electric cell will give a larger electromotive force than lead and copper in solution in a cell.

ELECTROMOTIVE SERIES

Element	Symbol
Potassium	K
Sodium	Na
Calcium	Ca
Magnesium	Mg
Aluminum	Al
Manganese	Mn
Zinc	Zn
Chromium	Cr
Iron	Fe
Cobalt	Co
Nickel	Ni
Tin	Sn
Lead	Pb
Hydrogen	H
Copper	Cu
Arsenic	As
Bismuth	Bi
Antimony	Sb
Mercury	Hg
Silver	Ag
Platinum	Pt
Gold	Au

A metal higher in the series (more electropositive) will displace a metal lower in the series (less electropositive). If magnesium metal is put in a solution of zinc sulfate, magnesium sulfate will be formed, and free zinc metal will be deposited. If nickel metal is placed in a solution of zinc sulfate, no displacement will occur. Nickel is less electropositive than zinc. Using the series, one can predict whether any metal will displace another metal from its compounds.

Metals less electropositive than hydrogen will not react with water or dilute acids to liberate hydrogen. Metals high in the series will react violently with cold water or with acids and will liberate hydrogen. Metals from magnesium through iron will displace hydrogen from steam and dilute acids. Metals from cobalt through lead will displace hydrogen from dilute acids.

When one metal displaces another or displaces hydrogen, there is a transfer of electrons. When magnesium metal is added to a solution of zinc sulfate, the magnesium atoms have 12 electrons each. The zinc ions in solution have 28 electrons each, two less than a zinc atom would have. When magnesium displaces zinc, the magnesium atoms each lose two electrons to become ions with 10 electrons each, and the zinc ions each gain two electrons to become zinc atoms with 30 electrons each.

ELECTRON. An electron is a very small particle of matter and energy. Electrons are particles making up most of the volume of an atom—all of it outside the nucleus. Electrons are important to electricity, to electronics, and to the composition of

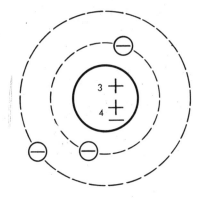

How electrons are arranged in an atom is shown by this diagram of the lithium atom. Three electrons (−) orbit in rings around a nucleus of three protons (+) and four neutrons.

chemical substances. The motion of electrons makes up an electric current. The activity and control of electrons is the science of electronics. The electron structure of the atom determines its ability to combine with other atoms to form molecules.

The electrons within the atoms of all substances are in constant motion. Some of these electrons tend to leave the atoms to which they belong and move to other atoms. Some atoms have more of these "free" electrons than others and tend to lose them to atoms with fewer free electrons. Substances that lose electrons become positively charged. Those that gain electrons are negatively charged. When an atom shares an electron with another atom, a molecule is formed. See ATOM; ELECTRICITY; ELECTRONICS; MOLECULE.

ELECTRONIC BRAIN, also known as an electronic computer, a calculating machine that uses electronic tubes or transistors in place of the gears of mechanical calculators. It can perform operations for large groups of figures and at very high speeds. An electronic computer has five principal elements: an input device to feed data to the machine; a storage system, such as a magnetic tape, to hold the information; a control unit, which indicates the type of answer required; an arithmetic unit, which performs the high-speed computations; and an output unit for recording the answer to the problem. The arithmetic unit can add, subtract, multiply, and divide. Complicated calculations are merely combinations of these operations. The instructions to an electronic brain are called the program.

One of the earliest applications of electronic brains was the use, beginning in 1948, of this automatic message-accounting equipment. It stores up information on telephone calls made. Bell Telephone Laboratories

Since the operations are all with numbers, these instructions are in the form of a code based on numbers. There may be a few hundred or many thousand instructions, depending on the problem.

Electronic computers make possible the solution of mathematical problems for which ordinary techniques are available but would take too long to be practical. For example, the solving of a problem in aircraft-wing design requires eight million steps. Since each step depends upon a previous step, only one man can work on the problem at a time. A modern electronic computer, averaging 14,000 mathematical operations a minute, can solve the problem in a matter of hours. Electronic computers replace mechanical, routine operations of the human brain. However, the problems requiring solution arise from creative thinking by the human brain. The availability of the electronic brain makes possible the solution of many more problems and therefore gives a wider range to creative thought.

Courtesy of Ford Motor Company

This electronic brain helps farmers work out the most profitable crop rotations and fertilizer applications for their farms.

This electronic data-processing system is made compact by using printed transistorized circuits like the one held by the engineer.

Courtesy of Burroughs Corporation

OCCUPATION: Programmer

NATURE OF WORK: Preparing instructions for electronic computers, specifying exactly what steps these machines should take to get the desired results

PERSONAL FACTORS: ABILITIES, SKILLS, APTITUDES: A logical and systematic approach to the solution of a problem, the ability to work with extreme accuracy, and imagination are needed.

EDUCATION AND SPECIAL TRAINING: Training is usually given at a company's expense, often in schools established by the computer manufacturer. College graduates are usually selected for this training.

WORKING CONDITIONS:

1. INCOME:
   COMPARED WITH OTHER CAREERS WITH EQUAL TRAINING: Average to high
   COMPARED WITH MOST OTHER CAREERS: Average to high

2. ENVIRONMENT: Well-lighted, air-conditioned, modern offices with various kinds of electronic computing equipment

3. OTHER: Regular hours; occasional evening work; usual benefits; excellent opportunities

WHERE TO FIND MORE INFORMATION: Large companies that have electronic computing systems; manufacturers of electronic computing systems

---

ELECTRONICS is a term that originally referred to the branch of physics explaining the theory of electrons, their behavior, and their movement through space. It has now come to mean the science of electronic tubes and the industries that are applying them to a rapidly widening variety of uses. From early developments of radio, sound films, and X-ray, the industry grew almost overnight to huge proportions, keeping pace with the development of many different kinds of tubes, transistors, and other devices. Because the technology includes electric wiring, insulation, and many electrical devices, there is some tendency in the industry to refer to the whole field of electrical engineering as electronics.

There are several kinds of electronic tubes, and their applications are many and varied. Among the more familiar applications are radio, television, X-ray, radar, electron microscopes, and electronic brains. Articles on these and many other electronic subjects may be found in this encyclopedia. See CATHODE RAY.

ELECTRON MICROSCOPE uses electrons instead of light waves to magnify objects up to 200,000 times. An ordinary microscope cannot magnify much beyond 2,000 times. But the waves associated with moving electrons are far shorter than

A powerful electron microscope is shown below. The cabinet has been opened to reveal some of the electronic apparatus inside.

Courtesy RCA

light waves and are thus capable of much greater magnification.

In an electron microscope the cathode structure from a cathode-ray tube is used to produce a beam of electrons (which behave in many respects like waves), which is directed toward and upon the object. The final image is projected upon a fluorescent screen or sometimes upon a photographic film.

Under an electron microscope the scale of magnification is such that the dot of an *i* would be as large as a baseball diamond, and one hair of your head would be 4 feet wide. Many hitherto invisible viruses can now be studied, and even molecules have been photographed.

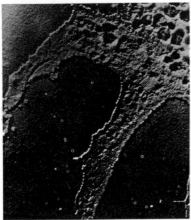

Courtesy RCA

The electron microscope enables scientists to see many viruses, such as this bean virus.

ELECTRON SYNCHROTRON. See PARTICLE ACCELERATOR.

ELECTROPLATING, the process of coating a piece of metal with another metal by electrolysis. (See ELEC-TROLYSIS.) It is used commercially to plate base, or inferior, metals with more valuable ones or to plate iron with zinc or copper or chromium to prevent it from rusting. In copper plating, for example, the positive plate (anode) is composed of pure copper. It is inserted in a solution (electrolyte) of copper sulfate, and the object to be plated is attached to the negative pole, forming the cathode. When the current is turned on, the sulfate ions of the solution, which are negative, are attracted to the positive plate. A reaction takes place, as a result of which the copper atoms of the positive plate go into solution as copper ions. The copper electrode is gradually dissolved. Meanwhile the positive copper ions of the original solution have been attracted to the

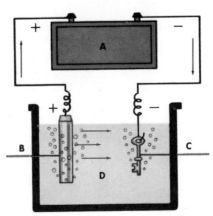

In electroplating a metal key with copper, the positive pole of a battery, **A**, is connected with a copper bar, **B**, and the negative pole is connected with the key, **C**. Both bar and key are submerged in a copper sulfate solution, **D**. The net transfer of copper, indicated by the arrows, is opposite in direction to the electron flow.

negative cathode and arriving there are deposited on the metal object in the form of copper atoms. Those copper atoms that attach to the metal object are immediately replaced in the solution by the copper ions torn from the copper plate.

Of course, if we wish to do gold plating, the anode will be a bar of gold and the electrolyte some salt of gold; if silver plating, a bar of silver for the anode with a salt of silver for the electrolyte.

A current of small amperage is used so that the deposit on the object is made slowly and evenly. If the deposit is made too fast, it is liable to crystallize. Plating with metallic mixtures or alloys, such as chrome-nickel, tin and lead, or brass can be done in the same way.

Electroplating is used to make printing plates, called electrotypes, that last through thousands of impressions and may be stored and used again and again. The type page, set in the usual manner, is impressed into wax; and the wax is coated with graphite to make it a conductor. A copper printing plate is then built up on the wax through electroplating.

ELEGY, a love poem or lamentation for the dead, written in a lofty style. In ancient Greece the elegy was distinguished not by its subject matter but rather by its metrical form. This consisted of couplets in dactylic rhythm; the first line contained six feet and the second line, five feet.

(See POEM.) Various subjects were rendered in the elegiac style—banquet poems, military addresses, epitaphs, declarations of love, and of course the funeral song. The character of the speaker was strongly evident in these works, so that the usual tone of the elegy was personal and reflective. Among the Greek elegiac writers, Theocritus and Bion exerted the most influence on English poets.

Of Latin poets, Ovid is the best known writer of elegies. Like the other poets of the empire under Augustus Caesar, he devoted himself primarily to love elegies.

English poets used both the Greek lament and the Latin love poem as models for the elegy. Most of Donne's poems called elegies are passionate love poems. After the Renaissance, however, the funeral song becomes increasingly important. Its classical associations make it a favorite subject for the pastoral mode. Thus in his poem *Lycidas* Milton represents his friend Edward King as a shepherd. The diction of the poem is formal and artificial; the tone, as befits the occasion, is plaintive and stately throughout. Shelley immortalizes the poet Keats in the elegy *Adonais*, resembling classical elegies in form. Matthew Arnold also uses the pastoral convention in his poem *Thyrsis*, which was written upon the death of his friend Arthur Hugh Clough.

Probably the most famous elegy in English is Thomas Gray's *Elegy Written in a Country Churchyard*. Written as a protest against governmental restrictions on public burials and monuments, this poem mourns not one man but every man who dies in obscurity. Surely everyone is familiar with at least one of the poem's stanzas: "Full many a gem of purest ray serene,/The dark unfathomed caves of ocean bear:/Full many a flower is born to blush unseen,/And waste its sweetness on the desert air."

Besides the poets of England a number of other poets on the Continent wrote in the elegiac strain. Poems of lament and melancholy reflection may be found in the work of the French poets Villon and Ronsard. The 17th-century Italian poets Chiabrera and Filicaia also wrote elegies. Pushkin, Russia's most cherished poet, wrote an elegy on the portrait of Prince Barclay de Tolly, a Russian field marshal of Scottish descent. The modern Spanish poet Ramón Jiménez wrote poems of lamentation entitled *Elegías* and *Rimas de Sombria*.

ELEMENT, in chemistry, a fundamental substance that cannot be decomposed into a simpler substance by ordinary chemical means. It may be a solid, a liquid, or a gas. Over 100 elements are known; together they make up all forms of matter. Many elements, such as copper, gold, iron, sulfur, and carbon, have been known for as long as there have been written records, although they were not at first recognized as elements. The ancient Greeks considered the elements, from which all other substances were made, to be earth, fire, air, and water. This idea persisted for many centuries. Alchemists frequently considered other substances, such as mercury, salt, and sulfur, as additional or replacement elements. Antoine Lavoisier in the 18th century was probably the first whose list of elements bears any strong similarity to the present lists, although he included light and "caloric" as elements. Lavoisier was the inventor of the chemical equation and the father of analytical chemistry, the science that determines the chemical composition of materials. Robert Boyle, in his book *The Sceptical Chemist*, published in 1661, ridiculed the alchemists' ideas and insisted that the word "element" should be applied only to those substances that could not be (chemically) decomposed. Boyle's qualitative analysis and Lavoisier's quantitative analysis made possible the later discovery of other elements and their differentiation from the elements already known. Using these principles, many other elements were discovered. The invention of electrolysis, the use of electric current to isolate elements, made possible the identification of such active metals as sodium and potassium, and the later use of the spectroscope disclosed the presence of still rarer elements. Dmitri Mendeleev's periodic table of the elements indicated the probable nature of other still undiscovered elements. The last elements, those beyond uranium. were discovered, not in nature, but in atomic reactors. See ATOM; PERIODIC TABLE OF ELEMENTS.

ELEPHANT, the largest and heaviest of all land animals. When full grown, it is usually 8 to 11 feet tall at the shoulders and weighs 3 to 6 tons. It is found only in southern Asia, Sumatra, and the wilds of central Africa. The brownish-gray elephant, which is usually seen in circus parades and in menageries, is of the Asiatic kind.

The elephant has a tough skin about an inch thick. Its trunk is an elongation of its upper lip and nose and is sometimes 7 feet in length. The elephant can bend it in any direction and can make it longer or shorter. On the end of the trunk is a small finger-like feeler with which the elephant can pick up objects as small as a pin. With its trunk the animal also picks up and carries heavy burdens. The elephant's food is gathered with its trunk and put into its mouth. By sticking the trunk in water and inhaling the air from it the elephant fills the tubes of the trunk with water, which is then poured into its mouth or squirted over its body for a bath. Through its trunk the elephant utters its trumpet-like call, which is equivalent to any noise made through or by the nose. The trunk is also a strong weapon of defense. The hard tusks are other weapons. They are really modified teeth, growing one on either side in the upper jaw. They are often 7 to 9 feet in length and are formed of ivory.

Elephants are used as beasts of burden in India, Burma, and Thailand, where they drag logs and do all sorts of heavy work. Since very early times they have been used in warfare and for hunting. They are intelligent, are easily taught, and seem to have good memories. When tamed, they often seem to have real affection for their masters, but they cannot be entirely trusted. Since the time of the Romans elephants have been taught to do tricks, just as they do today in the circuses and animal shows.

ELEVATED RAILROAD, called the el, is an electrically powered railroad elevated above the street level. The height of the structure enables large vehicles to pass beneath. The supporting structure for the rails is made up of strong steel beams and steel pillars. Electric power is furnished by a third rail, which transmits the power through a special contact on the train. The power for the system is generated at a powerhouse and is kept at a uniform level throughout the system.

Elephants are zoo and circus favorites. The trunk of the Indian elephant, **1**, ends in a single fleshy process, whereas the trunk of the African elephant, **2**, ends in two processes.

Walter G. Chandoha

Robert Bradley

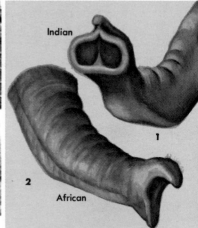

Indian

1

2

African

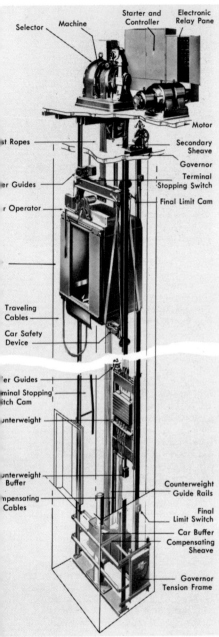

Otis Elevator Co.

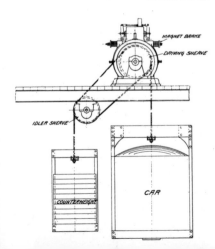

A gearless traction electric elevator (cutaway, top left) is called gearless because the driving sheave in its machine is mounted on the armature shaft of a slow, high-torque motor rather than connected to a motor through a reduction gear. A traction elevator is especially safe because its hoist ropes slacken when car or counterweight hits the buffers, thus preventing the other from being drawn through overhead mechanism. The side view below shows how hoist ropes are looped to increase traction.

Because of the congested traffic that plagued big cities after the Civil War, the elevated railroad became a popular means of transportation. It first came into being around 1875, and by 1876 New York had 40 trains running daily. These trains were powered by steam engines. Toward the close of the century Boston and Chicago had joined New York in building these railroads. Electric-traction motors were developed for these trains just prior to 1893 and have been in use ever since. The elevated railroad is being replaced by the subway, or underground railroad. New York has torn down its elevated structure, and a subway system handles most of the public transportation.

ELEVATOR, a car that moves up and down inside a shaft and is used to transport passengers or freight to different levels of a building or other structure.

Two years after the invention of a crude platform hoist in 1850, Elisha Graves Otis produced in America a machine run by a steam engine. In 1854 the elevator was first equipped with safety devices to prevent the car from falling if the cables should break. The first successful electric elevator was installed in New York by Otis Brothers and Company in 1889. It had a speed of 450 feet per minute as compared with the 600-foot speeds attained by hydraulic elevators at that time.

The first gearless traction electric elevator was developed in 1903. It had a car speed of 550 feet per minute and was free of limitations on potential speeds and heights attainable. Thereafter nearly all elevators installed were of the electric type, geared or gearless. The latter can be operated with speeds of 1,200-1,400 feet per minute and have effective safety devices and an automatic signal control for operating the car, from either the floor or the car.

The first automatic elevator was developed in 1892. It can be called to a floor by pressing a button; another button in the car is pressed to send the car to the floor desired. The collective automatic elevator was developed in the 1920's. It is designed to pick up and deposit passengers without regard to the order in which the floors are selected. These self-service elevators are being increasingly used in all types of buildings.

ELF. See FAIRY.

ELGAR, SIR EDWARD (1857-1934), a British composer, was born at Broadheath, Worcestershire. He received some training as a pianist and organist, but he was primarily self-taught as a musician. He was conductor of the Worcester Instrumental Society and a church organist until 1889 when he resigned to devote himself exclusively to composing. His important works included the *Enigma Variations* (1899), the five "Pomp and Circumstance" marches (1901), two symphonies (1908 and 1911), concertos for violin (1910) and cello (1919), and the oratorios *Lux Christi* (1896), *The Dream of Gerontius* (1900), *The Apostles* (1903), and *The Kingdom* (1906). He was knighted in 1904 and was made master of the king's music in 1924.

EL GRECO (1548?-1614?), a painter, was born at Candia, Crete. His real name, in Greek, was Kyriakos Theotokopoulos; in Spanish, Domingo Teotocópuli.

In Venice he studied with Titian

"Vision of St. John the Divine," by the Greek-Spanish master El Greco, hangs in the Metropolitan Museum of Art, in New York.
Courtesy of The Metropolitan Museum of Art, Rogers Fund, 1956

and was influenced by Tintoretto and Jacopo Bassano. In 1570 he went to Rome to study Michelangelo's works. Before 1577 he settled in Toledo, Spain, where he lived out his life.

Ranked as one of the masters, El Greco became famous and wealthy. His art was known for its religious fervor, imagination, boldness, and rich coloring. He foreshadowed the expressionists in his distortion of form and expression of mood.

"Burial of Count Orgaz" was considered his masterpiece. His other paintings included "Saint Martin and the Beggar," "View of Toledo," and "Christ Driving the Money Changers from the Temple."

L. C. Page & Co.

George Eliot

ELIOT, GEORGE (1819-1880), was the pseudonym of Mary Ann, or Marian, Evans, an English novelist, poet, and essayist. She was born near Nuneaton, Warwickshire. She received an ordinary education until the age of 17; thereupon she pursued in private a study of Italian, German, and music.

Her first literary undertaking was a translation of David Friedrich Strauss's *Life of Jesus* in 1846. After her father's death she went to live in London, where she became assistant editor of the *Westminster Review*. This brought her into contact with such literary figures as Thomas Carlyle, Herbert Spencer, and George Henry Lewes.

It was Lewes who discovered her talent for fiction and encouraged her to write novels. Her first work, *Scenes from Clerical Life*, began publication in *Blackwood's Magazine* in 1857 under her pseudonym. Her identity remained a secret until after the publication of her first full-length novel, *Adam Bede*, in 1859.

George Eliot was instantly successful as a novelist. Among her most famous novels are *The Mill on the Floss, Silas Marner, Romola*, and *Daniel Deronda*. Her finest novel, *Middlemarch*, is a study of the social complexities of English rural life. George Eliot's poetry and essays never attained great popularity, but in the novel she is regarded as the equal of Dickens and Thackeray.

In 1880, two years after the death of Lewes, with whom she had lived for 24 years, George Eliot married the banker John Walter Cross. She died that same year at the age of 61.

ELIOT, T. S. (1888-), properly Thomas Stearns Eliot, contemporary American poet, born in St. Louis, who in 1927 became a British subject. Eliot was graduated from Harvard in 1910 and later studied at the Sorbonne and at Oxford. He taught philosophy for a year at Harvard, but in 1914 he returned to Europe. In 1917 he published his first volume of poetry, *Prufrock and Other Observations*, and in 1920 his first volume of criticism, *The Sacred Wood*. In 1919 his second volume, *Poems*, was published. This included his noted poem "Gerontion." In England Eliot carved a career for himself as both banker and publisher. In 1923 he became editor of the quarterly *Criterion*.

Eliot's most famous poem, "The Wasteland," was published in 1922. In 1925 came "The Hollow Men" and in 1930 his "Ash-Wednesday." In 1932 Eliot returned to the United States and lectured at Harvard. These lectures are included in his volume *The Use of Poetry and the Use of Criticism*.

Eliot's first cohesive writing for the theater was in 1934, when he wrote the dialogues and choruses for a pageant called *The Rock*. In the following year he wrote his first play, *Murder in the Cathedral*, written in verse. Other verse plays of Eliot's are *The Family Reunion, The Cocktail Party, The Confidential Clerk*, and *The Elder Statesman*.

In 1943 Eliot published his *Four Quartets*. Other works include his *Collected Essays; Notes Toward a Definition of Culture*, a book of social criticism; and *Old Possum's Book of Practical Cats*, a book of light verse. Eliot was awarded the 1948 Nobel prize in literature.

ELIZABETH I (1533-1603), Tudor queen of England and Ireland from 1558 to 1603, daughter of Henry VIII and Anne Boleyn, was born at Greenwich. Elizabeth was a preco-

Courtesy of The Metropolitan Museum of Art, Gift of J. Pierpont Morgan, 1911

Elizabeth I

cious child and received an excellent education. Her tutors included John Cheke, William Grindal, and Roger Ascham. She read Greek and Latin and spoke German, Italian, and French.

Elizabeth had an older half sister, Mary (later Mary I), and a younger half brother, Edward (later Edward VI). Her mother was beheaded in 1536, and her father died in 1547. Elizabeth's claim to the throne was based upon her father's will and upon an act of Parliament. According to Roman Catholic canon law she was illegitimate and not in the legal line of succession. The child of a condemned marriage, Elizabeth was consequently raised a Protestant—or, more correctly, she was raised under her father's particular brand of Catholicism, for although Henry VIII had proclaimed himself "supreme head of the church of England after God," he remained Roman Catholic in all other points of doctrine.

When Elizabeth came to the throne in 1558, she inherited the religious unrest that existed in England between the Protestants and the Catholics. This unrest had been intensified by the persecution policies of her Catholic predecessor Mary I, called Bloody Mary. Elizabeth favored a return to Protestantism, but because her claim to the throne was in dispute and because she was supported by many Catholics and Protestants only through fear of civil war, she had to move carefully.

The chief danger to the Elizabethan Reformation came not from within the country but from foreign intervention. Of prime importance was the hostility of the pope in Rome, who had a Catholic candidate for the English throne in Mary, Queen of Scots, an ally of France through marriage. Provided Elizabeth made no open move against Catholicism, she could count on Philip II of Spain to exert his powerful influence in her favor at Rome. As good a Catholic as he was, the last thing Philip wanted was French political domination of England.

With consummate skill and courage Elizabeth played off these conflicting interests against one another to avoid foreign wars and to gain the time she needed. As she felt her hold on the throne becoming firmer through increased popular support, she let her religious policy slowly unfold. Elizabeth did not have the kind of strong religious conviction that had led Mary to persecute non-Catholics. Her devotion was primarily to her country and people. Her policies for a religious settlement were designed to unite behind the throne (by avoiding extremes) all moderate-minded men in the realm. She showed great judgment in selecting councilors to aid her in restoring peace to England. William Cecil was her chief adviser.

The laws that finally severed England from the Roman Catholic Church were framed in 1559 by Elizabeth's first Parliament. The supreme jurisdiction in spiritual and temporal matters was given back to the crown by the Act of Supremacy; Elizabeth had herself designated "Supreme Governor." The Uniformity Bill reintroduced the Book of Common Prayer of 1552 as the directory for public worship; this represented a return to the work of the reformation under Edward VI. In 1563 Edward's Forty-two Articles (1552) were revised to be less extremely Protestant; the new Thirty-nine Articles of Faith became the doctrinal basis of the Anglican Church.

Elizabeth never married, and she produced no heir. Throughout her reign this problem occupied the attention of the kingdom. Her near death from smallpox in 1562 caused a great deal of alarm, but with the exception of this one grave illness, Elizabeth enjoyed exceptionally good health and a long life. The unfortunate consequences of Mary Tudor's marriage to Philip of Spain remained uppermost in the public mind and produced the fear that Elizabeth too might imperil the kingdom by union with a fanatically Catholic foreign prince. Such fears appear to have been groundless, for

although Elizabeth allowed herself to be courted by Philip and a number of Austrian and French princes, she did so as a part of her national policy and with no real intention of marrying.

Considerations of political security seem also to have been principally responsible for her often-condemned treatment and execution in 1587 of Mary Stuart. If any of the conspiracies to put Mary on the throne—the Ridolfi plot of 1571, the Guise conspiracy of 1584, the Babington conspiracy of 1586—had succeeded, it would have meant the restoration of Roman Catholicism in England and foreign political domination.

The one attempt at insurrection that was personally most painful to Elizabeth was that instigated by her chief favorite Robert Devereux, second earl of Essex. She was forced to send him to the scaffold (1601).

Elizabeth was finally excommunicated in 1570, but excommunication was infinitely less dangerous at that time than it would have been in 1559. War with Spain eventually came in 1587; its effect was to unite further the people behind Elizabeth. Elizabeth had been preparing for this war, and when it came, England was in a position of economic and military strength. With the defeat of the Spanish Armada in 1588, Elizabeth's navy became the strongest in Europe.

Elizabeth's reign was a period of great cultural achievements also. The Elizabethan Age is the richest in English literary history; it was an age of such illustrious poets and dramatists as Edmund Spenser, Sir Philip Sidney, Christopher Marlowe, John Webster, Ben Jonson, and William Shakespeare.

Elizabeth died at Richmond in Surrey and was buried in Westminster Abbey.

ELIZABETH II (1926-   ), queen of Great Britain and Northern Ireland and head of the Commonwealth, was born in London, the daughter of the then Duke of York and the former Lady Elizabeth Bowes-Lyon. The course of her life was changed in 1936 when her uncle Edward VIII abdicated and her father became king as George VI. During World War II Princess Elizabeth and her sister Princess Margaret lived at Royal Lodge at Windsor Castle in Berkshire. In November, 1947, the Princess Elizabeth married Prince Philip, duke of Edinburgh, son of the late Prince Andrew of Greece. The young couple were on a tour of

Africa, Australia, and New Zealand in 1952 when on February 6 in Kenya they received the news of her father's death. Elizabeth was formally proclaimed queen on February 8, and was crowned at Westminster Abbey, June 2, 1953. She is the sixth woman to occupy the English throne by right of succession. Her predecessors were Mary I, Elizabeth I, Mary II, Anne, and Victoria.

The queen has three children: Prince Charles, duke of Cornwall, born in 1948; Princess Anne, born in 1950; and Prince Andrew, born in 1960.

The oval-shaped leaves and the winged fruits of the American elm are shown above.

ELM, any of a number of moderate to large deciduous trees with simple, alternate leaves and blades that are unequal at the base and toothed at the margins. The white, or American, elm is found in the woods throughout the United States east of the Rockies. It probably is used more than any other American tree for planting in streets and yards and is regarded as one of the most beautiful shade trees in the world. It is a tall tree, growing to a height of 60 to 125 feet, with a tall, thick, rough-barked trunk. The elm fruit is a small, winged capsule containing one seed. The tree has large ascending limbs that form a wide spreading crown. When planted on both sides of a street or a road, the branches of old trees often meet high overhead and interlock, giving a vaulted, cathedral-like effect.

The Dutch elm disease, a serious disease of elms carried by a bark beetle, is causing widespread destruction. The only method of control is the eradication and destruction of the diseased trees.

San Vicente is one of many volcanoes in El Salvador. Coffee is grown in the rich soil of its lower slopes.

Ripe coffee berries are unloaded from a car by workmen in El Salvador. An ideal climate aids the coffee crops.

Herbert Lanks—FPG

EL SALVADOR is the smallest but the most densely populated of the Central American republics. It is the only one without a Caribbean seacoast. Earthquakes are frequent and sometimes cause serious damage. The people of El Salvador are mainly persons of mixed Indian and Spanish blood (mestizos). Their language is Spanish, and they are Roman Catholics. The country's area has been estimated at about 8,300 square miles, but some estimates are larger. The population numbers about 2,500,000.

1838; El Salvador became independent. For detailed map, see MEXICO.

El Salvador is a land of mountains, hills, and upland plains. Two mountain ranges cross the country from west to east. One lies along the coast and the other, along the northern border. Between them is the fertile plateau region, about 2,000 feet above sea level. Here are the republic's chief cities, including San Salvador, the capital, and the principal farmlands. The mountains are not high. The highest peak rises to about 7,800 feet in the volcano Santa Ana. Along the Pacific is a narrow coastal lowland. Of the many rivers the most important is the Lempa, navigable by small ships for a short distance. Ilopango and a few other beautiful crater lakes lie on the plateau.

Except for the small coastal strip El Salvador's climate is warm rather than hot. On the plateaus and hills that cover most of the country the climate is marked by warm days and cool nights. The year is divided into two seasons, wet and dry. The wet season extends from June to October.

El Salvador is an agricultural country. One crop, coffee, dominates the economy and is the principal export. It is grown on the fertile mountain slopes. Foreign trade is mainly with the United States. There is some manufacturing of light consumer goods for domestic use, but industrial activity consists chiefly of the processing of agricultural products. Mining is not important. Native to El Salvador is the tree that yields balsam of Peru, which is used in medicines and perfumes.

The first European to arrive in what is now El Salvador was Pedro de Alvarado. He founded the city of San Salvador in 1525. The region remained a Spanish colony under the captaincy general of Guatemala until the captaincy declared its independence in 1821. Two years later El Salvador and the four other

Courtesy of the Pan American Coffee Bureau

former Spanish provinces formed a federation called the United Provinces of Central America. Civil war caused the union to break up in 1838, and El Salvador with the others became a separate republic.

EL SALVADOR

Area: 8,300 sq. mi.
Population: 2,500,000
Capital: San Salvador
Largest cities: San Salvador, Santa Ana
Highest mountain peak: Santa Ana Volcano (about 7,800 feet)
Chief river: Lempa
Chief lakes: Ilopango, Coatepeque, Guija
Climate: Generally warm to cool in highlands covering most of the country—hot in narrow, coastal lowland—seasonal rainfall
National flag: Three horizontal stripes of blue, white, blue—coat of arms in center
National anthem: *Saludemos la patria orgullosos* (Let Us Proudly Salute the Fatherland)
Form of government: Republic
Unit of currency: Colon
Language: Spanish
Chief religion: Roman Catholic

Chief economic activity: Agriculture

Chief crops: Coffee, corn, beans, sugarcane, sorghum, cotton

Chief minerals: Gold, silver

Chief exports: Coffee, cotton

Chief imports: Petroleum products, textiles, machinery and vehicles, wheat flour, various manufactures

EMANCIPATION PROCLAMATION

was issued by President Lincoln on Sept. 22, 1862. The proclamation declared that all slaves in any part of the Confederacy in rebellion against the United States on Jan. 1, 1863, should be forever free. The order did not apply to the four border states or to those parts of the Confederacy under the control of the federal armies. Thus the Emancipation Proclamation actually freed no slaves.

Lincoln had worked out a plan for gradual emancipation, full compensation for the slaveholders, and the sending of freed slaves to Liberia or Latin America. But the abolitionists in his party and the majority of the North demanded immediate action.

The Northern victory at the Battle of Antietam enabled Lincoln to issue the proclamation. Emancipation was actually completed on Dec. 18, 1865, by the ratification of the 13th Amendment, which forbade slavery anywhere in the United States.

EMBARGO,

in international law, prohibitions on shipping. The word originally referred only to the prohibition of ships leaving a country. The embargo enforced against Germany in World War I, however, amounted to a veritable blockade. There are, therefore, two forms of embargo. The civil embargo affects only ships of the nation applying the embargo. The international embargo applies to ships of other nations.

Until World War I the international embargo, the seizing of foreign ships, was uncommon. At one time ships were seized as a form of reprisal against other nations, to be released when wrongs were righted. The practice of seizing ships in anticipation of war was condemned by the Hague International Peace Conference of 1907, but an international embargo was applied during World War I. In that war, ships of foreign nations were taken and forced to deliver munitions.

The civil embargo might be levied for reasons purely domestic. The shutdown of coal mines caused Great Britain to embargo its coal-

carrying ships in 1926. President Thomas Jefferson sought to maintain neutrality with warring European powers in 1807 by placing an embargo on American ships. The embargo forestalled war with Great Britain, a power which had made itself unpopular by the impressment of American seamen. The embargo was partially effective, which showed a degree of national unity that surprised some skeptics. American trade suffered, but the embargo gave an impetus to American manufacturing enterprises. Against strenuous opposition, Jefferson maintained the embargo, but when he left office in 1809 the embargo was lifted. In the 1930's the United States maintained an embargo on munitions of war to states engaged in conflict or civil war. In 1950 the United States, as a result of the war in Korea, placed a total embargo on trade with the People's Republic of China. See BLOCKADE.

EMBARGO OF 1814. See WAR OF 1812.

EMBROIDERY,

needlework done in a variety of stitches and used for ornamenting clothing or household articles made of cloth. Embroidery stitches are flat, looped, chained, or knotted, but the individual variations of each of these types run into the hundreds. The materials necessary for embroidery, besides needle and thread, are a set of hoops, scissors, thimble, and of course the fabric to be stitched. Linen has long been a favorite material in western Europe, and because it is firm yet

This diagram shows a number of basic embroidery stitches, including the running stitch, 1; outline stitch, 2, used for design outlines; feather stitch, 3, used in borders; spoke stitch, 4; zigzag stitch, 5; blanket stitch, 6, used for edges; lazy-daisy stitch, 7, used to form flower petals; French knot, 8; and cross stitch, 9, an old sampler stitch.

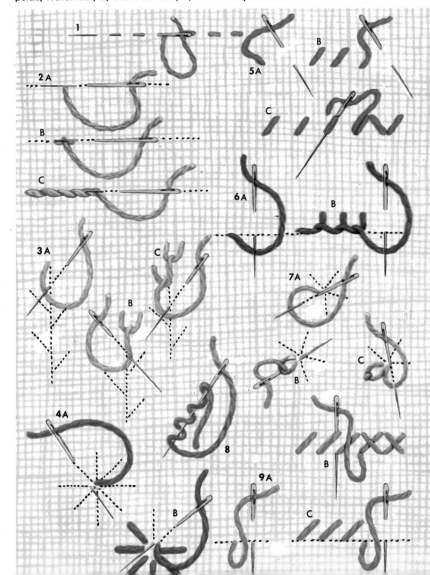

easy to work with, it is a good material for the beginner. Embroidery threads have been made of silk, cotton, wool, and even metal, but nowadays mercerized cotton that separates easily into strands is most widely used.

Embroidery has been known to nearly every country in the world since the Chinese first began to decorate their robes with silken threads 3,000 years before the birth of Christ. In the Middle Ages some of the most beautifully embroidered designs were made on European church vestments and coverings. Nearly every country has had its distinctive style, the peasant classes in Europe and the East having kept to traditional designs for generations. In England and France, however, embroidery was an art practiced by the leisure classes, and hence it developed in accordance with the educated taste of each generation.

Every young girl in colonial America was expected to practice her embroidery on a sampler, a piece of material that managed to incorporate all the different stitches in a single, unified design. This custom has, of course, died out since the industrialization of America, but many young girls are still able to embroider designs in the simpler stitches. Although clothing is not usually embroidered in this country, table linens, napkins, pillowcases, mats, and towels often are.

Material with a variety of patterns stamped on it can be bought. A person can thus begin immediately with the stitching. But for those who prefer to use original designs or to make their own copies, there are a number of ways of transferring a design from paper or cloth to the fabric that is intended for embroidery.

EMBRYOLOGY, the biological science that studies the development of an animal from its beginning as a fertilized ovum, or zygote, until it is hatched from its egg or is born from the maternal uterus. Before hatching or birth the developing animal is called an embryo.

The embryonic development of a frog, chick, or human being comprises many complex phenomena. First the single-celled zygote divides into many cells by a process called mitosis. Soon these cells form three distinct layers, the primary germ layers, which are called the ectoderm, mesoderm, and endoderm. All the structures of the body develop from the germ layers. From

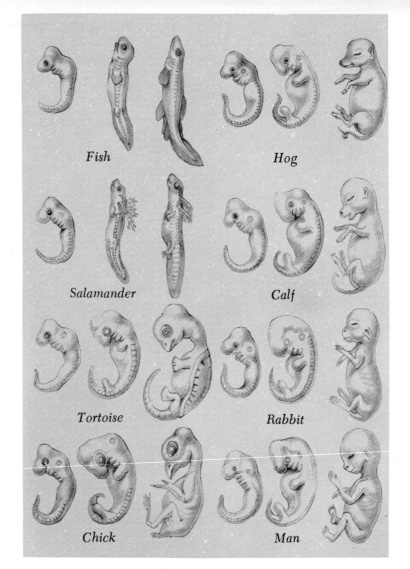

Embryology studies the similarities and differences in the development of different animals. As may be seen above, the embryos of various animals are very similar in early stages.

the ectoderm come the animal's epidermis, its nervous system, and its sense organs. From the mesoderm come the skeleton, the muscles, the circulatory system (heart, arteries, blood), and the lining of the body cavity. From the endoderm come the lining of the digestive tract, the lungs, the liver, the pancreas, the pharynx, and the middle ear.

A mammalian embryo is termed a fetus after the foundations of its organ systems have developed from the germ layers. A human embryo can properly be called a fetus after its eighth week of development.

A principal method of embryology is the comparative study of the embryonic development of the organs and organ systems of various animals of different phyla and classes, such as the starfish, earthworm, shrimp, grasshopper, spider, shark, frog, turtle, chicken, rabbit, pig, and man. Comparative em-

bryological studies sometimes reveal that apparently dissimilar animals undergo similar embryonic stages and therefore are really related to each other. Adult barnacles, which do not resemble crustaceans, were properly classified as crustaceans only after they were observed to pass through embryonic stages that are similar to those of other crustaceans.

Embryologists conduct laboratory experiments to discover the factors that initiate and influence the embryonic development of tissues and organs. For instance, they might remove a rudimentary leg or tail from its normal position on the body of a frog embryo and either put it in a chemical solution or graft it onto another part of the frog's body in order to determine whether or not it will develop normally. They might transplant rudimentary epithelial, muscular, or nerve tissue from a rat embryo to a cat embryo in order to determine how its future development will thereby be affected. They might alter the normal chemical environment of a frog or chick embryo in order to determine how such alteration affects the development of the embryo.

Studies of embryological development enlighten doctors as to the processes involved in the healing of wounds, in the replacement of red blood cells, and in the development of cancer cells.

EMERALD, a clear green form of the mineral beryl. Emeralds have always been highly prized for their beauty and scarcity and are among the most costly of gems. During the times of Alexander the Great and Cleopatra they were mined in Egypt and were elaborately carved. Modern excavations have revealed the exact locations of these operations. The Spaniards found emeralds of rare quality in Peru, but no one has ever located the place from which these were taken. At the present time the finest emeralds come from mines near Bogotá, Colombia, in South America. The stones are also found in the Ural Mountains, in Norway, in Australia, and in North Carolina.

Emerald in nature (left) and cut emerald

EMERSON, RALPH WALDO (1803-1882), American essayist and philosopher, was born in Boston. Many of his forebears, including his father, were Unitarian ministers. When he was eight years old, his father died. Emerson and his brothers underwent hardships in order to secure an education. He entered Harvard in 1817, was graduated in 1821, and then taught for three years in his brother's school. Finding the work uncongenial, he entered the theological school at Cambridge and became pastor of the Second Church of Boston in 1829. He was popular with his congregation. In 1832, however, he no longer agreed with its members about the validity of the sacrament and left the pulpit. Depressed by the death of his wife, he made an extended trip to Europe. Upon his return he married again and settled in Concord, Mass. His first published essay, "Nature," contained the nucleus of his philosophy. He believed in the essential goodness of man and in the soundness of his instincts as guides to life. For this philosophy he drew upon many ancient and modern sources.

Courtesy of The Art Institute of Chicago
Ralph Waldo Emerson, writer and lecturer, advocated self-reliance and individualism.

After the delivery of two addresses, "The American Scholar" to the Phi Beta Kappa Society at Harvard and a speech on religion to the Harvard Divinity School, Emerson became widely known as a lecturer. He made yearly tours, attracting everywhere large appreciative audiences. They were drawn as much by the charm of his manner and personality as by his lofty subjects. Meanwhile there clustered about him in Concord a group of men and women who called themselves Transcendentalists. Emerson, although he edited their periodical, *The Dial*, for two years, did not identify himself with them or with their experiment in communal living at Brook Farm. In 1847 he made a second trip to Europe and was cordially received by Thomas Carlyle and others. The rest of his life was spent in lecturing, writing, and contemplating. He made his third and last trip to Europe in 1872. In the same year his house in Concord burned, and his fellow townspeople showed their affection by rebuilding it for him. Emerson's best known books include *Essays*, *Representative Men*, *The Conduct of Life*, and *Society and Solitude*. He also wrote many poems, including "Threnody," in which he mourned the death of his son, "The Humble-Bee," and "Compensation."

EMERY is a mixture of grains of corundum and grains of iron oxide or iron aluminum oxide. Emery is used as an abrasive in grinding and polishing operations. It is mined in Asia Minor and on the Greek island of Naxos.

Particles of emery are used as an ingredient in some grinding wheels. To make a grinding wheel the emery particles are mixed with a bonding substance. The mixture is shaped and then subjected to heat to complete the bonding. Very little emery is now used in grinding wheels: Manufactured Carborundum is used instead.

Abrasive papers and cloths may contain emery particles. The particles are fastened to the cloth by glue or by a special adhesive. Abrasive cloths are used for metal and glass polishing. Papers are used on the surfaces of soft materials.

EMOTION is a disturbed condition of behavior resulting from an animal's lack of habitual adjustment to a situation. It is manifested in outward behavior, internal changes, and conscious awareness. Emotion often helps an animal to survive, but it may also make the animal unable to cope with a situation. Many kinds of emotions may be distinguished according to the changes in behavior that accompany them.

Outwardly an emotionally responding animal is excited and restless. It shows signs of unusual muscular tension. Internally, changes occur in the vital systems of the body. Breathing becomes heavy, the pulse quickens, and blood pressure increases. Finally, the individual has a peculiar sort of conscious experience. It also becomes unable to think clearly and deliberately.

Emotions may either help or hinder an animal in an emergency. For example, fear may make an animal capable of feats it could not otherwise perform. Fear stimulates the adrenal gland and causes it to release adrenaline. The adrenaline causes the liver to release stored sugar, supplying large amounts of energy to the animal. However, if the fear is intense, it may paralyze the animal. Such paralysis has survival value for some animals because it helps them to escape detection, but it may jeopardize other animals by making them unable to meet the emergency.

When emotional states are prolonged in man, they may become chronic. These chronic emotional states may not only become permanent personality traits but they may lead to various kinds of mental illness.

Our everyday language distinguishes many different kinds of

Russell Clarke, Inc.

As a child develops, emotion, at first displayed as a state of general excitement, gradually becomes differentiated into recognizable responses, ranging from extreme pleasure (lower left), through mild displeasure (left), to extreme displeasure (bottom).

Photo, Three Lions

Photo, Tom Dewberry

emotional behavior. These include surprise, delight, love, jealousy, fear, anger, hate, disgust, disappointment, and grief. Emotions are generally divided into two types: pleasant and unpleasant. Thus love is a pleasant emotion, while fear and hate are unpleasant emotions.

EMPIRE, any territory and people whose ruler has the title of emperor or empress, a title carrying the implication of complete monarchical power. The Babylonian and Egyptian empires, the earliest in history, began as several small kingdoms. Later came the Assyrian, Median, and Persian empires, which grew to enormous size through gradual conquest. The Athenian Empire, in the 5th century B.C., achieved lasting significance because of its cultural contributions. The Macedonian Empire made possible the Hellenization of the ancient world. The Roman Empire began officially in 31 B.C., continuing to A.D. 395, when it was divided into Eastern and Western empires. The Western Empire fell about A.D. 476. Charlemagne was made emperor of the territories he had conquered in 800. After Charlemagne German kings became the rulers of what was

known as the Holy Roman Empire, a loose confederacy of German states, which, with the advent of Napoleonic power in 1806, ceased to exist. Napoleon I and Napoleon III took the title of emperor, and in 1871 the German states formed an empire, which lasted until the end of World War I. The British Empire, which became the British Commonwealth of Nations, grew from small beginnings in the early 17th century to cover a vast area with colonies, dominions, dependencies, and crown territories throughout the world.

EMPIRE DAY is a holiday celebrated in Great Britain and throughout the Commonwealth on May 24. It began as Victoria Day, the birthday of Queen Victoria. After her death the day continued to be celebrated with special emphasis on the unity of all the people of the Empire. All over the world, wherever there are British subjects, Empire Day is observed with processions, fireworks, toasts, and speeches.

ENAMELING, a process in which a glassy coating is applied to the surface of metals. The enamel, the material that makes the glassy coating, is an easily fusible, colorless silicate or glass. Metallic oxides are added to produce color. Before enamel is heated, it has the consistency of coarse powder or tiny flakes of stone. This flaky material, or flux, is melted at a high temperature until

a glass is produced; the glass may be opaque or transparent, depending on the intensity of the heat. After the glass is cooled, it is ground to a fine powder, laid on the metal surface, and then reheated (or fired) in a furnace until the enamel melts and adheres to the metal.

Copper, gold, and silver are usually used for the ground metal in decorative work. Steel and cast iron serve as the ground metal in the enameling of such household appliances as bathtubs, sinks, refrigerators, ranges, and water heaters. Porcelain enamel offers such qualities as hardness, abrasion resistance, heat resistance, and durability and is of great value in the dairy, canning, chemical, brewing, and pharmaceutical industries.

Enameling is an ancient craft, one that was known to the early Egyptians and Babylonians. In Europe from the 12th to the 17th century the most famous center for enameling was Limoges, France. Here enamel was first used for decorating brass reliquaries and church articles. The enamel coating was opaque, but the colors were intense and the designs very beautiful. Around the 16th century the Limoges artisans began to use copper instead of brass and restricted their colors to black and white, with flesh tints for parts of the body. The commonest types of enameled pieces were miniatures and pictures.

ENCEPHALITIS is inflammation of the brain, occurring in epidemic and nonepidemic forms. The cause is viral or bacterial infection of the central nervous system: the meninges, the gray and white matter of the brain, and the spinal cord. In epidemic viral encephalitis, the virus is carried by arthropods (for example, a mosquito or tick), whose bite transmits the virus to man. The symptoms are basically those of a severe febrile infection and nervous-system involvement, with death or recovery in two to three weeks. Nonepidemic encephalitis may be caused by the mumps virus and may also follow other infections.

ENCKE'S COMET travels around the sun in less time than any other known comet. In three and three-tenths years it completes its elliptical path, passing inside Mercury's orbit when closest to the sun and penetrating far into the asteroid belt when farthest from the sun. It was discovered in 1786, and since 1819 it has been seen at each approach to the sun.

ENCOMIENDA, a means of regulating the Spaniards' use of Indian labor in Latin America. Though Queen Isabella of Spain proclaimed the encomienda scheme in 1503 in order to end the Spaniards' enslavement of the Indians, the scheme merely continued the enslavement and also brought about the seizure of the Indians' lands.

Under the encomienda system, deserving Spanish colonists were entrusted with a group of Indians. The Spanish conquerors of Latin America Cortés and Pizarro were each given 100,000 Indians. The Indians owed the colonists a specified number of days of work, and the colonists, in return, were responsible for the physical and spiritual welfare of their charges.

The colonists' abuse of the system called forth from the churchmen, particularly the Dominicans, many protests and from the Spanish kings attempts to reform or do away with the system. However, protests and even revolts by the colonists caused the kings to abandon their attempts. The encomienda system was not outlawed until the end of the 18th century. By that time the descendants of the colonists and the Roman Catholic Church owned all the best land, and most of the Indians had become peons.

ENCYCLOPEDIA, a reference work that gives information, generally, about the various branches of knowledge in separate articles arranged alphabetically. It may also be restricted to the branches of one general topic, such as an encyclopedia dealing exclusively with the arts or with the social sciences. To keep abreast of the times encyclopedias must be constantly revised. Some publishers of encyclopedias issue supplementary yearbooks, which include the most recently compiled facts.

The celebrated French *Encyclopédie,* edited by Diderot and d'Alembert in the 18th century, printed articles written by some of the best minds of the century — Voltaire, Rousseau, and Montesquieu, among others. Some years after the French *Encyclopédie* appeared, a "Society of Gentlemen in Scotland" published the *Encyclopaedia Britannica.* For its famous 11th edition the Britannica solicited articles from some of the most eminent English scholars of the late 19th and early 20th centuries. Since 1929 the *Britannica* has been published in the United States. A number of modern encyclopedias in Europe and America are modeled on the condensed but comprehensive *Brockhaus' Kleines Konversations-Lexikon,* a 19th-century German encyclopedia.

Recently there has been a trend among encyclopedia publishers toward the production of simplified general reference works in a single volume. The publication of encyclopedias prepared especially for children is another development of the 20th century.

HOW TO USE AN ENCYCLOPEDIA

To find out what information a particular encyclopedia includes, what it emphasizes, and how it is organized, you should read the preface, the explanatory section at the very beginning of the set. Most encyclopedias are arranged alphabetically, but you will find some sets that are first grouped under large headings (such as Arts, Biographies, Science, and so on) and are then subdivided alphabetically. Suppose you want some information about Abraham Lincoln. First, of course, you would look up the biography entry — Lincoln, Abraham. This would mention the important events in his life, but there might also be more detailed information under other headings — Emancipation Proclamation, Gettysburg Address, and Lincoln-Douglas Debates. These related entries would probably be referred to in the entry itself or listed at the end of the entry. Such headings are called internal cross-references. If you had looked for information about Lincoln under the heading "Great Emancipator, The," you might have found what is called an external cross-reference: "Great Emancipator, The. See LINCOLN, ABRAHAM." Sometimes it is best to begin with the index of the encyclopedia, for that section lists all the headings and topics related to the subject you are investigating. For example, under the index title LINCOLN, ABRAHAM you might find the volume and page numbers of the following topics: "assassination," "election cartoon," "Gettysburg Address," "quotation on government," and "wartime role."

ENERGY is the ability to do work. It is inherent in all matter. The energy of matter in motion is called kinetic energy. (See KINETIC ENERGY.) The energy of matter at rest is called potential energy, that is, the capacity to do work is stored. The wind, running water, a ball moving through the air, and an automobile in motion are all examples of kinetic energy. Energy stored in coal or in oil, in the water behind a dam, or in a tightly wound watch spring is potential energy, and under the right conditions it can be changed into kinetic energy. For example, the potential energy of the watch spring is changed into kinetic energy as the watch runs.

There are many different kinds of energy; some are mechanical energy, electrical energy, radiant energy, heat energy, and atomic (or nuclear) energy. The many forms of energy are interchangeable. The radiant energy from sunlight is used by plants to make food, which is chemical energy. When eaten, the food is converted by the body into heat energy, mechanical energy, and electrical energy. With these various forms of energy we are able to maintain life and do work.

The sun's energy comes from transformations within its atoms. By learning how to make similar transformations in atoms, man has produced a new source of energy, that is, atomic energy. See ATOMIC ENERGY.

ENERGY, CONSERVATION OF, the principle that energy cannot be created or destroyed, sometimes called the first law of thermodynamics. According to this principle the total quantity of energy within a system remains the same even when energy changes from one form into another, as long as no energy is added from outside the system or withdrawn. Part of the mechanical energy applied in braking a wheel, for instance, is converted into heat energy, which dissipates into the air. This dissipated energy, however, is not destroyed but remains part of the total energy system of the earth and its atmosphere.

The law of conservation of energy was first announced in general terms by Hermann Helmholtz in 1847. It is recognized as one of the great scientific generalizations of the 19th century and occupies an equal place beside the law of conservation of mass, which was developed late in the preceding century. However, according to the special theory of relativity published early in the 20th century mass and energy can be converted into one another. The law accommodating this discovery is called the law of conservation of mass-energy. (See MASS-ENERGY, CONSERVATION OF.) But where no conversion between mass and energy is involved, the law of conservation of energy remains true.

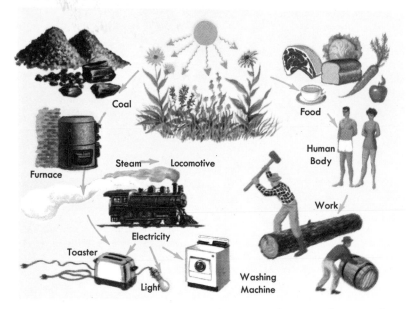

Radiant energy from the sun, stored as chemical energy by plants, is used in various forms by both men and machines. This chart shows some of the ways such energy is used.

ENERGY FROM SUNLIGHT. All life on earth depends for its existence on energy from the sun. The only process that makes the radiant energy of the sun available to life on earth is called photosynthesis. In photosynthesis the radiant energy from sunlight is converted to chemical energy that is stored in food in the plant. It is from this stored chemical energy that the entire world of living things draws its energy for life. In addition, the stored energy of plants of past ages provides the energy of such fuels as coal and oil. See ENERGY; PHOTOSYNTHESIS.

The sun is also the source of the energy of windpower and waterpower and even of part of the energy of tides. Through its effect on air pressure the heat of the sun rules the winds, and through the cycle of evaporation and precipitation it provides the water in streams for conversion to waterpower. While it is true that tidal energy is mainly derived from the moon, it is also influenced by the position of the moon in relation to the sun. Finally, the energy of the sun is used directly in the so-called solar furnace and solar battery. See SOLAR BATTERY; SOLAR FURNACE.

ENGELS, FRIEDRICH (1820-1895), a social theorist and the founder, with Karl Marx, of Marxian socialism. He collaborated with Marx in writing the *Communist Manifesto.* Engels' writings are quite important in the history of socialism.

Friedrich Engels was born in Barmen, Germany, of a prosperous business family. Young Engels, however, broke with his family, discarding their strict Protestant outlook. At the university he came under the influence of several radical movements characteristic of Germany at that time, among them the Young Hegelians and the Young Germany movement. Writing from the standpoint of the Young Hegelians, Engels published in 1842 his first book, which was an attack on the philosopher Friedrich von Schelling. He also wrote articles on a variety of subjects for German periodicals.

In 1842 Engels sailed for England to work in a Manchester company, of which his father was part owner. As a result of his observations of the laissez faire economy (the economy with no government interference) of his time, Engels wrote a critical essay in 1844. He also contributed to Owenite and Chartist papers. In 1844 Engels renewed a friendship with a young man by the name of Karl Marx. This began the literary collaboration that ended only with Marx's death in 1883. Engels published in 1845 his *Situation of the English Workers*, which made him known throughout Europe. In the years until 1850 Engels worked with revolutionists in Germany, France, and Belgium. The failure of the revolutions led him to return to England, where he reentered business and supported Marx, who was writing *Das Kapital.*

Following 1869 Engels devoted all his time to writing and socialism. He belonged to the General Council of the First International, an organization of Socialist and workers' groups. He was a central figure in the Socialist Second International in its early years. After Marx's death Engels edited and published the notes and drafts Marx had left for the last volumes of *Das Kapital.* He also wrote several books developing the principles of dialectical materialism, the philosophy of many Marxists. See MARX, KARL.

ENGINEERING. The first great engineers, men like James Watt of steam-engine fame, blended mechanical skill with practical craftsmanship. Modern machines, however, have to withstand such tremendous stresses and must perform such complex operations that an engineer can no longer rely on a mixture of experience and a good eye. Today engineers must be extremely exacting in their methods. In the field of engineering, the basic information that scientists have discovered about matter and energy is applied to the design, production, and operation of materials, machines, devices, and structures.

Engineering is such a wide field that it is difficult to set up a satisfactory or complete classification of its many branches. Partial descriptions of the major branches follow.

Mechanical engineering deals with the design, production, care, and applications of machines and with the power needed to make the machines operate. Mechanical engineering is a broad field. It includes such divergent subjects as metal processing and the manufacture and analysis of lubricants. Mechanical engineers are concerned with the properties of all materials that are used in or by machines or that are processed by machines. Mechanical engineers help design and manufacture such different products as airconditioning and refrigeration units, machine tools, simple tools, fans, pumps, conveyors, steam engines and turbines, and internal-combustion engines. All these are types of machines or contain machines. The mechanical engineer may work in a steam, hydroelectric, or nuclear powerplant or help to design the machinery in such a plant.

Electrical engineering deals with the production, distribution, and use of energy produced by electricity. An electrical engineer might help in the design and manufacture of electric generators or other powerplant equipment. He might deal

OCCUPATION: Engineer

NATURE OF WORK: Transforming natural resources into forms useful to mankind and doing this in the most efficient manner possible.

PERSONAL FACTORS—ABILITIES, SKILLS, APTITUDES: Aptitude for the sciences and mathematics, attention to detail, accuracy, and an interest in a special field are essential.

EDUCATION AND SPECIAL TRAINING: Bachelor's degree in engineering is the minimum requirement, with special courses in a particular field of study. Advanced degrees are important, leading to positions as aeronautical, ceramics, metallurgical, civil, mechanical, communications, chemical, and design engineers.

WORKING CONDITIONS:

1. INCOME:
   COMPARED WITH OTHER CAREERS WITH EQUAL TRAINING: Average
   COMPARED WITH MOST OTHER CAREERS: High.

2. ENVIRONMENT: Mostly indoor work in laboratory, factory, educational institution, or office, with private industry employing most engineers; civil, utilities, and petroleum engineers also needed

3. OTHER: Hours usually regular; usual benefits in industry; wide chance for advancement; opportunities excellent

WHERE TO FIND MORE INFORMATION: Engineers Council for Professional Development, 29 West 39th Street, New York 18, N.Y.; National Society of Professional Engineers, 2029 K Street, NW, Washington 6, D.C.; Engineers and Scientists of America, Munsey Building, Washington 4, D.C.

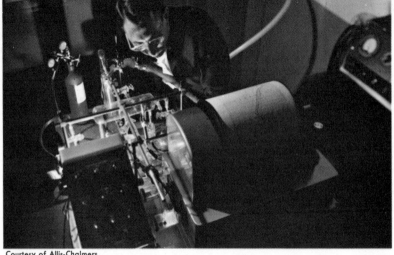

Courtesy of Allis-Chalmers

A research engineer, working in a particular branch of engineering, carries out experiments designed to improve products or production methods or to discover new products or methods.

with electric transmission lines or wiring, with the design or study of electric motors and other electric machinery, with telephone and telegraph transmission, or with radio or television transmission and reception. Electronics is a branch of electrical engineering. See ELECTRONICS.

Chemical engineering is concerned with methods of refining, manufacturing, transporting, storing, and using chemicals. For example, a chemical engineer might work in a petroleum refinery or in a plant for extracting chemicals from brine wells.

Civil engineering is concerned mainly with building stationary structures. Civil engineering includes such branches as surveying and topographic mapping; the study and design of structures such as roofs, beams, and columns; the study of construction methods, ma-

terials, and equipment; soil mechanics, the study of behavior of soils under different conditions; hydraulic engineering—the construction of dams, piers, jetties, canals, irrigation systems, and so on; bridge building; and road and railroad construction. There are several other subdivisions of engineering.

Most engineering work requires college-trained engineers well grounded in physics and mathematics. Engineering in the United States is one of the largest professional occupations, exceeded in size only by teaching and nursing; for men, it is the largest profession. Engineers give technical and, frequently, managerial leadership in industry. They develop new products and processes, design many types of structures, devise the most efficient ways of obtaining minerals from the earth, and contribute in countless ways to the technical progress of our civilization.

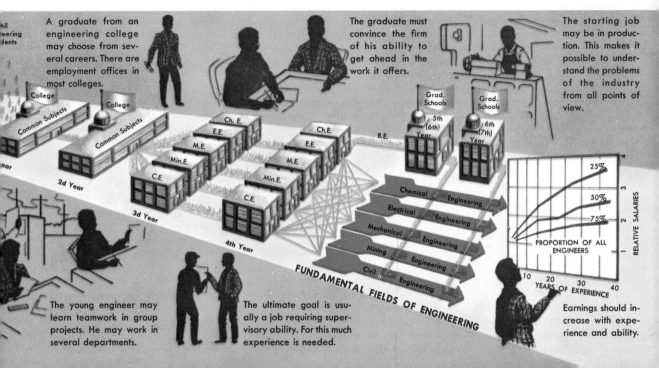

A graduate from an engineering college may choose from several careers. There are employment offices in most colleges.

The graduate must convince the firm of his ability to get ahead in the work it offers.

The starting job may be in production. This makes it possible to understand the problems of the industry from all points of view.

FUNDAMENTAL FIELDS OF ENGINEERING

PROPORTION OF ALL ENGINEERS

The young engineer may learn teamwork in group projects. He may work in several departments.

The ultimate goal is usually a job requiring supervisory ability. For this much experience is needed.

Earnings should increase with experience and ability.

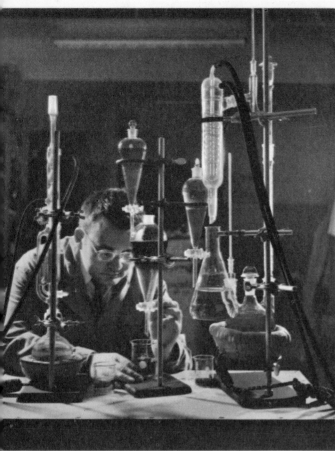

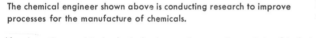

Courtesy of Allis-Chalmers

The chemical engineer shown above is conducting research to improve processes for the manufacture of chemicals.

Courtesy of Allis-Chalmers

Engineers may specialize, as these pictures show, in many fields. The engineer above is working on nuclear powerplant research.

Courtesy of Martin Company

New inventions and technological advances increase the variety of tasks to which the engineer may apply himself. The missile program (right) engages many engineers.

Below are several sales engineers. The sale of chemical, mechanical, and electrical equipment often calls for professional and technical knowledge.

Courtesy of Allis-Chalmers

Monkmeyer

A nation's roads, irrigation projects, airports, bridges, and harbors are the realm of the civil engineer.

Courtesy Molybdenum Corporation of America

These mining engineers (above) examine a molybdenum ore sample. They will determine whether the mine will be profitable, and they will lay out plans for its development after a study of the character, type, and size of the deposits.

The electrical engineer (below) works with electric-power generating plants, electrical machinery, and television.

Courtesy of Allis-Chalmers

The metallurgical engineer (below) is concerned with the processing of metals and their conversion into commercial products.

Courtesy of Allis-Chalmers

ENGINEERS, ARMY. The United States Army Corps of Engineers not only is an important part of the nation's defense system but also is responsible for construction and maintenance of many of the nation's most important civil-engineering projects.

In combat the mission of the engineers is to aid in the advance of friendly forces by removing or overcoming both manmade and natural obstacles and to assist in defense by building barriers and obstacles. Their duties involve, among other things, building roads, bridges, airstrips, and fortifications; laying and clearing minefields; demolishing enemy fortifications and bridges; purifying and distributing water; providing the maps necessary for military operations; and supplying electric power where needed. Often they must work under enemy fire, and during severe enemy attacks they may be pressed into service as infantry.

In peacetime the Corps of Engineers is responsible for all aspects of construction required by the Army and much of that of the Air Force, the Navy, the Atomic Energy Commission, and other defense agencies. This includes building such varied projects as Nike batteries, barracks, airfields, churches, pipelines, theaters, and harbor facilities.

The civil-works aspect of the activities of the Corps of Engineers stems from the early years of the republic when the engineer corps was the only available group of trained civil engineers. Since that time their responsibilities have increased many times over and now include flood-control projects and hydroelectric-power projects, as well as all construction, maintenance, and regulation of 28,600 miles of inland waterways (rivers and canals) and regulation of all harbor facilities on the Atlantic, Pacific, and Gulf coasts and in the Great Lakes. Other important projects of the Corps of Engineers have included construction of the Panama Canal, the Alaska Highway, the United States portion of the St. Lawrence Seaway, and many of the government buildings and monuments as well as the streets, schools, sewage-disposal and water-supply systems, and fire and police stations of Washington, D.C.

ENGLAND occupies the southern part of the island of Great Britain. Often the term *England* is used loosely to denote the entire United Kingdom of Great Britain and Northern Ireland, of which England is the principal part. Although small in size, England is one of the world's most important nations. Its influence has been felt in all continents, and at the beginning of the 20th century it possessed the greatest empire on earth. London, one of the world's largest cities, is its capital and leading seaport. Liverpool is also an important seaport. Other important cities include the steel centers of Birmingham and Sheffield and the textile centers of Manchester and Leeds. England's area is about 51,000 square miles. Its population is about 43,000,000. The Church of England is the established church.

Except for the lowland plains in the east, the surface of the country is generally hilly and is divided by wide valleys. The Cheviot Hills lie on the boundary with Scotland. Southward from the Cheviot Hills extends the Pennine Chain. Scafell Pike, in a northwestern offshoot of the Pennine Chain, rises to some 3,200 feet, the highest point in England. Here is the famous Lake District, known for its picturesque scenery.

England is well supplied with rivers. Many of them are of great importance to commerce and industry. The Thames, navigable by ocean ships to London, is the most important. The greater part of the country's irregular coastline consists of cliffs, in some places rocky, in others clayey. The most extensive stretches of flat coast lie in the east. England's climate is mild, with neither cold winters nor hot summers. Fogs are frequent.

Coal mining flourishes in northern and central England. The largest iron mines are in the east. Important fishing grounds are found in the North Sea. For a fuller discussion of the economy, see UNITED KINGDOM.

The recorded history of England begins with the Roman invasion under Julius Caesar in 55 B.C. After the Romans left in the 5th century A.D., the territory gradually came under control of the Angles and the Saxons, who with the Jutes had come from the Continent. The Danes later invaded the island. Saxon and Danish kings ruled the country until William the Conqueror arrived from Normandy and defeated the English king in the Battle of Hastings in 1066.

The feudal system was introduced

The Avon River flows through England's Wiltshire. In the distance is Salisbury Cathedral, which has the tallest spire in all of England.

Courtesy of the British Information Service

in the island. In 1215 the powerful nobles forced King John to grant the Magna Charta, which curbed the king's power. Protestantism came to England when Henry VIII, who ruled from 1509 to 1547, quarreled with the pope and declared the English church independent of Rome. Under Henry VIII Wales was politically united with England. During the reign of Elizabeth I England gained supremacy of the seas by defeating the Spanish Armada in 1588. The kingdom was abolished (1649-1660) after the unpopular king Charles I was defeated by Oliver Cromwell in a civil war and was beheaded.

The kingdoms of England and Scotland were united in 1707 under the name of Great Britain. Great Britain's victories in wars with Spain and France contributed to the expansion of the British colonial empire, which played such an important role in the history of the 19th century. But in the American Revolutionary War Great Britain lost the richest of its colonial possessions. Great Britain and Ireland were joined in 1801 as the United Kingdom, but the southern part of Ireland separated from the kingdom in 1922.

The reign of Queen Victoria, which lasted from 1837 to 1901, was one of the longest and most prosperous in the history of the nation.

B.I.S.

Micklegate Bar is the main surviving gateway in the walls that surrounded the English city of York during the Middle Ages. On it the head of the slain Duke of York was exposed in 1460.

Colonial development was fast and steady, and it was a great era in literature and science. The 20th century saw the United Kingdom take part in World Wars I and II, fighting on the side of the Allies. After World War II great changes occurred in the British colonial empire. A large part of it became self-governing within the British Commonwealth. Other parts became completely independent nations. In this encyclopedia you will find separate entries on English rulers and events in English history. For detailed map, see UNITED KINGDOM.

The women in the picture below are stripping hops off vines in Kent, a county in southeastern England. Hops are used in making beer.

David Forbert—Shostal

London's Westminster Bridge is near the Houses of Parliament. The clock tower houses the giant bell Big Ben.

Courtesy of TWA—Trans World Airlines

Holywell Street in the upper left is in the famous English university town of Oxford. In the upper right we see the colorful mounted guard of London's Whitehall, where Whitehall Palace, which burned during the 17th century, formerly stood. The photograph at the left shows the docks of the port city of Bristol, in southwestern England; they run into the center of the city. Below to the left is a picture of London's Trafalgar Square, dominated by the tall Nelson Column. Trafalgar Square commemorates Admiral Horatio Nelson's victory over Napoleon in 1805. The lower right photograph shows the level fields and ancient church that typify the countryside of southern England.

B.I.S.

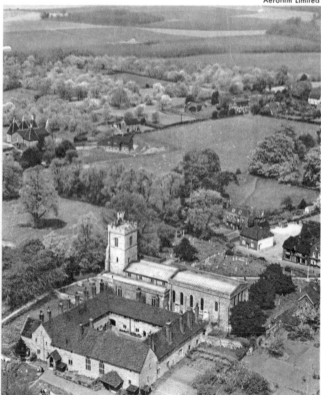

ENGLISH, the most widely spoken language in the world, now the national language of Great Britain, Canada, Australia, New Zealand, South Africa, and the United States. English originated from Anglo-Saxon, the language brought into the British Isles and developed there by Germanic invaders of the 5th century A.D.

English is spoken by some 250 million persons, about one of every ten in the world. Today it is a compulsory part of the curriculum of higher education in most countries. It is the language of trade and business transactions and the language most used in international scientific exchange.

Although the English spoken around the world varies little in other respects, it may be divided into distinct dialects according to vocabulary, usage, pronunciation, and spelling. For example, what an American calls a sidewalk is called a pavement by an Englishman. Similarly, a frying pan is known as a spider in certain areas of the United States.

Pronunciation is judged in Britain by the standard of the king's English, which is mostly the language of the cultured Londoner. There are, however, a large number of local dialects, including the cockney in London. In America there are three chief dialects, the New England, the southern, and the general American, but there are often variations from county to county. The Australian, New Zealand, and South African forms of the language are close to the British, supplemented with many words from the native tongues.

English is a member of the Indo-European family of languages and of the Germanic subfamily. It is closely related to German, Dutch, and the Scandinavian languages. English is a descendant of the language of the Angles, Saxons, and Jutes, who invaded Britain from northern Europe and conquered the Celts. The invaders' tongue replaced the Celtic tongue, although a few Celtic words persisted. Latin words were added by the invaders, chiefly those of the ruling class, who had felt the Roman influence on the Continent before they left it to live in the conquered country. However, most of the Latin adopted in this early period was brought by Roman missionaries to the British Isles. After the Normans conquered England in 1066, many French words were added to the English language. Thus English gained a rich French vocabulary; however, the basic Germanic structure of the language remained unchanged.

The history of the English language is usually divided into periods according to changes in vocabulary and spelling and the loss of inflection. The period of Anglo-Saxon, or Old English, lasted until around 1100. Middle English, the language of Chaucer, was spoken and written approximately from 1100 to 1500. The English in use since 1500 and still in use today is commonly called Modern English.

ENGLISH DERBY, the most important and popular horserace of the year in England. It is run on the first Sunday in June at the Epsom Downs racecourse in Surrey. On an average, 20 three-year-olds, selected from among the finest racehorses in the world, run over a twisting and hilly course of 1½ miles. The winner is usually considered the best horse of his day. The race was first run in 1780. The Derby was founded by Edward Smith Stanley, the 12th earl of Derby.

ENGLISH HORN, a double-reed instrument of the oboe family and a fifth lower in pitch than the oboe. (See OBOE AND BASSOON.) It has a mellower tone than the oboe and a large, pear-shaped bell instead of an open, slightly flaring bell. The reed is in a metal section bent to meet the player's mouth. It has a compass of over two octaves, and its music is written in a key a fifth higher than it is to sound. The name English horn, or *cor anglais*, is a corruption of *cor angle*, "a horn with an angle." Invented in Italy in 1760, it replaced an earlier, similar instrument called the *oboe di caccia*.

The English horn (below) is not really a horn, but rather a woodwind instrument.

ENGLISH LITERATURE. The earliest known works of English literature were written in a language called Old English, or Anglo-Saxon. This was the language of the Germanic tribes (Angles, Saxons, Jutes) that began to invade England about A.D. 449.

THE ANGLO-SAXON PERIOD

The principal stimulus to the writing of this period was the mass conversion of the people to Christianity. Some of the commonest literary forms employed were the biblical epic (mostly paraphrases of passages from the Old Testament), the religious lyric, ecclesiastical narrative (stories of the lives of saints and martyrs), the psalm and hymn, the allegory, and gnomic verse.

The religious lyrics of Caedmon and Cynewulf show a great Christian awareness. To these two almost legendary poets are generally attributed the fine poems called *Genesis B*, *The Dream of the Rood*, and *The Phoenix*.

Culver Pictures

The scholar and historian Bede wrote a famous history of England in the 8th century.

It was not until after the 7th century, however, that religious works became numerous. Throughout the Anglo-Saxon period the secular epic, which drew heavily for its material upon the Germanic mythology brought by the invaders from the Continent, remained a popular form. *Beowulf* is the best known example of this type. It consists of a series of heroic scenes and incidents illustrative of early Teutonic ideals and manners. This epic is a curious mingling of pagan and Christian elements.

Rhyme was rarely used in Anglo-

Saxon poetry, alliteration being employed instead, as is true of the older Teutonic poetry generally. The most valuable of the Old English prose writings is the *Anglo-Saxon Chronicle*, a collection of historical records. The early British and Anglo-Saxon historians, Gildas, Nennius, and Bede, wrote in Latin.

THE MIDDLE ENGLISH PERIOD
1100-1500

The Anglo-Saxon period ended in the 11th century with the Norman conquest of England. England became trilingual: Norman French was spoken by the aristocracy, Latin was spoken in the church, and the people spoke a confusion of Anglo-Saxon dialects.

The ascendancy of Anglo-Norman (the form of Old French spoken and written by the Normans who lived in England) over Anglo-Saxon interrupted the normal literary development and forced English prose and poetry into the background during the 12th, 13th, and 14th centuries. French culture and thought were introduced in England, and a considerable number of French words enriched the English language.

Brown Brothers

Ben Jonson, the Elizabethan dramatist, was a master of realistic satirical comedy.

It was not until the middle of the 14th century that English, and specifically the East Midland Anglo-Saxon dialect of London, from which modern English is derived, became the dominant language in the country.

This was the language in which Chaucer, the first great English poet, wrote *The Canterbury Tales.* (See CANTERBURY TALES.) Another outstanding work by this influential

poet is the poem *Troilus and Criseyde*, considered by some critics to be his greatest artistic achievement.

The period between 1350 and 1400, the year of Chaucer's death, was marked by an important revival of alliterative poetry. The finest examples of this type are *Pearl, Purity* (or *Cleanness*), and *Patience*, all believed to have been written by the same unknown poet; *Sir Gawain and the Green Knight*, one of the best Arthurian romances in English; and *The Vision Concerning Piers Plowman*, attributed to William Langland, generally considered second only to *The Canterbury Tales* as the greatest poem of the Middle English period. The best known English prose writer at the end of the 14th century was John Wycliffe, who initiated the first complete English translation of the Bible.

The poetry of the 15th century was dominated by the influence of Chaucer. There is very little to recommend in the poems of John Lydgate, Thomas Hoccleve, and their contemporaries. These poets continued treating the themes and using the forms of the 14th century and contributed nothing new. In drama, however, the 15th century was a period of great activity and originality. The miracle, or mystery, plays included the great cycles known by the towns in which they were performed: the York plays, the Chester plays, the Coventry plays, and the Wakefield plays (also called the Towneley plays). The other important dramatic form was the morality play, of which type *Everyman* is the best known example. See MIRACLE PLAY; MORALITY PLAY.

The first appearance in English of the Arthurian legend had been Layamon's *Brut* (about 1200). In the latter half of the 15th century Sir Thomas Malory wove the many stories about King Arthur into one great comprehensive prose narrative. His *Morte d'Arthur* supplied the inspiration for many of the later treatments of this legend.

By the close of the Middle English period the ballad, a type of folksong passed on from generation to generation by word of mouth, was flourishing. "Sir Patrick Spens," "Edward," and "Barbara Allen" are three of the most popular ballads composed during this period. See BALLAD.

THE ENGLISH RENAISSANCE

The spirit of the Italian Renaissance spread to England in the 16th century and stimulated literary activity. The outstanding achieve-

Brown Brothers

John Wycliffe is noted for work on a 14th-century English translation of the Bible.

ments in prose included the works of the influential humanists Thomas More (*Utopia*), Thomas Elyot (*The Boke Named the Governeur*), and Roger Ascham (*The Scholemaster*). The 16th century also saw the beginnings of English journalism in the topical pamphlets of Robert Greene and Thomas Nash. The first formal literary criticism in English appeared in the writings of Sir Philip Sidney ("The Defence of Poesie"), Ben Jonson, and others. The prose romances of Sidney, Nash, Greene, and John Lyly (whose *Euphues* started a new prose style) were the forerunners of the English novel.

Exceptional work was also done in poetry and drama. Thomas Wyatt and Henry Howard, earl of Surrey, studied the Italian master Petrarch and introduced the sonnet form into English poetry. (See SONNET.) The result was an outburst of lyric expression that made the 16th century one of richest periods in English literary history. Various collections of poems were published, the two most important being *Tottel's Miscellany* (1557) and *England's Helicon* (1600). The latter included poetry by Sidney, Sir Walter Raleigh, Edmund Spenser, Michael Drayton, Thomas Lodge, Christopher Marlowe, and Robert Greene. Other gifted poets of the period were John Skelton, Thomas Sackville, and Samuel Daniel.

The greatest narrative poem of the Renaissance was Spenser's *Faerie Queene*, a long unfinished allegory designed to teach moral and religious lessons and to glorify Queen Elizabeth I.

The great period of English drama

extended from the reign of Elizabeth I to that of Charles I. Many excellent plays were contributed to the English theater by Lyly, Thomas Kyd (*The Spanish Tragedy*), Greene, George Peele, George Chapman, Thomas Dekker, Thomas Middleton, Thomas Heywood, Philip Massinger, Francis Beaumont and John Fletcher, and John Webster (*The Duchess of Malfi*). Christopher Marlowe, who is considered the father of English tragedy, wrote *The Tragedy of Doctor Faustus* and *Tamburlaine the Great*. Ben Jonson, who wrote *The Alchemist* and *Volpone*, was the great classicist of the Renaissance theater.

What his contemporaries did well, Shakespeare excelled in every way. His sonnets are the finest in the language. As a dramatist he is supreme; his many masterpieces include *Hamlet*, *Othello*, *King Lear*, *Macbeth*, *Romeo and Juliet*, and *Julius Caesar*.

THE 17TH CENTURY

The 17th century was marked by a new emphasis on reason and scientific inquiry. This new intellectual spirit was first expressed in the philosophical works of Francis Bacon, *The Advancement of Learning* and the *Novum Organum*.

It was also a century of great religious and political controversies. John Milton, the great poet of the time, wrote political tracts as well as great religious epics: *Paradise Lost*, *Paradise Regained*, and *Samson Agonistes*. John Bunyan's great Christian allegory *The Pilgrim's Progress* was one of the most influential works of the latter half of the century.

John Milton, one of England's greatest poets, was both a Puritan and a classical humanist.
Brown Brothers

Milton's contemporaries, such as Robert Burton, Thomas Browne, Thomas Fuller, and Izaak Walton, bent English prose to topics as diverse as fishing, biography, and religious meditation. The Cavalier poets—Robert Herrick, Richard Lovelace, and John Suckling—wrote delicate, intensely personal lyrics. The metaphysical poets — John Donne, George Herbert, Richard Crashaw, and Henry Vaughan — wrote an entirely new kind of poetry, characterized by intellectual brilliance and subtle language.

The restoration of the Stuart monarchy after the grim experiences of the Civil War and the Puritan Commonwealth was accompanied by a desire on the part of many to relax and enjoy life rather than to concern themselves with serious problems. The theaters, closed in 1642 by the Puritans, were reopened in 1660 and soon were dominated by what is known as Restoration comedy, characterized by gay and witty dialogue. Its best writers were William Wycherley, William Congreve, and George Farquhar. Restoration life was chronicled by Samuel Pepys in his entertaining *Diary*.

The age was neoclassical in the sense that it found its literary ideals in the Latin classics and its great example in the perfection of French culture under Louis XIV. The leading thinker of this age was John Dryden, equally gifted in poetry, prose, and drama.

THE 18TH CENTURY

The early decades of the 18th century are referred to as the Age of Pope. Great emphasis was placed on form and reason rather than on the use of the imagination. The work of Alexander Pope, the era's dominant poet, is distinguished by its wit, which he used to great effect in satirizing his many enemies. The prose writers Joseph Addison and Richard Steele were friends of Pope, and they reflected his attitudes in their influential periodicals *The Tatler* and *The Spectator*.

The literary leaders thought very highly of themselves, as indicated by their naming their era the Augustan Age after the greatest era of ancient Rome. But the greatest figure of the day distinguished himself by reacting with disgust to virtually everything he saw about him. Jonathan Swift expressed his ideas in the famous satire *Gulliver's Travels*.

The English novel, which was eventually to displace poetry as the principal form in English literature, began its great tradition in the 18th

Brown Brothers

Alexander Pope was the author of the mock-epic poem *The Rape of the Lock*.

century. The novel was foreshadowed by the works of Daniel Defoe (*Robinson Crusoe*, *Moll Flanders*); they purported to be reports of actual events but were in reality the products of Defoe's imagination. The first true novel was Samuel Richardson's *Pamela*, a sentimental work parodied by Henry Fielding in *Joseph Andrews*. Fielding, the first of England's great realistic novelists, reached his peak in his masterpiece *Tom Jones*. Other 18th-century novelists were Tobias Smollett (*Roderick Random*, *Humphry Clinker*), Laurence Sterne (*Tristram Shandy*), and Oliver Goldsmith (*Vicar of Wakefield*).

The second half of the century was dominated by Samuel Johnson. Johnson is important not so much for what he wrote as for what he believed, talked about, and demonstrated by his own example. One of the masterpieces of the Age of Johnson is the monumental biography of him by James Boswell. Other masterpieces include the plays of Richard Sheridan (*The School for Scandal*, *The Rivals*) and the poetry of Thomas Gray ("Elegy Written in a Country Churchyard"). These authors continued the strict classical forms of the Age of Pope, but in their subject matter, which was more concerned with individual men than with abstract ideas, they presaged the coming of the romantic period.

AGE OF ROMANTICISM

As the 18th century drew to a close, an intense reaction set in against much that it stood for. This

The romantic poet William Wordsworth wrote many lyrics about the beauties of nature.

reaction was marked by an enthusiastic individualism, and it had a bewildering variety of results. (See ROMANTICISM.) The English literary movement to which the name romanticism is attached placed particular emphasis on the concerns of ordinary man and nature, on replacing the inflated poetic diction of the previous period with the language of ordinary speech, on individual freedom (as promised by the French Revolution of 1789), and on self-expression.

This movement is considered to have been officially launched with the publication of *Lyrical Ballads* (1798), a small collection of verse by William Wordsworth and Samuel Taylor Coleridge. Wordsworth's famous preface to the second edition became the manifesto of English romanticism.

The other principal romantic poets were William Blake, Percy Bysshe Shelley, John Keats, and Lord Byron. Sir Walter Scott is also identified with the romantics as a poet and a novelist (*Ivanhoe, The Bride of Lammermoor, Quentin Durward*). Scott is credited with having created the historical novel.

Among the outstanding prose writers of the period were Charles Lamb (*Essays of Elia*), William Hazlitt, and Thomas De Quincey (*Confessions of an English Opium Eater*).

THE VICTORIAN AGE

The literature of the Victorian Age, named for the English queen who reigned from 1837 to 1901, was conditioned by the Industrial Revolution, the impact of Charles Darwin's theory of evolution upon theology, and the development of the democratic state. Human values were set forth in the Victorian novel,

the richest genre of the age. Charles Dickens and William Makepeace Thackeray were the first of the great Victorian novelists. Of Dickens' many novels, *Oliver Twist, David Copperfield, A Tale of Two Cities,* and *Great Expectations* are the most widely read. Thackeray's great masterpiece of Victorian middle-class life is *Vanity Fair.*

Other important novelists were George Eliot (*Adam Bede, Silas Marner, Middlemarch*), Jane Austen (*Pride and Prejudice, Sense and Sensibility, Mansfield Park, Emma*), Thomas Hardy (*The Return of the Native, The Mayor of Casterbridge, Jude the Obscure*), Charlotte Brontë (*Jane Eyre*), Emily Brontë (*Wuthering Heights*), Samuel Butler (*The Way of All Flesh*), and Robert Louis Stevenson (*Treasure Island, Kidnapped, The Master of Ballantrae*).

The two principal Victorian poets were Robert Browning and Alfred Tennyson. The exploration of the human soul was a central theme of Browning's poetry, whereas Tennyson's poetry was largely concerned with philosophic ideas. Hardy, Elizabeth Barrett Browning, Algernon Charles Swinburne, Dante Gabriel Rossetti, Oscar Wilde, and Matthew Arnold all wrote memorable verse.

Many of these and other writers sought to harmonize traditional culture with the materialism of the industrial state—John Henry Cardinal Newman, from the point of view of Roman Catholicism; Thomas Carlyle, from that of German romanticism and hero worship; John Ruskin, Walter Pater, William Morris, and Oscar Wilde, from that of aestheticism and the fine arts.

THE 20TH CENTURY

One of the most important developments of the later 19th and early 20th centuries was the revival of the

Charles Dickens was one of the severest critics of Victorian industrial society.

drama, which had been languishing since the time of Sheridan. Oscar Wilde (*Lady Windermere's Fan, The Importance of Being Earnest*), James Barrie, and Bernard Shaw (*Major Barbara, Man and Superman, Saint Joan*) all wrote successful plays. William Butler Yeats, John Millington Synge, and Sean O'Casey, leaders of the so-called Irish renaissance, wrote excellent plays on Irish themes. After World War II poetic drama reemerged with the plays of Christopher Fry and T. S. Eliot.

H. G. Wells (*Tono-Bungay*), Arnold Bennett (*The Old Wives' Tale*), John Galsworthy (*The Forsyte Saga*), and Aldous Huxley (*Brave New World*) dedicated the modern novel to social themes. D. H. Lawrence (*Sons and Lovers, Lady Chatterley's Lover*), Virginia Woolf (*Mrs. Dalloway, Orlando*), James Joyce (*Portrait of the Artist as a Young Man,*

James Joyce was a 20th-century master of the stream-of-consciousness technique.

Ulysses), Joseph Conrad (*Lord Jim, Victory*), Graham Greene (*The Power and the Glory, Brighton Rock*), and Somerset Maugham (*Of Human Bondage*) explored the depths of human emotions and motivations, sometimes with a stream-of-consciousness technique, sometimes with quiet humor, and sometimes with biting satire.

In the 1930's a group of poets, W. H. Auden, Cecil Day Lewis, and Stephen Spender, and the novelist Christopher Isherwood approached social problems from a Marxist point of view. The political satirist George Orwell later wrote *Animal Farm*, a biting satire of Soviet communism, and *1984*, a novel depicting life in a totalitarian state of the future.

Other important poets of the 20th century include Gerard Manley Hopkins, Robert Bridges, Francis

Thompson, A. E. Housman, Rudyard Kipling, John Masefield, W. H. Davies, and Walter de la Mare. Particularly identified with World War I are Rupert Brooke, Wilfred Owen, and Robert Graves. The Welsh poet Dylan Thomas possessed amazing lyric gifts.

In the 1950's a considerable stir was created by several writers known as the Angry Young Men, of whom the most noteworthy were the novelists Kingsley Amis (*Lucky Jim, Take a Girl Like You*) and John Braine (*Room at the Top*) and the playwright John Osborne (*Look Back in Anger, The Entertainer*).

Additional novelists worthy of mention are E. M. Forster (*Howards End, A Passage to India*), W. H. Hudson (*Green Mansions*), Kipling (the *Jungle Book* and *The Second Jungle Book, Kim*), Joyce Cary, Evelyn Waugh, Henry Green, C. P. Snow, and Angus Wilson.

This encyclopedia contains separate entries on many of the authors mentioned here.

ENGLISH SPARROW, or house sparrow, is not really a sparrow. It belongs to a family of finchlike Old World birds known as weaverbirds. It was introduced at Brooklyn, N.Y., in 1850 and has spread across the continent until it is one of the commonest North American birds. It is numerous wherever people live. It occurs also in parts of Central America and South America and in the West Indies, Europe, Asia, northern Africa, and elsewhere.

Almost everyone recognizes the male, with his black bib, white cheeks, and chestnut nape. The female, however, is nondescript—dull brown above, dingy white below. Young birds resemble the females.

The English sparrow feeds on almost anything edible; in winter it lives mostly on weed seeds and grain and on rations placed out at bird-feeding stations. Its voice is a monotonous chirp. Its nest is a bulky mass of grass, feathers, and trash,

The English sparrow may nest in a bird box.

usually tucked into a bird box or a cavity about a building; when in a tree, it is domed and has a side entrance hole. Five or six eggs are laid, and there are several broods annually.

Because of their aggressive habits and rapid increase in numbers, English sparrows are usually regarded as undesirable birds. They tend to preempt the available nesting sites and to drive away useful and attractive birds.

ENGRAVING, the art of representing designs and pictures on wood, glass, precious stones, and metals by means of incisions made with special instruments. Since the introduction of the related techniques of etching, mezzotint, aquatint, and drypoint, however, the term has been used for all works of art executed on plates and intended for printing on paper, by whatever means they are produced. Impressions from wood are called woodcuts. Those printed from metal plates, such as copper, steel, and zinc, are called engravings, or prints.

Such archaeological finds as writings on slabs of stones found in the ruins of ancient Greece, Rome, and the Near East prove that engraving is an old art. As early as the 10th century printing from engraved wooden blocks was common in China. In Europe it has been practiced since before the 15th century. The best early engravers were Germans, especially Albrecht Dürer. He made both woodcuts and copperplates and used the techniques of etching (designs engraved into the copperplate by means of nitric acid) and of drypoint (pictures incised with a steel or other metal point). The art of etching reached perfection in the works of the Dutch masters, notably Rembrandt and Vandyke.

About the middle of the 17th century the German Ludwig von Siegen introduced the mezzotint, which was extensively used both for the creation of original pictures and for the reproduction of paintings, including portraits and landscapes. This technique employed the instruments of the rocker, which has many sharp teeth, and of scrapers.

The aquatint came into use about the middle of the 18th century. This technique produces an effect similar to watercolor drawings. Like etching and engraving it was used for book illustration, as well as for landscape and portrait subjects.

Beginning with the 19th century,

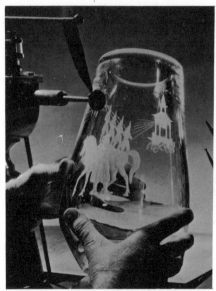

Courtesy of Corning Glass Works

Copper-wheel engraving requires great skill. The engraver presses the glass against small copper grinding wheels fixed to a lathe.

the growing necessity for large numbers of good impressions from one plate led to the increasing use of steel as a substitute for copper. Engravings in steel reproduce sharper lines than those in copper. See ETCHING; PHOTOENGRAVING; WOODCUT.

ENLIGHTENMENT, the term applied to a primarily philosophical movement that reached its height during the 18th century. Basic to the so-called enlightened outlook was the conviction that man is a rational being, capable of comprehending and understanding the world about him through the exercise of his reason alone. The Enlightenment was characterized by a vigorous criticism of the existing social structure in general and the church and monarchy in particular; by great intellectual productivity, especially in the fields of social, economic, and political theory; and by an emphasis on the empirical method in the sciences. Near the core of enlightened thought were the doctrines and theories expounded by John Locke and Pierre Bayle and the concepts implicit in Isaac Newton's work. Those associated with the movement in France included Voltaire, Jean Jacques Rousseau, and the Encyclopedists; in Germany, Gotthold Lessing and Hermann Reimarus; in England, Samuel Johnson; and in America, Thomas Paine, Benjamin Franklin, and Thomas Jefferson. See VOLTAIRE.

ENVELOPE, a piece of paper cut, folded, and sealed in such a way that it can enclose a very small object or other pieces of paper. Some envelopes do not enclose anything at all, the message being written on the inside surfaces of the envelope itself.

According to the *U.S. Postal Manual* envelopes may be used in any color that does not interfere with the legibility of the address and postmark. As a rule, brilliant colors should not be used.

Although they are permissible, envelopes larger than 9 by 12 inches are not recommended, as they tend to get bent and injured in handling. Standard-size envelopes are best as they fit the sorting and canceling machines. The post office will no longer accept for mailing envelopes that are less than 2¼ by 4 inches.

For regulations concerning the addressing of envelopes to members of the armed forces and for matters concerning other details of postal regulations, you should consult your local postmaster.

ENVIRONMENT, in relation to human beings, the natural and manmade physical surroundings, the institutions, and the opinions and ideas that surround individuals. Obviously the environment is very important to people. It affects the way people live, down to the smallest detail. Environment does not control the choices man makes with regard to his goals, but it limits the possibilities open to him. People who stress the importance of environment in human development and behavior are called environmentalists. Environmentalists used to debate heatedly with those who stressed the importance of heredity. Both these viewpoints can be carried to the extreme. Most scholars are probably of the opinion that human behavior is affected by an interplay of environment with heredity.

Environmentalism was expressed by the ancient Greek historian Herodotus, who showed the importance of geography to the development of Egyptian civilization. The modern viewpoint on the importance of environment dates from the French political economist Jean Bodin in the 16th century. In the 19th century Charles Darwin propounded a theory of the evolution of living beings that stressed the importance of environment in evolution's direction. The discovery of genes renewed the environment-*vs.*-heredity argument. (See EVOLUTION.) Toward the end of the 19th century psycholo-

gists seized on the idea of environment as an explanation of human behavior. Certain of the behaviorists, ignoring individual uniqueness, claimed that by education they could produce the sort of individual they set out to produce. This idea is akin to John Locke's view that human minds are a blank slate "written upon" by experience and education. If expressed in a less extreme way there is some truth in these ideas, and scientists have studied the effects of environment on identical twins. Identical twins are indeed an ideal human laboratory, for they have an identical genetic heredity. The studies are incomplete, but they seem to show that within the limits set by heredity there can be a great difference in the outlook and personality of twins reared in different environments.

Environmentalism has influenced social doctrines. Some forms of aristocratic government were founded on the idea that certain groups, generally those already in power, inherited their ability to govern. Those of democratic convictions seemed to feel that most men, if given the proper education, could develop the traits necessary for self-government. Thus, within democratic nations there were movements toward universal education. The English social reformer Robert Owen also felt that character is the result of the social environment. Karl Marx laid great stress on the impact of the economic environment on human behavior. Many social welfare projects, such as slum clearance, are attempts to alter environment so that human beings can develop into more constructive citizens.

It should always be kept in mind that heredity and environment interact. Man's heredity determines his ability to perceive colors. In this manner colors become a part of his environment and influence him. To go a step further, it must not be forgotten that man also acts on his environment. A society may choose to use a channel as a barrier between itself and other groups. Or it may use the channel as an easy way to communicate with others. See HEREDITY.

ENZYME, an agent that controls chemical reactions of living plants and animals. Enzymes are complex chemical agents produced by living cells and are called organic catalysts because they influence chemical reactions without being permanently changed themselves. En-

zymes influence the chemical reactions of digestion and of synthesis of all compounds produced by the organism. They are also necessary to reactions for the production of energy.

Enzymes are specific, that is, an enzyme works on a particular substance in one type of reaction. Since the chemical structure of most enzymes is not known, they are usually named for the substance or type of substance upon which they act (carbohydrases accelerate digestion of carbohydrates, and oxidases promote oxidation). Enzymes, to be most effective, require special conditions of acidity and temperature. They are destroyed or inactivated by too much or too little acid or by too high or too low a temperature.

Bacteria, molds, and yeast secrete enzymes. Some of the reactions involving enzymes are useful in industry—in fermenting alcohol, making cheese, and leavening bread.

EOS. See AURORA.

EPIC, a long narrative poem concerned with heroic actions of legendary or historical figures. Homer's *Iliad* and *Odyssey*, the most ancient epics known to us, still rank as the greatest ones ever written. Their date of composition dates from at least the 8th century B.C. So many later writers of epics have taken their cue from Homer that it might be well to consider the epic form as he handled it.

Since the subject and style of the classical, or Homeric, epic are exalted, the hero must be better than the ordinary man. Both Achilles (hero of the *Iliad*) and Odysseus (hero of the *Odyssey*) are brave; both are men of action; and both have largeness of soul, a quality akin to nobility. In other ways the two present an interesting contrast. Achilles is a sort of splendid barbarian. A warrior of great pride, he is quick to feel injury, furious in revenge, wild in grief. But he is also compassionate, capable of great generosity, and scrupulously honest. Odysseus, though no less brave than Achilles, is prudent and farseeing. He can control his anger and await the opportune moment for action. He is valued by the other fighters for his wise counsels and is often consulted on matters of policy. Odysseus will even resort to cunning and lies if it serves his purpose to do so. The subject of the *Iliad* is the wrath of Achilles; that of the *Odyssey* is the adventures of Odysseus and his revenge upon his wife's suitors. The single-minded and impetuous Achilles has the warrior's passion for glory in battle. Odysseus, on the other hand, has a many-sided character: He is fighter, counselor, ship's captain, father and husband, and statesman.

The verse form of Homer's epic poetry is based on the Greek hexameter line. Within the epic form he observes certain narrative and literary conventions: invocation of the Muse, rivalries among the gods, description of the hero's shield, funeral games, and the visit to the underworld. Although the narratives in both poems begin in the middle of things, they are unified by single, continuous lines of action. At appropriate points in each poem Homer is able to backtrack to earlier incidents that form a background for the present action. Throughout both the *Iliad* and the *Odyssey*, Homer freely mixes the narrative manner with dialogue and conversation.

Virgil's *Aeneid* continues the tradition of epic poetry established by Homer. His hero, Aeneas, is constantly referred to as *pius*, although like Achilles and Odysseus, he has fought in the Trojan War. To the ancient Roman *pietas* was not Christian piety or holiness. It meant reverence for one's parents, for one's city and country, and, above all, for the gods. Aeneas, with firm belief in his own destiny, leaves the Trojan battlefield to found a new nation. Like Homer, Virgil states the subject of his poem in the first line: "Of arms and the man I sing." He uses the Latin hexameter line and also makes use of various epic conventions established by Homer. The visit to the underworld in Book VI is one of the most memorable of these borrowings.

The earliest epic poem in English is a work of about the 8th century A.D. entitled *Beowulf*. Though outside the classical tradition, it shares the epic themes of avenging wrongs and of courage in battle. See BEOWULF.

In the Christian epics of Dante and Milton we are confronted with a continuation of the classical tradition and at the same time with a sharp break from the classical spirit. The admiration of both writers for Homer and Virgil is quite obvious, as are also their borrowings of classical myths and narrative devices. Milton chooses to use a pentameter line rather than a hexameter line since this is the traditional meter for the high style in English poetry. (See POEM.) Dante goes so far as to make Virgil his guide through Hell. But the hero of the *Divine Comedy* is not a warrior, ruler, or adventurer. He is a troubled man in the prime of life, primarily concerned with the salvation of his soul. The very titles of each section —*Hell, Purgatory,* and *Paradise*— reflect the theological values that determine the structure of the poem.

The hero of Milton's *Paradise Lost* is Adam. Satan is his mortal enemy, but their conflict cannot be resolved in physical combat. It is Adam's (and Eve's) obedience to God that is at stake, and when Satan makes Adam betray that trust, neither is the victor. When Adam falls, he loses Paradise for all of mankind. God curses Satan for his treachery and condemns him to eternal imprisonment in the body of a serpent. Thus, neither the "I" of the *Divine Comedy* nor Adam of *Paradise Lost* is a hero in the classical sense: They are not concerned with courage in battle, honor among men, or glory; rather, their concern is with sin, redemption, and eternal life.

A number of lesser epics modeled on the styles of Homer and Virgil were written through the centuries after the Golden Age of Rome under Augustus. Lucan's *Pharsalia* is the best of these early Latin imitations of Virgil. Most of the epics of his contemporaries were extremely artificial and pretentious. The *Lusiads* (1572), written by the Portuguese poet Camoëns, is one of the most interesting epics of the Renaissance. The *Chanson de Roland* of medieval France, like the chivalric tales of 16th-century Italian writers (Tasso and Ariosto, for example) are really romances rather than epics. See AENEID; DIVINE COMEDY; ILIAD AND ODYSSEY; PARADISE LOST.

EPICUREANISM, a philosophy based on the idea that pleasure is the chief goal of human beings. Its founder was Epicurus, who lived in Greece from 342 to 270 B.C. In 307 B.C. Epicurus established a philosophical school in Athens. The school was held in a garden, which Epicurus had purchased. His pupils lived in a community at the garden and put Epicureanism into practice. The life of the community was very plain, water and barley bread being the staple food and drink. Epicureanism was therefore not the sort of immoderate pleasure seeking that the Stoics claimed it to be.

Epicurus was not a systematic philosopher like Plato and Aristotle. He accepted the atomic theory of Democritus, which is very different from the modern atomic concept. Infinite space is a void, he said, except for the uncountable numbers of solid, moving particles called atoms. These atoms came together to form worlds, but these worlds constantly dissolved, and new ones arose to replace them. Epicurus also denied that the Greek gods had anything to do with the operation of the world or that Fate directed the lives of men. In this universe of atoms, truth for human beings, said Epicurus, lay in sensation. Evidence was based on feeling and what a person perceived with his senses or with his memory of sense experiences. Thus, Epicureans quarreled with Aristotelians, who valued reason above sensation.

The ethical doctrine of Epicurus was the really important aspect of his philosophy. Epicureanism was a form of hedonism, or a pursuit of pleasure. However, pleasure to the Epicureans was a tranquil feeling. With great care the true Epicurean weighed his choices, and he chose only the path that would be most conducive to pleasure in the long run. The Epicurean was therefore rational and even a bit solemn.

Epicureanism was popular among the Romans. It was one of the four chairs of philosophy established by the Roman emperor Marcus Aurelius at Athens. Lucretius wrote one of the greatest works inspired by the Epicurean philosophy, *De rerum natura*. Epicureanism was also a major influence during the Renaissance, during which period Pierre Gassendi revived and systematized the philosophy. The French writers Molière and Voltaire were also inclined toward Epicureanism. See ETHICS.

EPIDEMIC. An epidemic is the outbreak of a disease that attacks many persons at the same time at different places. It spreads with great rapidity, being extremely virulent and fatal at the first onset and gradually becoming spent and feeble so that the early cases are usually the worst. The plague, cholera, smallpox, encephalitis, poliomyelitis, influenza, and other infectious diseases may become epidemic. The lower animals are also subject to epidemic or, more properly, epizootic influences. Epidemics seldom run simultaneously. An epidemic of smallpox may be followed by one of measles, then scarlet fever, and so on. Medical science has greatly reduced the occurrence and mortality rate of epidemics.

EPSTEIN, SIR JACOB (1880-1959), English sculptor and artist. Epstein is known for his lifelike statues, his religious figures, his bronze portraits, and his drawings.

Epstein was born in the lower East Side of New York. After studying at the Art Students' League and under sculptor George Grey Barnard in New York (while working for a foundry for bronze casting at night), Epstein made up his mind to go to Europe. In England he met Mrs. Hamilton Fish, a wealthy patron of the arts, who financed his studies in Paris. After three years in Paris he went to London. Eventually he settled in England and became a British subject.

Epstein executed many controversial works, including those based on biblical themes: the "Ecce Homo," a huge marble "Genesis," an alabaster "Adam," "Jacob and the Angel," "Madonna and Child," a large bronze "Visitation," and "Christ in Majesty" (Llandaff Cathedral in Wales). The bronze group "Social Consciousness" in Philadelphia and the marble tomb of Oscar Wilde in Paris are also noteworthy. He also did numerous portraits, including those of George Bernard Shaw, Joseph Conrad, John Dewey, Somerset Maugham, and Albert Einstein. Examples of Epstein's work are in many places, including private collections, the Tate Gallery of London, the Brooklyn Museum of New York, and the Metropolitan Museum of Art of New York.

Epstein wrote two autobiographical works, *Let There Be Sculpture* and *Epstein: An Autobiography*. Arnold Haskell recounted his conversations with Epstein in *The Sculptor Speaks*. Epstein was knighted in 1954.

EQUATION. One mathematical expression connected to another by the sign of equality (=) is called an equation. A mathematical expression alone may involve operations like addition, subtraction, multiplication, and so on, but never an equal sign. An equation, on the other hand, is a statement about two such expressions asserting that they are equal. It equates one expression with the other, hence the term *equation*.

An equation is like a balance scale that has equal weights on its two sides. The expressions on either side of the equal sign in an equation are, in fact, called the two sides of the equation. Any change on one side must always be exactly compensated by an equal change on the other side in order to preserve the equality or balance.

An equation may be as simple as the statement in arithmetic that $1 + 1 = 2$. In this example the expression $1 + 1$ is the left side of the equation, and 2 is the right. More often the equation expresses a more general idea algebraically, as in $a = 2b$, which states that one quantity is equal to twice another quantity. Algebraic equations can, of course, be much more complicated, but they always consist of two expressions, one on each side of an equal sign.

Using equations to solve problems usually requires changing the form of the equation. There are many ways to change the form, but all of them rest on the principle that an operation performed on one side of the equation must be balanced by performing the same operation on the other side. The equation $a = 2b$ expresses a in terms of b. If we wanted to express b in terms of a, we could divide $2b$ by 2 and obtain b. To maintain the equality of both sides of the equation we would have to divide the other side, a, by 2 also, which would be written $\frac{a}{2}$. The new form of the equation would then be $\frac{a}{2} = b$. Other operations, such as addition, subtraction, and multiplication, can be performed on both sides of an equation in a similar way.

EQUATOR, the imaginary circle drawn around the earth midway between the North Pole and the South Pole. It is the earth's greatest circumference, 24,902 miles. Latitude is measured north and south from the Equator.

EQUATORIAL AFRICA consists of the four republics of the French Community located in north-central Africa. They formerly were known as French Equatorial Africa. Chad lies in the north, the Central African Republic (formerly Ubangi-Shari) in the middle, and Gabon and Congo (formerly Middle Congo) in the south. The four republics cover an area of about 970,000 square miles, much more than three times the size of Texas. Most of the approximately 5,000,000 people are Negroes, who belong to many different tribes.

Equatorial Africa has lowlands and mountainous regions, forests and grasslands, swamps and deserts. Its resources are mostly undeveloped. The Congo River and its tributary, the Ubangi, form the area's southeastern border.

Congo and Gabon, situated on the Equator, have high temperatures and heavy rainfall, which support thick tropical forests. Gorillas, monkeys, and leopards are some of the animals that live in these forests. Mineral resources include diamonds, gold, lead, and manganese. Coffee, cocoa, and palm oil are produced.

Much of the Central African Republic consists of open grasslands, where elephants, buffaloes, antelopes, and lions roam. The climate is hot, and there are wet and dry seasons. Livestock is raised. Cotton and peanuts are important crops. Chad is largely desert—very hot and very dry—but there are some areas where livestock is raised.

Although the Portuguese discovered the coast of Equatorial Africa in the 15th century, the region was not settled by Europeans until the French came to the Gabon area in 1839. Explorations steadily expanded the French sphere. First known as the French Congo, the region in 1910 was divided into separate colonies. During World War II it was an important part of the Free French territory. The republics lost their colonial status when the new French constitution was adopted in 1958.

EQUINOX, a moment when the direction of the sun from the earth's center is exactly toward the celestial equator. (See CELESTIAL SPHERE.) Every year there are two equinoxes. The vernal equinox, about March 21, marks the end of winter and the beginning of spring. The autumnal equinox, about September 23, marks the end of summer and the beginning of autumn.

The direction of the sun from the earth's center is always toward some point on a huge, imaginary circle in the sky called the ecliptic. As the earth revolves around the sun, the sun's direction among the stars

gradually shifts around the circle of the ecliptic. The earth's direction from the sun is, of course, also toward the ecliptic but in the reverse direction.

All the directions from the earth's center through the Equator establish a second circle in the sky called the celestial equator. The sun would always be in the direction of the celestial equator if the earth's axis were not tilted. But because the axis is tilted, half of the celestial equator is tilted above the ecliptic and half below it. The two circles cross only at two points, and an equinox is the moment when the sun lies in the direction of either of these two points. The points themselves are also called equinoxes.

At the moment of an equinox the earth's tilt is sideways to the sun, neither toward it nor away from it. Therefore both the northern and southern halves of the earth rotate an equal length of time in sunlight, and day and night are approximately equal in all parts of the world. This explains why it is called equinox, because the word *equinox* comes from two Latin words meaning "equal night."

Because the direction of the earth's axis is changing very slowly, the position of the equinoxes is also changing. This effect is known as the precession of the equinoxes. While in ancient times the equinoxes were in the constellations Aries and Libra, today they are in the constellations Pisces and Virgo.

The constellation Equuleus, represented above by a horse's head, is found in the sky near Pegasus, the great Winged Horse.

EQUULEUS, or the Little Horse, is a small, faint northern constellation between Pegasus and Delphinus near the celestial equator. It is visible in the evening sky from mid-northern latitudes between July and December.

ERA OF GOOD FEELING, the name used for the presidency of James Monroe, 1817-1825, when there was no rivalry between political parties. Political rivalry died out because Monroe's party, the Democratic-Republicans, adopted many of the policies of their old opponents, the Federalists. The Democratic-Republicans now agreed with the Federalists that the federal government had many powers to which they had previously objected. Members of both parties favored construction of roads and canals by the federal government and the establishment of tariffs to protect the new industries of the United States from European competition. The name Era of Good Feeling is misleading, for the place of the national parties with real principles was taken by a multitude of factions in various economic groups and sections of the country, which hated each other bitterly. During this period the split between North and South became evident in 1820, but it was temporarily smoothed over by the Missouri Compromise. See MISSOURI COMPROMISE.

ERASER, material to remove pen or pencil marks from paper or to remove chalk marks from chalkboards.

Erasers for pen or pencil marks are compounds made in different degrees of hardness, using either natural or synthetic rubber as a binder for cleaning and abrasive materials. The main compounding ingredient is a vulcanized oil known under the name of Factice. Gum erasers are made from Factice alone without a rubber binder and are therefore brittle and break into pieces. Ink erasers differ from pencil erasers by their content of a coarser abrasive, which is mostly pumice stone. A plastic or kneadable type of eraser is used for charcoal work and general cleaning. Typewriter erasers are sometimes made in disk form; sometimes they are wood cased and can be sharpened like a pencil. A new type of eraser especially suited for erasing coated drafting material is made of polyvinyl chloride.

Chalkboard erasers may be made of vertical layers of heavy wool felt sewed or glued to rigid felt backing or glued to wood backing; they may also be made of foam rubber to which lambskin or similar material is glued on one side of the eraser. The United States is the only country in the world producing rigid felt backing for chalkboard erasers; the United States and Canada are

the only nations producing sewed-felt chalkboard erasers. For removing chalk dust from erasers there is an electric vibrating vacuum cleaner that deposits the dust in a removable bag. There is also a revolving brush eraser cleaner operated by hand.

The brilliant 16th-century scholar Erasmus was a leading figure in the renaissance of learning in northern Europe. He sought to reform the Roman Catholic Church without destroying its basic order.

ERASMUS, DESIDERIUS (1465?-1536), Dutch scholar and writer, born in Rotterdam. He was educated at the Latin school in Deventer and later at the seminary in 's Hertogenbosch. He was ordained a priest in 1492.

The next year he became secretary to the bishop of Cambrai, but in 1495 he went to Paris to study. In 1499 he visited England and met men who became his lifelong friends, such as Thomas More and John Colet. The latter awakened his interest in Christian antiquity.

Until 1517 Erasmus was constantly abroad, first at Turin, in Italy, where he was made a doctor of theology. Later he was given a doctorate of theology at Cambridge, England, where he also taught.

It was in England that he wrote *Moriae encomium*, or *Praise of Folly*, a biting satire on human nature. From 1517 to 1521, the years beginning the Reformation, he was at Louvain, France. Urged by both Protestants and Catholics to take sides, the tolerant Erasmus feared for his personal safety and fled to Basel, Switzerland. There he completed work on his Greek-Latin edition of the New Testament.

ERICSON, LEIF, the discoverer of North America. He was a Norseman, probably born in Iceland in the latter half of the 10th century. He was the son of Eric the Red, who colonized Greenland. Leif's early years were probably spent in Greenland, whence he went to Norway. He embraced Christianity and about 1000 was sent as a missionary to Greenland by King Olaf I. According to one saga he was blown off his course on the voyage to Greenland and as a result discovered the eastern coast of North America. He named the place Vinland after the grapevines found there and proceeded to Greenland on his religious mission. Another saga states that he went first to Greenland, performed his work of conversion, and then set out deliberately on a voyage of discovery. Scholars generally agree that Leif Ericson landed on the North American coast, but they are unable to determine the exact location of Vinland. Some consider it to have been as far south as Virginia; others, as far north as Nova Scotia.

ERIC THE RED (flourished 10th century), founder of the first Norse settlement in Greenland and the father of Leif Ericson. The accounts of his voyages are found in the sagas of Iceland. According to these accounts he had to leave Norway after killing a man and fled to Iceland. There he got into more trouble and was sent into temporary exile. In the year 982 Eric sailed from Iceland in search of a land farther west that had been sighted a hundred years earlier by another Norse sea rover. He discovered the new country and named it Greenland. After living there for three years, he returned to Iceland and organized an expedition for permanent settlement. Eric landed his colonists and their supplies in 985 on the southwestern coast of Greenland, and they established the first Norse settlement near the present town of Julianehaab.

ERIDANUS, or the River Po, is a southern constellation lying south of Taurus. It begins near the celestial equator just west of the brilliant star Rigel in Orion and winds westward. It then turns in a great horseshoe curve and streams far to the south two-thirds of the way to the south celestial pole. It ends with the first-magnitude star Achernar. The northern part of Eridanus is visible in the evening sky from midnorthern latitudes between November and February.

ERIE CANAL. This historic waterway in the state of New York extends for more than 350 miles— from Albany, which is on the Hudson River, to Buffalo, on Lake Erie. It now is part of the New York State Barge Canal System.

The Erie Canal was the first great canal in the United States. It had an important effect on the country. It opened Eastern markets to the farmers of the Great Lakes region. Numerous large cities were established along the route. A stream of settlers used the waterway as a means of transportation to the lands of the Middle West. Finally, it confirmed the financial and commercial leadership of New York City and opened the interior of the country to the commerce of that city.

Under the steadfast leadership of DeWitt Clinton, work was started on the canal in 1817. The first section was completed in 1820. The canal was opened in 1825. It was a toll waterway until 1882.

ERINYES. See FURIES.

EROS. See CUPID.

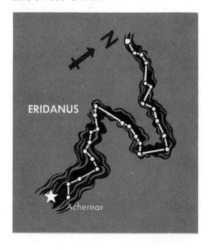

EROSION. When a landmass is gradually worn down toward sea level, the process of removing the material is called erosion. Weathering, which is the breaking up and decay of rock resulting from exposure to atmospheric agents, is a necessary preliminary to some kinds of erosion. Some of the chief agents or erosion are running water, wind, glaciers, and waves and currents.

Where the protective cover of vegetation has been removed, running water may carry away the topsoil, and each year thousands of acres of agricultural land are destroyed or rendered less productive by this type of erosion. Rivers cut canyons and wear away their banks and carry away material. Ocean waves batter the shores and cut cliffs in them. Wind removes loose particles from plowed fields and along shorelines.

Erosion is a matter of great importance to man. When erosion removes topsoil, the fertility of the land is destroyed, and farming becomes unprofitable or impossible. Much can be done to prevent erosion by proper cultivation of the soil, the building of dams, and the planting of trees and grass.

Erosion by waves and currents is seen on the face of this retreating shoreline.

The slow grinding of glaciers (below) erodes mountain ravines and valleys.

Eridanus, or the Po River, is associated with the legend of Phaethon, who begged his father to let him drive the sun's chariot across the sky. When he was finally given the chance, he could not control the chariot's horses, and Jupiter hurled him into the Po River to prevent a catastrophe.

Erosion by running water (above) gradually smooths irregular features of a landscape.

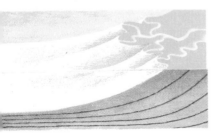

Debris from water erosion is finally deposited at the mouths of rivers.

ESCAPE VELOCITY is the minimum speed an object must have if it is to escape the gravitational attraction of a planet or other body by unpowered flight. This requirement applies not only to rockets and space vehicles attempting to leave the earth, the moon, or another planet but also to molecules of gas in a planet's atmosphere and to planets and other bodies orbiting the sun. The escape velocity varies according to the masses of the objects that are separating and to the distance between their centers. Escape velocity is normally stated in terms of launching velocity from the surface of a planet or other body.

For an object to escape the gravitational attraction of the earth the object must be given a launching speed of about 7 miles per second, or 25,000 miles per hour. The escape velocity from the moon is much less —only 1.4 miles per second. From the giant planet Jupiter it is 37 miles per second.

The earth is in the gravitational field of the sun and travels in orbit at about 19 miles per second. If an object is launched from the earth at greater than escape velocity, it will take up an independent orbit around the sun. If the launching is in the same direction as the earth's motion, the object's final velocity after being slowed by the earth's gravitation will still be greater than the earth's orbital speed. The object's orbit will then extend outside the earth's orbit. If the launching is in the opposite direction from the

earth's motion, the object's final speed will be somewhat less than the earth's, and its orbit will extend inside the earth's orbit.

The sun itself has an escape velocity, as do other stars also. At the earth's distance from the sun this velocity is much less than near the sun. From the earth's surface an object must be launched at a speed of about 10.2 miles per second or more if it is to escape from the solar system altogether.

Escape velocity is closely related to types of orbits. If the velocity of a space vehicle is greater than escape velocity, it will describe a hyperbolic orbit, **A**, in relation to the planet or other body, **D**. If the vehicle's velocity is less than escape velocity, it will describe an elliptical orbit, **C**, the normal orbit of a satellite. If its velocity is precisely escape velocity, it will describe a parabolic orbit, **B**.

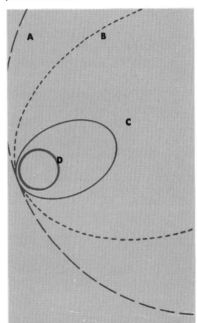

ESKIMO. About 2,000 years ago the Eskimos moved from Siberia across the Bering Strait into the New World. From Alaska they spread across the entire arctic coast of North America to Greenland.

The Eskimos call themselves the Innuit, meaning "the people." They are of short stature, muscular build, and light-brown complexion, with broad, flat faces and straight, dark hair.

From Asia the Eskimos brought with them the knowledge of how to live in an extremely cold climate without firewood. Therefore they were able to live in a previously uninhabited part of the earth. Their major tools for survival were the

Donald B. Marsh

Two Eskimos sit before a newly built igloo.

blubber lamp, tailormade clothing, intricate fishing equipment, and the famous snowhouse (igloo). For the blubber lamp (a lamp carved out of soapstone or made of pottery, in which the blubber of the whale is burned for fuel and light) they had to discover how blubber could be used in this way. They also had to fashion tools, mostly out of flint, with which to carve the lamps. And they had to develop the complex harpoons and other fishing equipment that would yield them a good supply of whale, walrus, and seal.

Perhaps even more important is the fur suit made by the Eskimo woman. The suit is made with an ulu, a semilunar knife much like that used by leatherworkers elsewhere. The suit consists of 12 pieces, including a parka with a hood, a pair of trousers, mittens, and boots, each of which is made in duplicate, skillfully tailored with the fur of one suit facing the skin, and that of the other facing the outside.

The hunting and fishing devices of the Eskimo are considered to be highly ingenious. To make the springlike apparatus used to kill wolves or polar bears the Eskimo shapes a strip of whalebone into a flat, double-edged skewer, rolls it tightly into a ball, freezes it into the center of a ball of fat, and throws it in the path of the oncoming animal. The animal eats it, and when the fat melts, the whalebone springs open, killing him.

The harpooning instrument is an ingenious combination of a harpoon head mounted on a bone or ivory foreshaft lashed into a socket fixed to the end of a wooden shaft. When the head has gone into the hide and blubber of the animal (seal or walrus), the foreshaft separates from the head (which remains in the animal) and floats free, while the fisherman holds his catch on a line connected only to the head. For whale catching, the Eskimo adds to this apparatus a pulley attached to the shore through slots carved in the solid ice.

Other important hunting and fishing devices are the kayak, or skin-covered canoe, and the dog sledge with its carefully iced runners for moving swiftly over the snow. The Eskimo's ingenuity is illustrated by his use of all the parts of the animals he catches. Skin becomes clothing, tents, and boat covers. Sinew becomes thread, cord, and bow. Waterproof clothing is made from the intestines. Sled runners, joints, and harpoon sockets are made from the bones and teeth.

The snowhouse is used as a regular home on the central Canadian coast but only as an emergency home in other regions. It is made by setting tapered blocks of snow in a spiral form. Each block is supported by the blocks at the sides as well as those beneath it. It is lined with hides. The blubber lamp supplies heat and light. In winter several families may live together in one snowhouse. A village may be composed of from 80 to 200 people. In the summer, however, the village breaks up, some families joining other groups or living by themselves in tents.

The social organization of the Eskimo is simple. There is no elaborate family structure. The wives and all their children share the work and the food equally. There are no formal political associations and

William W. Bacon—Rapho Guillumette

These Eskimos have killed a whale. They are cutting its meat and transporting portions of the meat on dogsleds to their homes. However, seals rather than whales are the Eskimos' chief source of meat. Seals also provide fur for clothing, bone for tools, and oil for fuel. Eskimos subsist mainly by hunting, as their homeland is too cold for agriculture.

little formal religious ceremony. Life is based on food getting, and the ideal of every Eskimo man is to be a good hunter.

Aside from the division of labor between men and women, there is no hierarchy of tasks. Each man hunts by himself or with a team, except for special cooperative projects in which the whole village shares the work equally. There is little thought for property. If one family has more than another, it shares with others equally, keeping no more than the bare necessities.

The Eskimo believes that there are a number of gods and spirits, who symbolize the various aspects of the weather and hunting and affect all people alike. When the weather or hunting is not good, they believe the particular god or spirit involved is angry, and they attempt to placate it. In former times the shaman was called upon to bring about better weather conditions or to improve hunting.

Nowadays the living conditions of the Eskimo, particularly in the region about Point Barrow, have changed substantially. Location of a U.S. naval base there has brought many Eskimos from other places, so that the village of Barrow is the largest community of Eskimos in Alaska—around 1,000 in 1953. There Eskimos work for wages, live in wooden houses, and own stoves, sewing machines, radios, and other items of the white man's culture. Eskimo children attend boarding schools; some go to college. The Eskimo makes use of outboard motors with traditional boats. He has become accustomed to air transport, and some young Eskimo women have prepared for the career of an airline hostess.

An Eskimo is stretching a piece of sealskin in a frame before the tent in which he lives.

Standard Oil Co. (N.J.)

ESPERANTO, a constructed language. Esperanto has been derived from several languages of Europe. It has been suggested, and to some extent adopted, as an international auxiliary language.

Esperanto was invented by Ludwig Zamenhof. As a boy, he lived in Bialystok, Poland, where Russians, Germans, Poles, and Jews lived together with no language in common. He tried to construct a new, neutral language. First he tried to revive a dead language. Then he experimented with roots of words from European languages.

As much as possible, Zamenhof based the words of Esperanto on words that were used in many nations. For example, *teatro* means "theater" in Esperanto.

Here is the Lord's Prayer in Esperanto.

Patro nia, kiu estas en la ĉielo,
sankta estu via nomo; venu
regeco via; estu volo via, kiel
en la ĉielo, tiel ankaŭ sur
la tero. Panon nian ĉiutagan
donu al ni hodiaŭ; kaj pardonu
al ni ŝuldojn niajn, kiel ni ankaŭ
pardonas al niaj ŝuldantoj;
kaj ne konduku nin en tenton,
sed liberigu nin de la malbono.

ESSAY, a literary composition in which a topic is discussed or an assertion proved. The form was given its name (the French word for "attempt") by the French writer Michel de Montaigne in a book published in 1580. It was adopted by the English author Francis Bacon a few years later and has since become a principal form of expression for many authors.

An essay may be on any subject whatsoever and is usually written in a brief, informal manner, much as if it were a conversation. A number of works called essays, however, might readily be classified in some other way. For example, John Locke's *Essay Concerning Human Understanding* is a lengthy philosophical treatise. Alexander Pope's *Essay on Man* is a long didactic poem in heroic couplets. John Dryden's "An Essay of Dramatic Poesy" is presented as a dialogue among four different speakers.

The commonest type of essay, however, follows the pattern established by Montaigne: brief, irregular, and with constant interruptions and digressions that appear to be random thoughts of the author brought to mind by, but not necessarily logically connected to, the subject he had begun to discuss. This air of informal wandering from thought to thought is almost always a deception, for a well-written essay

requires as much careful writing as any other form of literature. However, it is responsible for the essay's principal charm, which is the impression conveyed to the reader that he is sitting with the author by a fireplace or at the kitchen table having a pleasant talk.

The essay as a literary form has had a particularly rich and varied development in England. The essays of Francis Bacon, a name as great as that of Montaigne in the history of the essay, differ in that they are simpler and more direct and unornamented than those of Montaigne. Terse, pithy sentences characterize his essays on such subjects as "Truth" (" 'What is Truth?' said jesting Pilate; and would not stay for an answer") and "Death" ("Men fear Death, as Children fear to go in the Dark").

The periodical essays of Joseph Addison and Richard Steele are regarded by many as the most perfect expression of the essay form. These lively social commentaries, written in a simple, clear style, are among the best and most enjoyable works of the 18th century. The writings of Addison were well known in translation in Russia and his style was cultivated by essayists in that country.

The English familiar essay continued to flourish in the 19th century, beginning with the humor and grace of Charles Lamb, perhaps the best loved of all essayists, and the vigor and versatility of William Hazlitt. The great English tradition was carried forward by, among others, Thomas De Quincey, Thomas Babington Macaulay, Thomas Carlyle, John Ruskin, Matthew Arnold, Walter Pater, and Robert Louis Stevenson and into the 20th century by Max Beerbohm, G. K. Chesterton, T. S. Eliot, Aldous Huxley, and Virginia Woolf.

Although the essay is considered an essentially English form, it has been adopted into the literatures of many other countries. The first great American essayist was Ralph Waldo Emerson, whose essays are, like Montaigne's, a record of the author's quest for self-knowledge and the nature of reality. The principles evolved by Emerson were tested by Henry David Thoreau, who reported the results of his experiment in simple, self-reliant living in the long essay *Walden*. Their contemporary, Oliver Wendell Holmes, amused many with his humorous essays in *The Autocrat of the Breakfast Table*.

In the 20th century the vigorous

essays of H. L. Mencken smashed many American idols, while the more familiar, humorous essay reached a new high level in the work of James Thurber, John Mason Brown, and E. B. White. George Santayana's philosophical essays and Lionel Trilling's critical essays on literature and politics are examples of the more formal scholarly type of essay.

French essayists of distinction include Sainte-Beuve, Théophile Gautier, Paul de Saint-Victor, Anatole France, Jules Lemaître, Ferdinand Brunetière, Emile Faguet, and André Maurois. Ideas and loftiness of purpose are never missing from the essays of such German essayists as Goethe, Schiller, Jean Paul Friedrich Richter, Heinrich Heine, and Thomas Mann.

ESSEX, EARL OF. See ELIZABETH I.

ESTER. In chemistry the term *ester* is used for compounds formed by the reaction of an acid and an alcohol with the elimination of water. To define it another way, an ester is a compound that reacts with water, an acid, or an alkali to form an alcohol and an acid.

Many esters are found in natural materials such as animal fats and vegetable oils and waxes. In addition, a great many alcohols and acids may react to form esters; an extremely large number of esters is thus theoretically possible.

Esters are widely used in solvents, plasticizers, perfumes, flavors, and medicines. Some polymerized esters (those of high molecular weight) are useful as resins and plastics.

One of the oldest known chemical reactions is the hydrolysis (decomposition in water) of esters with alkali. This reaction is called saponification and is the basis of the soap industry. Romans and Gauls made use of this reaction when they treated fats with wood ashes to make a solution which had cleansing properties.

ESTIVATION, a state of torpidity undergone by the frog and other coldblooded animals in order to survive during periods of summer heat and dryness. Coldblooded animals must somehow cool their bodies during the heat and dryness of summer in order to survive. Semiaquatic amphibians and reptiles normally cool their bodies in summer by submerging themselves in the cool water of ponds or streams. However, if a pond or a stream dries up during an especially hot, dry summer and if migration to another one is impossible, the frogs and other amphibians and reptiles that inhabit the pond or stream bury themselves deep in the mud of its bottom in order to cool their bodies and survive. Such summertime immersion is one aspect of estivation.

Another aspect of the estivation of frogs is a torpid state similar to the dormancy they undergo during their wintertime hibernation. They do not eat or move their bodies, and apparently their metabolism and the rate of their heartbeat are decreased. When the weather becomes cooler or water returns to the pond or stream, the frogs emerge from estivation and resume their normal activities. Salamanders, turtles, tortoises, and other amphibians and reptiles undergo a similar state of estivation during hot, dry weather.

ESTONIA, a Baltic state and a former independent nation, is now incorporated in the U.S.S.R. as a member republic. The United States does not recognize the legality of that incorporation. The country is in northeastern Europe on the southern shore of the Gulf of Finland. It commands the Soviet route of entry into the Baltic Sea. Tallinn is the capital and the chief city. Paldiski is a naval base and a major port.

The country has an area of approximately 18,400 square miles. It is about half the size of Austria. Its population is about 1,000,000.

Estonia has for the most part a flat surface, but the land rises in small hills in the south. The coastline is indented by numerous bays, with cliffs on the northern coast. There are several islands, of which

These women dressed in colorful native costumes are the wives of Estonian fishermen.
Sovfoto

the most important is Saare. About one-fourth of the surface is covered with forests. The only important river is the Narva in the east. Estonia has a humid, moderate, continental climate.

Farming, especially dairying, is the principal occupation. There are many pastures and meadows. Much butter is produced. Hogs, poultry, and cattle are raised. Fodder crops and potatoes are the major crops. Fishing is common along the coast.

Textiles are the chief manufactured item. Other products include electrical equipment and wood products. Exports include butter, meat, eggs, bacon, timber, and electrical equipment.

The Estonians are of Ugro-Finnic origin. Their language is closely related to Finnish. Many speak Russian.

In the Middle Ages Estonia belonged to Denmark and later to Sweden. Russia seized it in 1721. It was occupied by the German army during part of World War I. In 1918 it declared its independence. Aided by the Allies, it resisted Bolshevik attacks and in 1920 made peace with the U.S.S.R. To combat various internal and foreign intrigues, the country was put under martial law in 1934.

On Jan. 1, 1938, a new constitution was adopted. The actual government, however, continued to approximate a dictatorship. With the German invasion of Poland in September, 1939, Estonia was forced to grant concessions to the U.S.S.R., including air and naval bases on some of the islands.

In 1940 the country became an autonomous republic in the U.S.S.R. It was occupied by the Germans in 1941-1942 but was recaptured and reannexed by the U.S.S.R. in 1944. Since annexation almost all farms have been collectivized. For detailed map, see UNION OF SOVIET SOCIALIST REPUBLICS.

Above are shown the flag and coat of arms of Estonia, since its incorporation into the Soviet Union as a constituent republic.

ETCHING, a type of engraving on a metal plate in which acid is used to eat out a faintly sketched design. Both the process and the print made from the metal plate are referred to as etching. The fundamental difference between etching and other types of metal engraving is that etched lines are made by biting out an exposed surface with acid, while in other types of metal engraving lines are cut with a sharp metal point.

The etching process is begun by coating a polished metal plate with a wax preparation that resists acids. Then a steel point is used to make the drawing on the wax surface, leaving the metal surface underneath lightly scratched. The plate is then put in a dish of acid solution, which eats into the exposed metal surfaces without affecting the wax covering. The longer the acid is allowed to corrode the metal, the wider and deeper the lines will be. After the corrosion process is finished, the wax coating is removed, and the metal plate is rubbed with a thick, oily ink, which fills in the lines of the design. When the excess ink has been wiped away, the plate is ready for making prints.

Etchings can be made to exhibit pure line; to contrast line and shading, as in a water color; or to suggest the shades and textures of painting. To achieve some of these effects the artist may "stop out" his etching, that is, remove the plate from the acid bath at various intervals and coat the lines intended to be finer and lighter with an acid-resistant varnish, or he may combine etching with some of the other metal-engraving processes for even richer and more varied tones.

Etching used expressly for making prints did not begin until the 15th century in Germany. The 17th-century Dutch painter Rembrandt executed landscapes, portraits, and groups of figures with such skill and in such a variety of styles that he is still considered the master of this art. Etching has also been used in reproducing paintings and for illustrating books, but etchings made by artists as an independent art—Vandyke, Goya, and William Blake, for example—are more highly regarded. In the late 19th century the American painter James M. Whistler proved to be another master of the art with his fine portraits and series of river and canal scenes.

"Prodigal Son," an etching by the Dutch painter Rembrandt, dates from 1636. In the hands of Rembrandt the art of etching achieved its greatest importance. His subjects included almost every variety—scenes from the Old Testament and New Testament, genre, landscape, portrait, and still life. Estimates of the number of his etchings vary. One expert places the number as high as 300. Beside and below the work of the master are shown the tools employed in engraving and processing the metal plates used in the art of etching.

1. Needle
2. Needle
3. Roller
4. Plate
5. Oil Rubber
6. Diamond Point
7. Scraper
8. Balanced Point
9. Burnisher

ETHER, in chemistry, has several meanings. It is used to designate organic compounds in which a single oxygen atom is connected to two organic radicals. Ether also refers to a particular member of this series of compounds, diethyl ether, also sometimes called sulfuric ether.

All ethers contain the group —C—O—C—. Ethers can be considered to be derivatives of alcohols in which the H of the OH group has been replaced by an organic radical. A simple ether has two identical radicals. A mixed ether has two different radicals. Dimethyl ether is a simple ether.

$$H-\overset{\displaystyle H}{\underset{\displaystyle H}{C}}-O-\overset{\displaystyle H}{\underset{\displaystyle H}{C}}-H$$

Methyl ethyl ether is a mixed ether.

$$H-\overset{\displaystyle H}{\underset{\displaystyle H}{C}}-O-\overset{\displaystyle H}{\underset{\displaystyle H}{C}}-\overset{\displaystyle H}{\underset{\displaystyle H}{C}}-H$$

Diethyl ether is a colorless volatile liquid with a characteristic odor. It is used as an anesthetic by inhalation of the vapor and is a good solvent of oils and fats.

ETHICS, the branch of philosophy concerned with moral principles. Among the words most commonly discussed in ethics are *good*, *bad*, *right*, and *wrong*. Ethics is about the conduct of men. It tries to arrive at principles that tell men how to act.

One of the first great thinkers about ethics was Socrates. Socrates arrived at the principle that virtue, or doing right, was knowledge. He thought that men would act virtuously if they knew how. See SOCRATES.

Eventually, Greek thought on ethics developed into two schools. One was taught by the philosopher Epicurus, who thought that pleasure was the important thing in human life. But pleasure to Epicurus was quite different from what it was to other philosophers of his own day. Pleasure, said Epicurus, was tranquillity. It was freedom from physical pain and troubling thoughts. Epicurus thought that the true seeker of pleasure was the thoughtful philosopher who weighed very carefully the evils that might result from pleasure. Virtue to the Epicureans was a means toward pleasure, not a good thing in itself, as it was

for Socrates. Epicurus himself was both moderate and prudent. He and his disciples lived a simple life in the community he established. Their meals consisted usually of barley bread, cheese, and water. Epicurus taught informally and with great warmth. He was very kindly and even admitted one of his slaves to his community of philosophers. Epicureanism certainly does not deserve the reputation for gluttony the modern use of the word has given it.

Opposed to Epicureanism was a system of ethics founded earlier in Greece by Zeno. Zeno taught his system of philosophy in a corridor (stoa) in the marketplace in Athens. The group that gathered to hear him were therefore called Stoics, from the word *stoa*. The Stoics believed with Socrates that knowledge was good. The wise man had complete well-being. His wisdom was displayed in his indifference to extreme emotions, such as sorrow or joy. So loyal was the Stoic to wisdom that he was not disturbed even by great physical pain. His wisdom taught him that pain was not a concern of his real self. Although he was inclined to believe that man's life was subject to Fate, the Stoic also taught that man had the power to do good if he used his reason. Evil acts were the result of ignorance. And one could escape from ignorance by reason. But man did not live all by himself. Therefore, the Stoics tried to discover how men should act in relation to other people. They felt that if men really tried to act as Nature intended them to, they would act justly and ethically.

Thus, the Stoic was a calm individual, who had a strong sense of duty. He would direct his actions, not toward personal pleasure like the Epicurean, but toward what he thought duty demanded. Brutus, one of the men who stabbed Julius Caesar, acted as he did, even though Caesar was his friend, because he felt that it was his duty to Rome to do so. An Epicurean would not have done as Brutus did, unless he thought that not to have done so would have afforded him less pleasure or less tranquillity of mind. Of course, these two schools, the Stoic and the Epicurean, did not agree. In fact, the conflicts between them have continued, with other new ethical ideas, down to the present day. See CHRISTIANITY; CONFUCIUS; JESUS; JUDAISM; MOSES; RELIGIONS OF THE WORLD; TEN COMMANDMENTS.

ETHIOPIA is a constitutional monarchy in northeastern Africa. Abyssinia is another name for the country. Ethiopia also includes the federated state of Eritrea, a prewar Italian colony. The capital, Addis Ababa, is situated in the approximate center of the country at an altitude of 8,000 feet. Other important towns include Harar and Diredawa. Ethiopia has no ports, but the Eritrean ports of Assab and Massawa are connected to the country by highways. The port of Djibouti in French Somaliland is connected to Addis Ababa by the country's only railroad.

Ethiopia, including Eritrea, has an area of about 395,000 square miles. It is nearly as large as Texas and California combined. The country's present population is estimated at 20,000,000.

Ethiopia is generally mountainous, with high tablelands rising to over 15,000 feet. Formidable mountains are found in the north, west, and south. The Great Rift Valley cuts through the country from the northeast to the southwest. The valley is studded with lakes. The Danakil Desert is in the northeast. Most of the country has a temperate and invigorating climate. The low regions (up to 5,500 feet) have a semiarid to arid climate. The country's population is concentrated in the 5,500-foot to 8,000-foot region. It enjoys a mean annual temperature of 62° F.

Ethiopia has great natural resources that have not been fully exploited. Mineral resources of chief importance are gold and potash salts.

Farming and livestock raising are the main occupations. About 17 percent of the land is fertile, but only about 10 percent is used. Because of Ethiopia's diversity of altitude and climate, a large variety of crops can be raised. The chief crops are cereal grains, coffee, fruits and vegetables, tobacco, sisal and other coarse fibers, and cotton. Many cattle, sheep, goats, ponies, and mules are raised.

Ethiopia's flag has three colors. The conquering lion of Judah is the coat of arms.

Ethiopia's industry is concentrated on the processing of agricultural products. There is some production of small consumer goods for local consumption. Coffee (of high quality), hides and skins, grain, and beeswax are the principal exports.

Chief imports include cotton textiles and yarn and petroleum products.

Ethiopia is a constitutional monarchy. A democratic constitution was adopted in 1955. Haile Selassie I has been emperor since 1930, except from 1935 to 1941 when Ethiopia was occupied by Italian forces.

Ethiopia is comprised of a number of earlier kingdoms. The majority of the people are descendants of ancient Hamite and Semite tribes. The present dynasty dates from 1000 B.C. Map under UNITED ARAB REPUBLIC.

Ethiopia is generally a land of rugged highlands and mountains. The northeast is a desert, and the southeast is a semiarid plateau.   W. Kuls

Martin Simpson—Annan Photo Features

These tribesmen in dry eastern Ethiopia are pulling a goatskin bag of water from a well to supply their herd of thirsty animals.

ETHIOPIA

Area: 350,000 sq. mi. (including Eritrea, 395,000 sq. mi.)

Population: 20,000,000

Capital: Addis Ababa

Largest cities: Addis Ababa, Asmara (capital of Eritrea), Harar, Dire-dawa

Highest mountain peak: Ras Dashan (about 15,150 feet)

Chief rivers: Blue Nile, Webi Shebeli

Chief lakes: Tana, Rudolf

Climate: Hot in lowlands, cool in plateau, cold in mountains—rainfall light in east, heavier in west, especially in summer

National flag: Three horizontal stripes of green, yellow, red, with lion in yellow stripe

National anthem: *Ityopya hoy dass yiballish*

Form of government: Constitutional monarchy (empire)

Unit of currency: Dollar

Languages: Amharic, English

Chief religions: Coptic Christian, Moslem

Chief economic activity: Agriculture, including livestock raising

Chief crops: Coffee, teff (a grain), barley, wheat, corn, millet

Chief minerals: Gold, potash salt

Chief exports: Coffee, hides and skins

Chief imports: Textiles, petroleum products, machinery and vehicles

ETHNIC GROUP, a community remaining distinct within another, usually dominant, surrounding group and bound together by any or all of the following factors: race, language, nationality, or religion. Such a community has a common culture and a strong feeling of identity. It perpetuates its own culture and is recognized as a distinct entity by surrounding groups.

Racial differences may also be reinforced by social factors. The entrance of the Negroes into the United States as slaves caused them to be regarded as a different and subordinate group. In many former colonies of Spain and Portugal racial differences were not emphasized; there resulted a mixing of the various populations. The attitude of the dominant group usually determines just how separate an ethnic group will be.

A common religion may hold a group together for a long time. The German Mennonite farmers are a separate group bound together by customs and traditions. Other German farmers who are not members of this religious community are assimilated more quickly into the surrounding culture.

Especially since the growth of modern natoinalism, language has served to symbolize a national group and to carry on its traditions. Foreign-language newspapers and radio programs are a symbol and a vehicle of a separate culture. A feeling of loyalty to a homeland may in itself serve to perpetuate an ethnic group.

Members of a dominant culture may try to assimilate ethnic groups. Americanization programs and other community activities that include all interested individuals enable members of ethnic groups to become acquainted with members of the dominant group. Intermarriage further breaks down the distinctness of ethnic groups.

Some countries have tried to remove groups that are considered difficult to assimilate. In Europe national governments have at times attempted to move ethnic groups within their jurisdiction back to their homelands or to exchange populations with other countries. In the U.S.S.R. local ethnic identity is encouraged, and ethnic groups are granted some autonomy.

Government or business policy may perpetuate an ethnic group. Restricted housing may limit the area where certain groups may live. Thus a group mixes primarily with its own members. The placing of

American Indians on reservations is another instance of isolation of an ethnic group. These reservations are usually owned by the Indians, either as individuals or as tribes. They are not bound by law to remain on them; they may live elsewhere if they so desire. See MINORITY.

ETHNOLOGY. See ANTHROPOLOGY.

ETIQUETTE, forms of behavior on official occasions and in everyday affairs that indicate good breeding. It is usually the affluent members of society that establish the proprieties generally observed in social life. However, various social and national groups have different ideas about what is acceptable social behavior.

In most countries, the etiquette for formal occasions is different from that for ordinary situations. Weddings, funerals, and gatherings of high-ranking members of the government, the armed services, the church, or of wealthy families require a show of respect and deference. On the other hand, courtesies observed in one's own home, among friends, or in the street—everyday manners—are more informal. Yet all social situations demand certain amenities of everyone in regard to speech, dress, table manners, making introductions, sending invitations, entertaining, traveling, and the like.

Each country has its own rules of etiquette, down to the smallest detail of how to butter a piece of bread properly. On the whole, however, etiquette in America is more flexible than etiquette in Europe, since we have no remnants of an established aristocracy or ruling class. However, since the 19th century, the financially successful families of America have taken a strong lead in establishing social proprieties. What was once a set of rules to be observed by these families, the average American now learns in order to make himself socially acceptable.

For the young, etiquette is often a distressing matter, since so many social situations arise for the first time during adolescence. Every teen-ager wants to know what to say when meeting someone for the first time, how to introduce a friend to his parents, what to wear to a wedding or a formal dance, and how to word a thank-you note or written invitation. The standard books on etiquette by Emily Post and Amy Vanderbilt are helpful guides. The feature sections of many newspapers also devote a column or an occasional article to matters of etiquette.

ETRUSCAN, an inhabitant of ancient Etruria, an area of the Italian peninsula roughly corresponding to the modern provinces of Tuscany and Umbria. The exact origin of the Etruscans even today remains a matter of speculation. However, it has been established that the Etruscans emigrated from somewhere in Asia Minor to the Italian peninsula by way of the sea about 900 B.C. After conquering the native Umbrians the Etruscans founded a number of settlements that were later united into a loose federation. As the centuries passed, the Etruscan civilization expanded. Shortly before 500 B.C. penetration had been made as far south as modern Salerno and as far north as the Alps. Remains of Etruscan settlements have been found on the neighboring islands of Corsica and Elba. At this time the Etruscan navy dominated the western Mediterranean area. Until 510 B.C., when the last of the semilegendary Tarquin kings was overthrown, the city of Rome was intermittently under Etruscan control. Very soon after the Etruscan civilization reached its maximum extension geographically, it began to crumble. Naval supremacy was broken at the battle off Cumae in 474 B.C. Northern settlements fell to Celtic invaders from the Alps, and during the 4th century members of the Etruscan federation of cities fell to the Romans one by one. By the end of the 1st century B.C. the Etruscan civilization had been completely absorbed into that of Rome.

The Etruscan culture, at its height during the 6th century B.C., was un-

Courtesy of The Metropolitan Museum of Art, 1916

This is a terra cotta head of a helmeted Etruscan warrior. The Etruscans were expert and inventive artists, and they produced works in a distinctive artistic style. They were especially skilled in the casting of bronze sculpture. Many brilliantly colored Etruscan mural paintings still exist and are on display in museums throughout the world.

doubtedly the most brilliant to flourish on the Italian peninsula until the time of classical Rome. However, our knowledge of certain areas of Etruscan culture is quite limited. Although there is evidence that a literature was produced, no body of Etruscan literature has yet been unearthed. In fact, the Etruscan language itself still remains undeciphered.

The Etruscans were a wealthy people. Although agriculture was an important pursuit, more characteristic was the brisk commercial trade, both overland and maritime, that was built up with the Greeks, Phoenicians, and other Mediterranean people. Much of Etruria's wealth depended on the exploitation of the peninsula's mineral resources. Even today ancient slag heaps mark the sites of Etruscan mines.

Etruscan art produced before the 7th century B.C. seems to indicate that there was a close cultural association with the civilizations of the Near East, such as Syria and Egypt. After the 7th century, however, the Greek influence on art became quite strong. In addition to metalwork of superior quality, the Etruscans are noted for work in terra cotta and pottery. Although little of what the Etruscans built remains standing, they are renowned as architects and engineers. Vivid murals decorate the walls of tombs, which are storehouses of Etruscan art.

Because of the lack of a written record, Etruscan religion has remained largely a mystery to us. However, we do know that it was strongly influenced by Greek mythology and, in turn, exerted a significant influence on Roman religion. That the Etruscans were greatly concerned with death and believed in life after death is evident from the care with which they built and furnished the tombs for their dead. Prophecy and divination were also important elements of Etruscan religion.

Politically and socially the population was divided into a princely aristocratic minority, which exercised control over the city governments, and a plebeian majority, which consisted primarily of slaves and freemen of low status. The Etruscan cities, like the Greek city-states, were bound together by cultural ties but never achieved real political solidarity. Uprisings of the lower class were fairly common, as were wars between cities. Consequently, in later years the Etruscan cities were easy prey to the invasions of the Greeks, the Celts, and the Romans.

ETYMOLOGY, a branch of philology, is the study of the origin and derivation of words through analysis of their components and through comparison with similar forms in parent languages. An etymology, an account of a word's development, is usually included under each word entry of a dictionary.

The Etruscans were clever and industrious architects. They were the first to design and build arches consisting of a series of wedge-shaped stones held together by pressure upon one another. Below are the remains of two ancient Etruscan columns.

Artha Hornbostel

Taking the word *recur* as an example, we discover that it is derived from the Latin elements *re*, meaning "back" or "again," and *currere*, meaning "to run." Hence, the word *recur* means literally "to run back" or "to run again." In addition to the origin of words and their meanings, the etymologist is interested in the way in which words (such as *recur*) undergo changes in meaning.

Etymology not only gives us a more comprehensive understanding of a word's meaning but also reveals relationships that exist among certain languages of the world. Words that share common elements and a parent language are called cognates. For example, the English word *mother* comes to us from the Anglo-Saxon *modor*. Cognate forms include the German *Mutter*, the Swedish and Danish *Moder*, the Greek *meter*, the Latin *mater*, and the Romance language forms. Not only the words but the languages themselves are cognate, all being members of the Indo-European language family.

EUCALYPTUS, the name of many species of trees grown principally in Australasia but found also in California. More than 250 species grow in Australasia; about 90 species, in California. The rapid growth of eucalyptus trees and their pleasing appearance have made them popular.

The commonest species is the one usually known as blue gum. This is said to be the fastest growing tree in the world. It is not unusual for a five-year-old tree to be 50 feet in height. The leaves are silvery gray to dark green, often with a distinct blue cast. Those on young trees differ in size, shape, and arrangement from those on old trees. The leaves of the young shoots are heart shaped, white, and waxy; they are without petioles. The leaves of the older shoots are lance shaped. Flowers vary from white to red. Eucalyptus trees have four or five petals, which, with the calyx, fall off and expose yellow or red stamens, which then become the conspicuous part of the flower. The flowers of the blue gum are either solitary or in groups of two or three. They are about $1\frac{1}{2}$ inches across.

The eucalyptus is grown for more than ornament. In Australia it is one of the most important of the timber woods. The wood is also used for flooring, inside finish, and furniture. Oil of eucalyptus is distilled from the leaves and small twigs. The dried juice of several Australian species is known as red gum and is used in medicine.

EUCHRE, a popular card game of the United States first played about 1825 by the Pennsylvania Dutch. Two to seven persons may play, but the four-handed game described here is the most popular. It is played with a deck consisting of all cards above six. The highest card is the jack of trump suit (called right bower). The jack of the other suit of the same color as trump (left bower) ranks next, and the other cards rank in the usual order.

Five cards are dealt (in batches of three and two) to each player, and the next card is turned up as the proposed trump suit. The players, beginning with the one to the left of the dealer, accept or reject the proposed trump suit by either "I order it up" or "Pass." The dealer's partner passes or accepts the trump by saying "I assist." However, if the three other players pass, the dealer indicates a pass by placing the card face down under the pack. He indicates acceptance by discarding one card, face down, from his hand. If the dealer passes, the player to his left begins another round by naming another suit as trump or by passing. If all pass on the second round, the cards are shuffled and dealt again. The player making trump (by ordering it up, assisting, accepting, or naming a new suit) may declare "I play alone." His partner then discards his hand and does not play. When the turn-up is accepted, the dealer takes up the turn-up card and discards one from his hand.

The leaves, flowers, and fruits of a eucalyptus tree are shown above. Eucalyptus trees are aromatic evergreens that belong to the myrtle family. Oil of eucalyptus, which smells like camphor, is sometimes inhaled to alleviate respiratory infections.

When the maker of trump plays alone, the opening lead is made by the player to his left; otherwise it is made by the player to the left of the dealer. Any card may be led, and the other players must follow suit if they are able. If they cannot, then they may play any card. The highest trump wins a trick, or if no trump is played, the highest card of the suit led wins the trick. The player winning a trick leads to the next trick.

Only the side winning a majority of the tricks scores. The side making trump scores one point for three or four tricks and two points for all five tricks (called march.) The maker who plays alone scores one point for three or four tricks and four points for march. If the maker's side wins fewer than three tricks, it is euchred, and the other side scores two points. Game may be set at five, seven, or ten points.

EUCLID (flourished 323-285 B.C.), famous Greek mathematician, lived in Alexandria, Egypt. His chief work was his *Elements*, which deals with geometry and the theory of numbers. He collected all the fundamental principles of pure mathematics that had been advanced by Thales, Pythagoras, and other mathematicians before him and put them in order, with many others of his own. On this account he is said to have been the first to reduce geometry to the form of a science. His work is still the basis of all modern geometries. No other book dealing with science has been kept unaltered as long as has Euclid's *Elements*. Attributed to Euclid is a famous remark made to Ptolemy I, in which he told the ruler that "there is no royal road to geometry."

EUGENICS, the application of scientific principles to the improvement of human inherited characteristics. The word was invented by Francis Galton, who began the modern eugenics movement. The principle is not a new one. The harsh military society of ancient Sparta practiced a form of eugenics. Sickly infants were destroyed, and the strict military training of the children probably caused the death of those unable to stand up under the severe conditions of war. Influenced by the example of Sparta, the philosopher Plato also advocated certain eugenic measures in his ideal republic.

The modern eugenics movement is based on the theories of Francis Galton and his successors, Karl Pearson and Leonard Darwin. Galton founded the Laboratory of National Eugenics at the University of London in 1904. In the United States the movement was pioneered by Alexander Graham Bell. An American Eugenics Society was founded in 1926. The International Federation of Eugenic Organizations was created to coordinate the numerous national groups.

The purpose of eugenics is to improve the human race. Negative eugenics deals with the task by preventing certain grossly defective traits from being passed to the next generation. It proposes, for example, that hemophilia, an inherited disease known as bleeding, be stopped by preventing the marriage of affected individuals. This could be done either by voluntary decisions based on education or by legal measures. Many states have laws for the segregation of defectives or the prevention of their marriage. The effects of certain negative eugenics are known, but other effects are difficult to trace genetically. The causes of certain types of feeble-mindedness cannot be traced; thus the defect cannot be eliminated. Negative eugenicists often mistake traits resulting from environment for inherited traits. For example, individuals with criminal traits are often changed by altering the social environment. Positive eugenics is the attempt to produce more people who are "superior" human beings. However, human beings generally do not want to be as strictly controlled as would be necessary for the development of a positive eugenic program. Obviously, health and intelligence are desirable traits, but dissension arises when eugenicists try to define superior or desirable traits more exactly. See EN-VIRONMENT; HEREDITY.

EUGLENA, a genus of microscopic protozoans that show important characteristics of both animals and plants. The individual euglena is a single-celled, oblong, green organism that inhabits fresh-water ponds and streams. It swims by waving back and forth a long hairlike flagellum that is extended forward from its anterior end. It can also move by alternately pulling its posterior end forward and pushing its anterior end forward. This method of locomotion is called euglenoid movement.

The outstanding plant characteristic of the euglena is its manufacture of food from carbon dioxide and water by a process known as photosynthesis. Photosynthesis oc-

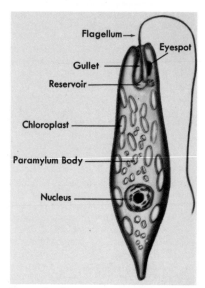

The euglena's eyespot is sensitive to light.

curs within minute intracellular bodies called chloroplasts. The chloroplasts contain the green pigment chlorophyll, which is necessary for photosynthesis and which imparts to the euglena its green color. The euglena carries on photosynthesis as long as it is exposed to light. However, if it is placed in darkness, its photosynthesis ceases, and it proceeds to absorb dissolved organic substances through its external membrane in a manner typical of animal cells. Some euglenas eat bacteria. The bacteria are swallowed by a gullet, through which they pass to a cavity called a reservoir, where they are digested and assimilated. Besides locomotion and the ingestion of food, another outstanding animal characteristic of the euglena is its capacity for sensing light. It senses light by means of a tiny red eyespot located at its anterior end. Its eyespot enables the euglena to seek the light that it requires for photosynthesis.

Because within it are united important activities of both animals and plants, the euglena is regarded as a connecting link between the animal and plant kingdoms.

EULER, LEONHARD (1707-1783), a distinguished Swiss mathematician, was born in Basel. He was educated at the University of Basel. In 1727 he was called to St. Petersburg (now Leningrad) by Catherine I to become professor of physics and mathematics at the Academy of Sciences. In 1741 he accepted an invitation from Frederick the Great to become professor of mathematics in the Berlin Academy of Sciences, but

in 1766 he returned to St. Petersburg to become director of mathematics at the academy. He applied the analytic method to mechanics and greatly improved the integral and differential calculus. He also did work on acoustics, optics, and hydrodynamics.

EUPHRATES RIVER. See TIGRIS AND EUPHRATES RIVERS.

EURATOM, the European Atomic Energy Community, an organization to develop the peaceful uses of atomic energy and to facilitate the creation and growth of peaceful nuclear industries. The treaty creating Euratom was signed in 1957 at Rome with the treaty creating the European Economic Community. These treaties were signed by The Six: Belgium, The Netherlands, Luxembourg, France, German Federal Republic, and Italy.

To accomplish its aim, Euratom purposes to develop research and to interchange technical information. It receives reports of progress from national atomic-research programs, which it aids by financial assistance and by supplying free fissionable materials. In addition, its Joint Nuclear Research Center operates Euratom's own research program.

The need for united efforts in the development of atomic energy for peaceful uses so impressed the United States and the United Kingdom that they signed cooperative agreements with the organization.

EURIPIDES (480?-406? B.C.), one of the three great Athenian dramatists, was probably born on the island of Salamis. Little is known of his life, and the legends recounted about it seem hardly credible.

Of the 92 plays that Euripides reputedly wrote, 17 tragedies, 1 satyr play, and numerous fragments survive. Euripides won five victories in the festivals. Of his plays, the most noted are *Orestes, Electra, Medea, The Trojan Women, Hecuba,* and *Bacchae.* His *Alcestis* and *Ion* are noteworthy romantic dramas, and his *Helen* is brilliant high comedy.

Euripides used the three actors Sophocles had established for Greek drama and a much more restricted chorus. However, his great innovation was the prologue, distinct from the usual *prologos,* which summarized the story that had occurred before the play began. After his death, a monument was erected to him at Athens.